The Goldsmith's Rant

A New Song.

Composed By John Aitken.

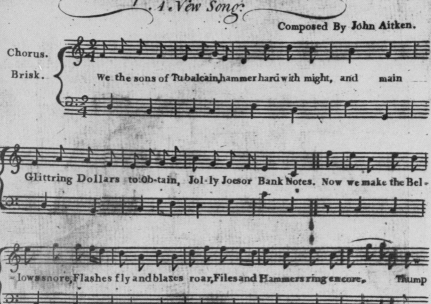

Chorus.
Brisk.

We the sons of Tubalcain, hammer hard with might, and main

Glittring Dollars to obtain, Jolly Joes or Bank Notes. Now we make the Bel-

-lows snore, Flashes fly and blases roar, Files and Hammers ring encore, Thump

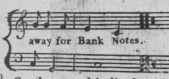

away for Bank Notes.

Chorus
O the bonny O the bonny
O the bonny Bank Notes,
Clinkum clink brings the chink
And the silken Bank Notes.

2
Smack! The're gone as sleek's a rat!
Here and there for this and that
Gammon and I dont know what,
All slip off the Bank Notes,
Cho.
O the bonny O the bonny
O the bonny Bank Notes,
Mind your eye watch 'em sly
Grapple well the Bank Notes.

3
Gentlemen and Ladies dear
Charming trinkets we have here
Take and welcome never fear
Tip us but the Banck Notes.
Cho. O the bonny O the bonny
O the bonny Bank Notes,
Polish'd gold of neatest mould
Shall bow before the Bank Notes.

4
Justic ballances our Scales!
Hope the Fairy never fails!
Still to whisper coazing tales
Yonder come the Bank Notes.
Cho.
O the bonny O the bonny
O the bonny Bank Notes,
Fal lal lay! thump away!
This will bring the Bank Notes.

I. AITKEN,

GOLDSMITH & JEWELLER,

N. 33.

South Second Street.

PHILAD.

N.B. Silver Cyphers for Carriages.

Early American Music Engraving and Printing

A History of Music Publishing
in America from 1787 to 1825 with
Commentary on Earlier
and Later Practices

Richard J. Wolfe

Published in cooperation with the
Bibliographical Society of America by the

University of Illinois Press

Urbana   Chicago   London

Publication of this work was supported in part by
a grant from the Bibliographical Society of America,
with assistance from the Lathrop Colgate Harper Litt. D. Trust Fund

FRONTISPIECE: *The Goldsmith's Rant, A New Song, Composed by
John Aitken.* Philadelphia: J. Aitken, 1802. The song appeared
on the front of one leaf only, with vignettes on the back showing
a metalsmith (probably Aitken himself), Aitken's wares, and
Muses. From the copy in the New York Public Library.

LIBRARY OF CONGRESS CATALOGING IN PUBLICATION DATA

Wolfe, Richard J.
    Early American music engraving and printing.

    (Music in American life)
    Bibliography: p.
    Includes index.
    1. Music printing.   2. Publishers and publishing—
United States.   3. Music—United States—History and
criticism.   I. Title.
ML112.W64   686.2'84'0973   79-12955
ISBN 0-252-00726-3

For CARLETON SPRAGUE SMITH

I give thee all I can no more.

From the song *My Heart and Lute*,
by Thomas Moore

CONTENTS

PREFACE

T HE TYPICAL MUSIC PUBLISHER of the birth and cradle period of American music publishing was an English or German musician and music teacher who had emigrated to the United States after the Revolution and had begun to engrave and issue music as an adjunct to his performing and teaching activities. His entry into the publishing field was purely incidental. He was inspired probably by a desire to supplement his income through exploiting a market which had not previously been satisfied locally and to supply his pupils with music necessary for their instruction and improvement. Or he may have been motivated by the need to establish a convenient outlet for the publication of his own compositions. Possibly he had engraved a little music as a side activity before leaving his native land, and had brought a kit of cutting and stamping tools with him on his voyage across the Atlantic. Generally, his venture into music publishing was short-lived, lasting less than two or three years, and the sheets he produced look naive and crude when compared with those of an average English or European music publisher of the day.

Less typical in either extreme were such publishers as Joseph Carr of Baltimore on the one hand and John Aitken of Philadelphia on the other. Carr had been an active music publisher in London before his emigration. He possessed all the modern tools and the know-how needed to engrave and print a product whose excellence would assure him a reasonably long life in music publishing. Aitken, who in 1787 had been the first to employ metal punches to engrave music plates in the United States, was an immigrant metalsmith and jeweler with little musical knowledge and no prior music engraving or publishing experience at all. His initial output represented little more than the groping attempts of an artisan working out of his medium, and the arrival of more skilled musician-engravers soon pushed him into the background; even though his later efforts show greater refinement he remained only an indifferent publisher who imitated the work of his more sophisticated contemporaries.

The musician-publishers who were among the thousands of people going out to America in the period following the Revolution brought with them English and European traditions of music publishing as part of their cultural baggage. These two traditions, which were almost identical in theory and practice, had developed over several centuries and at the time of their transference to the New World had been fully established for less than a hundred years. The high point of this Anglo-European tradition was the engraving technique, which utilized metal dies or punches to strike notation into soft, pewter plates from which impressions were ultimately transferred to paper by means of the copperplate or rolling press. This stamping process had superseded the technique of freehand engraving on copper shortly after the beginning of the eighteenth century; and, because of its superiority for reproducing chords and passages of rapid movement requiring many small notes, the stamping process had very nearly supplanted the still older method of printing music from movable type, which by the latter part of the eighteenth century was mostly restricted to the publishing of large collections, especially of sacred music. Both of these earlier methods had been employed in America for a number of decades before the arrival of the musician-publishers in the post-Revolutionary period, but only casually and with little enduring effect. Only after the introduction of the punching and stamping technique about 1787 did a permanent music-publishing industry begin to develop in this country.

The chapters which follow are an outgrowth of work I carried on between 1958 and 1964 in compiling my bibliography *Secular Music in America, 1801–1825*. Early in the course of that project it became evident to me that I was going to have to learn a great deal about the techniques and customs of our early music engravers and publishers, particularly if I was to date correctly the music produced within that period. Lack of dates on early music sheets, reissue of new editions from older plates of prior publishers, and other complicated and complicating factors of this early trade made the comprehension and control of such data extremely difficult, and, in some cases, seemingly impossible. So far as I could determine at that time, there existed no guide or body of information on the manners and customs of early music publishers—in America, or elsewhere—which would help me interpret the ways of their trade and assist me in assigning dates to our early music editions. It soon became apparent that if my journey through the musical landscape of this period was not to be made blindly, it was I who would have to throw light on the path ahead.

The idea of doing the present book developed slowly. Lack of source materials on early American music publishing made it appear initially that the task was beyond doing. As a result, during my first year of work on the 1801–25 bibliography I failed to record bits of valuable evidence which began to emerge along the way. It was only during the second year, while I was recording musical imprints in the Maryland Historical Society, that I determined to undertake the work which follows herein. The specific incident that precipitated the decision was my encounter of an English music sheet of the late 1780s or early 1790s bearing the name "B. Carr" as engraver. Benjamin Carr was one of our foremost pioneer composers and music publishers, but his work as an engraver of music before his immigration to America was previously unknown. Unfortunately, a day or two intervened between that find and my ultimate decision, and later attempts to relocate the Carr sheet proved unsuccessful. Thus, another valuable scrap of evidence was lost.

Upon my return to the New York Public Library, I began to search for all available data relevant to early American music engraving and publishing. Fortuitously, I soon made a valuable discovery among the manuscripts of Frederick Rausch, one of our earlier publishers, in the Manuscripts Division of the library. Finding a receipt for the purchase of metal music plates among the Rausch Papers set me off on a frenzied search, which resulted in a substantial essay on this esoteric subject. (This essay forms the basis of Chapter 6 herein.) A few other essays followed before I completed the 1801–25 bibliography and left the New York Public Library in 1964 to assume a position with the Lilly Library of Indiana University. Because this move placed me at a great distance from sources, I had to postpone further work on this study until I could obtain outside assistance for travel and research. I received small grants from the American Philosophical Society and the American Council of Learned Societies when, in the spring of 1965, I was offered a position in the Harvard University library system.

The assumption of that position and the weighty responsibilities connected with it, as well as the reestablishing of my family in the East, prevented further work on the book immediately. While I worked on the book intermittently after 1968, it was not until I had a meeting with A. Hyatt King, Keeper of Music in the British Museum, and with James Mosley, librarian of the St. Bride Institute and editor of the *Journal of the Printing Historical Society*, during a trip to London in June 1972, that I recommenced serious work on this project. King made me aware that I had much valuable information about early music publishing that should be made known to others. Mosley brought to my attention a trade card of Richard Austin, an English engraver of the late eighteenth century who cut music punches, which set me off on a new course of investigations into the origin of these little-known tools. The identity of the manufacturers of these instruments had remained a principal stumbling block to further progress on the book, and my talk with Mosley suggested possible breakthroughs on that particular problem.

As a result of my contacts with King and Mosley, I resolved to resume work on this project and to complete it. Investigations into the nature and origin of early music punches and into other aspects of the early American trade were carried on—sometimes in bursts of activity that flamed into white heat—during the remainder of that summer and during the summers of 1973 and 1974, and the work was concluded just before Thanksgiving of that year. If the book suffers from an off again–on again manner of research and writing, it has gained all the more from a continually maturing viewpoint and from a slow and systematic growth of knowledge of this and analogous subjects. Some parts of it could not have been written in the 1960s; the elucidation of these subjects had to be the by-products of longtime thought and continual reevaluation, and, of course, of later discoveries.

When I initially conceived the idea of this work I patterned its organization and scope after Lawrence Wroth's study of the colonial American printer (*The Colonial Printer*, 1931), attempting to accomplish for our early music-publishing trade what he achieved with regard to the early letterpress printing industry. Like the nest of a magpie, my study had to be woven together from bits and pieces, often from seemingly unimportant material. For this reason, I have included only a selective bibliography of frequently cited works, restricting citations of other sources to bibliographical footnotes.

This work is intended to serve as a companion piece to the Sonneck-Upton bibliography of eighteenth-century American music and to my own continuation of that bibliography. It attempts to answer such questions regarding the engraving, printing, publishing, and selling of music in America during the colonial and federal periods as a collector, librarian, musicologist, historian, bibliographer, researcher, or other interested person would be likely to ask. The main part of the work is concerned with the publication of music from about 1787 until about 1830, the period when professional musicians and music publishers came to America in increasing numbers and began to form a music-publishing industry here. However, to place these endeavors in proper perspective, I have also included chapters on music publishing and its techniques during the colonial phase of our history, as well as information, wherever possible, on later innovations and practices. I shall be pleased if this book encourages others to undertake more detailed studies of the points herein, and hope that it may prompt investigation as well into other related aspects of this subject.

ACKNOWLEDGMENTS

BECAUSE THERE WERE no fundamental sources upon which to base such a study, and no individuals or colleagues within my orbit with whom I could discuss problems and work out possible solutions, the compilation of this work has been a lonely task. However, I am particularly grateful for the many bits and pieces contributing substantially to the work that were brought to my attention by associates and friends, some of whom also read the manuscript and made substantial and constructive criticisms. Therefore, my debts are many.

My indebtedness to A. Hyatt King of the British Library of the British Museum and to James Mosley of the St. Bride's Institute in London have already been acknowledged in the Preface. Several bibliographer or musicologist friends read the manuscript and offered scores of suggestions and criticisms which have been woven invisibly into the fabric of this work. Chief among these were Rollo G. Silver, Richard A. Crawford, and Nicholas E. Tawa. Marcus A. McCorison of the American Antiquarian Society informed me of the work of William Norman, who about 1783 cast probably the first music types produced in America. In addition, McCorison equipped me with a number of the illustrations which appear herein. Jacob Blanck, the distinguished bibliographer of American literature and a good friend, supplied me with a music plate which also forms one of the illustrations herein. Two music engravers, Frank Cappiello of Jersey City, and Walter Bolke of Hillsdale, New York, took time out from their work to discuss past and current customs and techniques of their trade and to show me tools and processes. In addition, Bolke provided me with tools of nineteenth-century American manufacture, some of which have been reproduced as illustrations herein. Crawford should be mentioned again, both for having turned over to me some information, previously unpublished (and unknown to me), on the earliest music printing from type in this country, and for sharing with me some of his vast knowledge of early American psalmody, a service similarly provided by Irving Lowens, who also brought to my attention the account book of Simeon Wood, which makes up Appendix A herein. Several music collectors, most notably Lester S. Levy, William Lloyd Keepers, Harry Dichter, and Saul Starr, also gave advice, encouragement, materials for illustrations, and, most important, warm friendship. Edwin Wolf 2nd of the Library Company of Philadelphia, which holds unique copies of several of the colonial tunebooks discussed in Chapter 2 herein, allowed free use of those materials and gave valuable advice with regard to their printers and printing. Several former colleagues at the New York Public Library, especially John Edmunds, Sidney Beck, the late Frederick Freeman, and David V. Erdman, provided advice and assistance. Roger Stoddard of the Houghton Library of Harvard, in addition to informing me of an important collection of unpublished materials that shed light on early American music vending, kept reminding me of my obligation to conclude this work and so served as the Socratic gadfly that kept the horse from sleeping. (He read the completed manuscript, as well.) David Gunner of the Warren Anatomical Museum of the Harvard Medical School was responsible for reproducing several of the composite illustrations here. The administrators and curators of the Boston Public Library, the Essex Institute in Salem, Massachusetts, the Houghton Library at Harvard, the Philadelphia Museum of Art, and the New York Public Library allowed me to reproduce materials from their collections. Other individuals who provided assistance were: Gilbert Chase, who gave major assistance in bringing the manuscript to the attention of Richard L. Wentworth, Director of the University of Illinois Press; Stuart C. Sherman, formerly John Hay Librarian at Brown University; Whitfield J. Bell, Jr., and Murphy D. Smith of the American Philosophical Society; H. Earle Johnson; Jacob Kainen, formerly of the Division of Graphic Arts at the Smithsonian Institution; William Lichtenwanger, formerly of the Music Division of the Library of Congress; Richard Jackson, Curator of the Musical Americana Collection at the New York Public Library; John Tasker Howard; Hannah D. French; A. N. L. Munby of King's College, Cambridge; and librarians of the Bodleian Library, Oxford, the Dundee Public Library, the Mitchell Library, Glasgow, the Cardiff Public Library, and the John Rylands

Library, Manchester. The indirect assistance, through their pioneering efforts and important publications, of Virginia Larkin Redway and Rita Susswein Gottesman must also be acknowledged. (The same may be said of compilations of printers and allied tradesmen of Philadelphia, New York, Boston, and elsewhere, by Rollo Silver, H. Glenn and Maude O. Brown, and others.) My deep gratitude is owed to the American Philosophical Society and the American Council of Learned Societies for providing me with financial assistance necessary to underwrite the expenses of research, and to the Bibliographical Society of America for generously advancing funds to allow this work to come into print. My thanks also go to Doris J. Dyen, who edited this work for publication with intelligence, sympathy, and understanding. Finally, to Carleton Sprague Smith the deepest acknowledgment of all: the inspiration for beginning this work (as well as *Secular Music in America*). His breadth of musicological knowledge and his interest in promoting greater understanding and appreciation of early American music were beacon lights which guided me throughout.

*Early American
Music Engraving
and Printing*

CHAPTER I

Anglo-European Background

꽃꽃

BECAUSE OF THE nature of his subject matter, the printer of music must cope with a great many problems not encountered by the everyday letterpress typographer. The latter has only to set meaningful text in a single, horizontal direction. The music printer, on the other hand, works with symbols instead of words, which have to be positioned vertically as well as horizontally and must fit into measured schemes in either direction. Instead of one line, he deals at once with five, on or about which he must arrange his symbols in up and down positions in order to denote pitch; vary them, in both form and spacing, in order to show changes in time value; and frequently situate them one above the other so as to depict chords for the production of simultaneous sound. Finally, in vocal music, he must establish a relationship between notes on the staff and words underneath. Because of the multiplicity of forms inherent in music, a variety of methods have arisen over the centuries for reproducing it in print. These have included the printing of music from movable type, from wood and metal blocks, from engraved plates, and, beginning in the early nineteenth century, by the process of lithography. Some of these methods were carried on simultaneously, with one at times more dominant than another. And some of them became restricted to the production of particular types of musical works. The following brief outline, derived in large part from the prior work of others, traces the development of these varied processes from the period of the earliest

[3]

music printing down to the time when music printing was transferred from the old world to the new.[1]

Musical notation found its way into printed books within a few years after the invention of movable type, the first such example occurring in the famous *Psalterium* of 1457, printed by Fust and Schoeffer.[2] But until the beginning of the sixteenth century, the art of printing music involved only the production of simple service books and the inclusion of musical examples in books of theory and instruction. While great advances in the composition of polyphonic music paralleled the invention and early development of letterpress typography, the crude techniques of early printing were incapable of reproducing elaborate polyphonic notation and rhythms. As a result, not one book containing polyphonic compositions printed from type emanated from any press in Europe before the close of the fifteenth century. During this period, liturgical books were in most demand. These contained simple music, usually monodic plainsong. In order to reproduce such works, printers resorted to movable type. For the less numerous books dealing with musical theory and instruction, in which brief examples only were needed, printers mostly used engraved blocks, usually wooden but sometimes metal. When using movable type, the printer had to devise a system of correlating staves, notes, and text, for he was limited by the simple concepts of the earliest typefounders, who had not yet conceived the idea of casting anything but a single form—that is, a single letter, a single note, a single sign, a single line—at any one time. The earliest printers surmounted this problem by using engraved blocks or separate lengths of rules for printing staves together with text beneath at a first impression, and subsequently printing notes and signs at a second impression, meticulously justifying the two so that the notes and signs registered in their proper positions on the staff.

1. Major sources here include A. Hyatt King, *Four Hundred Years of Music Printing* (London, British Museum, 1964; 2nd ed. 1968); H. Edmund Poole, "New Music Types," *Journal of the Printing Historical Society* I (1965) 21–38, II (1966) 23–44; chapters 2 and 3 of William Gamble's *Music Engraving and Printing*; Kathi Meyer and Eva Judd O'Meara, "The Printing of Music," in *The Dolphin* (New York, Limited Editions Club, 1935), pp. 171–207; Charles Humphries and William C. Smith, *Music Publishing in the British Isles from the Earliest Times to the Middle of the Nineteenth Century* (London, Cassell, 1954); Frank Kidson, *British Music Publishers, Printers and Engravers* (London, Hill, 1900); William C. Smith, *Bibliography of the Musical Works Published by John Walsh during the Years 1695–1720* (London, Bibliographical Society, 1948); and an anonymous article "Music and Music Printing" which appeared in the *Printing Times and Lithographer* in 1875. An excellent pictorial presentation of the advance of this art appears in *The Printed Note*, a catalog published by the Toledo Museum of Art in 1957 in conjunction with its exhibition covering 500 years of music printing and engraving, which was held between January 14 and February 24 of that year.

2. Only the text and three black lines of the staff were printed; the fourth line was drawn in by hand in red, and the notes were written in, also.

Recent scholarship has theorized that the first book of music printed from specially designed type is a Gradual of which the only extant copy is in the British Museum (I.B. 15154). This book lacks both a date of issue and a printer's name, but its production has been assigned to the year 1473 because the type employed to print it is similar to that of another work which is known to have been printed at that time, and its origin has been ascribed to an unidentified press in southern Germany. The next work containing music—and the first music book bearing its date of issue—is a Missal produced at Rome by the German printer Ulrich Han on October 12, 1476. The music here is printed in Roman notation, with text initials in red or blue, and touches of yellow in the capitals, all added by hand.[3] From these beginnings the printing of music from movable type spread rapidly throughout most of Europe, so that by 1501 nearly 270 such works had appeared. However, the skills acquired by the early printers were not applied with equal consistency, nor did music printing undergo much technical development within this initial period. Even as late as the final decade of the fifteenth century, methods were sometimes crude and uneven. Printing at two impressions, with its need for meticulous justification, still posed an insurmountable problem for some printers, for in many cases only notes were printed, with the staves later added by hand. Or sometimes staves were first printed from woodblocks or from lengths of rules, and then left blank for the notes to be added by hand. And infrequently, both staves and notes were so added.

The earliest use of movable type for printing music other than liturgies occured in 1473, when Conrad Fyner of Esslingen printed five identical square notes in descending sequence to illustrate the mystical meaning of certain words in Charlier de Gerson's *Collectorium Super Manificat.*[4] The earliest known printing both of secular music and of mensural notes occurred in Franciscus Niger's *Grammatica*, issued at Venice in 1480 by Theodor of Würzburg. In this book, the notes were printed from type and the staves added later by hand. In the second edition of this work (Basle, ca. 1485) the same notes were printed from a woodblock, the first

---

3. Pages from both the Gradual of 1473 and the Missal printed by Han are reproduced in color in King's *Four Hundred Years of Music Printing* (Plates II and III).

4. As King has noted, the importance of this passage has been exaggerated. The notation was stamped, probably with metal and perhaps by inverting type pieces, while the staff lines were left to be supplied by hand. This same technique was employed in the second edition of Ralph Higden's *Polichronicon*, which contains the first music printed in England. The first edition (1482) was printed by William Caxton, who did not possess music types and consequently left a space for music to be filled in by hand. In the second edition, printed by Wynkyn de Worde in 1495, the musical notes were printed with quads or inverted letters, while the staff lines were printed with type rules.

[5]

such occurrence for secular music. More extended use of the woodblock is found in Nicholas Burtius's *Musices Opusculum*, issued at Bologna in 1487, which includes what is thought to be the first printed polyphonic music. Woodblocks were continually employed for the printing of music throughout the first half of the sixteenth century, particularly for books requiring only musical examples or for reproducing polyphonic quotations. They continued in use, though with diminished frequency, for 200 years afterward.

The slow progress made in the printing of music from type throughout the fifteenth century is sharply contrasted with the fine craftsmanship achieved by Ottaviano dei Petrucci during the very first years of the next. A native of Fossombrone, Petrucci moved to Venice in 1491 and established a printing house there (which he moved back to Fossombrone in 1513). Having received in 1498 from the Venetian Republic a patent for printing music by movable type, he published in 1501 his first book, entitled *Odhecaton*, a collection of ninety-six secular songs for several voices. This was tastefully printed in lozenge-shaped notes. Petrucci worked by triple impression, printing first the staves, then the text, initial letters, and signatures, and then the notes. His presswork was so meticulous that he was able to achieve perfect register of notes, text, and staves. His punchcutting and typecasting were also of the highest caliber, so that the resulting typefaces were elegant and appealing. In all, Petrucci produced sixty-one publications, which consisted of partbooks, each voice being printed separately. The technical difficulties he overcame in reaching this standard of perfection in layout, composition, and printing were considerable. Petrucci's work represents a high-water mark in early music publishing, unrivaled during his own lifetime and for a long time afterward. Even today, one marvels at the esthetic beauty of his pages. When one considers the conditions and circumstances under which he worked and the limited knowledge and implements of printing at his time, his achievement appears all the more remarkable.

It is obvious that the sheer perfection of Petrucci's process must have made it a slow and costly way to issue music. Triple impression is rarely found elsewhere, although Petrucci's methods and style were widely and often successfully imitated by various printers who used only double impression. The difficulties presented by printing in several impressions were alleviated about 1525 by the introduction of a process needing but one press operation. This method embodied the principle of casting each note and its line, together with its stem, if any was required, on one piece of type. Types were cast for every note and for any necessary time variations of notes, as well as for rests, clefs, and other necessary signs. The compositor arranged his types one after the other following his copy as always, but as he worked he assembled not only the notes but the staves too, resulting in a complete composition from which copies could be struck off at a single impression. The invention of this process is unknown, although it was long attributed to Pierre Haultin of Paris. This method of printing was probably first employed by Pierre Attaingnant of Paris, printer of music to the King (1538–52), in a collection of *chansons* issued in April 1527.[5] Single-impression printing of about this period is also found on two anonymous pieces of music printed by John Rastell of London, which survive in a single copy each in the British Museum. Neither of these bears a date, but both have been assigned to the years immediately after 1525.[6] For a long period thereafter, the accepted method in musical typography was single-impression printing from movable type.[7]

After the invention of printing music at a single impression, there still remained the need to adapt this method to chord figures and to quick-moving music containing many small notes. The single-impression method was best suited to monodic music, but by the sixteenth century polyphonic composition had begun to flourish freely, and the question of reproducing it in score arose. The earliest manuscripts containing instrumental music in several voices were written in tablatures, that is, in a system of notation which represents chords by means of letters or numbers. This type of notation was necessary for polyphonic compositions, such as those for the organ, lute, and clavichord, in which the chords had to be played by one person. But while the columns of numbers and letters in tablatures indicated the notes which were to be played together, they did not show the movement of the individual parts and

5. Our knowledge of Attaingnant has recently been enlarged through the publication of Daniel Heartz's *Pierre Attaingnant, Royal Printer of Music; a Historical Study and Bibliographical Catalogue* (Berkeley, University of California Press, 1969).

6. A Hyatt King, in his "The Significance of John Rastell in Early Music Printing," *The Library* 5th ser XXVI (1971) [197]–214, has reviewed the Haultin claims and their fallacies, and has analyzed the remaining Rastell fragments of music in an attempt to date their publication more precisely. His conclusions here constitute the latest thinking on this problem which is far from being resolved.

7. Guy A. Marco's *The Earliest Music Printers of Continental Europe; a Checklist of Facsimiles Illustrating Their Work* (Charlottesville, Bibliographical Society of the University of Virginia, 1962) provides a key for anyone who wishes to locate republished specimens of the work of many of the earliest music printers. His booklet lists a great many examples of early music printing which have been reproduced in modern critical literature, ranging from the year 1457, when Fust and Schoeffer issued their famous *Psalterium*, through 1599. *The Printed Note*, cited before, is of special value for showing, in one convenient location, a great range of specimens of early music printing.

did not allow the score to be read easily. Nor were these requirements fulfilled by the single-impression printing of the day. However, they were satisfied from the first by engraving, a method of printing music especially suited to instrumental music.

The year 1586 is generally accepted as the date of the introduction of engraving to the reproduction of music, for in that year Verovio published at Rome the *Diletto Spirituale*, which contained the first practical music to be issued through the engraving process.[8] By 1608, Verovio had published a dozen engraved books, mostly anthologies. He sometimes employed as his engraver a fellow countryman, Martin van Buyten (Verovio had emigrated from Holland in 1575 and had Italianized his name). Verovio's tradition was carried on in Rome by Nicolo Borbone, who issued magnificent volumes of Frescobaldi's keyboard music from 1615 onward. From this time on, the engraving method spread slowly over northern Europe, where it was the sole method of reproducing music in score until after the middle of the eighteenth century. At the same time, the printing of music by single impression also flourished, being used to produce instrumental and vocal partbooks and large quantities of church music. Outside Italy, the first country in which engraved music appeared was England. There William Hole prepared an anthology of virginal music by Byrd, Bull, and Orlando Gibbons entitled *Parthenia*, which was published between November 1612 and February 1613 to celebrate a royal wedding. *Parthenia* was followed in November 1613 by Angelo Notari's *Prime Musiche Nuova*, by Orlando Gibbon's *Fantasies of III Parts* about 1620, and by *Parthenia In-Violata* about 1625. In Holland, the next country to receive the process, several engraved books of lute tablatures appeared between 1615 and 1620.

Copperplate engraving is thought to have originated from *nielo* engraving, a process in which an engraved intaglio upon a metal surface was filled with a black substance to show up the engraving. The statement of Vasari, attributing to Maso Finiguerra, a Florentine goldsmith, the first transfer of impressions from an engraved surface to paper about 1460, has been disproved, for later research has shown that engraving was carried on in the north Alps for several decades before this date. In any event, the

---

8. King, in *Four Hundred Years of Music Printing* (1964 ed., p. 17), notes that this process was previously applied to music in 1581, when Giorgio Marescotti of Florence printed the first edition of Galilei's *Diologo . . . della Musica Antica e della Moderna*. In this work, all the musical examples were set from type but two, each of which was printed from an engraved plate. Examples of engraved music also appeared in a number of prints issued between 1584 and 1587. These contain short phrases of music being sung or played by saints or angels from open music books.

art of engraving progressed rapidly after the middle of the fifteenth century and was used extensively after 1500 for printing both pictures and text. Its transfer to music printing, where its freehand methods could be well employed in the reproduction of polyphony, was undoubtedly a natural one.

By about 1700, engraving had gained ascendancy over typography throughout most of Europe for producing music. In England, whence sprang most of the traditions of our own trade, Thomas Cross is given much credit for spurring the growth of this method. He not only popularized the process, but he set a standard of artistic workmanship that was rarely equaled by his contemporaries or successors. Between 1683 and 1733, he turned out a great amount of engraved music, nearly all of it of the highest quality in design and execution. He also popularized the publication of single song sheets, which he issued in considerable numbers.

At first, music was engraved on copper with a graver and other tools, in a freehand style. But soon after 1700 radical changes were introduced, for economic reasons. Instead of copper, which was hard and costly, pewter, which was softer, less expensive, and easier to work, began to be used; concurrently, freehand engraving was superceded by stamping. The punch or stamp, in limited use as early as about 1660, was first used for the heads of the notes, and later for accidentals, clefs, time-signatures, and, in vocal music, for the text. The graver was retained for cutting the stems of notes and for cutting ties and slurs. The staves were usually drawn on the plate with a five-pronged instrument called a scorer, though they were infrequently scratched in with the graver one line at a time.

The two countries principally concerned with the development of these changes were England and Holland. Priority seems to belong to Holland, where, about 1700, a method was discovered for softening copper, probably through combining one or more metals with it, so that notation could be stamped in instead of drawn in by hand. King points out that the Dutch publisher Estienne Roger took full advantage of this new method well before 1710. His great rival in England was John Walsh the elder, who adopted pewter and punching before 1710. With the arrival of these methods, English music publishing and music selling underwent a revolution. Walsh not only lowered the price of music by employing these less expensive methods and materials, thereby giving the music an appreciably larger circulation, but also used various methods of advertising to bring it to the widest possible audience. He started off by issuing cheap instructors and music sheets and was soon publishing collections of

[9]

songs and instrumental works, theater music, operas, sonatas, and even musical periodicals.[9] From the early eighteenth century on, new firms were constantly springing up, both in England and on the Continent, to share in the ever increasing market for printed music. By the middle of the century the cheap music plate, partly punched, partly engraved, was recognized as the medium used by the majority of English and European publishers for printing music.

Just after the middle of the eighteenth century, concurrent with the almost universal adoption of the punched plate by the music-publishing industries of England and the Continent, there occurred a revival in the printing of music from type. This method had never really gone out of use, but its lack of flexibility restricted it to certain types of publications: hymn- and songbooks, larger collections of secular songs, and theoretical works; it was employed only by publishers and printers who specialized in one or more of these types of books. Credit for the revival of the method is owed to Johann Gottlieb Immanuel Breitkopf, who in the mid-1740s began a long period of research and experiment to overcome its limitations. Breitkopf had inherited from his father a fairly important printing office at Leipzig, which was equipped to produce music from punched plates. Though not himself an engraver, he was an experienced printer and a lover of music; by 1754 he had perfected a new font of type of much improved appearance, which was based on a radical departure from the principles of design that had remained almost unchanged since the days of Attaingnant. Breitkopf abandoned the usual idea of a type unit composed of a note-head, stem, and staff on a single piece. He broke the unit down into separate pieces for the head and stem, attached to staff segments of varying length. And he devised another piece that could be positioned at the end of the stem, with one, two, or three flags for the alteration of time value.

As his first large work, Breitkopf printed the score of a pastoral drama, *Il Trionfo della Fedeltà*, composed by the Electress Maria Anna Walpurgis of Bavaria and published in 1756 under her pseudonym Ermelinda Talia Pastorella Arcada. The type here is clean, the presswork crisp, the pages are surrounded by tasteful borders, and the openings of the acts are decorated with ornamental headpieces to give the production an elegance

---

9. Some idea of the importance and extent of the activity of the John Walshes, father and son, can be judged from an examination of William C. Smith's *A Bibliography of the Musical Works Published by John Walsh during the Years 1695–1720* and of Smith and Charles Humphries's *A Bibliography of the Musical Works Published by the Firm of John Walsh during the Years 1721–1766* (London, Bibliographical Society, 1968). Smith ascribes Walsh's use of punches to as early as the year 1695.

seldom achieved again. Between 1755 and 1761 Breitkopf printed fifty-one musical works, including operas, keyboard compositions, and songs. His types were a great success, and other publishers adopted or adapted them. With the introduction of Breitkopf's fonts, the modern system of printing music from type was achieved. Nothing essential has been altered since that time. The main disadvantage of typeset music—a factor which has been largely responsible for restricting its use to works originally produced by single impression—is the great number of sorts of type needed to complete a font. While the French typefounder Fournier succeeded in reducing the number of these to 160, Gamble states that about 400 are now needed (i.e., as of 1923) to make up the usual font, and in many cases the number is still higher.[10] The setting itself is also difficult, requiring, in addition to skill, a great amount of patience and accuracy. Finally, music printed from type has never attained the esthetic beauty of the engraved product.

This, then, was the approximate state of English and European music publishing toward the end of the eighteenth century, when the American industry began to flourish on a continuing basis by emulating these examples and traditions. The printing of music sheets was effected almost entirely through the agency of the stamped plate, while typography was usually restricted to the publication of large collections, mostly of sacred music, and of theoretical works and books of instruction containing mostly textual matter but with a few musical examples. (In general, the engraved and punched plate was adaptable to the issuance of small editions of publications consisting of a few pages only, while the typographic process was better suited to the publication of bulkier works which were printed in great quantity from one setting of type.) The punching technique for printing music which was introduced in America within a few years after the Revolution, and the concurrent springing up of typographic music presses for the publication of sacred collections and the like marked the beginning of a music-publishing industry or trade in this country. Within a few years after its inception this trade had dwarfed the feeble attempts to publish music in America during the previous ninety years.

---

10. Breitkopf's original font contained 257 characters. H. Edmund Poole's article (see n. 1) explains in greater detail the Breitkopf method of printing music. It also provides excellent accounts of the various experiments which were being carried on at the same time by other persons—J. F. Rosart, P. S. Fournier le jeune, J. M. Fleischmann, and Johannes Enschedè—to perfect a method of printing music from types that would parallel the results of the engraved and punched plate.

CHAPTER II

Music Publishing in the American Colonies

APPROXIMATELY 175 years separated the pioneer settlements at Jamestown (1607), Plymouth (1620), New Amsterdam (1626), and Boston (1630) from the beginning of a permanent music-publishing industry in America shortly after the conclusion of the Revolutionary War. During this century and three quarters—a period about as long as the existence of that industry from its inception to the present time—comparatively little music was published in America. What did appear here was usually either printed from woodcuts, if included within the text of a book, or engraved on copper in a freehand style, when issued in collection. At present, we know of only a handful of music books which were printed from type in America before 1786, when Isaiah Thomas set up the first enduring typographic music press at Worcester, Massachusetts; all of these date from the 1750s on. While the history and motivation behind the publication of these books is frequently unclear, it appears from the evidence at hand that most if not all were printed to satisfy some local need, from type that had been imported specifically for that purpose. None represented the product of a long-continuing music-publishing effort.[1]

1. Allen P. Britton has estimated, in his dissertation "Theoretical Introductions in American Tune-Books to 1800" (p. 120), that "during the period beginning in 1698 (when a collection of two-part tunes was first added to the *Bay Psalm Book*) and extending to the close of the year 1800, there were published in the United States at least 319 separate editions,

Our first music publishing was naturally related to the spiritual requirements of the early settlers and resulted from their desire for a more satisfactory translation of the scriptures than was found in the standard European psalters of the day. The Pilgrims of 1620 brought to the Plymouth Colony their own psalter, the *Book of Psalmes*, prepared by Henry Ainsworth for the congregations of Separatists who fled from England to Holland.[2] When the small group of Hollanders who settled New Amsterdam began to hold services in the Dutch church in 1628, they sang the songs of the Dutch psalter printed at Amsterdam. The Puritans of the Winthrop fleet, who settled the Massachusetts Bay Colony in 1630, carried with them the psalter of Sternhold and Hopkins, which had dominated the English field since its publication in 1562, though the more cultivated early New England settlers may at times have used Thomas Ravencroft's *Whole Booke of Psalmes*, published in 1621, or Richard Allison's *Psalmes of David* of 1599.[3]

In time, dissatisfaction arose over the translations of Sternhold and Hopkins, who were thought to have taken too many liberties with the meaning of the original Hebrew, and a committee of thirty New England divines was appointed to prepare a more literal metrical translation. Their efforts resulted in *The Whole Booke of Psalmes Faithfully Translated into English Metre*, better known as the Bay Psalm Book, which was first published at Cambridge in 1640. Between that date and 1762 the book went through twenty-seven American editions, with some twenty more editions appearing in England; the last dated British issue that has come

representing 152 individual titles, of works containing religious vocal music." The majority of these appeared in the period after 1787, following the formal introduction of typographic music printing. But with few exceptions, which are discussed in Chapter 3 herein, all works produced before that date were printed from copperplates which had been freely engraved by hand, or, in the very beginning, had been reproduced from woodblocks. The list of such tunebooks or sacred collections in Britton's dissertation has been revised and enlarged by Richard Crawford of the University of Michigan, and his reworking of this material is scheduled for publication by the American Antiquarian Society in the near future under the tentative title, *Bibliography of Sacred Music Through the Year 1810 Published in America*.

2. This book contained thirth-nine psalm tunes, about half of them extracted from English psalm books with the remainder comprising French and Dutch tunes in a variety of meters. Ainsworth's psalter was superior, musically, to any English psalm book then available. It remained in use at Plymouth until 1692, when it was abandoned in favor of the Bay Psalm Book, because the children of the emigrant generation were no longer able to sing the more involved tunes to which their fathers had been accustomed.

3. The Sternhold and Hopkins psalter, or the "Old Version," as it was frequently called, had been produced by English Protestant exiles in Geneva on the model of the French Genevan psalter of 1562, and it was used in the worship of the Church of England for about a century and a half, gradually giving way to the *New Version* (*A New Version of the Psalms of David, Fitted to the Tunes Used in Churches*), produced by Nahum Tate and Nicholas Brady in London, 1696.

to my attention is the twenty-first (Edinburgh, Printed by Adrian Watkins) of 1756.

The earlier editions of the Bay Psalm Book contained no music (probably for lack of anyone capable of engraving woodblocks for printing it) and, in fact, restricted the use of psalm tunes to only those tunes which conformed to its six meters. The earliest known edition of the Bay Psalm Book containing musical notation was the ninth, published in 1698. This crudely printed book, with its thirteen tunes at the back in two-part harmony, in diamond-shaped notes printed from wood, is the earliest existing music of American imprint.[4]

The limitations placed by the Bay Psalm Book upon the number and variety of psalm tunes which could be sung to its words is thought to have resulted in a lessening of the psalm-tune repertory. At the same time, the lack of printed music in the book's earlier editions resulted in a widespread decline in ability to read music, so that the majority of people came to sing by ear. This condition led to a continuation of the earlier English practice of "lining out" the psalms. In New England churches it became the custom for the deacon to "set the tune." He would sing the psalm, line by line, pausing for the congregation to repeat the line he had just sung. The quality of singing, then, depended upon the ability and quality of the leader. It was probably the practice of lining-out more than any other factor which, toward the end of the seventeenth century, led to the great confusion regarding the tunes themselves and the manner of rendering them.[5]

In the initial decades of the eighteenth century the need for reform in psalm singing became evident, and several divines set about achieving it.[6]

---

4. As Donald W. Krummel has noted (p. 218) in his article "Graphic Analysis, Its Application to Early American Engraved Music," the music contained in this work has been the basis of considerable controversy. Extant copies are in poor condition, making it difficult to conclude where and how they were printed. In later editions, copperplates were used for printing the music. The Bay Psalm Book soon came into wide use, not only in New England, but, in its 1751 form, as far south as Philadelphia.

5. In the preface to their work *William Billings of Boston: Eighteenth-Century Printer* (Princeton University Press, 1975), Richard Crawford and David McKay try to deal with the tricky problem of lining-out and setting the tune in early New England psalmody. They claim here that they found no evidence that deacons set the tune, that is, sang it line by line, followed by congregational response. Crawford and McKay have concluded that lining-out, as practiced by New England deacons, was more likely a chanted reading of the text, pitched but not in the pitches of the tune.

6. In a yet unpublished work entitled "Music in the American Experience," Nicholas E. Tawa of Boston ascribes this call for reform in psalm singing to the urban young. The principal reasons for reform, Tawa reasons, were the desire of the youth of early eighteenth-century Boston to be able to sing together with one another and to sing in harmony. Tawa has looked into this controversy in great detail and has sorted out the various

About 1721 the Reverend John Tufts published a little work entitled *A Very Plain and Easy Introduction to the Singing of Psalm Tunes*, though no edition earlier than the third (Boston, 1723) has been located. This was a modest pamphlet of only twelve pages, containing thirty-seven tunes set in three parts, with instructions for singing adapted to Ravenscroft and John Playford. Though this work went through eleven editions up to 1744, Tufts's "easy method of singing by letters instead of notes" was not widely adopted.[7] Tufts's work was followed in 1721 by another instruction book, also produced by a New England divine. This was the *Grounds and Rules of Musick Explained: or An Introduction to the Art of Singing by Note*, compiled by the Reverend Thomas Walter of Roxbury, Massachusetts, a nephew of Cotton Mather. This book was issued from the Boston press of James Franklin, the older brother of Benjamin (who was then an apprentice in James's printing establishment). Walter's book went through at least eight editions, the last in 1764.[8] It was highly regarded, and it exerted wide influence for more than forty years. It was the first music book to be printed with bar lines in the American colonies. At about the time Walter's book first appeared, a controversy occurred, with the reformers advocating and trying to impose "regular singing" (i.e., by note), while the common folk preferred their own way of singing, handed down through oral tradition. The progressive element eventually won out and singing societies, where instruction could be obtained, were ultimately formed throughout New England, the first such appearing in Boston in 1721. The years which followed saw a gradual broadening of interest in psalm singing, and by the 1740s a number of churches (but not

arguments, and the pamphlets and other publications supporting them, for and against the method of "regular singing" or "singing by rule," as it was termed.

7. Until less than ten years ago the fifth (Boston, 1726) was the earliest known edition of the Tufts work. A report of the discovery of a unique copy of the third (Boston, 1723) edition was made by Theodore M. Finney in the *Journal of Research in Music Education* XIV (1966) 163–70. Instead of musical notation, Tufts used letters to indicate the notes of the scale, with time value indicated through a system of punctuation. A letter standing alone was equal to a quarter note; a letter followed by a period was equal to a half note; and one followed by a colon, to a whole note. The initial publication of this work has been ascribed variously to the years 1710, 1712, 1714, and 1715. However, its first appearance in 1721 seems most likely, for the earliest known reference to it appeared in the *Boston News-Letter* of January 2 of that year. For a resumé of the earliest editions of this work see Allen P. Britton and Irving Lowens, "Unlocated Titles in Early Sacred Music," Music Library Association *Notes* 2nd ser XI (1953) 33–48. A detailed discussion of Tufts's work was later published by Lowens, "John Tufts' *Introduction to the Singing of Psalm-Tunes* (1721–1744): The First American Music Textbook," in the *Journal of Research in Music Education* II (1954) 89–102. This article was republished under the same title in Lowens's *Music and Musicians in Early America*, pp. 39–57.

8. Matt B. Jones, "Bibliographical Notes of Thomas Walter's *Grounds and Rules of Musick Explained*," *Proceedings of the American Antiquarian Society* XLI (1932) 235–46, provides a complete history and description of all editions.

Congregational churches) in New England and elsewhere had introduced organs for its accompaniment.

Previous to this reform, the Bay Psalm Book had reigned supreme in the New England congregations, as had Sternhold and Hopkins among the Presbyterians and Episcopalians of the other colonies. However, with the revival of singing toward the first quarter of the eighteenth century, other influences arose which occasioned a decline in the popularity of both of these works. This decline began with the appearance of Tate and Brady's *New Version* of the psalms in 1696 and gained impetus in 1711 through the publication of Isaac Watts's *Hymns* and in 1719 through his *Psalms of David Imitated.*[9] An appreciation of Watts's hymns and psalms spread rapidly, so that by 1800 Watts completely dominated the hymnody in most American churches. Concurrent with the growing popularity of Watts's hymns and psalms was the emergence of local and native compilers and composers. From the middle of the eighteenth century on, a number of sacred collections began to be published in the colonies which greatly increased the singer's repertory. In 1761 appeared the Reverend James Lyon's *Urania, or A Choice Collection of Psalm-Tunes, Anthems and Hymns*, the first Philadelphia musical publication of historical importance. This contained seventy wordless psalm tunes, fourteen hymns, and twelve anthems, making it the largest collection of music thus far published in the colonies. The 1764 publication, *A Collection of the Best Psalm Tunes*, compiled by Josiah Flagg of Boston, constituted the most significant collection issued up to that time in New England. This work was notable not only for containing lighter music intermingled with the psalm tunes but also because the plates for it were engraved by Paul Revere. In the mid- and late 1760s appeared a number of collections compiled or published by Daniel Bayley of Newburyport, Massachusetts, and the 1770s and early 1780s witnessed the publication of several works of William Billings, said to be the first American composer to make music his profession. All of the foregoing and, in fact, nearly all other music books issued in the American colonies were printed from engraved copperplates, the engraving having been effected in a freehand style by a local engraver or silversmith, as noted before in the case of Paul Revere. The handful of music books printed from movable type during this period will be discussed separately in the following chapter.

9. An edition of Tate and Brady was published in Boston in 1713, being the second known American imprint to contain musical notation. Richard Crawford has reported to me that he recently located a copy of this work, which had previously been unknown in an extant copy, in Yale University's Beinecke Library. For the most part, however, various editions of this and other music books needed for services in American churches during the eighteenth century were imported from abroad, as need dictated.

It is necessary to make a number of observations here regarding the involvement of the ordinary engraver or silversmith in the production of music books in the American colonies. In his classic work on early American printing, *The Colonial Printer*, Lawrence C. Wroth has devoted several pages to the subject of the silversmith as engraver, pointing out that Thomas Sparrow of Annapolis, Paul Revere of Boston, and Amos Doolittle and Abel Buell of Connecticut represented a well-known type among American engravers: the silversmith who practiced engraving as a subsidiary craft, employing in it the techniques he used for incising coats of arms and decorative designs of coffeepots, urns, and other products of his manufacture. As Stephen De Witt Stephens has aptly observed in *The Mavericks, American Engravers*, "silversmithing leads naturally to engraving, for cutting a design on a silver teapot is little different from cutting it on a flat copperplate, and the task of taking off an impression on paper follows easily."[10] Since there existed no established music-publishing industry in colonial America, the silversmith and the general engraver inherited almost all of the responsibility for producing the music published in America before the punching method was introduced by John Aitken of Philadelphia in 1787 (and Aitken, too, began his music-publishing career as an errant silversmith and worker of metals).

Although I have not examined copies of every musical work issued in America before the close of the Revolutionary War—the fact that many of the works exist in rare or unique copies in scattered locations and the earlier custom of binding music indiscriminately into sacred texts have made this task impractical—I have examined as many as were available to me at the Houghton Library of Harvard University, the American Antiquarian Society, the Massachusetts Historical Society, and other neighboring repositories. This investigation has convinced me that the names of the engravers of a great many of our earliest music publications are likely to remain unknown forever.

The Bay Psalm Book had gone through at least twenty-seven editions in Boston by 1758, the year in which the last edition appeared. Yet, for the last fourteen editions (between 1709 and 1758), the name of no individual can be assigned to the production of the music.[11] John Tufts's *Introduction*

10. P. 16. Again, in Chapter 7 on "American Silversmiths" in his book *The American Craftsman* (New York, Crown Publishers, 1940), Scott G. Williamson has mentioned (p. 113), while discussing the process of engraving, that "the craft of engraving on silver is so familiar to the fine art of engraving on copperplate for printing, that this accounts for the number of silversmiths who practiced both arts."

11. Copies of the thirteenth (Boston, 1706) and the seventeenth (Boston, 1716) editions of the Bay Psalm Book contain music, printed probably from woodblocks or less probably from relief cuts, which is signed "F. M. Sculpt." The owner of these initials remains unidentified.

to the Singing of Psalm-Tunes appeared in at least eleven editions between 1721 and 1724 (admittedly, a few of these are known through advertisements alone), and again we are unable to identify any hands that cut the plates for them. Attempts to assign specific engravers to the production of any of these works would qualify as mere speculation. Thomas Walter's *The Grounds and Rules of Musick Explained* came out in seven or eight editions between 1721, the first, and 1764, the last. Yet it is only with the final two (or three) editions, issued in 1760 and 1764 respectively, that we can associate a definite engraver with the production of the music (Thomas Johnston, about whom we shall know more presently).[12] A number of reasonably proficient engravers and metalsmiths were present in Boston during the period from 1715 to 1760, any or all of whom could have been responsible for effecting the plates needed to print these various titles and editions: Francis Dewing, William Burgis, Nathaniel Hurd, and Peter Pelham are most prominent in this respect, as is Thomas Johnston, who was active after 1728. Yet there is no evidence whatsoever to connect any of these men with the production of music plates before the mid-1750s, and only Johnston has a proven relationship to this medium. During the earlier half of the eighteenth century, the engraving of music plates was undoubtedly looked upon as just another job, and one which carried

12. With regard to the 1721 edition of Walter's instructor, the first book known to contain music printed from metal plates, we might hazard a guess that the plates for this could have been executed by James Franklin, for the imprint here reads, "Boston: Printed by J. Franklin, for S. Gerrish, near the Brick Church in Cornhill. 1721." As Sinclair Hitchings has recently pointed out in his essay, "Graphic Arts in Colonial New England" (p. 83), Franklin is known to have engraved relief cuts on wood and on type metal, and it would not be entirely unreasonable to conjecture that he might have scratched out the plates for the initial edition of Walter's work also. Hitchings's observation of Franklin's engraving is actually based upon the prior work of Lawrence C. Wroth and Marion W. Adams published in their *American Woodcuts and Engravings, 1670–1800* (Providence, Associates of the John Carter Brown Library, 1946).

The fact that I was able to locate and examine every known edition of Walter's *Grounds and Rules of Musick Explained* in the Houghton Library at Harvard has enabled me to make the following observations on interpolations, addenda, recut plates, and other anomalies in the publishing history of this important work. The second edition of the work, "Printed by B. Green, for S. Gerrish, 1723," uses the music plates of the initial edition. Both of these works are in oblong quarto format. The third edition, "Printed by J. Draper for S. Gerrish, *MDCCXL*," was produced in an upright octavo format and introduced newly engraved plates containing additional music as well. The next edition, "Printed for Samuel Gerrish, 1746," reverted to the oblong quarto format and reemployed some of the plates of the initial two editions, together with some additional plates containing new music. The 1760 edition, "Printed and sold by Benjamin Mecom," is also in oblong quarto format, but is larger than the earlier oblong editions. Its plates were newly engraved by Thomas Johnston, who had to cut many more to produce it. Johnston used these plates to imprint another edition or variant state of the 1760 Mecom edition wherein the imprint reads, "Printed by Benjamin Mecom, for Thomas Johnston." The final edition, issued in 1764, contains the imprint, "Printed for, and sold by Thomas Johnston." This edition reemploys the plates of the earlier 1760 edition (or editions), but contains additional music printed from still more new plates.

insufficient distinction (and perhaps insufficient remuneration or profit) for engravers or metalsmiths to bother identifying themselves with it.

As the eighteenth century wore on, engravers did begin to add their names to plates or imprints of American music books. The first engraver whose name has been noticed imprinted on an American music book was James Turner. Turner described himself as engraver, printer, and seller in 1752 of a small collection entitled *Tunes, with an Introduction "To Learn to Sing."* Turner was working in Boston as early as 1743. Though little is known of his early career, it is thought that he acquired his training as an engraver in England. He described himself, when setting up in business in Boston, as a silversmith and engraver, and he called himself an engraver of copperplates and a cutter of stamps for printing, coats of arms, and crests, a maker of watch faces and seals, and a cutter of stamps for saddlers and bookbinders. Turner eventually migrated to Philadelphia, where he worked as an engraver until his death from smallpox in December 1759. *Tunes, with an Introduction "To Learn to Sing"* is his only known attempt at music engraving.

The most energetic and interesting of our early engravers who directed some of their energies to cutting copperplates for printing music in pre-Revolutionary America was Thomas Johnston. More documentation exists on Johnston's career than on that of almost any other early American engraver and craftsman. The many extant records of his wide-ranging activities have recently been surveyed by Sinclair Hitchings in a lengthy essay which represents the most definitive statement on Johnston to date.[13] Johnston not only typifies the colonial engraver and metalsmith who extended his activities into the medium of music engraving (and the engraving of maps, views, bookplates, certificates, currency, and book illustrations as well), but he further exemplifies the early American artisan who worked in a multiple of crafts in order to earn his daily living. Hitchings has described Johnston as a house painter and decorator, a japanner, an engraver, a painter of coats of arms, a church singer, a publisher of singing books, and a pioneer New England organ builder. According to Hitchings (pp. 84–85),

> Johnston would see to the painting of your garden fence or sitting room, sell you gilt papers for a screen, color and varnish your wall maps, sell you a frame for a picture, paint a bedstead for you, stain and varnish a table, provide a stand for your clock or a "desk" for your spinnet; he would paint you a coat of arms and have it framed, glazed, and delivered to your house; he would provide funeral

13. Sinclair Hitchings, "Thomas Johnston," pp. 83–131.

decorations on behalf of your family, if you had suddenly departed this life leaving the means for an expensive funeral.

The exact year of Thomas Johnston's birth is unknown, but he is thought to have been born in Boston in 1708, and he died there in 1767. Hitchings says that Johnston learned engraving from William Burgis, one of the first printmakers to come out from England. Johnston's first signed piece of engraving was, in fact, Burgis's map of Boston of 1728, which was engraved in a skillful copperplate hand and signed: "Engraven by Thos. Iohnson Boston N.E." Reference is made by Hitchings to other maps undertaken by Johnston, as well as to other engraving jobs, including trade cards, views, prints, bookplates, and the like. Hitchings also relates that Johnston had in 1753 been a member of the committee appointed by the Brattle Street Church to issue a revision of the *Psalms of David* and that possibly, as part of this enterprise, he engraved sixteen pages of music, beginning with instructions entitled *To Learn to Sing, Observe These Rules* and carrying the imprint, "Engrav'd Printed & sold by Thomas Johnston Brattle street Boston 1755." (Reference has already been made to an earlier but separate work of the same title by James Turner.) This little publication could be bound in at the back of any singing book which provided the words of hymns only (printed by letterpress). It has been found bound into editions of Tate and Brady's *New Version of the Psalms of David* (1754, 1755, 1757, 1758, 1760, 1763, and 1765), into the 1763 edition of Watts's *Psalms of David, Imitated in the Language of the New Testament*, and into Thomas Prince's edition (Boston, 1744) of the Bay Psalm Book. Hitchings speculates that Johnston may have engraved as many as four sets of plates for this publication, which proved to be a financial bonanza. On his deathbed, Johnston specifically willed to his wife Bathsheba these plates and his press in addition to what her proportionate part of his estate might be.

As has been noted previously, Johnston also engraved the plates for the 1760 and 1764 editions of Walter's *Grounds and Rules of Musick Explained*, the last to be issued, and possibly for the earlier, third (1740) edition also. He was also responsible for engraving in 1760 an edition of Tate and Brady's *New Version of the Psalms of David*, which probably resulted from his work on the Brattle Street Church committee in 1753. And finally, his name appeared imprinted on the Boston, 1766, edition of Daniel Bayley's *A New and Complete Introduction to the Grounds and Rules of Music*. An original copperplate of Johnston's making, carrying four pages of music of this work, still exists in the Essex Institute in Salem, Massachusetts, and is reproduced as Illustration 1a herein. On the other side of the plate is a clockface (Illus. 1b), engraved and signed by Johnston for Preserved Clapp, exemplifying how copperplates were utilized to the utmost in early America.

Johnston's work in music engraving and publishing was not accidental, for he is known to have had an active interest in music. His name appears in the records of the Brattle Street Church as a leader of singing and as a singer, probably a soloist, at King's Chapel in 1754 and 1756. Thomas Johnston also turned his talents as a cabinetmaker and jack-of-all-trades to the repair and construction of organs. The first evidence of his interest in the construction of organs comes in 1743, when he overhauled the first organ used by Christ Church. (This instrument had been purchased by the church from William Claggett of Newport in 1736.) Later, in 1752, he built an organ which replaced this one, and he also completed, in 1754, an organ for St. Peter's Church in Salem. Finally, among the effects listed on a lengthy inventory of his estate in 1767 were "part of an Organ," valued at 80 shillings, and "an Organ unfinished."

Paul Revere has already been mentioned as the engraver of the plates for one of our most notable early tunebooks, the *Collection of the Best Psalm Tunes* of Josiah Flagg (Boston, 1764). Revere, the leading goldsmith of New England, is also held responsible for the engraving of two other collections of music: Josiah Flagg's *Sixteen Anthems, Collected from Tans'ur, Williams, Knapp, Ashworth & Stephenson* (Boston, 1766), and William Billings's *The New-England Psalm Singer* (Boston, 1770), the latter containing 116 pages of engraved music and the famous engraved frontispiece showing seven men seated around a table, with singing books before them.[14]

The next producer of plates for early American music books in order of chronology, John Ward Gilman, appears to have been neither a professional engraver nor a metalsmith, though very little is actually known about him and his activities. Born in Exeter, New Hampshire, in 1741, Gilman is reported in scant genealogical references to have served as

14. For a description of Revere's association with music engraving see Clarence S. Brigham's *Paul Revere's Engravings* (Worcester, Mass., American Antiquarian Society, 1954): pp. [14]–15 relate to Flagg's *Collection of Psalm Tunes*; pp. [29]–30 to the *Sixteen Anthems;* and pp. [65]–70 to the Billings publication. Facsimiles of title pages and of pages of music of each of these works are reproduced there. Several leading authorities on early American music have recently expressed doubt as to Revere's responsibility for the music plates of Billings's *New-England Psalm Singer*, believing that he probably engraved only the frontispiece, while some as yet unidentified engraver cut the plates containing music. Crawford claims (pp. 44–45) in his and David McKay's recent book on Billings (see n. 5 above) that Josiah Flagg engraved the plates for *The New-England Psalm Singer*.

postmaster to that town for forty years, dying there in 1823. Exeter is about 15 miles distant from Newburyport, Massachusetts, where much of the music that Gilman engraved was published. It was Gilman who executed the plates for Daniel Bayley's *The Psalm-Singer's Assistant* (Newburyport, 1767, 1785) and for the Boston, 1764 and 1768, editions of Bayley's *New and Complete Introduction to the Grounds and Rules of Music*. Gilman also issued in Exeter in 1771 a compilation of his own making entitled *A New Introduction to Psalmody*, and he denominated himself as engraver of the plates for the edition of William Tans'ur's *American Harmony, or Royal Melody Complete*, which Bayley published in Newburyport in 1771. It is also probable that Gilman engraved a number of other works issued by Bayley on which no engraver is designated.[15] Nothing else is known of Gilman. Letters of inquiry to sources in Exeter have gone unanswered, and Gilman genealogies and histories of Exeter have provided nothing substantial. If and when information on Gilman eventually emerges, I am sure that it will associate him in an important way with church music in Exeter, as in the case of Thomas Johnston in Boston. Gilman obviously had more than a purely commercial interest in music, and he is worthy of study.

Amos Doolittle (1754–1832) of New Haven falls more directly into the category of the engraver-silversmith who turned out occasional music books. Doolittle learned the trade of silversmithing from Eliakim Hitchcock of Cheshire, Connecticut, and later moved to New Haven. His initial entry into publishing occurred in 1775, when he engraved and offered for sale a series of four illustrations depicting the Battle of Lexington. As a supplement to his work as a silversmith in New Haven, Doolittle turned out a succession of prints which included portraits, views, plates for books, maps, and the like, as well as several music publications, the first being *The Chorister's Companion, or Church Music Revived*, which was printed and sold by Simeon Jocelyn and Doolittle. According to William A. Beardsley, Doolittle's most complete biographer to date, this work appeared in 1782.[16] *The Chorister's Companion* was

---

15. Many of the editions issued by Bayley, both of his own works and of the Tans'ur compilations, are bibliographical nightmares. Parts of works were obviously reused in other works through the interpolation of plates and the like. The problems inherent in the Bayley publications were pointed out by Irving Lowens and Allen P. Britton in their article, "Daniel Bayley's 'The American Harmony': A Bibliographical Study," *Papers of the Bibliographical Society of America* XLIX (1955) [340]–54.

16. William A. Beardsley, *An Old New Haven Engraver and His Work: Amos Doolittle* [N.p., 191–?). This contains an extensive but incomplete list of Doolittle's engravings.

followed (May 1786 to September 1787) by volume I of the *American Musical Magazine*, a collection of music (mostly sacred) which was issued in twelve monthly numbers by Doolittle and Daniel Read. Doolittle is also recorded as having executed an involved work entitled *The Art of Singing*, by Andrew Law, which was issued at Cheshire in 1792–94; Daniel Read's *Columbian Harmonist* (New Haven, 1793); and possibly other of Read's works. The engraving of Jocelyn's *Collection of Favourite Psalm Tunes* (New Haven, ca. 1787) is also attributed to him, as is (by Richard Crawford) the engraving of Daniel Read's *The American Singing Book* (New Haven, 1785).

John Norman (1748–1817) commenced engraving plates for music almost immediately after arriving in Boston in 1781, and he probably engraved all of the Boston sacred music imprints between 1781 and 1793. In 1781 William Billings's *The Psalm Singer's Amusement* had appeared, with title page and music executed by Norman. In addition to issuing three pieces of secular music—probably the first cut on metal in America—in the *Boston Magazine* in 1783, his name is attached to the engraving of the following music books: *The Suffolk Harmony* by William Billings (Boston, 1786); *The New American Melody* by Jacob French (Boston, 1789); and the 1794 Boston edition of the *Federal Harmony*. Norman appears to have been born in England and to have emigrated to Philadelphia in 1774. Upon his arrival in Philadelphia he advertised himself as an architect and landscape engraver. Norman was also something of a jack-of-all-trades. While in Philadelphia he conducted a drawing school, engraved illustrations for books, and executed portraits and maps. He earned his living in Boston by publishing books, by issuing the *Boston Magazine*, and by executing portraits and illustrations of various kinds. He also brought out the first Boston city directory in 1789.

Of the several men mentioned here, Joel Knott Allen probably comes closest to Thomas Johnston in typifying the general craftsman who took on music engraving as just another of his many jobs. Born in Southington, Connecticut, in 1755, Allen followed a variety of trades and pursuits. He is said to have been a spoonmaker, engraver, brass worker, carpenter, general storekeeper, and tinker. In his shop he sold jewelry, books, dry goods, groceries, drugs, meats, and hardware. In 1790 Allen moved to Middletown, where he initially supported himself by engraving for silversmiths. In addition to repairing the organ in a local church, he engraved a map of Connecticut (1792), made bookplates, engraved seals and coats of arms, painted and gilded chairs and mirrors, and is attributed, in the most complete biographical account that has come to my notice,[17] with the lettering of the coffin of the silversmith Jonathan Otis, following Otis's death in 1791. Several American music books published in the last decades of the eighteenth century carry the designation "Joel Allen" or "J. Allen" as "sculptor" or "engraver." These include Andrew Law's large publication, *A Select Number of Plain Tunes Adapted to Congregational Worship* (1781), and the same author's *Select Harmony* (1779) and *Collection of Hymns, for Social Worship* (1783).[18] Allen's name also appeared on Joseph Stone and Abraham Wood's *Columbian Harmony* (1793) and on Griswold & Skinner's *Connecticut Harmony* (1796).

17. George Munson Curtis, *Early Silver of Connecticut and Its Makers* (Meriden, Conn., International Silver Co., 1913), pp. 68–69. While there is no mention of music engraving here, the "J. Allen" who signed his name to some of our early music publications and Joel Knott Allen were obviously the same person, for there is no other silversmith of that name and period in Connecticut or its environs. Another extensive reference to Joel Allen is published in Albert C. Bates's *An Early Connecticut Engraver and His Work* (Hartford, 1906). This volume is devoted to the life of Connecticut's first engraver, Richard Brunton, but Allen is mentioned (p. 6) as the second Connecticut engraver, being preceded only by Amos Doolittle of New Haven. Bates's resumé of Allen has so much flavor—and this time he *is* connected with music engraving—that I have reprinted it here in full:

"The second Connecticut engraver was Joel Allen, who was born in Farmington, now Southington, Conn., in 1755, the son of Daniel Allen, a store and tavern keeper of that town. Joel assisted his father in the store and kept the books, which he wrote in a beautiful 'copper plate' hand. Later he seems to have lived in Middletown, where he owned property, as much of his engraving was done there. He was very versatile and did many things of interest besides engraving, such as regulating and repairing clocks, making 'tooth instruments,' repairing the pipe organ for Christ Church Society in Middletown and 'making a read for a hautboy.' The earliest dated work of his that has been noted by the writer is the elaborately engraved title of 'Select Harmony' by Andrew Law which is signed 'Farmington 1779. J. Allen Sculpsit.' He also engraved other music books. His most ambitious work was a map of Connecticut bearing the following title and imprint, 'A New and Correct Map of the State of Connecticut one of the United States of North America from actual survey—Humbly Dedicated by permission to His Excellency Samuel Huntington Esquire Governor and Commander in Chief of said state. Joel Allen Script. et Sculpt. Printed at Middleton for the Publisher March 1792.' It measures 28 by 36 inches. Another map of Connecticut engraved by him of the same size and probably printed from the same plate has a slightly different title, being dedicated to the governor by William Blodget and undated. He printed 301 impressions of the map of Connecticut for William Blodget in March to July, 1792. Whether this number included impressions of one or both varieties of the map it is impossible to say, but probably it was only of the dated variety. He also engraved book-plates; one for Joseph Parry, one for Maj. George Phillips, both armorial, and others are said to be known to collectors. Akin to these was the 'advertisement to put on snuff bottles' which he engraved for Nathaniel Shaler. In 1790 he charged 'Boardman' for '2 Miniatures 13–12,' from which it would seem that he tried his hand at portrait work. His engraving was done with bold free strokes. He was of an artistic temperament, idealistic and sensitive, traits which he transmitted to his descendants. During the Revolution he served as a fifer in the company of Noahdiah Hooker of Farmington. His death occurred in 1825."

18. The engraved music of Law's *Collection of Hymns* was accompanied by a forty-eight-page book of texts. Allen signed the title page of the engraved part, but the music on pp. 1, 4, and 36 is signed "Daniel Hawkins." Allen may have engraved the title page and ornate materials but left some or all of the other engraving to Hawkins.

The names of a few other engravers and silversmiths can be identified with occasional music engraving. Most notable among these was Henry Dawkins, an English emigrant, who executed the plates for James Lyon's *Urania*, published in Philadelphia in 1761, and probably the plates for Francis Hopkinson's *A Collection of Psalm Tunes* (Philadelphia, 1763). Dawkins, a professional engraver, enclosed the title-page information here within a beautifully executed ornamental border showing at top center a woman (the Muse Urania?) holding a tunebook in one hand and evidently beating time with the other. Isaac Sanford, a native of Hartford, Connecticut, was an engraver and occasional portrait painter and miniature painter from about 1783 to 1822. About 1783 he engraved the plates for Oliver Brownson's *Select Harmony, Containing the Necessary Rules for Psalmody, Together with a Collection of Approved Psalm Tunes, Hymns and Anthems*, issued in 1791. It is noted in Sanford's biography in *The New-York Historical Society's Dictionary of Artists in America, 1564–1860* that Sanford was also an inventor and spent some years in England between 1799 and 1808 attempting to advance his inventions. He later settled in Philadelphia and died there about 1842.

The foregoing discussion has attempted to illustrate the casual and matter-of-fact manner in which music engraving and publishing were carried on in America before the establishment of an active publishing industry. In the absence of any organized effort, means directly at hand were utilized, and an available engraver or silversmith was engaged to produce the necessary copperplates for a planned publication. Such publications usually grew out of a desire by a particular congregation or denomination for a particular text or version of a collection of hymns which would not otherwise be obtained, and the output of such works became more frequent after the middle of the eighteenth century, when native composers and compilers introduced new music into the repertory.

The above-mentioned engravers were not responsible for all of the music published in America during this early period. The task of engraving plates for music publications was sometimes undertaken so casually that anonymous engravers and silversmiths continued to add to the flow. For example, Francis Hopkinson's *A Collection of Psalm Tunes*, issued in Philadelphia in 1763, failed to identify the agent who produced the plates to print it, and it was by no means unique in this respect.

Although for American music publishing in general, engraving continued to grow in importance during the late eighteenth century, for sacred music it actually began to give way to letterpress printing. From 1786, which witnessed initial efforts in New England and Philadelphia to issue music from type in an organized manner, typographic printing for hymnbooks and sacred collections was on the ascendancy. In spite of this, occasional attempts continued to be made to publish sacred music from freehand engraved plates. (In such enterprises, it should be remembered, the engraver lined off and cut notation and text onto polished copperplates in a freehand manner.) Such publications include Griswold and Skinner's *Connecticut Harmony* (Charles Evans in his *American Bibliography* dates this 1796, adding that it was advertised "for sale in Stockbridge, Massachusetts, September 19, 1796") and Stephen Jenks's *The Delights of Harmony*, issued at New Haven as late as 1804. And, as has been noted here, Amos Doolittle, John Norman, and Joel Allen all issued engraved collections after 1786.[19]

19. In his article "Connecticut Sacred Music Imprints, 1778–1810," Music Library Association *Notes* 2nd ser XXVII (1971) 445–52, 671–79, Richard Crawford made the point that conservatism of Connecticut musicians is in some sense reflected in their failure to print or have music printed from type after this form had come into vogue and use for issuing tunebooks.

CHAPTER III

Printing Music from Type Before 1825

❧❧

THERE EXISTED no relationship or similarity of interests between the few printers who issued music from type in early America and the small group of musician-engravers of the post-Revolutionary period who produced the thousands of song sheets and instrumental pieces intended for instruction as well as for parlor entertainment. The typographic music printer, restricted to printing collections of sacred music and hymns, was allied more with the ordinary publishing industry than with the few scattered musicians who specialized in issuing sheet music through the punching and engraving process upon pewter (or type-metal) plates. Those printers who actually produced sacred collections and books of theory containing musical examples were usually much more involved in the process of general letterpress printing. Their work with music fonts usually constituted only a portion of their total activity, since they published books, pamphlets, and sometimes magazines and newspapers as well. When such printers set musical texts, their customs, methods, and materials differed only slightly or not at all from those of the general typographer, whose story has already been outlined in Lawrence C. Wroth's *The Colonial Printer* and continued in Rollo G. Silver's *The American Printer, 1787–1825*. However, a few historical facts have emerged during the last few decades, which relate to the first examples of typographically printed music in America. A discussion of these will help clarify the record, and will provide a proper perspective to the concurrent

[27]

activities of our musician-engravers and music typographers in the period before 1825.

As recently as thirty years ago *The Worcester Collection of Sacred Harmony*, supposedly compiled by Isaiah Thomas and printed by him at Worcester in 1786, was generally considered to be the first book containing music that had been printed from movable type in America. (This book's title begins with the phrase *Laus Deo*, but the work is generally known by the phrase that follows, *The Worcester Collection of Sacred Harmony*.) Recent research, particularly by Britton and Irving Lowens, has moved the date of this event back some thirty years and has shown that at least six other works, issued in about a dozen editions, actually preceded the Thomas publication. In several cases, facts concerning the origin and history of these publications are sketchy or lacking altogether. However, it seems reasonable to conclude from available information that most if not all of these were issued casually to remedy some existing deficiency—perhaps linguistic, perhaps denominational—which imported or domestic hymn-books could not satisfy.

The two earliest American publications known to contain music printed from movable type are *Kern Alter und Neuer, in 700. Bestehender, Geistreicher Lieder* and *Neu-Vermehrt- und Vollstaendiges Gesang-Buch*. These were issued by the pioneer German-American printer Christopher Sower (Saur) in Germantown, Pennsylvania, in 1752 and 1753 respectively, from type which, in the opinion of Britton, was "probably cast by Sower himself."[1] The first-named publication was reissued in 1753 as the second part of the *Neu-Vermehrt- und Vollstaendiges Gesang-Buch*, as, in fact, were all later editions of it. The *Neu-Vermehrt- und Vollstaendiges Gesang-Buch* was itself reissued in 1763 and 1772 by Christopher Sower II and in 1774 by Ernst Ludwig Baisch in Philadelphia, this edition also possibly emanating from the Sower printing establishment.[2] The title page and an internal page of the *Kern Alter und Neuer, in 700 Bestehender, Geistreicher Lieder* are shown in Illustration 2 herein. This work was almost an exact reprint of another work of the same title printed in Marburg by Johann Heinrich.

1. Britton, "Theoretical Introductions," p. 562. *The Printed Note* is even more positive in this respect, stating (p. 133) that "The type was cast by Saur himself." This catalog reproduces a page of music from the Sower publication on p. 134.

2. Evans's *American Bibliography* identifies Baisch as a bookseller only, resident in Philadelphia in 1774 and 1775. The imprint of this last edition, which reads, "Philadelphia: zu finden bey Ernst Ludwig Baisch, in der Zweiten-strasse, nahe bey der Rees-strasse. 1774," implies only that the work could be obtained from him. He may have had nothing to do with its printing. A comparison of this with the earlier Sower editions arouses the suspicion that all were printed in the same establishment, or from the same type. While the 1774 edition appears more refined, it nonetheless bears a resemblance to the earlier Sower printings.

Based on all available evidence, there seems to be little justification for attributing to Sower himself the casting of the music types used in printing these works, though the crude aspects of the images they left make their local manufacture seem likely, and Sower seems the most appropriate candidate. However, the elder Sower is not known to have engaged in letter founding at all, and, as Wroth has pointed out in *The Colonial Printer* and elsewhere,[3] his son, Christopher Sower II, did little more in this area than import matrices or molds from which letter types were cast by his journeyman, Justus Fox, in the period around 1770. Upon comparison, the music in the Sower songbooks does not seem unlike that contained in a great many German and European psalters of the day, its crude appearance being easily attributable to bad or indifferent composition, inking, and presswork, and perhaps to its printer's inexperience in working with music types. It would seem more likely that Sower imported the necessary music font or possibly matrices for casting it from Germany. For, as we shall see shortly, the importation of music types occurred several times in colonial America.[4]

The music which Sower had inserted in his editions of 1752 and 1753

---

3. "The First Work with Music Types," in *Typographical Heritage; Selected Essays by Lawrence C. Wroth* (New York, The Typophiles, 1949), p. 142ff.

4. Rollo Silver has reminded me that several sources, including Edward W. Hocker's *The Founding of the Sower Press* (Germantown, Pa., Germantown Historical Society, 1935) and Felix Reichmann's *Christopher Sower Sr., 1694–1758, Printer in Germantown; an Annotated Bibliography* (Philadelphia, Carl Schurz Memorial Foundation, 1943), have reported that during his early printing career Sower obtained his necessary types from the foundry of Ehrenfried Luther in Frankfurt. In his book on the Luther foundry, *Die Egenolff–Luthersche Schriftgiesserei in Frankfurt und Ihre Geschäftlichen Verbindungen mit den Vereinigten Staaten von Nordamerika* (Frankfurt, Schriftgiesserei D. Stempel AG, 1926), Gustav Mori devotes some pages to the Luther–Sower relationship and reproduces several letters from Sower to Luther in the period before and around 1740. Mori and other authors say nothing about the origin of Sower's types in the period after 1750 and nothing at all about the source of the small amount of music type which he employed to print musical examples in the two above-named hymnals of 1752 and 1753. Mori is silent with regard to the manufacture of music types by the Luther foundry, except to note that in 1757 Luther employed the punchcutter Schmidt, who had cut the new-style notes for Breitkopf in 1754, to effect a similar font for him. Mori states that Sower never involved himself in typefounding (p. 31: "ausserdem hat er [Sower], entgegen früheren Nachrichten, niemals eine Giesserei betrieben".) In a more recent study of Sower and his publications by Anna Kathryn Oller, "Christopher Saur, Colonial Printer: a Study of the Publications of His Press, 1738–1758"(Doctoral Dissertation, University of Michigan, 1963), is the statement (p. 29), "that the elder Saur cast his own music types is without documentation. There is some foundation for the assertion, since from time to time he would make single pieces of type to facilitate the printing of a particular item." Oller incorrectly relates that only one of the nine hymnals which Sower published, the *Neu-Vermehrt- und Vollstaendiges Gesang-Buch*, contained music, for we know that musical examples were also included in the *Kern Alter und Neuer, in 700 Bestehender, Geistreicher Lieder*. It seems logical to assume that the Luther foundry manufactured music types of the pre-Breitkopf type in the period before 1757 and that Sower probably obtained those he used from this source. At least, this seems a better assumption than the ascription of his music types to his own manufacture.

(and later) amounted only to random and brief examples of simple melodies within his printed pages. Nowhere did he print full pages of music either singly or in quantity. The first American imprint which actually contained whole pages of tunes was issued in Philadelphia about two years later, in 1754. This work, which has an elongated title, *The Youths Entertaining Amusement, or A Plain Guide to Psalmody. Being a Collection of the Most Usual, and Necessary Tunes Sung in the English Protestant Congregations in Philadelphia, &c. In Two Parts, viz. Treble and Base, with All Proper and Necessary Rules, Adapted to the Meanest Capacities*, commences with twenty-seven pages of instructions on music and singing, followed by nineteen pages of music and thirteen final pages entitled "Supplement," this last part containing words only. The work was compiled by one William Dawson, who listed himself on its title page as "Writing Master and Accomptant [accountant], at the Hand and Pen in Third-Street, Philadelphia," and its imprint stated that it had been printed at the German Printing Office on Third Street in Philadelphia and that it was sold by its author. Little is actually known about Dawson, who according to an advertisement in the *Pennsylvania Gazette* of April 1, 1756, was also a teacher, bookbinder, and stationer. From this information, it seems logical to conclude that Dawson mainly made his living from teaching handwriting and probably by performing scribal duties, that is, by writing letters for the illiterate and keeping books and performing the other duties of an accountant. This business naturally brought him into contact with paper and blank books, and he undoubtedly sold these also, possibly making them up and lining and binding them.

The address on the imprint of *The Youth's Entertaining Amusement* provides sufficient evidence to identify its printer. Of all the printers at work in Philadelphia at this time—William Bradford, James Chattin, William Dunlap, Franklin & Hall, Solomon Fussell, and the rest—only one, Anton (or Anthony) Armbrüster, worked at this address, and he was the major (if not sole) German printer in Philadelphia at this time. However, the source of his types and his reasons for acquiring them remain unknown. Inasmuch as he worked in partnership about this time with Benjamin Franklin in publishing the *Philadelphische Zeitung*, the local German newspaper, and because the types employed in printing this music appear to be of English manufacture, one is tempted to theorize that Franklin obtained them for him. But such an inference is purely speculative. It seems reasonable to conclude, however, that Armbrüster's music types were imported from abroad, which lends credence to the earlier assumption that Sower's types also emanated from a foreign foundry.

The third title containing music printed from type in America before the publication of *The Worcester Collection* also came from the press of Anton Armbrüster, though a period of eleven years elapsed before he attempted music printing again. This work, entitled *Tunes in Three Parts, for Several Metres in Dr. Watt's Version of the Psalms*, is a small collection of less than fifty pages. It is known in two editions, each extant in a single copy only, in the collection of the Historical Society of Pennsylvania now in the keeping of the Library Company of Philadelphia. (The Dawson compilation is likewise extant in a unique copy in the Library Company in Philadelphia.) An examination and comparison of the two editions of this title, which were issued by Armbrüster in Philadelphia in 1763 and 1764, show the second to be merely a reissue of the original sheets of 1763, with the addition of a cancellans title page, six pages of instructions following it, and two interpolated leaves intended probably to cancel misnumbered leaves in the 1763 edition. As mentioned before, the physical appearance of the music in this book, said by Britton (before the recent discovery of the unique copy of *The Youths Entertaining Amusement*) to be the first English-language book published in America containing music printed from type, strongly suggests that the font of music type used was brought in from abroad. As far as we now know, Armbrüster restricted his music printing to these two titles only and did not reemploy this font for publishing any other music before leaving the Philadelphia printing scene in 1768. The fact that eleven years lapsed between his issuance of *The Youths Entertaining Amusement* and *Tunes in Three Parts* indicates that he might have encountered some difficulty in working with music types, though a limited market for music, and other factors, could have kept him from expending greater energy in this sideline. There appears to have been no particular linguistic or religious motive connected with the publication of either of these two titles. Both were undoubtedly intended to capture some of the Philadelphia market which, until the appearance of these two titles, had been supplied almost entirely through the importation of tunebooks from abroad. Tunes included in these two books were undoubtedly selected to please the Philadelphia tastes for church music.

The remaining two sacred works in this category have piqued the curiosity of competent investigators. Consequently, we need only mention briefly the main aspects of their publication. *The Psalms of David, with the Ten Commandments, Creed, Lord's Prayer, &c. in Metre*, the fifth such undertaking, was versified by Francis Hopkinson, America's first poet-composer, and was printed for the use of the Reformed Protestant Dutch Church in the City of New York by James Parker in 1767 from music types which had been ordered from Daniel Crommelin of Amsterdam at a cost of 557 guilders and 12 stavers.[5] The sixth and last music book produced typographically in America before 1786 was *A Collection of the Psalm and Hymn Tunes Used by the Reformed Protestant Dutch Church in the City of New York*, which was printed by Hodge and Shober in New York in 1774. The sole account of the compiling and publishing of this work does not refer to the origin of the music types employed to produce it.[6] However, a comparison of this book with its immediate predecessor, the Parker printing of 1767, shows that the same types were common to both. Most likely the identical music font was used to produce both titles, or possibly similar types were imported from Amsterdam. The fact that James Parker had died in New York on July 2, 1770, lends credence to the theory that Hodge and Schober, who had only begun as printers in New York City in 1773, acquired Parker's music types from which their 1774 tunebook was printed.

The only other known instance of music printing from type in America before the entrance of Isaiah Thomas into the field in 1786 occurred in 1783 with the publication of a secular piece entitled *A New Song, Set to Music by A. Hawkins* in the October issue of the *Boston Magazine* (Illus. 3). This event is all the more interesting because the three other pieces of music within this publication were engraved on copper by the previously mentioned John Norman, publisher of the magazine, in the usual freehand manner of the day. And all of these pieces followed the publication of the Hawkins song. Most interesting of all, however, is the manuscript note which Isaiah Thomas himself wrote on the lower margin of this song in the American Antiquarian Society's copy of the *Boston Magazine*, this copy unquestionably emanating from Thomas's own library. His note reads: "The types for the above Music, were cast in Boston by Wm. Norman, and tho' ordinary, are a proof of his great ingenuity in the first, and only attempt made in this country, excepting a few sorts that I cast some time after to compleat a font I had from Lon-

5. See "The First English Psalm Book," in the *Year Book of the [Collegiate] Reformed Protestant Dutch Church of the City of New York* III (1882) 72–77, and Virginia Larkin Redway's "James Parker and the 'Dutch Church'," *Musical Quarterly* XXIV (1938) 481–500. Both articles contain illustrations of music.

6. Carleton Sprague Smith, "The 1774 Psalm Book of the Reformed Protestant Dutch Church in New York City," *Musical Quarterly* XXXIV (1948) 84–96. The only known copies of this psalter are in the New York Public LIbrary and the Huntington Library.

don. Norman cut the punches, and made every tool to complete the above types."[7]

While Thomas's statement seems conclusive regarding the initial founding of music types in America, his attribution of this achievement to "Wm" Norman comes as a surprising revelation indeed. Although William Norman actually does figure in early Boston music publishing (as we shall see in the next chapter), he does not formally enter the scene here until about 1796. John Norman, on the other hand, plays an active role in this enterprise in the period under discussion, having engraved the copperplates for William Billings's *The Psalm-Singer's Amusement* in 1781 (as well as other such works noted before) and having inserted three pieces of music which he had engraved in the 1783 *Boston Magazine*. Inasmuch as a twelve- or thirteen-year interval separates this music-typefounding endeavor from the later music-publishing efforts of William Norman, who issued music that he had engraved in a freehand style in Boston between 1796 and 1799, we cannot but wonder whether Thomas confused the two Normans, especially in view of the fact that he may have penned this note some years after the occurrence.[8] A curious aspect of this initial and quite early venture into American music typefounding is that Norman—whichever one it was—resorted to printing from these types only once, for the three songs published after it in the 1783 *Boston Magazine* were engraved in the usual manner of the day. When looking at the *New Song, Set to Music By A. Hawkins* (Illus. 3), one can readily speculate that the composition and presswork (and undoubtedly the punchcutting and typecasting) must have caused Norman great difficulties, perhaps

7. I have Marcus A. McCorison of the American Antiquarian Society to thank for bringing Thomas's note to my attention. McCorison assures me that the authenticity of his authorship here cannot be doubted. Isaiah Thomas was founder of the American Antiquarian Society, and he contributed his personal library to it.

8. It is impossible to date Thomas's statement regarding this initial effort to produce music types in America. A considerable but from our point of view unsatisfactory biography of John Norman appears in the *Dictionary of American Biography*, and a checklist of his known engravings can be found in D. M. Stauffer's *American Engravers upon Copper and Steel*. (vol.2, pp. 383–91). The death of one "William Norman," age unspecified, was reported in the Boston *Columbian Centinel* of November 21, 1807, but no legal papers regarding his demise are extant in the records of Suffolk County, Massachusetts. The fact that there existed at about the same time and in the same place two engravers named Norman and that both can be connected with music engraving suggests a relationship between them. The entry for William Norman in Rollo G. Silver's "The Boston Book Trade, 1790–1799," in *Essays Honoring Lawrence C. Wroth*, p. 295, states that "according to *Lord*, William Norman was the son of John Norman." Silver's sources here are unpublished manuscript notes of Melvin Lord in the American Antiquarian Society. On an inventory of possessions left by John Norman upon his death in 1817 (Probate Records, Suffolk County, Massachusetts, No. 25285) appears a box of type metal valued at 10 dollars, but the exact nature of this is unknown.

convincing him that the final result was not worth the effort. His music types, of the single-impression type noted in the first chapter, are poorly aligned, and the braces are awkwardly out of position. How curious it is that Norman, after going to the trouble of cutting punches and casting types, did not use this font again, especially for the three other pieces which he issued right after the Hawkins piece. Equally curious is the fact that Thomas made no mention of this undertaking in his *History of Printing in America*, which he published in 1810.

The publication by Isaiah Thomas in January 1786 of *The Worcester Collection of Sacred Harmony* marks the first real effort by an American publisher to issue music on a continuing basis, for it constituted the beginning of a long succession of music publications issued by him in Worcester and, after 1789, by the firm of Isaiah Thomas and Ebenezer T. Andrews in Boston.[9] The music types employed in printing *The Worcester Collection* had been purchased two years earlier from the Caslon Foundry in London, and Thomas had previously used some of them to print "Tewkesbury," a hymn included in the specimen book of his available types, which he issued about April 1785 (see Illus. 4).[10] *The Worcester Collection* was without doubt the finest music book the country had seen up to that time. It went through eight editions between 1786 and 1803, and between 1789 and 1800 Thomas and the firm of Thomas and Andrews issued at least seventeen major music collections in addition to it, some reprinted in several editions.

Also in 1786 appeared the first of a long series of music publications issued by another important early printer, John M'Culloch of Philadelphia. This was *A Collection of Church Music, No. 1*, "printed Typographically by Young and M'Culloch, corner of Second and Chestnut-street," noted in Evans's *American Bibliography* (19563), though no copy is now known to exist.[11] The firm of Young and M'Culloch published two other

9. Isaiah Thomas's activity as a music publisher has recently been the subject of a paper by Karl Kroeger, "Isaiah Thomas as a Music Publisher," *Proceedings of the American Antiquarian Society* LXXXVI (1976) 321–41. While this concentrates on the publication and contents of Thomas's *Worcester Collection*, it does contain a checklist of all of Thomas's musical publications.

10. The title page here reads, *A Specimen of Isaiah Thomas's Printing Types. Being as large and complete an Assortment as is to be met with in any one Printing Office in America. Chiefly Manufactured by that great Artist, William Caslon, Esq; of London. Printed at Worcester, Massachusetts, by Isaiah Thomas. MDCCLXXXV.* His dedication here is dated April 1785. Thomas had previously announced his acquisition of music types in his newspaper, the *Spy*, on December 30, 1784, and in the Boston *Independent Chronicle* of January 26, 1785. Copies of this specimen book are in the New York Public Library, at Harvard, and in the American Antiquarian Society. The last-named owns two copies, one of them Thomas's own.

11. Evans probably based his description upon an advertisement, and it is possible that this book never advanced into publication.

musical works in 1787 before dissolving, and later M'Culloch, who was to contribute a substantial amount of information to Thomas's *History of Printing in America*, carried on alone, publishing a great many music collections throughout the 1790s and into the second decade of the nineteenth century. His most ambitious work was undoubtedly *Selected Music*, a 136-page collection of national music which he issued in 1806 and 1807 (see Wolfe, no. 7878).

The 1790s saw a number of additional typographic music presses spring into existence, and from that time on, the publication of music from type became a rather routine business in America, carried on by a handful of printers and publishers who possessed the necessary fonts and who usually specialized in producing one type of music or another. The majority restricted their output to sacred collections, though a few turned out instrumental instruction books, and some did both. Of our early printers and publishers of music from type, the following were most active during the 1790s and the first years of the nineteenth century: Manning and Loring, and Joseph T. Buckingham, Boston; Herman Mann, Dedham, Massachusetts, and later Providence, Rhode Island; Henry Ranlet, Exeter, New Hampshire; Norris and Company, Newburyport, Massachusetts, and later Exeter, New Hampshire; Andrew Wright, Northampton, Massachusetts; Joshua Cushing, Salem, Massachusetts. Printers and publishers who specialized in issuing music from type during the first three decades of the nineteenth century included, in addition to some of those just mentioned: Packard and Van Benthuysen (O. R. Van Benthuysen), Albany; Dobbin and Murphy, and Henry S. Keatinge, Baltimore; Denio and Phelps, Greenfield, Massachusetts; Ezekial Goodale, Hallowell, Maine; David Hogan, and Henry C. Lewis, Philadelphia; William Williams, Utica, New York; Thomas Badger, Jr., and J. H. A. Frost, Boston.[12]

Music publishing started west in 1816 with the publication of John Armstrong's *The Pittsburgh Selection of Psalm Tunes*, printed by Robert Ferguson for Cramer & Spear, Pittsburgh, and in the same year with Timothy Flint's *The Columbian Harmonist*, printed in Cincinnati by Looker, Palmer and Reynolds for Colman and Philipps. It is possible that

12. In addition to the publications of the larger printing houses, enumerated above for the most part, there occurred infrequently the publication of a hymnbook or tunebook which had been produced on a less than professional level to satisfy the needs of a particular community or language group. The article by R. B. Brown and Frank X. Braun on "The Tunebook of Conrad Doll," *Papers of the Bibliographical Society of America* XLII (October 1948) 229–38, described the publication of a single edition of a tunebook by Conrad Doll, the local schoolmaster and church organist of Lancaster, Pennsylvania, to satisfy the needs of the German settlement there in 1798.

other hymnbooks were published beyond the Alleghenies before these. However, copies of them are either nonexistent today or have escaped my notice. All the preceding music books were printed from types which contained one note on the staff for single-impression printing, in the style that has been attributed to Pierre Haultin and first employed by Pierre Attaingnant of Paris. Krummel has noted in his "Philadelphia Music Engraving" that the music font, based on the improvements of Breitkopf and Fournier, which allowed for the printing of chords, was not introduced into America until the nineteenth century, the first work printed from such type that has been noted by him being Jonathan M. Wainright's *Music of the Church* (Philadelphia, Printed for Samuel F. Bradford and Peter C. Smith, New York, 1828).[13]

As Wroth in *The Colonial Printer* makes no mention of the local manufacture of music type in America before 1800, we may conclude that the necessary fonts were brought in from abroad. The earliest advertisement that has come to my attention regarding the casting of music type in America, aside from the previously noted observation of Isaiah Thomas, occurred in the Baltimore *American* of December 25, 1809, when the Baltimore Type Foundry announced that it was "prepared to execute orders for sizes from Diamond to French Canon, including Music," so that we may assume that it was available through local manufacture after that date, at least.[14]

It should be reemphasized here that while typographical music printing continued throughout the nineteenth century, the employment of this medium was mostly restricted to the publication of large sacred collections and to printing musical examples within the texts of books. The musician-engravers who issued sheet music using the punched plate far outstripped the typographers in the amount of music produced. Although the printers frequently turned out large editions—for this was, after all, the advantage of type in the first place—the volume of music produced in sheet form virtually dwarfed that machined from type. One has only to go

13. P. 78.

14. Rollo G. Silver's *Typefounding in America* makes only two cursory references to the casting of music fonts. Silver reprints (p. 45) the advertisement of the Baltimore Type Foundry which I have noted before and he requotes (p. 43) a letter of Samuel Sower (grandson of the first Christopher Sower and tenth son of the second, who had commenced typefounding in 1804 as Samuel Sower & Company or as the Baltimore Type Foundry) of December 7, 1808, wherein Sower stated that his organization had received a firm order from Albany for a note-type for a book of hymns, 1,500 pounds for $2,587. Doubtless, the availability of music types from a local source was responsible for the publication of a number of American hymn- and tunebooks from this time on, including probably the Pittsburgh and Cincinnati collections of 1816. The tracing of these types to the printing of American books of that period would prove an interesting study.

into the stacks of our larger libraries holding sizable collections of sheet music to visualize the vast activity that went on (and still goes on today) to bring the vocal and instrumental favorites of the times to the American music public. While editions of sacred collections issued in the nineteenth century number over 1,000, editions of sheet music number in the many tens of thousands, and their volume and form reflect the industry of a small but enterprising trade which contributed much to the flavor of American culture and life, not only as an expression of musical and social activity but also through the quaint pictorial illustrations they bore. It is with the specialized musician-engravers and musician-publishers, who produced this vast amount of sheet music from 1787 on, that the remainder of this work is concerned.

CHAPTER IV

The Arrival of Musician-Engravers and the Establishment of a Music-Publishing Industry

S O LONG AS THE American colonists needed only church music, their requirements for printed texts could be fulfilled through importation or, on occasion, by metalsmiths and engravers at hand. However, the interests of the early settlers began to expand to include secular music as the eighteenth century advanced. This interest eventually culminated in a demand for theater, opera, and instrumental performances following the cessation of hostilities with England in the 1780s. In order to satisfy this demand, actors and musicians began to filter to these shores in increasing numbers, and a few of them commenced to import and later to publish music sheets which were a necessary concomitant to this activity.

While religious life predominated in the musical life of the early settlements, the first decades of the eighteenth century saw a gradual growth of interest in both private and public entertainment. The singing societies established in the early 1700s by the clergy in an attempt to improve psalm singing fostered music societies which became the forerunners of the large, semi-professional choral organizations of the late eighteenth century. In the 1730s public concerts were established in almost all major American cities, the first such performance taking place in Boston in late 1731 and in New York, and Charleston, South Carolina, within a few years. (Philadelphia lagged behind in this respect, for no public concerts are on record there before 1757, though private concerts were given as early as 1734.) Ballad operas were probably performed in New York from 1732 on, and Charleston was the locale in 1735 of the first recorded performance of an opera in America, though the real beginnings of American theater belong to the decade following 1750. The 1740s found an increase in the number of concerts given and the places where they occurred; during the 1750s, concerts began to rely more and more on the theater, both for performers and repertory; and the 1760s continued the trends already noted. While fewer amusements were given during the Revolution, the years following the war saw a rapid increase in the number and an improvement in the quality of theatrical and concert programs, due to the influx of musicians from abroad. Added to these were such entertainments as dancing, both private and public, the circus, and puppetry, all performed to the accompaniment of music.

During the seventy-year period between the 1720s and the late 1780s, when interest in nonreligious music was emerging, almost total reliance for secular performance was placed upon imported music and transcriptions of it.[1] Practically no secular music was published locally, except for occasional broadsides containing verses to be sung to the tune of a well-known air but no music. In a very few cases, patriotic music was published separately or appeared in magazines before the Revolution, having been printed from hand-engraved copperplates or from wood-blocks. However, such publications were unusual and had no aim other than to arouse nationalistic feelings on the eve of the rebellion.[2]

The musical and theatrical activities that had been all but suspended during the conflict with the mother country resumed with renewed vigor after the cessation of hostilities in 1783; and the flow of foreign musicians

1. Actually, great reliance was placed upon importation, especially from England, for music needed for both sacred and secular performance. A collection of eighteenth-century music in the library of the College of William and Mary in Williamsburg, Virginia, which contains a great many materials emanating from the homes of the gentry, provides a striking example of this dependence. From this collection, which contains English psalm books and bound volumes of English instrumental and vocal music, one can obtain a good insight into the musical life of the wealthy and well-bred of that locality and period.

2. For a list of broadsides and music published in periodical form from 1759 through 1781 see Dichter and Shapiro, *Early American Sheet Music*, pp. xix–xxii. Only a few pieces were published separately, outside the covers of magazines. These are known today only through advertisements, for no copies of them are extant. For a commentary on one such publication, the *Liberty Song*, the first separate song issued in the American Colonies, see William Arms Fisher's *One Hundred and Fifty Years of Music Publishing in the United States* . . . (Boston, Ditson, 1933), pp. 20–21. As was previously noted, four additional songs appeared after the Revolutionary War in the *Boston Magazine* in 1783, one printed from type.

and music teachers to America, which had amounted to little more than a trickle before the war, grew into a rapid stream in the years which followed it. With the arrival of this new group of performers and instructors and the concurrent increase in music and musical activities which they generated, there arose an ever-broadening demand for musical instruction and instruments and for printed copies of the pieces being performed on the stage and in the concert halls. Some of the more enterprising of the immigrant musicians—George Gilfert in New York and Peter Albrecht von Hagen in Boston were two such men—quickly recognized that profits could be made from the sale of imported musical merchandise and acted accordingly. In time, a few such musicians expanded their activities to include the engraving and printing of music sheets, a natural extension in view of the uncertain modes of transportation upon which they had to depend for supply. Eventually, some of the musicians who had commenced publishing and selling music as a sideline came to devote more and more of their time and energy to this occupation, until they were just about fully engaged in it. It was in this offhand way that our music-publishing industry began.

It is not difficult to explain the emigration of this group of professional musicians. Many of the men who were attracted here possessed too strong an ambition and too keen a sense of opportunity to be content with remaining obscure members of the pit orchestras in English and continental theaters. To them America offered possibilities and opportunities beyond their reach at home. Others were drawn by the reputed excellence of theatrical companies being engaged by New World impresarios for the opening of theaters in leading cities. Many fled social and political upheaval (in Hispaniola, in France, and in other countries feeling the backlash of the French Revolution). And a few came with the intention of making their fortunes and returning home but stayed on. Finding no established outlets for music publication—for many of these musicians were active composers as well as performers and teachers—a number of the immigrants had the good sense to begin producing music themselves. And although a few professional music engravers and publishers followed them to America to cater to the whims of a burgeoning music-conscious public, it was mainly these immigrant music masters who issued our earliest music and song sheets.

PHILADELPHIA

During the 1780s Philadelphia was the largest city in America and the political and economic hub. It had emerged from the Revolution as the most important port in the nation; and, as it was also the seat of government for many months of each year, it became the crossroads where new ideas were brought together by travelers, both native and foreign, especially by emigrants coming in from abroad. Inasmuch as the musical life of Philadelphia had advanced rapidly from about 1750 on, particularly with regard to the theater, it is not surprising that the city should establish itself first as the center of music publishing in the United States. Surprisingly enough, however, music publishing was not begun by an emigrant musician but by an emigrant silversmith, though the latter may have been moved to action by a newly arrived music master, for immigrant musicians played important roles in Philadelphia's early music-publishing supremacy. The first music to be engraved in America through punching tools—an event which marked the beginning of a music-publishing industry in this country—appeared in Philadelphia in mid-1787 and coincided with the recent settlement in that city of Alexander Reinagle, a member of the Society of Musicians in London, who had emigrated to New York during the previous year. The publication was Reinagle's *A Selection of the Most Favourite Scots Tunes with Variations for the Piano Forte or Harpsichord*, engraved by John Aitken, a Scottish metalsmith who had come to America before 1785, and was announced as "just published" in the *Pennsylvania Packet* of August 28, 1787. Between then and 1793, when a number of immigrant musicians began publishing in Philadelphia, Aitken was the sole producer of sheet music in America, his six-year catalog amounting to about sixteen individual publications, of which all but four were composed by, arranged by, or printed for Alexander Reinagle.[3] It is not my intention to discuss in depth the probable Aitken–Reinagle relationship at this time nor to theorize here regarding the origin of Aitken's punches and tools. Much more will be said about these later. However, one cannot but be impressed with the role which Reinagle appears to share in the majority of Aitken's early publications. His association here begs the inference that he may have prompted the obscure metalsmith to venture into music publishing in the first place. One can theorize that Reinagle, upon settling

3. These four exceptions are Francis Hopkinson's *Seven Songs for the Harpsichord or Piano Forte* (ca. November 1788); Aitken's own *A Compilation of the Litanies and Vesper Hymns and Anthems as They Are Sung in the Catholic Church* (ca. November 1787); William Brown's *Three Rondos for the Piano Forte or Harpsichord* (1787); and the second edition of the Aitken collection of 1787, noted just before. The first two were reissued in facsimile by Musical Americana, Philadelphia, in 1954. Thomas Dobson, a bookseller in Philadelphia from 1785, appears to have been involved in a number of Aitken's music publications, though his interest in them may have been merely financial, i.e., as a backer or as an agent for their sale. His advertisements of these usually read "just published and to be had of Thomas Dobson."

down in Philadelphia would have needed someone to engrave his compositions (in order to gain rapid fame as well as students in that strange city) and to produce music for his pupils. Finding no music engravers as such, he may have turned to the most immediate source available, either urging a willing engraver—albeit a metalsmith—to fashion the necessary tools to do musical work or helping him procure these implements from abroad.

It may have been the competition of newly arrived musician-engravers that forced Aitken into temporary retirement in 1794, for except for his *Scots Musical Museum,* a collection he advertised in January 1797, and *The Goldsmith's Rant* (copyright April 14, 1802), a composition of his own invention which shows several vignettes of him goldsmithing and reveals his slight musical knowledge (illustrated in the Frontispiece herein), he issued no more music until 1807, when he resumed publishing for a period of about four years.[4] Except for its historical importance, Aitken's career as a music publisher was of little significance. While he did issue some native music and a few collections in the years after 1794, including two between 1807 and 1811 (*Aitken's New Musical Museum* and *Aitken's Fountain of Music*), his later activity was spent almost entirely in emulating the work of George E. Blake, a later and more important publisher. Aitken retired from music publishing in 1811, probably returning to metalsmithing until his death in Philadelphia on March 19, 1831. The few facts that are actually known about his life and career in metalsmithing and music engraving are brought together in Chapter 7.

About March 1793 John Christopher Moller, a music teacher and organist who had settled in Philadelphia a year previously, and Henri Capron, a French cellist residing there since 1785, began publishing *Moller & Capron's Monthly Numbers*, a collection which came out in four separate issues before ceasing publication in mid- or late 1793 due to the serious illness or death of Capron. Moller produced a few music sheets in 1794

---

4. Until recently, *The Scots Musical Museum* was known only through a contemporary advertisement. A copy of this work has since been located in the private library of Ernst C. Krohn of St. Louis, and another is reported to exist in the Henry Francis du Pont Winterthur Museum in Winterthur, Delaware. This collection of music extends to about 230 pages, including printed interleaves, and it represents a substantial effort on Aitken's part during his otherwise barren "middle period," which extended from 1794 until 1806 or 1807. Cf. Sonneck–Upton, pp. 370–71, and Wolfe, *Secular Music in America,* pp. 1001–2. A few Aitken sheets also carry the name of Charles Taws, a well-known piano manufacturer of Philadelphia, as co-publisher. These were issued between 1807 and 1811, toward the end of Aitken's publishing career. Taws was also a musical-instrument maker in Philadelphia between 1789 and 1833, in which year he may have died. A Joseph C. Taws, possibly a son or nephew of Aitken's partner, composed a number of pieces of music which were published in Philadelphia after 1820 (see Wolfe, *Secular Music in America,* pp. 895–96).

before turning his business over to George Willig and moving on to New York, where he later engaged in music publishing and selling in addition to serving as organist to Trinity Church until his death on September 21, 1803. Sometime in 1793 John Young, who previously may have been a music publisher in New York, began issuing music in Philadelphia, his activity here extending into 1795. His only known Philadelphia publication is a collection of music in eight separate numbers (amounting to sixty-three pages) entitled *Young's Vocal and Instrumental Musical Miscellany*. However, it was really with the arrival of Benjamin Carr and George Willig that music publishing in Philadelphia (and in America) began to flourish on a permanent and solid basis, and it may have been the appearance of these two energetic personalities that forced all others into retirement or flight.

Benjamin Carr was descended from a long line of English music publishers. His father, Joseph Carr (who was to follow the son to America and establish his own music-publishing business in Baltimore in June 1794), had been proprietor of a music-publishing and music-selling establishment at Middle Row, Holborn, in London since about 1770. Born in 1768, Benjamin Carr received his musical education from some of the foremost church musicians of England and had participated in a number of concerts in London before departing for America. He had probably also engraved music for his father, for I have seen (but unfortunately did not record) one English song sheet bearing his name as engraver. Carr arrived in Philadelphia about the middle of 1793 and immediately threw himself into the musical activities of that city, performing at concerts, working as church organist, teaching music, acting on the stage, and establishing a "musical repository" for the publication of music and the sale of musical merchandise. Benjamin Carr was decidedly the most important and prolific music publisher in America during the 1790s (as well as one of its most distinguished composers), conducting, in addition to his Philadelphia business, a New York branch from 1794 to 1797, when it was acquired by James Hewitt.

Carr seems to have ceased publishing for two or three years after 1799, during which time he apparently devoted much of his time and energy to editing *The Musical Journal for the Piano Forte*, a collection of music amounting to five large volumes and containing much original material. This was the most important and the most ambitious musical publication issued in America to that time and for a decade or two afterward. Though initially published by Joseph Carr of Baltimore on a subscription basis, it could be obtained through booksellers in New York, Philadelphia, and in other cities. The Carrs issued their *Musical Journal* in two sections, one for vocal and one for instrumental music, a few pages appearing weekly. (The last number of it appeared about May 1804.) In 1803 Benjamin Carr had joined forces with George Schetky, a nephew of Alexander Reinagle and a good cellist, singer, and arranger, to issue the final volumes of *The Musical Journal* and to reprint some music from it. They also issued some fresh pieces (including an edition of Haydn's duet *The Master and Scholar* and a patriotic descriptive sonata by Carr himself entitled *The Siege of Tripoli*) and a few collections before dissolving their partnership around 1811.

Benjamin Carr is not identified with music publishing again until about 1822 or 1823, when he reentered the field to conclude *Carr's Musical Miscellany in Occasional Numbers*, a serial publication which he had edited and which had been published from 1812 by his father, who had since died. He undoubtedly took this over in order to complete it following the sale of his father's business in late 1822 or early 1823. Benjamin Carr continued publishing music intermittently in Philadelphia until a year or two before his death in 1831. His brother, Thomas, who inherited and subsequently disposed of the father's Baltimore business, issued a few music publications from a newly established music store and musical academy in Philadelphia between 1824 and 1827, and he may have had some connection with his brother Benjamin in this later enterprise.

In addition to composing or arranging a vast amount of vocal and instrumental music, Benjamin Carr found the time and interest to compile several major works, including: *Masses, Vespers, Litanies, Hymns, Psalms, Anthems & Motets, Composed, Selected and Arranged for the Use of the Catholic Churches in the United States of America* (1805); *A Collection of Chants and Tunes for the Use of the Episcopal Church in the City of Philadelphia* (1816); *The Chorister* (1820); *Sacred Airs, in Six Numbers* (1830); a *Mass, in Two Parts* (date unknown) and a pianoforte instruction book (1826). In 1820 Carr was a leader in the organization of the Musical Fund Society of Philadelphia and served as one of its early conductors. His sound musicianship and practical versatility made him extremely influential in early Philadelphia musical circles.[5]

Throughout the first thirty years of the nineteenth century, and possibly even later, George Willig and George E. Blake were the most active music publishers in Philadelphia, if not in America. Not only were their catalogs the largest and most varied and the most representative of

5. More information on the Carrs—Benjamin, Joseph, and Thomas—can be found in two important sources, Virginia Larkin Redway's "The Carrs, American Music Publishers," *Musical Quarterly* XVIII (1932) 150–77 and Joseph Muller's *The Star Spangled Banner*.

the musical vogues of the times; they continued in business for longer periods than did any of their contemporaries. Willig took over the business started by John Christopher Moller upon the latter's removal to New York in 1794, and by 1803, the year of Blake's entry into the field, had built up a sizable catalog, to which he continued to add into the 1840s. Little is known of Willig's life, except that he also worked as a music teacher. His name is conspicuously absent from contemporary music programs, indicating that he performed little or not at all. In 1845 his name appeared in a booklet entitled *Wealth and Biography of the Wealthy Citizens of Philadelphia*, published by G. B. Ziebler, with the description "a respectable and much esteemed teacher and seller of music." His fortune was indicated here to be $75,000, a considerable sum for the period. The exact source of his wealth remains a mystery. Willig, like his thrifty compatriot Christopher Meineke of Baltimore, might have amassed his fortune through hard work and wise investments in real estate and through other business ventures. His will remains on file with the Register of Wills in and for the County of Philadelphia (No. 18, 1852). This document, which I have examined, indicates that he was a fair-minded and businesslike man. George Willig's death occurred at Philadelphia on December 30, 1851. His son, George Willig, Jr., became an important American music publisher also.

George E. Blake, born in England in 1775 and a resident of Philadelphia from 1793, began his musical career in that city as a teacher of the clarinet, flute, and flageolet in a room above John Aitken's engraving shop. In 1802 he acquired the patent portable grand pianoforte manufactory of John Isaac Hawkins, an inventor and correspondent of Thomas Jefferson, upon Hawkins's recall to England on family business. Within a year he had moved into larger quarters, had opened up a circulating library, and had begun to publish music, all of which he was reported to have engraved himself during his early years as a music publisher.[6] Blake's business prospered from the very beginning. By 1810 he was able to boast on the imprints of several of his publications that he had the largest assortment of sheet music for sale in America. In addition to issuing the usual songs and instrumental works of the day, Blake published a complete edition of Thomas Moore's *Irish Melodies* (from about 1808 until about 1825); the songs and incidental music of several theatrical pieces (John Braham's

6. Krummel, "Philadelphia Music Engraving," p. 100, quoting from Blake's obituary in the *Philadelphia Evening Telegraph* of February 21, 1871. It is likely that Blake did engrave all of his own music publications, and print them as well, for both engraving and printing equipment were in his possession at the time of his death.

Narensky, John Bray's *The Indian Princess*, Michael Kelly's *The Music of Cinderella* and *The Foundling of the Forest*, and Raynor Taylor's version of *The Ethiop*); a large miscellany or series of music publication in eighty-odd numbers embodying the works of a great many native or naturalized American composers (being rivaled in this respect by Joseph Carr of Baltimore and to a lesser extent by Allyn Bacon in Philadelphia); the *Sacred Songs* and most of the *National Melodies* of Thomas Moore; and, during the late 1820s and into the early 1830s, the complete vocal works of Handel in piano score. This last endeavor amounted to fifteen thick folio volumes, and it was by far the most ambitious music-publishing effort undertaken in America to that time and for some time afterward. Blake lived to be nearly a hundred years old, his death occurring in Philadelphia on February 20, 1871. He had ceased publishing music by the 1850s and spent the remainder of his life selling earlier music publications, which by then must have been hopelessly out of date. He apparently kept all of his music plates and equipment, for on May 22, 1871, his entire plate stock and his engraving and printing tools were put up at auction by M. Thomas and Sons. Fortunately, a copy of the catalog of this sale has survived. It extends to fifty-four pages and lists all or almost all of his music publications, attesting to the vastness of his activity. The final pages from this catalog, containing an enumeration of his tools, form Appendix B of this work. Music publishing also proved lucrative for George E. Blake, as it did for Willig. Probate records of the estates of both of these publishers, on file at the Philadelphia County Courthouse, show that they were worth slightly more than $31,000 and $32,000 at the times of their deaths.

Blake's obituary, which appeared in the *Philadelphia Evening Telegraph* of February 21, 1871, affords much insight into his personal life and gives the flavor of the period in which he lived; it is reprinted here in full.[7]

The venerable George E. Blake, who has kept a music store on Fifth Street, a few doors above Chesnut, for so many years past, died at his residence in the same building, last evening. Mr. Blake has attained the extreme old age of ninety-five years, and has long been regarded as one of the celebrities of this city. He has been for so many years the oldest music publisher in the United States, and there is but one music house in the country whose original establishment antidates his. This is the music publishing house of Lee & Walker, Philadelphia, which was founded in 1772 [*sic*] by George Willig who died very old in 1851.

Mr. Blake left England, his native country, at the age of sixteen, coming to Philadelphia where he worked for a while as a carpenter and taught music, but

7. This obituary is quoted in full in Krummel's dissertation, cited in n. 6.

finally in 1802 opened a music store at 3rd. & Market Streets, from which he continued his business and residence for nearly fifty-seven years. The store is about 20 x 30 feet, and immediately in the rear is the small office in which the venerable non-agenarian was accustomed to pass much of his time. When Mr. Blake first started in business, he engraved with his own hands all the plates for the music which he published and this he continued to do for many years. Previous to starting in business as a music dealer, Mr. Blake has been a piano manufacturer, and the first piano made in the United States was constructed by him in this City, becoming when completed the property of Thomas Jefferson.[8]

In his day Mr. Blake was one of the most extensive music dealer[s] in the country, his shelves being loaded down with the best selections. His own publications likewise numbered among them many extensive and valuable works. An edition of Handel's oratorio of the "Messiah," which he published many years ago, is regarded as the best ever published in this country. But for many years past Mr. Blake has practically ceased to transact any business, and probably there has not been in his store a new piece of music during the past quarter of a century. But he still continued to beguile his leisure with show of work, going through the ceremony of taking down the shutters every morning, and of putting them up again about dark. The windows of his store were filled with the quaint old music sheets of the early part of the century, changed at regular intervals to impress the passing world with an idea of the extent of his stock. With the great bustling world he had nothing to do, and of its doings he knew nothing. To the day of his death he is said never to have heard of the existence of any other music store in the city. We have even heard him say, in a gossipy moment, that since Mr. Willig's death he was the only music publisher in the country that he knew of.

Mr. Blake for years lived almost entirely alone. A maiden daughter, now over sixty, who is said to have been a great belle in her young days, has long lived with her father. His wife died about twenty-one years ago; but, in addition to the unmarried daughter mentioned three other children out of a large family are still living—Colonel George A. H. Blake, of the United States Army; T. West Blake, the former secretary of the Fire Department, and now connected with the Water Department; and a married daughter.

Next door to his store has long lived Thomas Sully, the eminent painter of a past generation. Mr. Blake was but eight years his senior and the two venerable gentlemen were on the most intimate and friendly terms.[9]

8. The obituary confuses Blake with John Isaac Hawkins. It was Hawkins who, while living in Philadelphia between 1799 and 1802, invented, patented, and manufactured a portable upright piano. It was in connection with the sale of one of these instruments that Hawkins made the acquaintance of Thomas Jefferson, who wished to promote American invention and manufacture. Neither Blake nor Hawkins constructed the first piano made in the United States (see Spillane, *History of the American Pianoforte*), though Hawkins might have manufactured the first portable upright model. Inasmuch as Blake is identified as a carpenter in this obituary, it is possible that he worked with Hawkins in constructing pianos before assuming his business and venturing into music publishing.

9. Two points brought out in the obituary need explanation. Willig opened his music store in Philadelphia in 1794 and not 1772, the date given above being probably a typographical error. And the Handel *Messiah*, which Krummel mentions in his dissertation as unlocated by

The endurance of the Blake and Willig enterprises was not typical of our early music-publishing industry. In other cities business failures were far more frequent, especially in New York. It may very well have been the longevity of these two pioneer publishers that led to the eventual downfall of Philadelphia as the nation's music-publishing center, for in stifling competition they also stifled change. In other cities, particularly New York, which was to succeed to Philadelphia's eminence in this field, the influx of new men, frequently from abroad, kept the published output abreast of the vogues and changing tastes of the times. Blake and Willig, on the other hand, were issuing the same type of music in the 1820s and 1830s that they had been publishing for the previous twenty or thirty years, nor were they quick to decorate their sheets with lithographs and highly illustrative covers, a practice which arose in the 1820s and became the custom after 1840. By the time they retired from the field, the center of music publishing in the United States had shifted away from Philadelphia to New York, where it remained ever since.

During the 1790s Filippo Trisobio, R. Shaw (probably Ralph and not Robert, the other R. Shaw associated with Philadelphia music then) and William Priest were the only active music publishers in Philadelphia in addition to those five previously mentioned. Trisobio, an immigrant singing teacher and composer, issued a little music in Philadelphia between 1796, the year of his arrival there, and 1798, the year of his death. Shaw had been only moderately active there between 1794 and 1798, when he moved to Baltimore. After a three-year residence there, he reappeared as a Philadelphia music publisher in 1800, remaining there until 1807, when he moved on to Boston. His output in all three cities was slight, consisting of a few handfuls of songs. William Priest, an English bassoonist and trumpeter who in 1796 performed the obligato part of Raynor Taylor's *Trumpet Song* (see Sonneck–Upton, p. 438), issued only one title in his capacity as a Philadelphia music publisher, an edition of Taylor's arrangement of Philip Phile's *The President's March*, in 1795. Though his role as a Philadelphia publisher was insignificant, he did make an important announcement regarding his importation of punching tools which will be referred to in the discussion on implements. Priest also published an interesting account of his American experience, *Travels in the United States of America; Commencing in the Year 1793, and Ending in 1797*, after his return to London.

---

him (p. 101), was undoubtedly the edition which Blake issued as part of the complete vocal works of that composer between the late 1820s and the early 1830s. This is a magnificent edition, a major achievement of American music publishing before 1850.

Throughout the first decade of the nineteenth century, Blake, Willig, and the firm of Carr & Schetky held the field all to themselves. And in the next decade only Allyn Bacon and his associates (George Bacon, who may have been his son, and Abraham Hart) were able to challenge the supremacy of Willig and Blake. Bacon was in business for about seven years, from about 1815 until about 1821, and George Bacon, who possibly did all of the firm's engraving, published only a few pieces under his own name in Philadelphia in 1823 and 1824 before moving to New York. Allyn Bacon's catalog contained about 200 titles, with instrumental music predominating. His *American Musical Miscellany*, in twelve numbers, was the first series of musical publications devoted exclusively to the works of American composers. About 1823 John G. Klemm, a musical-instrument maker (who may have been descended from Johann Gottlob Klemm [1690–1762], a German organ-maker who came to Philadelphia in 1736 and made the first American organ for Trinity Church, New York, about 1740), bought Bacon's plate stock and began a publishing business that was to endure for approximately sixty years, reissuing almost the entire Bacon catalog under his own name.

Less active publishers in Philadelphia during the first quarter of the nineteenth century were G. Balls (ca. 1818), a relative of the London publishers of the same name; Gaetano Carusi (1819), father of Samuel Carusi, a music publisher of Baltimore and Washington from 1837 until 1854, and of Lewis Carusi, a well-known dancing master of Washington (Gaetano Carusi was also the disputed second director of the United States Marine Band); John Conrad (ca. 1804), whose few publications appear to have been engraved by Blake; Thomas De Silver, whose sole effort was an edition of *Jessie the Flower o' Dumblane* (ca. 1815); John L. Frederick, a general engraver and engraver of music who issued a few sheets between 1818 and 1822 and again about 1830, his large collection *The Ladies Musical Port Folio* appearing about that time; J. C. Homann, a prominent musician (1800–1810), and Charles Hupfield (Hupfeld), his son-in-law and a violinist of note (1804–12); John Morgan, whose only publication was *A Selection of the Most Admired Ballads* (1801); John F. W. Pchellas, a music teacher who in 1820 issued a set of three of his own sonatas for piano and violin and two other works, John Braham's *Fair Ellen* and his own setting of Thomas Moore's *Mary I Believ'd Thee True*; and Charles Taws (1807–19), the pianoforte maker and erstwhile partner of John Aitken. Several composers also issued or had issued one or more of their own compositions. Included in this group were Stephen (or Etienne) Christiani (ca. 1820); Peter Gilles, Jr. (1822); Anthony

Philip Heinrich (1820); John Huneker (ca. 1823), grandfather of the music critic James Gibbon Huneker; Francis Johnson, a black or mulatto bandmaster (1820–25); Pierre Nicolas Neveu (1804); and George Pfeiffer, whose song *The Chaplet of Fame* appeared in 1817.

A number of music engravers were undoubtedly active in Philadelphia within this period, but they remain for the most part anonymous and unidentified. John L. Frederick, mentioned previously as a publisher, may have engraved for George Willig. George Bacon's activity as a engraver has been noted previously. Thomas Birch (son or relative of the Philadelphia painter?), who established himself as a music engraver in New York in 1817 and as a publisher there a few years later, probably came from Philadelphia and in all likelihood learned music engraving there. And, finally, H. Glenn and Maude O. Brown's *Directory of the Book-Arts . . . in Philadelphia to 1820* carried a D. H. Mason as "music engraver" between the years 1805 and 1818, though his name does not appear on a single contemporary music sheet, nor is it known for whom he worked, if indeed, he actually did engrave music at all.[10]

NEW YORK

Due to a lack of positive information, no one person can be singled out with certainty at this time as the first to have issued sheet music from punched plates in New York. A few sheets published in New York by John Young, the man mentioned previously in the resumé of early Philadelphia publishing, are assigned in Sonneck–Upton to the years 1792–93. However, the exact dates of Young's residence in New York have never really been established; and, in view of a recently discovered New York collection of his which contains reprints from his Philadelphia *Vocal and Instrumental Musical Miscellany*, it seems more likely that his New York music-publishing career followed rather than preceded his residence in Philadelphia, for it was upon separate issues of the recently discovered work that Upton based his early dating.[11]

10. In view of the fact that Mason also advertised himself as an engraver on brass, and because he was connected in business with William Mason, who engraved brass ornaments for bookbinding and letterpress printing, it seems more likely that the description of him as "music engraver" here does not imply that he engraved music plates, but, more important, that he probably cut the necessary punches used in stamping them. Mason will be discussed at greater length in Chapter 7 herein, which deals with the engraving and stamping tools used in early American music publishing.

11. This recently located collection is a curious publication entitled *Volume, Consisting of Favourite Songs, Duetts, &c. New York, Published by I. Young & Co.* , the only complete copy of which is in the Grosvenor Library in Buffalo, New York (see Wolfe, No. 10351). A number of titles in this collection, carrying Young's New York imprint, were obviously issued

In view of this, the distinction of being the first publisher of sheet music in New York City probably passes over to James Harrison, who stated in an advertisement in the *New York Daily Advertiser* of July 29, 1793, that he was from London. Harrison's presence in New York had previously been made known through an advertisement which he published in the *Weekly Museum* on the 13th of that month. In this he had proposed to publish by subscription a "collection of the newest and most approved songs," which, he declared, was then in preparation. Harrison stated his intention to publish a number of popular songs and instrumental pieces that would eventually form a handsome folio volume of thirty pages. In his initial advertisement he stated that part of the plates for this were already finished, but, as noted in Sonneck–Upton (p. 75), no sheets from these "already finished" plates have survived. Harrison's notice of July 29 also informed the New York musical clientele that he had opened a music store at No. 38 Maiden Lane, two doors from Queen Street.

Only two of Harrison's publications are known today. Both date from the year 1794. The first is an edition of the elder Thomas Linley's *Primroses Deck*. According to the subtitle which Harrison added to this, it was sung by Mr. [Benjamin] Carr at the amateur and professional concerts. Publication of this piece was announced by Harrison in April 1794. According to another contemporary advertisement, his other extant publication, *A Christmas Hymn* (known only through a single copy in the New York Public Library), appeared in November 1794. This was written probably by an amateur composer named Page to words by Harrison himself and issued just in time to attract the Christmas trade.

Harrison's name can be found in New York City directories for the years 1794 and 1795 only, initially as a music seller and later as a print seller. He advertised in the December 28, 1793, issue of the *Weekly Museum* that he had recently opened up a musical circulating library (see Illus. 5), offering to loan music on a subscription basis. And in a similar advertisement on April 21 following, he noted that he carried on copperplate printing and engraving in all its branches, and, additionally, that he had a copperplate press for sale. In September 1793 he had advertised that he had just published a plan of Cape François in Haiti, and

---

separately before the collection was made up. All titles in it had been issued previously in *Young's Vocal and Instrumental Musical Miscellany*, which appeared in Philadelphia in the 1793–95 period. It seems likely that the Philadelphia collection preceded the separate New York issue of the songs in this collection and their later reissue within the collection itself. On a number of separate New York issues the earlier Philadelphia imprint has partly inked through where it was poorly effaced. In addition, I have not seen any parts of the *Miscellany* or separate issues from it with Young's New York imprint or traces of it.

in the New York *American Minerva* of May 25, 1795, and in *The Daily &* *Universal Advertiser* of January 8, 1796, he published a detailed proposal for issuing through subscription a set of twenty-four selected American views, executed in aquatint. Nothing more is heard or known of Harrison after that date, and it is to be assumed that he departed from the New York scene reasonably soon afterward. It is apparent that Harrison's successes did not measure up to his expectations or ambitions, and his attempts at publishing music in New York City—significant as they were from the standpoint of priority—cannot be considered as important or enduring. However, three additional efforts at publishing music in New York followed Harrison's rather feeble activity, all of which were successful and long-lasting.

Benjamin Carr of Philadelphia opened up a New York branch of his music-publishing and music-selling business in the late fall of 1794. George Gilfert, a string player and organist who had been selling musical merchandise in the city since 1787, commenced his publishing activity about November of 1794. And James Hewitt, a violinist who had emigrated from London in 1792, is thought to have issued some music in New York as early as 1794, though his activity as a publisher here was mostly confined to the period after 1797, when he acquired the Carr outlet. Of the three, Gilfert was the most prolific New York publisher throughout the 1790s, issuing well over 200 titles in the six or seven years before 1800. Carr's output in New York was slight by comparison. He probably maintained his New York branch mainly as an outlet for the sale of his Philadelphia publications, for those imprints which designate New York as their place of issue amount to only a few dozen items.

As was previously noted, George Gilfert was one of the first of the immigrant musicians to realize that profits could be made through the sale of musical merchandise and through the publication of music locally. Nothing substantial is known of his origin or of his life before about 1787.[12] In the period 1789–91 he was head of the Musical Society in New York, and he appeared as a violist at a few concerts. In the initial New York City directory, for 1789, he was denominated an organist, and in directories for 1794 and 1795 this description was lengthened to "organist at the New Dutch Church." In addition to being named as the proprietor

12. In the *New York Packet* of July 18, 1785, "George Gilford, lately arrived from Philadelphia, Begs leave to acquaint the respectable Public, that he strings and tunes piano fortes, harpsichords, spinnets, etc., etc. He also instructs gentlemen and ladies in the art of music, on either of these instruments, at a very moderate rate, and is willing to attend at such hours as may be·convenient either at their own dwellings, or at his house, No. 64 Nassau-street, next to the German Reformed Church."

of a "musical magazine," which was the contemporary way of saying that he kept a music store, he was also listed in directories as a tavern keeper (1791) and as the proprietor of a boardinghouse (1793–94). Although his origin is unknown, another Gilfert, Charles, who composed music at about the time of the War of 1812, is thought to have been born in Prague. It is likely that the two Gilferts were related, and the fact that George Gilfert served as organist at the New Dutch Church in New York suggests that he was Germanic (Austro-Hungarian?) in origin. Gilfert continued as a music dealer and publisher until about 1814, but his activity in issuing music diminished sharply after 1803 or 1804. Though no obituaries or news of his death are known, he apparently died in 1814, for his widow is entered in the city directory of the following year. His business relationship with Peter Albrecht von Hagen of Boston in the late years of the eighteenth century and early years of the nineteenth will be referred to later on (as will his slight connection with George Willig of Philadelphia). From contemporary advertisements we know that he imported pianofortes from London and other instruments and items of musical merchandise. At the outset of his publishing career he was in partnership with Frederick Rausch (1794–96), a figure who will loom prominently in later pages of this work.

Little attention has been afforded Gilfert as a major music publisher during this early period. Because of the notoriety given to Benjamin Carr and James Hewitt and other musician-composers who also dealt in music publishing in late eighteenth-century America, Gilfert's prodigious efforts by comparison have been overlooked or taken for granted at best. Yet, for the ten-year period from 1794 through 1803, at which time his output diminished sharply, he was the most active publisher of music in New York. He did little or no performing or composing, and as a consequence is hardly recognized by musicologists. In spite of this, he contributed significantly to New York's musical life by providing it with most of the music used for its early instruction and entertainment.

James Hewitt, like Gilfert, was an energetic publisher, producing slightly more than a hundred titles between 1797 and 1801. In 1798 or 1799 John and Michael Paff, whose origin and personal lives are obscure, opened up another musical warehouse for the publication of music and for the sale of musical merchandise. (They also advertised toys, prints, clocks and watches, and other non-musical items.) During the next decade and a half, theirs proved to be the major publishing outlet in the city, though during the period from 1801 until 1805 or 1806 James Hewitt may have run a close second. Less active publishers here before 1801 were Frederick

Rausch, a German-American organist who was in partnership with Gilfert in late 1794 and early 1795 and with Hewitt from about March to August 1797; William Howe (1797–98), an organ-builder who also maintained a music store from which he issued a few publications; John Christopher Moller (1797–1803), previously located in Philadelphia; and Peter Weldon (1800–1803 and 1808–11), who may have engraved some plates for the Paffs.

During the first decade of the next century the Paffs and James Hewitt dominated the music-publishing field in New York, though George Gilfert remained active as a publisher until about 1805 and continued to produce a few sheets and to sell musical merchandise until his death in 1814. Hewitt was the dominant figure in New York's early music life, and his story has been told in John Tasker Howard's *Our American Music* and elsewhere. Hewitt obviously published music to augment his income. He also earned his livelihood by participating in almost all of the musical activities of the city, performing on the violin and as organist at Trinity Church, serving as leader of the orchestra of the Old American Company (a theater group) and as director of several bands, giving music lessons, and composing a great deal of vocal and instrumental music, almost all of which he published himself. Born at Dartmoor, England, on June 4, 1770, Hewitt arrived in New York about September 1792 in the company of other "professors of music from the Opera house, Hanover-square and professional Concerts under the direction of Haydn, Pleyel, etc." He was energetically involved in New York musical circles until 1811, when he moved to Boston to assume the position of organist of Trinity Church and to take charge of music at the Federal Street Theatre. Although he reappeared in New York again in 1817, his later life was spent mostly in Boston or in traveling with theatrical companies. Hewitt died in Boston in early August 1827. His trade card, engraved about 1807 when he added a circulating library, appears as Illustration 6a here. The later whereabouts of the Paffs remain unknown. They disappeared from the New York musical scene just as they had arrived, quietly and without notice, Michael in 1810 and John in 1817.

Hewitt's departure for Boston apparently opened up opportunities for others to share in the profits of music publishing. Joseph Willson (or Wilson), an English singer, music teacher, and organist, commenced his publishing career in 1812 by reissuing music from the acquired plates of several earlier publishers, in addition to having some new music engraved for publication. He had emigrated from London in the final years of the eighteenth century and had initially settled in New Brunswick, New

Jersey, where he appears to have had some connection with Dr. George K. Jackson, one of the most erudite of our early music masters. By 1802 Willson was in New York, where he appeared as a singer at concerts and performed as organist at Trinity Church (1804–9). He had actually issued a few musical titles before 1812, but only randomly. Willson continued as a music publisher in New York until about 1820, after which time he moved to Roxbury, Massachusetts, to assume the position of organist to a local congregation, and he may have eventually returned to England. [13] Willson rivaled John Paff as the most active New York music publisher between 1812 and 1816, when his output began to slacken. Although he employed several engravers to produce plates for original works—Peter Smith and Uri K. or Frederick Hill—his activity was mainly directed toward reissuing the publications of earlier publishers.

Edward Riley, a music engraver, seller, publisher, and musical-instrument maker, had emigrated from London about 1805 and had initially set up in New York as a music engraver and instrument maker, producing music plates for the Paffs and others as well as issuing an occasional title under his own name. In 1812 he opened his own publishing establishment and music store at 23 Chatham Steet and by 1819 or 1820 had become New York's most active and important publisher, issuing a great quantity of music until his death in 1829, when the business was assumed by his widow, Elizabeth, and later by his sons, Edward C. and Frederick Riley, who conducted it until 1851. In his early career in New York, Riley also supported himself through music teaching (flute, flageolet, piano, and singing) and by appearing at numerous concerts as singer and flutist. Several flutes made by him are extant in the Dayton Miller collection of wind instruments at the Library of Congress.

John Appel was another whose publishing career began at about the time of Hewitt's departure. However, he remained in business for only three years and his output during this time was not significant. The few plates that he had engraved were acquired by Adam Geib in 1815, who used them to launch his own publishing endeavor. In 1816 Adam Geib took his nephew, John Geib, Jr., into partnership, and in 1818 they were joined by William, John's brother. (John Geib, Sr., and Adam were piano-makers who had appeared in New York in 1802, the sons of John Geib, one of the Germans who from 1760 established piano-making in England.) This firm published music under the name of J. A. & W. Geib

13. The records of the First Church in Roxbury, where he served as organist, indicate that Willson was appointed to his post and began his duties on November 17, 1822, and continued to serve in this capacity until April 1825. His activities thereafter are unknown.

until 1821, when it became A. & W. Geib. In 1829 the firm became known as Geib & Walker when Adam Geib took into partnership his son-in-law, Daniel Walker, who had married his daughter, Mary Anne (see Illus. 6b).

In 1817 John Paff, who had continued on alone after his brother Michael's retirement from publishing in 1810, sold his plate stock to William Dubois, a resident of New York from at least 1813, if not earlier. During the next year or two, Dubois reissued almost completely Paff's 1811–17 catalog and a number of titles published earlier by John and Michael Paff jointly. In late 1820 or early 1821 Dubois formed a partnership with William Stodart, who had dealt in music and musical instruments in Richmond, Virginia, and the firm issued music under the name Dubois & Stodart (and made and sold pianos, as well) until the mid-1830s, when Stodart was succeeded by George Bacon, mentioned earlier in Philadelphia publishing. During the 1820s Dubois & Stodart, Edward Riley, and the Geibs and their successors were the principal music publishers in the city. In 1824 Thomas Birch, who had worked in New York as a music engraver since 1817, established a music-publishing business which was carried on by him and his descendants until the 1890s.

Others who issued music on a lesser scale in New York during the first twenty-five years of the nineteenth century were Peter Erben (ca. 1801–20), a teacher of music, an organist, and an organ-builder, who issued about twenty publications; Sarah Territt, who had assumed the music store conducted by her husband, Charles, upon his death in 1802 or 1803 (she published a few titles between 1803 and 1805); John Butler, an instrument maker from London who published a number of sheets in 1808 and was probably associated with the music master George K. Jackson in this enterprise; Mrs. Bradish (1811), widow and keeper of a boarding-house, whose small catalog was, along with Butler's, reissued by Joseph Willson in 1812; Charles P. F. O'Hara, publisher of three sheets and a patriotic collection, *The Gentleman's Musical Repository*, in 1813; Raymond Meetz (1819–26), who acted primarily as the New York agent for George E. Blake of Philadelphia, but who published a small number of titles jointly with him or under his name alone; Joseph Willson, Jr. (1820); Nathaniel Thurston (1821–24); George Geib (1822), brother of Adam and a music teacher of distinction; Peter K. Moran, an Irish musician and music teacher who also conducted a music store in 1822 and 1823 from which he issued a number of titles, mostly his own compositions; Harris Sage (1823); William Plain (1824); and Charles and Edwin W. Jackson, sons of George K. Jackson, who also published music in Boston concurrently (their New York activity dates 1824–25). Three individuals in New York restricted their publishing activity to a single item: John Andrew Graham, later a musician in Philadelphia, issued *An Acrostic* between 1808 and 1810; Andrew T. Goodrich, a bookseller and stationer, reprinted one of Mrs. Bradish's titles in 1812; and Isaac P. Cole, professor of music, published Benjamin Carr's adaptation of an ode, *The Landing of Columbus*, to music from Mozart's *La Clemenza di Tito* in 1825. Musicians issuing one or more of their own works were Charles Burton (1825); Antoine Louis Chevallier, a dancing master (1820–23); John Davies (ca. 1819); "Mr. Demilliere" and Mark Desabaye, whose publications were engraved for them by Edward Riley between 1812 and 1818 (Demilliere actually published a composition of his daughter's); Charles Gilfert (1815); George K. Jackson and Theodore Marschausen (180–); Florent Meline (1821), later of Albany; Samuel Priestly Taylor (1809–10), an organist; Charles Thibault (ca. 1824); and Richard L. Williams (ca. 1825).

William Pirsson was the principal music engraver in New York City during the first seven or eight years of the nineteenth century. He ceased engraving about 1808, perhaps driven off by the arrival of Riley with his up-to-date methods and tools, for sheets pulled from plates engraved by Pirsson appear crude when compared with Riley's and evince a lack of skill. In addition to Riley, who was the major engraver for a decade or more following his arrival, other known engravers who were active in New York after 1808 were: Peter Smith (1812); Uri K. and Frederick Hill (1815–16);[14] Thomas Birch (from 1817); and Nathaniel Thurston (1821–24). Peter Weldon has previously been mentioned as a possible engraver for the Paffs in the 1801–03 period. And one publication of Peter Erben's, a set of six sonatas by Muzio Clementi, contains the note "L. Seymour, No. 35 Mott street, N.Y.," undoubtedly set there to identify the engraver of its plates. Seymour's name is entered in New York City directories between 1804 and 1820 with the occupation of teacher and proprietor of a hardware store. I have found no evidence that connects him with music or

14. A number of sheets issued by Joseph Willson and Adam Geib in 1815 carry the note "Engraved by Hill" or "Engraved by Hill, No. 8 Fair Street, New York." Number 8 Fair Street was the 1815 address of Uri K. Hill, a local music teacher, and we would normally assume that he was the actual engraver here. However, two contemporary titles, Peter Erben's edition of James Hook's *When Edward Left His Native Plain* and Philip Trajetta's *Periodical Publications No. 2*, containing his *Two Marches for the Piano Forte*, carry the note "Engraved by F. Hill." Inasmuch as Frederick Hill, a lawyer of Rutland, Vermont, was the father of Uri K. Hill and was probably living in New York at the same time, in all likelihood lodging with his son (Frederick Hill's name never appeared in contemporary directories), he may have actually done the engraving for the Willson and Geib publications also. The Boston *Columbian Centinel* of September 21, 1825, announced that Frederick Hill, "Counsellor-at-law, formerly of Vermont, died in New York, aged 72 years."

publishing. Of the publishers, probably James Hewitt, George Gilfert, Riley, Birch, and Thurston did their own engraving. Others who may have done so were John Butler and C. P. F. O'Hara. It seems fairly certain that Hewitt engraved his own plates. In addition to two sources to support this fact, it must have been he who trained James L. Hewitt, his son and longtime music publisher of a slightly later period, in the art of engraving music.[15] We know that publishers sometimes employed general engravers to assist them in finishing or decorating their plates, for a notation for March 23, 1795, in the diary of Alexander Anderson, the first known engraver on wood in the United States, states that Anderson went to George Gilfert's musical magazine and was engaged for 12 shillings to engrave letters for the title of a piece of music.[16]

In general, music publishing in New York during the first thirty years or so of the industry's existence there was a far from stable occupation. Unlike Philadelphia, no single publisher became sufficiently entrenched to gain a decided advantage over all others. Competition must have been fierce, and the mortality of music-publishing businesses was high. It appears that there was only enough demand to support a given number of publishers: one could not successfully enter the trade until another had dropped out, the latter usually relinquishing his stock of plates and perhaps his tools to the newcomer. With regard to instability, uncertainty, and change, New York was probably the most typical of the earliest centers of music publishing in the United States.

BOSTON

Although William Norman was the first to issue sheet music in Boston, his collection *The Musical Repertory* appearing there as early as 1796, the few works he published between then and 1799 were engraved freehand and not produced with punching tools.[17] Consequently, to Peter Albrecht

15. James Hewitt is denominated a music engraver in vol. 3 of William Dunlap's *History of Design in the United States* (1918 ed. p. 308) in the section containing a list of painters, sculptors, architects, and engravers at work in America before 1835 and in Mantle Fielding's *Dictionary of American Painters, Sculptors & Engravers* (Philadelphia, 1926, p. 168, under "Hewitt").

16. The manuscript of Anderson's diary is now in the Department of Special Collections of the Columbia University Library.

17. This was the same William Norman who was said by Isaiah Thomas to have produced the first music types in America. The few facts that are known about him are given in Chapter 3 herein. Norman more likely belonged to that class of engravers, discussed in Chapter 2, who cut the plates for our early psalters and hymn collections. In fact, one of his publications, the *Beauties of Music*, of which no copy is now known to exist (see Sonneck–Upton, p. 39), may have belonged to this class. In addition to the *Repertory*, Norman also published *Twenty-four Fashionable Country Dances for the Year 1799*, which was a reprinting of a London publication, and an edition of Stephen Storac's popular song, *Lullaby*.

von Hagen belongs the distinction of being the first to engrave music with the aid of punching tools in Boston and the first to publish music on a continuing basis in that city. Von Hagen was a Dutch musician and composer who had emigrated to America by way of London in 1774 and had been active in Charleston and New York as well as in New England. In January 1790, while residing in New York, he had advertised instruments and music for sale from his lodgings. In May 1798, in partnership with Benjamin Crehore, a maker of cellos and basses, harpsichords and pianos, he opened up a "Musical Magazine and Warranted Piano Forte Warehouse" at No. 62 Newbury Street (now part of Washington Street) in Boston, from which he issued music of his own manufacture. The von Hagen–Crehore partnership was dissolved in mid-1799, whereupon von Hagen took his son, Peter Albertus (1781–1837)—designated incorrectly in Sonneck–Upton as Peter Albrecht von Hagen, Jr.—into the business, the latter continuing on alone after the father's death in 1803. Von Hagen, his associates, and his successor published perhaps a hunderd or more titles from 1798 to 1804, including a number of patriotic pieces and some of their own compositions. Before his death in September 1803, he dictated a will that is reproduced as Illustration 7 here. The accompanying inventory of his estate, on file at the Probate Court of Suffolk County in Boston, is a valuable source of information on our early music publishing. Within a year after the death of the elder von Hagen, the enterprise which he had founded failed, due probably to the intemperate habits of his son, whom one contemporary source described as heavily addicted to alcohol.[18]

Early in 1802, probably coincidental with the diminishing activity of the von Hagens, there began what was to prove to be the major publishing business in Boston for the next fifteen to twenty years. This was the firm of Francis Mallet and Gottlieb Graupner, who had joined together to establish a "Conservatorio or Musical Academy" about November 1801,

18. George Handel Hill's *Scenes from the Life of an Actor* (New York, 1837), in recounting the author's early musical instruction on the flute at the hands of the younger von Hagen, refers to his teacher (pp. 49–50) in terms which can only be interpreted to imply that Peter Albertus von Hagen was a drunkard. Von Hagen, Jr. shared poorly in his father's estate, and one might assume, when reading the elder von Hagen's will and the inventory of his estate, that he had incurred the displeasure of his father. For incidentals on his later life, see the short biography of him that appeared in my *Secular Music in America* (p. 333). In his day, George Handel Hill was a famous comedian who was known on the stage as "Yankee Hill" (so named, possibly, because of his Vermont heritage but more likely because of the "Yankee" characters he portrayed on the stage). Coincidentally, he was the son of Uri K. Hill, mentioned as a New York music engraver, and brother of Ureli Corelli Hill, first conductor of the New York Philharmonic (as well as the grandson of Frederick Hill, referred to in n. 14 above).

whence they began to issue music within six months or so. The partnership continued until the following November, when Mallet dropped out. From that time on Gottlieb Graupner was the major—and frequently the only—music publisher in Boston until the mid- or late 1820s. Graupner had been born in Hanover, Germany, in 1767 and had been an oboist in a Hanoverian regiment. When he was twenty years old he obtained his discharge and journeyed to London, where, like James Hewitt, he played in the orchestra directed by Joseph Haydn which introduced the "Salomon" symphonies in 1791. He left England in 1794 or 1795 and, after some years of wandering in America, finally settled in Boston in 1798, where he taught music and engaged in orchestral activity, both as conductor and performer on the oboe, violin, piano, and double bass. He was one of the principal founders of the Philharmonic Society in 1810 and of the Handel and Haydn Society five years later. His efforts as a composer were slight. However, he did complete an instruction book for the pianoforte which he reissued several times, as well as methods for the clarinet, flute, and double bass.[19]

Graupner issued music from his "Musical Academy" between 1803 and 1806 or 1807 and from his "Music Store" between 1807 and 1817, at which time his activity as a publisher began to slacken. Between 1817 and 1820 he was in partnership with George Cushing, their publications bearing the imprint "G. Graupner and Company." Graupner continued publishing music in Boston until about 1827, and in September 1829 a clearance sale of a large part of his stock was announced. During the late 1820s John Ashton, a dealer in music and musical instruments from about 1818, became the agent for the sale of most of Graupner's publications, and Ashton's name is frequently found affixed to reissues of later and sometimes even earlier Graupner music sheets. Graupner died in Boston on April 16, 1836. After his death many of his music plates fell into the hands of other publishers, who continued to reissue music from them for many years afterward. In addition to the usual fare of the day and to the instructors mentioned before, Graupner published the following large collections: *The Musical Magazine* (1803–5), which was essentially a re-issue of William Norman's *Musical Repertory* with some material added; a large sacred compilation entitled *The Monitor, or Celestial Melody* (1806); and *The Anacreontic Vocalist* (1809), an eighty-page collection in oblong format of glees, catches, and rounds.

19. The fullest account of Graupner's overall activities, as well as the best treatment of the early Boston musical scene, appears in H. Earle Johnson's *Musical Interludes in Boston*.

Except for a very few sheets published by Francis Mallet independently between 1803 and 1807 and a single publication issued by R. Shaw (formerly of Philadelphia and Baltimore) in 1807, Graupner had no rival to speak of until 1811 or 1812, when the arrival of James Hewitt from New York brought Boston its second music publisher. However, Hewitt's activity in Boston was slight when compared with that of his New York period, only about three dozen titles appearing with his name on imprint by 1817, when he moved back to New York. About 1815 George K. Jackson, the music master who had moved from New York to Boston in 1809 and had resided at Northampton during the War of 1812, established a music store upon his return to Boston, from which he issued a few pieces of music. And in 1815 and 1816 five known sheets emanated from the music store of Hayts, Babcock, and Appleton, No. 6 Milk Street (at which address John Rowe Parker was soon to open up his Franklin Music Warehouse).[20] From about 1815 to 1818 Francesco Masi, an immigrant Italian organist and music teacher resident in Boston from 1807, engraved and issued a number of musical publications here, mostly consisting of his own compositions or arrangements. The title page of one of these, *The Battles of Lake Champlain and Plattsburg* (1815), carries a quaint patriotic scene which is reproduced herein (see Illus. 8a). In addition to playing the organ, Masi also taught music (piano, clarinet, violoncello, violin, French horn, trumpet, flute, and guitar). He removed to Washington about 1821. This same period witnessed the emergence of two other music publishers, Samuel Stockwell, a member of the Boston theater troupe and a founder of the Handel and Haydn Society, and S. H. Parker. Stockwell issued two known pieces about 1816, while Parker published *The Orphean Lyre*, a collection of glees, catches, and duets, that same year. In 1818 appeared the first of about thirty titles engraved by Simeon Wood, a bassoonist and double-bass player in the Philharmonic and Handel and Haydn Society orchestras. He would probably have emerged as a major music publisher in Boston had not his life been cut short in 1822. His manuscript account book, found in New England some years ago and acquired by the Library of Congress, forms Appendix A herein.

Samuel Wetherbee, whose name appears as engraver on some Graupner publications dating to 1820 and afterward, issued a number of sheets under his own name between 1820 and 1826. In 1821 Charles and Edwin

---

20. Hayts, Babcock, and Appleton also sold umbrellas, an item of merchandise that was handled by John Ashton and others of our early music sellers. Some even repaired umbrellas.

W. Jackson, sons of the learned music master, commenced publishing in Boston, opening up a New York branch in 1824 or 1825. Their activity was limited to the years between 1821 and 1827 and consisted mostly of reprinting some of the earlier Boston publications of James Hewitt and of compositions issued by Peter K. Moran in New York in 1822. James L. Hewitt, the second son of the pioneer publisher, began engraving and publishing music in 1824. However, his activity in Boston was mostly confined to the period between 1826 and 1829, when he removed his business to New York. S. H. Parker, referred to before as publisher of *The Orphean Lyre* in 1816, published a few sheets at No. 12 Cornhill in 1824 and 1825, and Louis Ostinelli, a violinist and son-in-law of James Hewitt, had two sheets engraved for him at the same time. The only composer issuing one of her own works during this period was Caroline Clark, an amateur, whose *LaFayette's March* was published in 1824 upon the occasion of the visit of the Revolutionary hero to the United States and specifically to Boston. It is my opinion that Thomas Spear, the self-advertised pupil of G. K. Jackson, and John Ashton did not publish music in Boston before 1826 and 1827 respectively. Although John Rowe Parker did not issue sheet music, he did edit and publish *The Euterpeiad*, one of the country's first magazines devoted entirely to music. This appeared between 1820 and 1823 and contained several dozen music sheets printed from type by Thomas Badger, Jr., and John H. A. Frost. Parker was also proprietor from about 1817 until 1821 or later of a large music-selling establishment which he called the Franklin Music Warehouse. Here were sold the sheets of publishers in Philadelphia and New York as well as Boston. In 1821 Parker issued a large catalog of the stock he had for sale, a list of over fifty printed pages.

Gottlieb Graupner must have engraved his own plates before about 1820, after which time he frequently employed Samuel Wetherbee to engrave for him. (It is interesting to observe that Graupner, like James Hewitt, taught his son the art of engraving music, for John Henry Howard Graupner was in charge of the music-engraving department of Oliver Ditson and Company, Boston music publishers, from 1850 or earlier until 1880.) Simeon Wood, who in 1817 engraved the musical appendix for *The Songster's New Pocket Companion* (a songster, containing some music at the end and published in Boston by T. Swan), engraved a number of plates for use by others between then and 1822, and James Hewitt probably engraved his own publications in Boston as well as in New York. The Harvard University copy of Anthony Philip Heinrich's collection (actually collections) entitled *The Sylviad*, published in Boston for the author by Graupner between 1823 and 1826, contains a presentation note in which Heinrich refers to Mr. George Haws, the donee, as a "rival engraver."

BALTIMORE

The dominant figure in early Baltimore publishing was Joseph Carr, who followed his son Benjamin to America in 1794 and set up a music-publishing and music-selling establishment which was to be continued for a few years after his death in 1819 by his son Thomas. Carr was previously mentioned as a music engraver and music publisher in London from about 1770 until his emigration. He was in Baltimore by June 1794, having first disposed of his stock before leaving London. Joseph Carr supplemented the income he received through engraving (probably mainly for Benjamin) and through publishing by conducting the musical affairs of Old St. Paul's Parish in Baltimore, his son Thomas, who succeeded him as a music publisher in 1819, being organist of Christ Church, an offshoot of St. Paul's, from 1798 until 1811. While Joseph Carr turned out a substantial number of musical titles during the quarter of a century that he was active in Baltimore, his main contributions to American music and music publishing were his publication in 1800 and 1801 of the first two volumes of *The Musical Journal for the Piano Forte*, edited by his son Benjamin, and *Carr's Musical Miscellany in Occasional Numbers*, a continuing series of vocal and instrumental pieces (which were for the most part composed or arranged by Benjamin also), the first of its genre in America. This was issued by Joseph Carr between 1812 and 1819 and by Thomas until 1822, being finally concluded by Benjamin himself at Philadelphia in 1825. Joseph Carr is especially esteemed by collectors of American sheet music for having published the initial edition of *The Star Spangled Banner*, after Thomas had adapted the poem by Francis Scott Key to the tune of *To Anacreon in Heaven*. A month or so before his death in 1819 Joseph Carr conveyed his publishing business to Thomas. Either because of lack of interest or for want of business acumen, the son abandoned music publishing in 1822, selling the Carr plate stock to George Willig of Philadelphia. Reference has already been made to Thomas Carr's slight music-publishing activity in Philadelphia between 1824 and 1827.

Any competition encountered by Joseph Carr during his twenty-five-year residence in Baltimore was negligible. Between 1797 and 1800 R. Shaw of Philadelphia published a few titles in Baltimore before returning to Philadelphia and reestablishing a music outlet there. And from about 1805 until 1812 Charles Hupfield (Hupfeld), later prominent in Philadelphia music circles, issued about half a dozen publications in Baltimore, sometimes singularly and sometimes jointly with Henry S. Keatinge, who, along with Dobbin and Murphy, was the principal publisher of music from type in that city. Charles P. Hupfield was a competent German violinist who from about 1815 joined Benjamin Carr and Raynor Taylor in Philadelphia in promoting chamber and orchestral music. He was one of the founders and early conductors of the Musical Fund Society. In 1810 and in early 1811 Madame LePelletier, a little-known member of the French community of Baltimore, published a sizable collection entitled *Journal of Musick.* The plates for this, her sole publishing effort, were engraved in Philadelphia by George Willig.

George Willig, who had acquired the Carr business in 1822, published music in Baltimore from 1823 or 1824. He was succeeded in the late 1820s by his son, George Willig, Jr., who became as successful a music publisher as his father had been, the firm being conducted by him and his descendants until 1910. In 1822, when the Carr enterprise was coming to an end, John Cole, a Scottish immigrant who had been working as a printer and bookseller in Baltimore since 1785, opened up a music store from which he issued a large quantity of music up to the time of his death in 1855. It was probably Cole—also a composer, arranger, and compiler of a number of books on singing—who edited *The Minstrel*, a large secular collection of music that had been printed from type by Dobbin and Murphy and published in 1812 by F. Lucas, Jr., for Cole's name appears as holder of its copyright. In the early 1820s Arthur Clifton issued a number of his own compositions in Baltimore, including most of the vocal score of his opera *The Enterprise*. However, he had Thomas Carr or George E. Blake of Philadelphia engrave his plates. Clifton had been born Philip Anthony Corri, the eldest son of Domenico Corri, the composer and London music publisher. Due to some sort of scandal at home, he emigrated to Baltimore and changed his name. Henri-Noël Gilles, a French oboist of some distinction, also had one of his compositions published in Baltimore at this time.

CHARLESTON

Charleston, South Carolina, ranks last among our main early music-publishing centers with respect both to time sequence and the quantity of music produced. Charles Gilfert, a composer and theater manager and probable relative of the early New York publisher, issued music here between 1813 and 1817, his major contribution being a large collection entitled *Chas. Gilfert & Cos. Monthly Publication of Rondos, Airs with Variations, Waltzes and Songs for the Piano Forte*, which appeared in six numbers about 1817. P. Muck was another publisher at work in Charleston during this period, the few titles he issued dating to the years between 1813 and 1819. In 1819 John Siegling opened up an establishment that was to become the major publishing house in that city and, in fact, is the oldest music house in America controlled by descendants of the original owner: the Siegling music store is still located in Charleston, having been at the same address since 1831. Siegling seems to have issued music in very small quantities during his initial years as a publisher, reissuing much of it later with an altered imprint. Consequently, sheets bearing his first address, 69 Broad Street, are scarce, allowing no definite conclusions to be formed about Siegling's early activity and about their dates of issue. Later on, perhaps in the early 1840s, Siegling opened up a branch store in Havana, Cuba, and issued a number of titles which carried both Charleston and Havana on their imprints. A fourth publisher who may have been in business here during the 1820s was H. Dunning, whose few known publications have so far defied positive dating. However, the plate-numbering system he used indicates that he may have engraved for Siegling concurrently and that his own publications were issued about 1828 or slightly later. The designation "Thornhill, Sc." appears on a number of music sheets issued in Charleston during the second and third decades of the nineteenth century. Thornhill's contribution to these was restricted to the engraving of illustrations, lettering, and fancy titles or title pages. He did not engrave music. Admittedly, a great many more Charleston imprints will have to be found before we can reach definitive conclusions concerning early music publishing in this city.

OTHER LOCALITIES

In additon to the music published before 1825 in the major centers, a small amount of music was issued elsewhere, usually either by a local musician and music teacher who had it engraved in one of the large centers (by Riley or Birch in New York or by Blake or Willig in Philadelphia) or by a musician carrying on engraving as a sideline who happened to settle in or pass through a small community. Less frequently, plates were prepared by a general engraver who was not a music engraver by profession or by an allied artisan, such as a jeweler. John Goldberg and

Florent Meline belong to the first category. Goldberg, a music teacher of Albany, published nearly two dozen titles between 1813 and 1819, all of which he had engraved by Edward Riley of New York. And Meline, also of Albany, published several of his own compositions there between 1822 and 1824 which were engraved by Thomas Birch of New York. Representative of the second group is Francesco Masi, previously cited as a music publisher in Boston, who migrated to the Washington area by 1822, where he published a handful of music titles for a few years. Some of his imprints bear the location "Washington City"; two pieces have the location "Alexandria, D. C." (Alexandria was part of the District of Columbia from 1789 to 1847.) Although primarily a musician and music teacher by trade, he engraved and published music on the side wherever he happened to settle. It is interesting to note that he eventually became a jeweler, an occupation which also required an ability to engrave on metal. (A receipt for goods purchased at his "Military, Jewelry, and Fancy Goods Store" in 1831 appears as Illustration 8b herein.) Frederick Bosler, engraver of a map of Virginia which was published in Richmond on March 4, 1807, illustrates the third class. About that time Bosler published in Norfolk a piece entitled *Fragments from Mrs. Ann Radcliffe's Ode to Melancholy*, which was composed by James Tomlins, a local musician. In this the music was punched and the title and text freely engraved, probably by Bosler himself. Also in this category was A. Lynn of Alexandria, Virginia, who in 1799 was inspired to engrave a *Funeral Dirge. Adopted for & play'd by the Alexandria Band at the funeral of Genl. Geo. Washington.* The composer of this piece was one I. Decker, undoubtedly a local musician connected with the band. In his revision of the Sonneck *Bibliography* Upton has appended the following note to his entry for this composition: "A. Lynn was probably Adam Lynn, who at that time had a jeweler's shop in Alexandria, Virginia. The combination of jeweler and engraver was far from uncommon in those days."

G. Balls, mentioned in the resumé of Philadelphia publishing, and T. Balls, active in Norfolk, Virginia, during the second decade of the nineteenth century, were members of the English family of music publishers whose firm was located at 408 Oxford Street, London, during most of the period under consideration. The plates for the music they issued may have been engraved in England for them. In addition, a number of publications of the parent firm specify that they could also be had of T. Balls in Norfolk and G. Balls in Philadelphia. Oliver Shaw, a blind singer who from 1807 was a composer and organist of Providence, Rhode Island, established a "Musical Repository" in that city about 1817, whence he issued a large number of his own compositions. One of these carried the notation that it was engraved by George Bacon of Philadelphia. Another, *Kill Deer*, issued about 1825, was engraved by James L. Hewitt & Company in Boston. The similarity of style between this and other Shaw publications indicates that Hewitt probably engraved most of the Shaw publications. Henry Stone, an Englishman who introduced lithography to Washington in 1822 (and remained active there until 1846), published a small quantity of music in the capital between 1823 and 1826, the first music to be lithographed in the United States. His most notable effort was an unidentified collection which ran to 104 pages.[21] And in 1827 L. C. Saxton of Cooperstown, New York, published a collection of ten pieces (five instrumental and five vocal) which was engraved by an unidentified "E. C. Tracy."

Other efforts at publishing music in out-of-the-way places were as follows. Joseph Willson, later a New York publisher, brought out his piano sonata and song *O, Yes, Sir, If You Please* in New Brunswick, New Jersey, about 1801, probably shortly after debarking from England. About 1805 "I. Goodman" (possibly John Goodman, whose arrangements were published by G. E. Blake in Philadelphia about 1817) issued an edition of James Sanderson's *Sandy and Jenny* in "Frankfort," which I interpret to mean Frankford, Pennsylvania (now part of Philadelphia), not the Kentucky city. An "A Willoughby" published an edition of *Kate Kearney* at Hartford, Connecticut, late in the second decade of the nineteenth century, which was reissued by the New York firm of Firth & Hall about 1827. In view of this reissue, it seems likely that Willoughby had his plates made in New York. William R. Coppock, a music teacher who lived in Brooklyn during most of the 1820s before migrating to Buffalo, where he died in 1863, had several of his own compositions issued for him by New York publishers in the period around 1825. However, he is known to have issued one work on his own, his *Favorite Waltzes*, from his own music studio at 49 Main Street, Brooklyn, about that time. J. Womrath, a local musician, had his *Thomas Jefferson's March* issued at Norfolk, Virginia, in 1801. And finally, *Three Favorite Mazourkas, as Danced at the Washington Societies* was published in the capital city by the arrangers F. A. and C. K. Wagler sometime during the second decade of the nineteenth century.

21. See Edith A. Wright and Josephine McDevitt, "Henry Stone, Lithographer," *Antiques* XXXIV (1938) 16–19.

CHAPTER V

The Early American Music-Publishing Firm

THE TYPICAL music-engraving, music-publishing, and music-selling establishment in late eighteenth- and early nineteenth-century America was probably little different in outward appearance from other small manufacturing and retail shops—particularly printing, bookselling, and bookbinding concerns—of the day. If would, first of all, be located within the publishing and bookselling district of its city. Here its proprietor could easily obtain paper, ink, and other supplies necessary to his trade. Hither the literate citizenry would be expected to come in order to procure books, stationery, and similar materials for their education and amusement. In Philadelphia, the shops of music publishers and sellers were to be found on Second, Third, Fourth, or Fifth streets in the neighborhood where Chestnut intersected them. The music trade in Boston centered on Newbury and Marlborough streets and on Cornhill (making up the present Washington Street). Market (also called Baltimore) and Gay streets contained the Baltimore trade. The potential purchaser of music in New York would proceed to that part of the city which today is termed the financial district, the area between lower Broadway on the west and Pearl Street on the east, extending north from Trinity Church to the vicinity of St. Paul's (at the beginning of Chatham Street), and including the crossways of Wall, Ann, and William streets and Maiden Lane.

We actually know little about the exact makeup of the early American music-publishing and music-selling establishment. However, we can achieve a fair reconstruction of one from evidence obtained through illustrations of music shops added to music sheets of later periods, from contemporary advertisements of proprietors of such concerns, from analogies drawn from the customs and practices of similar trades, and from commonsense inferences based upon the nature of the business. The establishment itself might have been contained within a private house, in a commercial building, or, as in the case of John and Michael Paff of this early period and of William Hall at a later date, within a hotel (see Illus. 9 and 10). Sometimes, as shown by the previously quoted obituary of George E. Blake, one building served as both the place of business and the residence of a publisher. The establishment normally occupied quarters on the ground floor of its structure so that there was direct access to it from the street. Above its main entrance might hang a sign—perhaps in the shape of some musical instrument—declaring the identity of the proprietor and the nature and quality of his business. On either side of its front entrance would be display windows in which were exhibited samples of merchandise on sale within: sheet music, both domestic and imported, musical instruments, and sundry musical merchandise.[1] Close by could be found bookstores, the shops of stationers and binders, warehouses supplying the printing trades with paper, ink, and other essentials, and perhaps one or more newspapers of the town.

The establishment of the typical early publisher and seller of music probably contained two or more rooms, depending upon the ambition and success of its proprietor, on whether or not he executed his own printing and therefore required space for a copperplate press and its appurtenances, and on other activities in which he engaged, as, for example, in the teaching of music or in making and repairing musical instruments. We know that George E. Blake, Gottlieb Graupner, James Hewitt, Edward Riley, George Willig, and other early music publishers gave music

1. The earliest picture of the exterior of an American music-publisher's establishment appeared as a caption illustration on John Cole's edition of a popular ballad, *Buy a Broom*, of 1826. This illustration, reproduced on p. 77 of Joseph Muller's *The Star Spangled Banner*, shows display windows with a few musical titles inside, but nothing else. From then until the 1870s a number of publications carried representations of the exteriors of music stores, intended as advertising. In only a few cases were interiors shown. A checklist of the more interesting of these scenes can be found in Dichter and Shapiro's *Early American Sheet Music*, pp. 89–91. The earliest picture of the interior of a music store that has come to my notice appeared in *Dwight's Journal of Music* XI no. 21 (August 22, 1857) 166–67, where a sketch of "Ditson & Co.'s New Music Store" is given. The Ditson establishment was a five-story building at No. 277 Washington Street, Boston. According to the description accompanying the picture, twelve presses were at work here printing sheet music alone, and the basement held a large safe containing from 50,000 to 60,000 music plates. The interior of another large music-selling establishment, dating to the year 1866, is shown in Illustration 10b herein.

lessons, and Riley, among others, advertised himself as a musical-instrument maker (the Dayton Miller collection of musical instruments in the Library of Congress contains several woodwinds of his manufacture). The front room of the establishment, which opened onto the street, was devoted to the retail aspects of the business. Engraving, printing, and other activities were confined to the rear of the store or to other areas of the establishment. (Blake, his obituary tells us, had a small office immediately to the rear of his store, in which he must have engraved and printed his publications.) In a few instances, publishers neither engraved nor printed the issues bearing their imprints, contracting for this work elsewhere. In such cases, there was no need for a workroom, unless the engraver worked on the publisher's premises, though it would seem more likely that this type of job might have been accomplished at home.

Upon entering the music store from the street, the customer would walk on the bare plank floors typical of stores at that time, and make purchases over a wooden counter having shelves for merchandise behind it. On these shelves music sheets would be stacked in neat piles, next to bound volumes of music, wind instruments such as flutes, oboes, clarinets, and flageolets, and brass and percussion pieces of varying sorts. From beams in the ceiling or from pegs projecting from the walls might be hung violins, guitars, and other string instruments. An upright piano or several might stand to the side, and somewhere about could be displayed lyres, hurdy-gurdies, bagpipes, and other musical merchandise then in demand.[2] Hung from a string stretched at ceiling level across the entire length of the counter would be the latest musical publications of the proprietor and perhaps recently imported "hits" of the London stage. In addition, the interior of the store would reflect other activities in which its

2. We can absorb much of the flavor of the early American music store from sources other than illustrations on later music sheets, for example, from advertisements which publishers appended to their imprints or placed in local newspapers. A typical example of the first type is a note which George E. Blake affixed to the imprint of *Blake's Preceptor for the Spanish Guitar and Lyre* (ca. 1825), reading, "A great variety of Spanish and English guitars, Harp Lutes, Harp Guitars, &c. &c. for sale as above." The second group is illustrated by the advertisement which Mrs. Sarah Howe, widow of the recently deceased instrument maker William, published in the *New York Gazette and General Advertiser* of January 19, 1799. This stated that she "still carries on the business at No. 320 Pearl-street, and has for sale, Barrel Organs, Piano Fortes, fine tone pedal Harp trumpets, &c. with a general assortment of all kinds of Musical Instruments, Fiddle strings, Wholesale or Retail, with a great variety of New Music, lately imported from London." Antther was the notice of new music published, which James Hewitt inserted in the New York *Daily Advertiser* of August 6, 1801. This concluded, "also . . . piano fortes, grand and small, with or without additional keys, warranted to stand the climate, violins, clarinets, oboes, bassons, horns, violincellos, flutes, of every description, tenors, tamborins, field drums, strings for the harp, violin, violincells, double bass piano forte, &c. and every article in the musical line on the lowest terms. Two capital organs, suitable for church or chapple, to be sold cheap."

owner engaged in order to eke out his living, such as general bookbinding (in the early days of music publishing at least), the handling of drygoods, toys, umbrellas, and even hardware.

Successful and sophisticated businesses, such as George E. Blake's and George Willig's in Philadelphia, which traded exclusively in musical merchandise on a large scale, might show neatly carpeted floors, finished and polished cabinetwork, and a more eye-catching and appealing overall arrangement. Nonetheless, even these shops were small, for the Blake obituary stated that the store he occupied on South Fifth Street from 1814 until the time of his death measured about 20 by 30 feet, hardly the dimensions of a large living room today. In Blake's store in Philadelphia, James Hewitt's in New York, and others, there might be racks or trays containing music to be rented out to those unwilling or unable to buy, for we know from advertisements that both men also conducted circulating music libraries as well. Some publishers—Gottlieb Graupner in Boston was one—at times connected their establishments with music schools at which they and others taught. The early American music publisher was at times performing musician, music teacher, engraver, printer, seller, instrument maker and repairer, piano tuner and merchant combined, and the exterior and interior of his establishment reflected every aspect of his varied activity.

The back room and other areas of the shop were undoubtedly reserved for technical aspects of the business, such as the engraving and printing of music, and the making and repairing of instruments. These areas might be lined with shelves for storing paper, ink, engraved plates, and other materials essential in the publishing of music, as well as any overflow of printed music which could not be accommodated within the store proper. If the proprietor executed his own engraving or employed one or more engravers to work for him on the premises (George E. Blake, for example, probably did both), there would be one or more work tables or benches usually to the side and near a window, containing engraving and punching tools which usually stood upright in wooden racks (see Illus. 11a). There might also be some sort of stand or support to hold in an upright position the manuscript or piece being copied. The presence of one or more copperplate presses would depend upon whether or not the publisher did his own printing or let this bothersome chore out to professional copperplate printers.

Probably because of the difficulties entailed in printing from the intaglio method, which shall be outlined shortly, some and perhaps many engravers and publishers preferred to abstain from this phase of publishing. Instead, they sent out their plates to professional printers who specialized in this method. Edward Riley, for example, who has been described as a major music publisher in New York during the second and third decades of the nineteenth century, must have restricted his role in the publishing process to the engraving of plates alone, leaving the actual printing from them to one Thomas G. Adams, a partner and professional copperplate printer. Why else would Adams be located in New York City directories between 1812 and 1820 at Riley's address, and the firm of "Riley and Adams, copperplate printers" be designated in the same list? Freedom from the printing task left Riley time to engrave many plates, to make instruments, and to teach. If we skip ahead to the "Account Book of Simeon Wood," reprinted in Appendix A herein, we can see that Wood also refrained from printing, employing the Boston copperplate printers Luther Stevens, Abel Bowen, and the copperplate printer and musicain (and sometime music publisher) Samuel Wetherbee to do this for him. Finally, the statement of David Edwin, an English engraver active in Philadelphia during much of the period under discussion, quoted on p. 104 herein from Dunlap's *History of . . . Design in the United States*, shows that the practice of sending out plates for printing was common among general engravers as well.

If, however, printing was done on the premises, the work area would also have a table or bench upon which plates could be inked and prepared. There would also be stools and waste receptacles and, somewhere about, a stove. In shops where printing was carried on, the ceiling of this work area would be crisscrossed with strings across which newly printed sheets were draped until they had dried, for it was a normal procedure in copperplate printing to wet paper before printing it (as seen in Illus. 11b). Additional rooms or perhaps the cellar of the structure might be employed for storing finished plates, though in this early period the plates probably were put somewhere within the work shop itself.[3] Some individuals restricted their

3. While underground areas might have been used as repositories for storing engraved plates from the very beginning of American music publishing, it was probably not until a later period—perhaps the 1820s, 1830s, 1840s, or later, when stocks began to mount up, that American publishers, like their English counterparts, maintained specialized "plate cellars." About one such plate cellar, *A Day at a Music Publishers*, an important but little-known brochure which was issued by the London firm of D'Almaine and Company about 1838 to explain to visitors the general aspects of music publishing, states: "These depositories of plates consist of intricate labyrinths underground, of immense extent, curiously constructed, with arched roofs. Some idea of the great space which they occupy may be formed, when it is known that plates, weighing several hundred tons, here are compiled as completely as possible. Each set of plates is corded round, and numerically labelled, and a correct catalogue is kept of the whole stock, which enables any party wanting a particular piece of music, to select from the mass at once. These cellars are rendered fire-proof, and the doors are made of

activities solely to publishing music (Simeon Wood was in this category) and others solely to selling it and other musical wares. An illustration which appeared in the first (1931) edition of John Tasker Howard's *Our American Music* (reproduced here as Illus. 9), gives a variation on this theme, showing the music-publishing and music-selling establishment of James L. Hewitt & Co., 137 Broadway (about 1831), with the pianoforte warehouse of R. & W. Nunn immediately above it.

Equipment employed in engraving and printing music was usually kept in the rear and other areas of the early American music-publishing establishment. It included the following materials, instruments, and utensils: flat plates of pewter or of type metal (which was of almost the same consistency as pewter) onto which were stamped and cut the musical symbols and accompanying text; engraving and punching tools, and racks for holding them; a punching stone, to support the plate during the stamping operation and to cushion it against the blows of the punches as these were tapped with the hammer;[4] a small anvil, used in the planishing process after the plate had been punched; ink, or the ingredients for making ink, and a pot and other utensils for boiling, preparing, and holding ink; an inkstone and muller for mixing ink during the printing process; a printing ball or "rubber" for spreading ink onto the engraved plate; a chalky powder called "whiting" which was rubbed over the surface of the plate so that any ink in its pores would not print black, and a receptacle for containing it; a supply of paper; a trough or tray into which sheets of paper were dipped in order to prepare them for the press; a copperplate or rolling press; blankets of broadcloth and blotters for enclosing the plate and paper after they had been placed on the sliding plank or table of the press; a screw press or bookbinder's press for pressing the paper after it had been imprinted, and wooden boards for enclosing it during the pressing operation; additional printing balls or rubbers for cleaning plates after impressions had been worked from them and for coating them with oil eventually for storage; a stock of lye for cleaning

iron; in winter they are properly heated and throughout the milder months of the year healthfully ventilated." (*A Day at a Music Publishers* will be invoked as a source of information many times later on; the only copy of this pamphlet that I have seen is in the Drexel Collection of the Music Division of the New York Public Library, though Hyatt King has told me that another can be found in the British Museum.) Note 1 above makes reference to a similar repository in the Ditson establishment (in Boston) in 1857.

4. The general engraver used a sandbag for cushioning his plate. This was usually a leather bag containing sand, and it was made to turn easily for the making of circular or curved lines. This oblong stone, something like a lithographic stone, was standard equipment for the music engraver of this period. Such an item of equipment is mentioned on the inventory of the estate of Peter Albrecht von Hagen: "1 Punching Stone 2 Dollrs."

plates upon conclusion of printing; and, finally, perhaps a palette knife, used for mixing ink and ultimately for removing it from the printing ball or rubber. A large quantity of rags were also kept handy for cleaning and handling plates during the various phases of the inking and printing operations. Frequently, a linen cloth hung from the printer's belt so that he could wipe his fingers clean before taking hold of the sheet of paper to be printed and when removing it from the bed of the press after the printing had been completed.

THE ENGRAVING PROCESS

The procedure of transferring musical notation from a manuscript or from a copy of an earlier edition onto fresh plates in order to issue or reissue a given piece involved the following steps. The publisher or his engraver would first read through the manuscript or printed piece to be copied and mark off the bars for each page, thereby determining the total number of pages required to accommodate the work. This operation is sometimes termed "casting off." By marking the bars on the manuscript, and in turn the lines, the engraver determined the number of plates necessary to accommodate it. (On the first plate the engraver would allow for two or three fewer lines, as it was necessary to reserve space for the title, performance identifications, and imprint.) If the piece extended over more than two pages, the person casting off had to determine also the most suitable places for turning over at the foot of odd-numbered pages so that the music would break in a convenient way. Once the casting off had been accomplished, the engraver took hold of a plate and, laying it flat on the punching stone, proceeded to "space it out." If plates showed any scratches or irregularities when received from the pewterer, these imperfections first had to be removed by burnishing and, in extreme cases, by scraping. Burnishing was done with the steel burnisher, a knife-shaped tool with a smooth, rounded surface for polishing. Scraping was effected with a thin, elastic strip of metal known as the scraper or busk, which was drawn over the plate at an angle so as not to cut deeply into it. Today, a plate is routinely scraped before the engraver commences to space it out, this task being frequently allotted to the lowest apprentice in the shop.

In spacing out, the engraver determined the outer limits of the piece to be copied, the points where the staves commenced and concluded, and the distance between the staves. He did this by noting and measuring off the predominant characteristics of the manuscript or edit-copy and then

[74]

locating their approximate positions on the plate by means of a marking device (usually calipers). Next, with a straightedge and a crook graver (in modern terminology, a T-square and a hook), he proceeded to rule off the plate, cutting lines for staves. The music engraver of today employs a "scorer," a device with a rakelike head of five equidistant teeth, and which can cut the five lines of the staff in a single motion. We know that this instrument, also referred to as a "staver," was in use in the eighteenth century, as a picture of one appeared in the famous Diderot *Encyclopèdie.*[5] However, this instrument appears not to have been universally used in early America, for we sometimes encounter sheets having irregularly spaced lines on the staff and lines which extend farther into the margins than other lines. The engraver, probably lacking a staver, must have cut each line onto the plate individually, most likely with the burin or graver and a ruler. It is a normal custom of music engraving to scrape the plate, once the plate has been ruled off, in order to remove the burr or excess metal thrown up around the lines by the cutting process.

In modern music engraving, the next step, after the necessary spacing out and ruling has been done, is to "mark out" the plate. We do not know for sure how—or indeed if—this was done by our early music engravers. However, the presence of a "Copper Ruling Pen" and "6 Markers" on the Blake inventory in Appendix B and the fact that marking out is, as Gamble states with regard to twentieth-century music engraving,[6] "not only a conventional thing, but a necessity in order that any workman can punch a plate drawn by another man," allows us to presume that marking out was probably a common practice in earlier music engraving as well. Marking out means to indicate on the ruled plate the position and character of the notes to be punched. This operation is considered to be the most difficult aspect of the entire engraving process, and it requires a knowledge of music, if errors are to be avoided, in order to position clefs, notes, signs, etc., in their proper spaces, form, and sequence.

Gamble describes the modern technique of marking out as follows. The engraver first draws light marks on the plate by means of a marking pin to indicate the signs, notes, and other data to be punched, as the manuscript

---

5. *Planches* V (1767). A similar instrument was in use in early nineteenth-century America for lining music paper. The Philadelphia Museum of Art owns a five-pronged music pen, cut neatly out of hardwood in a very expert manner (Zieget Collection, Accession 63–160). This is dated (i.e., attributed) 1836 and was used by a former Shaker owner to line out a sheet of paper for writing music in much the same manner as an engraver would use a "staver" for lining out a plate. The Shaker pen was dipped into a inkwell and drawn across the paper to form a staff.

6. *Music Engraving and Printing*, p. 125.

or edit-copy indicates. In order to do this, he employs a shorthand system which guides him in punching the proper notes in the proper locations. Different engravers used different systems, but the system Gamble outlines (p. 124) is the one that came to be used by most English engravers. Notes which are to lie on the staff lines, regardless of note value, are marked on the plate as circles; notes to be located within the spaces are indicated by a sign similar to the letter N. A cross through a circle shows a whole note, a single line through a circle shows a half note, and circles left without any mark show quarter notes. Smaller note values (eighth notes, etc.) have their hooks and ties shown. Each note can be recognized easily, thus avoiding errors in punching. It is necessary to indicate on the plate everything that is on the manuscript or edit-copy, including ties, signs, and the like, so that nothing is left out in the punching and cutting operation. With this system any engraver can complete any plate merely by following the indications drawn on it.

The indication of the spacing is first accomplished by a method called "pointing." For this, a compass—three are included in the Blake inventory—is used to measure the distance of the space required for each bar and to make a dot indicating this. The engraver first makes a guide line for the clefs all the way down the plate, using a straightedge and a marking pin, and afterward punches in the necessary key-signatures. Then he proceeds with the pointing. He sets the legs of the compass far enough apart to accommodate a given bar and then twirls the compass from one point to another, indicating the length of each bar. He continues doing this, lifting the compass from the plate only when allowing more or less space, according to the nature of time values within, until he reaches the end of the line. Each time he presses the points on the plate he makes a dot which indicates the spacing. The dotting is actually done in a space or upon one of the staff lines. Finally, guide lines are drawn through each dot, and the marking of the notes, rests, and other material follows. In vocal works it is necessary to mark out carefully the positions of the lyrics, as these are governed by rhythmical considerations. As we shall presently see, a compass was needed for correcting as well as for pointing.

After the necessary ruling and marking had been done the engraver selected a punch with its face shaped like a quarter note (●), of the design and shape required (or at hand), and holding it vertically between the fingers of his left hand, with its head positioned on the appropriate area of the staff, he tapped its base smartly with a striking mallet or hammer, thereby pressing its image into the face of the plate. If the plate had been marked out, as indeed it probably was, he would continue

[76]

putting in all of the quarter notes in a given line or throughout the plate. Gamble is our authority (p. 138), with regard to modern music engraving, for the statement that "the depth of the impression should not be more than 1/64 in., and the force of the blow must be such as to secure this depth uniformly for all characters." However, modern plates are thinner than those used in earlier times, so we cannot be sure on this point. It is obvious, however, from the thick impressions on some extant sheets, that early American music engravers were frequently careless or inexperienced in this operation, and that they probably struck the punches unevenly.

When a line of music or a number of bars had been completed, the engraver then placed tails or stems onto the quarter notes by means of another punch, and in a like manner formed eighth notes, sixteenth notes, or thirty-second notes, as the master copy would require. Half notes, whole notes, sharps, flats, naturals, dots, as well as clefs, braces, grace notes, and other marks of expression were similarly stamped onto the plate with different punches. Musical signs not readily stamped were cut into the plate with the graver. Among these were lengthened crescendos and diminuendos and the deep, dark lines by which notes are tied together. Lyrics and directions given by the composer to the performer were stamped also, as were, for the most part, titles, performance identifications, pagination, price, and imprint. The whole process was executed in reverse, from right to left, as transferring the impression onto paper reversed the image once again. The sheets of many of our early engravers display inexperience and crudeness, for it is not unusual to encounter sheets having their notes reversed, i.e., put onto the plate in a readable fashion in the first place, and text containing a capital letter within a word that is otherwise in lower case. After the plate had been punched, its surface was somewhat distorted, for there were bulges and ridges (burrs) around the outlines of notes caused by metal being forced up by the punch. The engraver smoothed these down by scraping or burnishing or by planishing, that is, tapping the face of the plate with a special leveling hammer. During this operation the plate rests face up on an anvil (again, such an item of equipment is noted on the Blake inventory).

The engraving operation, that is, the necessary freehand cutting, was done the same way as on a copperplate. The main tool used was the graver or burin. Bar lines, stems of notes, ledger lines, ties, swells, and slurs are usually the only parts that are cut, unless there are some unusual signs required for which no punches are available. Bar lines are customarily cut first, then the stems, ledger lines, ties, and finally swells and slurs.

[77]

Gravers having blades of different sizes and thicknesses are needed for cutting a number of these symbols.

Illustration 12 shows the condition of a music plate at the proof stage in contrast to its later finished form. The proof sheet reproduced here is one of a handful of pieces from a collection of music entitled *The Music of Erin*, which was compiled and published by James Hewitt in New York in 1807. These rarities, the only proof sheets that have survived from the early days of American music publishing, were bound into a volume of early published music that was purchased by the New York Public Library in 1958. (They have since been unbound.) The example shown here indicates, at first glance, that its publisher may have contemplated issuing it as a separate publication. However, it seems more likely that this proof merely represents the state of the plate at a time before its final form—as part of a music collection—had been determined. We can see that the proofreader, very likely James Hewitt himself, first added missing directional material and altered in ink incorrectly engraved notes, indicating errors or omissions within staves by prefacing each line containing discrepancies with an X. Those errors on the proof sheet which we find corrected or altered on the finished sheet must have been excised from the plate and emended in the following manner: the engraver located and indicated the errors on the back of the plate by measuring them off from the face of the plate with a compass or with calipers. He then turned the plate over, so that its engraved surface rested against the punching stone, and taking up a mallet and a medium-sized dot punch, he hammered and punched out the area of the incorrect impression until it again became even with the surface of the plate. He then turned the plate on its back and burnished the punched area so that the dots rubbed together and the old working became completely obliterated. If another sign had to be added in place of the one removed, it could then be punched in. Old imprints were undoubtedly removed in like manner when a subsequent publisher acquired the plates of an earlier firm and reissued editions from them. (The imprints of many of the publications reprinted by William Dubois in New York in 1817 and 1818 from the earlier plates of John and Michael Paff show dark splotches where the earlier names and addresses had been removed in a haphazard fashion in order to accommodate the identification of the new publisher.) The proof sheet illustrated here also indicates that like their modern counterparts, earlier engravers added titles, performance identifications, and probably also imprints at the last, as the concluding operation of the engraving process and subsequent to proofing.

Illustration 11a, taken from *A Day at a Music Publishers*, shows an English music engraver from about 1838. It is the only representation that I have encountered which depicts an early engraver at work. Though English, the workman here would undoubtedly be representative of a music engraver of any nationality at that time. Indeed, when I visited an American music-engraving shop in 1962, I was struck by the similarity between its interior and several scenes in that publication. Little had changed during the intervening decades with regard to the tools and methods employed in this age-old process. The workmen were positioned at benches before windows, as in Illustration 11a. And in spite of their modern attire, they had much of the appearance of the English engraver of 1838. Only an iron proofing press and a few modern appurtenances detracted from the similarity of the scenes. The English engraver in Illustration 11a is completing the process of lining out a plate. To his right are plates which have previously been scored, and before and around him are racks of punches, a burnisher, gravers, and other tools necessary for this work.

Before going on to the printing process, it would be appropriate to make a few additional observations which have reference to the engraving operation. The imprints which earlier publishers printed on their sheets, consisting of such phrases as "Engraved, printed and published [or "sold"] by," "Engraved for and printed by," "Printed and sold by," usually indicated the roles which their publishers played in producing them. For example, John and Michael Paff used the imprint "Engraved, printed and published by" when one or both of them were involved in all the publishing operations. However, they employed the phrase "Published [or "printed"] and sold by" when they employed William Pirsson and later Edward Riley for engraving their plates. On the other hand, James Hewitt and Gottlieb Graupner, who probably engraved their own plates—Graupner availed himself of the services of the engraver Samuel Wetherbee mostly in the period after 1818, when his output was declining—usually set the phrase "Printed and sold by" on their imprints. Edward Riley, who, it has been noted, had Thomas G. Adams print his plates for him, rarely used the phrase "printed by" on his imprints. George E. Blake of Philadelphia, whose auction inventory in Appendix B testifies to his involvement in all of the processes of music engraving, almost always used the phrase "published by" on his imprints, as did his rival George Willig, who also must have done most of his own engraving and printing.

It should also be noted that some phases of the engraving process were

[79]

contracted to others. The previously cited diary of Alexander Anderson, whom Dunlap denominates as the one "who introduced the art [of wood engraving] into our country and almost invented it," contains the following entries for the year 1795:[7]

[March]

23^d Went to Gilfert's Musical Magazine and engag'd to engrave letters for the title of a piece of music for 12/,–[;] left some type-metal at G. Youle's for a plate.

24th Began Gilfert's plate.

25th Finish'd Gilfert's plate & deliver'd to him after getting a proof at Burger's.—receiv'd 12/,–.

26th Called at Scoles's—he found much fault with my engraving Gilfert's plate too cheap.

George Youle was a plumber and pewterer who made music plates for a number of our early publishers. John Burger was a copperplate printer who was in business in New York City from about 1791 until the 1820s. John Scoles earned his living as an engraver and bookseller there from 1794 until late in the 1840s. The fact that he was critical of Anderson for underpricing his work implies that he too may have engraved titles for music publishers. The division of labor in this instance may have occurred more frequently than has been realized. We shall soon see that David Edwin, an English engraver who had emigrated to Philadelphia in 1797, performed a similar job for John Aitken in that year. And many artists and engravers, some of them outstanding and notable, picked up additional income by making cuts and illustrations for the decoration of music sheets.

Another aspect of the early trade, pointed out by the above-quoted references in the Anderson diary, is that separate plates were sometimes employed to print non-musical data on music sheets, and, of course, to print separate title pages. And sometimes subsequent imprints were added this way also. We know that Carr & Schetky added their imprint both to separate publications and to reprints of individual pieces from their collections—for example, from *Carr's Musical Journal for the Piano Forte*, from their *Applicazione Addolcita* and *Elegant Extracts from the Most Esteem'd English Operas*, and other works—from a separate plate, frequently changing this in order to add the names of additional agents who handled their publications outside of Philadelphia. Another interesting entry in the Anderson diary for 1795 occurred on April 25, when he recorded: "Be-

7. These entries are misdated in Spillane's *History of the American Pianoforte* as 1792. They can be found on p. 125 of Anderson's diary.

fore dark, I finish'd the border for Mr. Carr—He came for it and paid me 10/-." The "Mr. Carr" here was, of course, Benjamin Carr, who in 1795 operated a music-publishing outlet in New York at No. 131 William Street, from which he issued occasional publications.

THE PRINTING PROCESS

After all plates for a particular work had been engraved, they were inked and readied for the press. The first plate to be imprinted was laid onto the grate of a charcoal brazier with its back directly over the burning coals in the fire pan.[8] When the plate had become slightly heated, the printer took hold of one of its corners with his left hand and, holding it flat and steady over the grate, he picked up a printing ball or "rubber" (usually a wad of woolen rags) and began to ink it with his right and. The ink used in music printing, as well as in general copperplate printing, was not so viscous as that employed in typographical work, but had more of a pasty consistency. After dipping the printing ball into the ink vessel, the printer glided and sponged and beat it against the face of the plate in every direction, forcing ink into the minutest hollows of engraving on every part of the plate. When the ink had entered into all lines and recesses on the surface of the plate, the printer replaced the ink ball on the edge of the ink vessel and, still resting the plate on top of the grate, took up a cloth and proceeded to clean the plate. He wiped all excess ink from its surface, back, and sides. He then removed it to a part of his workbench sometimes called a "jigger" and began the cleaning process again, this time rubbing the plate in all directions with his bare hand, which he kept clear of ink by wiping it, from time to time, with a clean cloth. When no ink remained on the surface of the plate except that lodged in strokes or hatches and punched indentations of the engraving, he wiped the edges and borders clean. The printer concluded his inking operation by applying to the surface of the plate a coat of "whiting" or "Spanish white" (calcium carbonate, more commonly known as chalk, prepared by washing), which he laid on by passing his hand powdered with it over the surface of the

8. This phase of the operation rendered the business injurious to the health of the workmen, for the vapor arising from the charcoal was noxious. In the third decade of the nineteenth century steam was introduced as a substitute for the charcoal fire. For background information see T. C. Hansard's *Typographia* (London, 1825), p. 802. According to M. Bertilaud's *Nouveau Manuel Complet de l'Imprimeur en Taille Douce* (Paris, Roret, 1837), a manual of engraving techniques which also included a few pages on music engraving and printing, music plates were always printed cold; while the printer inked his plates on the grill of the brazier as before, he first removed its fire-pan. Bertilaud also states that plates were cleaned and degreased with a rag that contained a solution of potash (potassium carbonate).

plate. He did this so that the plate, which had absorbed a certain amount of ink that could not be wiped from its pores, would not print dark. (This last operation may have been done inconsistently or inexpertly, for many sheets produced by our early publishers, for example by the Paffs in the first years of the nineteenth century, have dark areas where ink was not removed from the surface of the plate.)

Preparing the paper was a simpler matter. This operation was usually begun a day in advance of the actual printing operation. The printer selected half a dozen sheets of paper at a time and dipped them into a trough or tray of clean water. He repeated this dipping two or three times, depending upon the strength of the paper and the quantity of gum in it. The sheets had to be kept exactly even and free of folds. After they had been sufficiently moistened, he removed them and set them individually between flat boards and then placed a weight on the uppermost board so that water was forced into all parts of the paper alike and any superfluous quantity was pressed out. (Stacks of these boards with weights upon them can be seen reposing between the cheeks of the copperplate presses in Illus. 11b.) He repeated this procedure as many times as was necessary to provide him with a sufficient stock for the proposed print run, and when the contemplated number of sheets had been prepared, they were left, usually overnight, to await the next day's printing. In order to achieve the best results, the paper had to be moist for printing.

All was now in readiness for the final press operation. The table of the press was adjusted and the rollers were checked in order to insure that they closed properly above and below. The printer then took up the prepared plate, touching only its back and sides, and selecting a piece of paper, he laid them together gently and evenly and placed them on the table of the press. He next laid a slightly moistened blotter over them and hung blankets of broadcloth onto the rollers of the press.[9] He then turned the cross of the press slowly and smoothly, sending the plate and its furniture through the rollers and over to the other side of the press. The pressure of the rollers and blankets forced the moistened paper into the indentations on the plate, causing ink (and ultimately impressions) to be imparted to it. Next, it was the custom of some printers to turn the cross in a contrary direction, returning the plate to where it originated and thereby securing an even sharper impression. This practice frequently

9. These blankets can be seen suspended from the rollers of the copperplate press shown in Illustration 27a. This is the first known illustration depicting that usage, which might have been fairly new to America at that time. An earlier and possibly commoner method in copperplate printing was simply to lay blankets onto the plate after it had been charged with paper.

depended upon whether or not the plate had been engraved and punched more or less deeply or whether, in the case of ornamented or illustrated title pages and captions, for example, the overall shade desired was to be lighter or darker. After the paper had been imprinted, it was removed from the press and carried to the fire-pan, where it was heated until it became slightly hotter than was the plate at the beginning of the printing operation. It was finally laid aside, and the printer returned the plate to the grate to be inked as before, beginning the procedure anew.

The process of printing from engraved plates (in intaglio) stands in direct contrast to the typographic method (in relief). In the former, impressions are produced by forcing paper into the indentations on the plate. In typographic printing, the typefaces project from the bodies and shoulders of the type pieces and stamp their images onto the paper directly. In printing from type, the form containing composed letterpress can be dabbed with ink rapidly before each pull of the press. If engraved plates were inked in such a manner, they would print almost entirely black. Printing from plates requires that they be removed from the press after each impression and that they be re-inked carefully and cleaned meticulously, as outlined before. Lithography, a planographic process introduced to American music publishing by Henry Stone of Washington, D.C., in 1823 (though its general application to the printing of music in America dates from about 1827), was the only other method of printing music in which ink could be applied directly to the surface of the printing medium, in this case stone.

The early printing of music directly from engraved plates was a tedious, repetitious, and expensive operation. The publication of a sonata of twenty pages, for example, required that the inking and printing procedure be repeated 1,000 times to produce a mere fifty copies of that work! Benjamin Carr's *Six Ballads from the Lady of the Lake*, issued by Carr & Schetky of Philadelphia in 1810 and containing a subscription list of 136 names, required that its printer go through 6,020 inking, cleaning, and printing operations in order to produce its forty-five pages, which included repeated title pages for each of the individual pieces within it. The same firm's *The Ladies Collection of Glees, Rounds & Chorusses for Three Voices* (ca. 1805), with a pagination of thirty-seven and a subscription list of sixty-four, indicates an inking, cleaning, and printing requirement of 2,368 operations. In view of this it is readily apparent why, during this early phase of American music publishing at least, works of considerable magnitude were not frequently undertaken or were undertaken only after their cost had been at least partly guaranteed through subscription. It is also clear why publishers such as Simeon Wood of Boston had only a few copies of a given title printed at one time, resorting to reprinting as demand required. The expense and risk involved in engraving and especially in printing large works did not accord with the feeble demand for them. For this reason the more ambitious compositions of many of our early composers—the sonatas of Alexander Reinagle and the larger works of James Hewitt, to mention but two examples—never passed beyond their original manuscript form.

When the printer had completed his entire run, he suspended from cords all prints taken off during the printing operation.[10] After all moisture had been drained from them, they were stacked together in a press—probably a bookbinder's or screw press, as two of the latter are listed on the Blake inventory—and left there for a day or two to remove creases and the superfluous impressions of the cord. They were then laid in a box to complete the drying process and to bring the ink to its proper color. Finally, the plates were cleaned and rubbed down with olive oil or with a mixture of tallow and olive oil and placed in storage until additional copies of the work were needed. If, during the printing operation, the strokes on the plates had become filled with hardened ink, these excesses were removed by boiling, usually in a lye solution, before oil was applied. All the plates of a given work were then bound together and labeled or coded to facilitate their rapid identification and recovery from the mass of stored plates. It was for retrieving and reprinting individual works that some publishers employed plate-numbering systems, which will be described in greater detail later.

After the period under consideration, more efficient processes evolved for printing music, particularly from the 1830s on, when music came into greater demand. In the mid-1820s there were attempts to introduce lithography to the printing of music. Because this process allowed rapid inking, music could be produced at considerable savings. However, this method was employed by a few publishers only, who specialized in it, and the esthetic result did not measure up to that produced by the punched plate. For this reason, lithographically produced music captured only a small percentage of the market, mainly in the period between 1827 and 1835, and by the 1840s the process of lithographing music had all but died out. In time, a more satisfactory process evolved which employed a

---

10. Illustration 11b, showing the interior of an English music-printing shop about 1838, points this out on a grand scale. Cords are stretched across the ceiling in a web-like fashion and printed music is lifted and hung over them by means of a long pole. Prints suspended in this fashion can also be observed in Illustration 27b.

combination of engraving and lithography. In this, plates were punched and engraved as before, but instead of issuing his edition from them directly, the printer used them to pull off a single copy only (exclusive of proofs), usually called a transfer copy. This was then transferred to a lithographic stone, from which the whole edition was worked. This process allowed the printer to ink the stone directly in much the same manner as a letterpress printer would ink his type, thus eliminating the tedious task of inking and cleaning the plate meticulously for each sheet printed. The engraving/lithographic process not only resulted in cheaper music, but it produced a clear, fine sheet. Publishers today still consider this the optimum process for producing really fine music.

This combined method was the dominant process employed by American music publishers from about the middle of the nineteenth century into the twentieth, though it was partly replaced by photolithography in the 1920s, a method which predominated from then until comparatively recent times. When the transfer method was employed for working the edition from a lithographic stone (eventually metal plates replaced the stone), a sheet of thin paper—Chinese handmade rice paper came to be commonly used—was applied to the engraved plate and an impression was taken from it. The paper was then coated with flour and glycerine and pressed onto a soft lithographic stone. The stone was subsequently rolled with ink, rosin, and nitric acid (the latter ingredients hold the impression fast) and the printing was then effected directly from the stone. Eventually larger stones were employed, so that by the 1920s each stone carried eight plate impressions. We do not know when this improved method was introduced into America, nor have I seen any information relating to its initial use in England or on the Continent. Its introduction into American music publishing probably occurred in the early or mid-1840s. The English pamphlet *A Day at a Music Publishers,* which describes the English trade about 1838, mentions (p. 6) a "new and very superior mode of producing printed music" which was then being employed to print Sir Henry R. Bishop's arrangement of Handel's *Songs, Duets, and Trios.* I have inspected the D'Almaine edition of this arrangement, which appeared in six volumes, the first in 1837, and I have concluded from the esthetic beauty of the printing here that it must have been produced through the combined method of engraving and lithography.[11] As regards other improvements of the English and German music-publishing trades, the transference to America of this superior

11. A complete set of this edition can be found in the Boston Public Library.

method of music printing probably happened within a few years after its introduction abroad. When lithographic stones had given up the maximum number of impressions desired from them, the images on them could be removed by rubbing them with sand and water and they could be used again and again until worn too thin for further work. As noted before, some of them might have ended up as punching stones, which were so necessary in the music-punching process.[12]

In photo-offset work, which became the major method for printing music in America from the 1920s, though it had been used for three or four decades earlier, India proofs were first made from the engraved plate (usually in groups of four, eight, or sixteen pages) and these were then mounted on a sheet of heavy paper which held four pages. The large sheet was then placed in a frame before a large camara and photographed. After the ensuing negatives had been developed and retouched, the next step was to put the negative on a sheet of zinc that had been prepared with a sensitive albumen coating. (Eventually, aluminum plates were introduced as a replacement for zinc.) When the photographic print had been made on the plate, the plate was covered with a special developing ink. This ink adhered to the portions of albumen solution which had been hardened in the making of the photographic print, and when the developing ink was washed from the surface of the zinc sheet, it took with it the albumen deposit, which did not form any part of the print. The zinc sheet, which was as thin as a piece of lightweight cardboard, was curved to fit onto the cylinder of a rotary press. In the printing process, the plate was moistened by another cylinder. This moisture stayed only on the metal, none of it adhering to the photographic print on the surface of the plate, so that when the plate next encountered the ink rollers of the press, ink adhered only to the photographic print on the plate. The moistened parts of the plate rejected ink, since water and oil do not mix. Paper was then fed into the press and music printing resulted.

The last decades have seen important innovations in music engraving and printing, including the use of typewriting machines and other instruments for putting music onto paper (for making the photographic transfer directly) and for doing away with the engraving process altogether. Computers are also coming into the field, as is the process of stamping music and accompanying text onto paper directly (again doing

---

12. Michael Twyman's "Lithographic Stone and the Printing Trade in the Nineteenth Century," *Journal of the Printing Historical Society* VIII (1972) 1–41, surveys the production of lithographic stones during the past century and stands as the published authority on this subject.

away with the engraving stage altogether). It seems likely that further developments will eventually result in the elimination of the engraving process altogether, or at least in its employment on a very minute scale. Though it may never be dispensed with altogether, its usefulness over a duration of about three centuries may be coming to an end. For a resumé of present-day processes and trends in music engraving, the reader is directed to Ted Ross's *The Art of Music Engraving and Processing*. While this work appears to be somewhat deficient in describing and predicting present and future mechanical trends in music engraving, it nonetheless presents a useful summary of processes now in use.

CHAPTER VI

Music Plates

꽃꽃

F ROM LATE IN the sixteenth century, when the idea of multiplying impressions from engraved plates was first transferred to the printing of music, until early in the eighteenth century, when the innovation of stamping impressions with steel punches supplanted the earlier method of cutting impressions freely by hand, copper was the principal metal employed in England and on the Continent for music plates. The hard composition and high price of copper did not suit it to the stamping process, and metals better adapted were needed. About 1700 the Dutch or English hit upon a method of softening copper. This method, in turn, soon gave way to the use of pewter for making music plates. Pewter proved to be the best-suited substance, for its softness and malleability rendered it pliable to the punch and graver, its cost was trifling compared with that of copper, and its durability greater. The use of pewter for music plates became universal after the middle of the eighteenth century and continued so nearly to the present time.[1]

Pewter is an alloy whose chief factor is tin. Other metals added singly or in varying combinations to make different forms of the alloy are copper, lead, antimony, and bismuth. Copper, antimony, and bismuth were used

1. Plates which I saw being engraved for music printing in the early 1960s were quite thin, as they were used for making transfer copies only, the resultant transfers being then photographed and put onto photolithographic plates from which the entire edition was worked. These plates were so thin that they bent downward naturally when suspended horizontally from the hand. According to the engravers working with them, these modern plates have a zinc alloy and are, in addition, much softer. Acid is used to clean them after inking.

to toughen, harden, and temper the tin; lead was used to cheapen it as well as to make it malleable.[2]

During the seventeenth, eighteenth, and early nineteenth centuries the tin mines of Cornwall and Wales produced the principal supply of this metal for the western world. In colonial times the British deliberately imposed handicaps on the American artisan in accordance with their policy of discouraging manufacturing in the colonies. By imposts on raw materials and taxes of varying kinds the British contrived to build up their own export of manufactured wares and keep the colonies dependent upon them. Finished pewter entered the colonies duty-free, while tin bars carried an ad valorem tariff. The American pewterer suffered additional disadvantages over his English counterpart whose stock of raw materials was close at hand. Being thousands of miles removed from his source of supply, he was forced to send to England for bars of tin, pay transportation charges, order in advance, and risk uncertain delivery. In view of their noncompetitive postion it is not surprising that only a handful of pewterers existed in the colonies before 1750.

In spite of these pitfalls, the number of pewterers in America began to increase after 1750. Utensils comprised the majority of wares manufactured from this alloy, and owing to the metal's short life under constant usage, the pewterer survived mainly by receiving old wares in exchange for new. From about 1750 into the first decades of the nineteenth century, when the importation of china and other substitutes from England all but wiped out the industry, every large town and many a village had its pewter shop. Although the pewter industry had started its decline about the time of the Revolution, immigrant musicians and journeyman

---

2. Bismuth was used by early pewterers to harden the alloy. However, because it lowered the melting point and caused brittleness, it was in time replaced by brass (the combination of copper and zinc), and finally both bismuth and zinc were replaced by antimony. Neither bismuth nor zinc appears in the chemical composition of early American pewter. In vol. 1 of his *Pewter in America: Its Makers and Their Marks* (Boston, Houghton Mifflin, 1940), Ledlie I. Laughlin gives a laboratory analysis (p. 7) of [dinner] plates made by two American pewterers, the brothers Joseph Danforth of Middletown and Edward Danforth of Hartford, Connecticut (late eighteenth–early nineteenth century), showing their composition to be:

	Tin	*Copper*	*Lead*	*Antimony*
Joseph Danforth plate	88.52	0.67	8.33	2.47
Edward Danforth plate	88.43	0.97	8.39	2.15

As regards music plates, the greater the ratio of tin to lead, the harder the plate; the harder the plate, the more impressions that could be secured from it. The frequent use of the description "type metal" (as mentioned, for instance, in the Alexander Anderson diary entry of March 23, 1795, quoted on p. 80 herein), when referring to music plates on early wills, inventories, and the like, suggests that the metallic content of early music plates was similar to that of early printing type. One source, Rollo Silver's *Typefounding in America*, actually describes type (p. 127) as made of pewter.

engravers of the 1780s probably had little difficulty in securing the necessary plates right at hand. Tin bars continued to be imported almost entirely from England following the break with the mother country, but now duty-free. The first discovery of tin-bearing ore in the United States occurred in 1829 at Goshen, Connecticut, but in negligible quantity only. Other metals requisite to the production of pewter were both mined and refined natively and imported in varying amounts and forms.

The process employed by the early pewterer in founding music plates was little different from the methods he followed when manufacturing other articles of his trade, particularly flatware. His first step would be the selection of metal, old or new, sufficient for the task at hand. This he would deposit in an iron cauldron or crucible over a fire and add to the bath such additional ingredients as he required. Next he would select a mold for the product desired and coat it with a preparation, if castings were to be finished on a lathe, or with soot, if only a minimum of finishing was required. The mold was heated, in order to allow the free flow of metal throughout its inner surfaces, and clamped. Molten metal was next ladled into the mold. When the metal hardened, the clamps were released and the casting deposited onto a piece of felt. The mold was then reheated, reclamped, and the process was repeated. Each piece came from the mold rough, and protrusions had to be melted off with a heated tool or cut away with nippers. Air bubbles and other indentations were filled with molten metal and the entire surface was then smoothed down. Finally, the piece was fastened onto a lathe and scraped, burnished, and polished. Flatware was usually planished—polished by hammering—in order to close the pores of the metal. When flatware was made in odd sizes for which no mold existed, such plates were hammered out of a flat sheet. The pewterer would cast a flat circle in a mold made for that purpose from which he would cut a blank of the size required.[3]

American music plates from the early nineteenth century and before have not withstood the attrition of time, as far as I know. Continual use of the same plates for striking off impressions resulted in the plates' gradual wearing down, and only a certain number of sheets could be worked from them before they became unsatisfactory for further imprinting. Other

3. Molds were usually made of brass, but owing to the high cost of this metal, iron and sandstone were substituted frequently. The rougher the surface of the mold, the greater was the amount of effort required to bring the castings to a finished form. We do not know whether early music plates were cast from molds made especially for that purpose or cut from patterns. Probably the latter was more true of the early trade. However, we do have the statement of David Edwin, an English engraver who emigrated to Philadelphia in 1797, that, as regards general engraving, "copperplates were finished rough from the hammer" at the time of his arrival into Philadelphia. See p. 104 herein.

plates saw too little service, for the music they contained never caught on and the demand for it never measured up to the expectations of the publisher. In both cases, such plates were eventually sold as scrap and melted down, and the metal they contained was reemployed for casting new plates or other objects. Although in this early period editions of sheet music were relatively small, some pieces were especially popular and the resultant demand for them called for more copies than the original soft plates were able to produce. Such a piece would be copied anew onto fresh plates and another edition issued. The frequency of the designation "new" and "second" and sometimes even "third edition" on the captions of Blake, Willig, and Dubois sheets, for example, attests to this practice. In two known cases, we can conclude with a reasonable degree of certainty that music plates ended up on the scrapdealer's heap while still in usable condition. In one instance, this was due to the sale of their owner's estate; in another, it was because they had been retained by their maker long after the demand had ceased for the type of music they contained.[4] Frequently, if plates had not been worn out by their original makers or owners, their reemployment by subsequent owners and publishers would bring about the same result.[5] But most frequently, plates became obsolete because the music they contained had gone out of style and there was a diminishing demand or need for their reuse.

Although these early plates are no longer extant, we can infer a great many details regarding their nature and characteristics. In addition to what we already know about their probable metallic content and about the method employed in founding them, we can conclude from general customs and practices of the early pewtering trade that they were finished on one side only and that this side was highly polished. Owing to the

4. The account of John Knapp, executor of the will of Joannetta Catharina Elizabeth von Hagen, widow of Peter Albrecht von Hagen, probated in Boston on June 11, 1810, contains the following entry (no. 4): "The accountant charges himself . . . with the net gain acquired . . . by the sale of the Type metal Musick Plates, appraised in the inventory at $43,87, & which he has sold to E. Ayres for $64,10." E. Ayres (Ayers) is not indexed among the many Ayres (Ayers) in contemporary Boston directories. He was probably not a pewterer, as he does not appear in any of the books devoted to the American pewtering trade. Nor had he any connection with music or with publishing. Most probably he was involved in the anonymous business of buying and selling old metal for scrap or in some allied trade, for instance, plumbing. Regarding the second point, the "large and valuable stock of music plates" belonging to George E. Blake, which were sold at auction after his death in 1871, approximately thirty years after he had ceased publishing, undoubtedly ended up on the scrapdealer's pile, for we know of no subsequent reissues from them. There would be little interest in the type of music they were capable of reproducing at that late time, for the songs which Blake published during the first four decades of the nineteenth century were hopelessly out of date by 1871. Little profit would ensue from their republication.

5. For a statement on the reuse of music plates by subsequent publishers, see pp. 200–205 herein.

nature of the copperplate printing process, in which the paper was jammed into the plate with such force as to cause its outline to be impressed into the sheet, we can determine from extant music sheets that the usual plate—that is, the plate ordinarily employed to print individual songs and instrumental works—measured about 11 inches from top to bottom and approximately 8 inches from side to side. (Gamble, in *Music Engraving and Printing* [p. 87], states that 8 by 11 is a standard plate size for the period around 1923.) Naturally, plate dimensions varied slightly from publisher to publisher and from period to period. In addition, plates intended for unusual purposes would have unusual dimensions: those employed for making a pocket edition, for example, with "oblong quarto" dimensions might extend only 4 or 5 inches in height and from 6 to 8 inches in width; plates employed to print a centered title page might measure only 8 inches square.[6] Extant sheets show us that edges were rounded off gently at corners, and by comparing plate outlines on sheets of publishers in different localities and varying periods we notice a startling near-conformity of measurements, which suggests that molds may have been used in the founding process. (The gray outline of two early music plates can be noted on the Hewitt proof and final sheets shown in Illus. 12.) I own an engraved and punched music plate dating probably from the very late nineteenth century or the early years of the twentieth, which was given to me by the late Jacob Blanck, the bibliographer of American literature (see Illus. 13 and 14). This plate is silver-gray and measures approximately 11 inches in height, 8 inches in

6. Examples of the first group include *The Musical Journal for the Flute or Violin*, published by J. Carr, Baltimore, about 1800 (Sonneck–Upton, p. 273) which measures approximately 6¾ inches in height by 8¾ inches in width, and *Riley's New Instructions for the German Flute*, issued by Edward Riley at 17 Chatham Street, New York, in 1811. This measures about 6 by 9 inches. (This size and the oblong-quarto format were common for pocket instructors.) Examples of small title-page plates include John Gildon's *Le Retour de Cambridge*, published by Willig at Philadelphia about 1865, and Thomas Thohpson's *Now at Moonlight's Fairy Hour*, originally published by J. Butler, 156 Broadway, about 1808 and reprinted, first by J. & M. Paff, Broadway, between this date and 1811 and again by Joseph Willson in 1814 or 1815. The plate for the Willig publication measures about 6 by 7¾ inches and that of the Butler issue about 4 by 6 inches. The shape and approximate size of two oblong-quarto editions can be seen on the front free endpaper of vol. 2 of my *Secular Music in America* in the form of *Aitken's Fountain of Music* and *Blake's Evening Companion*. With regard to the manner of imposing and printing books in oblong-quarto format, Gottlieb Graupner's *The Anacreontic Vocalist* (Boston, 1809) indicates that four pages were engraved on one plate in an upside-down fashion, and after the reverse of the sheet had been perfected, it was folded twice in book fashion and cut apart at the outer edges. On some pages of *The Anacreontic Vocalist* a dividing line, set on the plate by the engraver to indicate outer margins and the area of folding, is still visible, thanks to imperfect cutting by the binder. This manner of imposition and printing accords with the usage of Thomas Johnston over fifty years earlier (see Illus. 1a), and it was probably representative of common usage in music printing in general.

width, and ¹⁄₁₆ inch in thickness; its weight is just over 18 ounces. Its surface appears to be fairly hard, and I judge that it would be capable of throwing off a great many impressions, even at this late date.[7] Regarding the life expectancy of earlier plates, and the number of impressions that could be struck from them, we have only the comment provided by the English pamphlet *A Day at a Music Publishers*, which dates from slightly after the period under consideration but at a time when editions were still worked directly from plates. This pamphlet informs us (p. 5) that "music engraved from pewter will throw upwards of two thousand impressions, without flaw or blemish, if skillfully worked through the press."

Finally, to complete our sketch of the early American music plate, we have a contemporary receipt for the sale of music plates, and the information contained on this, though scanty, allows us to know, in one instance at least, who manufactured these implements, what they cost the publisher, how much they weighed, and in what measure they were sold. Frederick Rausch is known to have been active in New York publishing circles in the mid- and late 1790s, but not afterward. Now, a single document, included among his receipted bills from 1797 through 1810, has turned up to prove an extension of his activity in music publishing after 1797; it reads:

January 30, 1802

Mʳ Rausch

Bought of Geo. Coldwell
18 plates for Music wt. 32 lb @ 3/– Ĺ 4,,16,,0
Received payment in full
= Geo. Coldwell   [8]

7. The Blanck plate actually measures ⁵⁵⁄₁,₀₀₀ of an inch in thickness. The punched characters, especially the lettering of text, are neat and well done. This plate appears to contain a single page of a song, with words from the middle or final portion of verse. It bears no mark of identification regarding its maker or user.

8. Manuscript in the Manuscript Division of the New York Public Library, Rausch Collection. Only a handful of the sixty-odd items on file here have any association with music and these relate, for the most part, to the purchase of music and musical merchandise or are receipts for the purchase and repair of musical instruments. This item, another containing reference to the purchase of music paper, and a third acknowledging payment by Rausch to the English music-publishing firm of Preston for the engraving and printing of *A Russian Air*, a publication for which Rausch probably arranged and contracted while in London between 1804 and 1806, alone have a nexus to publishing. The non-musical accounts, which make up the major part of the file, comprise receipts for the purchase of books, wine, wearing apparel, board, lodging, etc. Rausch's negotiation with Coldwell for the purchase of music plates in January 1802 is especially interesting in light of the fact that there has heretofore been no known connection between him and music publishing after 1799, though Sonneck–Upton lists him as a publisher (p. 582) between 1800 and 1803 with the notation "no issues located." It is possible that he may have engraved music on the side for one of the then-active publishers, perhaps for George Gilfert or James Hewitt, with

George Coldwell first appeared in New York City directories in 1789, being listed as a pewterer at 218 Queen Street, the address of the pewterer Francis Bassett, to whom he was in all likelihood apprenticed. Subsequent listings and advertisements describe Coldwell as a manufacturer of spoons and candle-molds and as a maker of beer and wine measures, pots, and buttons. He apparently followed the trade of pewterer in New York City until his death in 1811, upon which he left a will that makes for interesting reading.[9] While none of the standard texts on early American pewtering associated him, or any other pewterer for that matter, with the casting of music plates, the obvious puzzlement of the authors of these texts concerning the fact that so few specimens of Coldwell's work remain today (only seven pieces with his "Liberty cap" touch are recorded)[10] suggests that he probably devoted most of his time and energy to the manufacture of baser materials and commodities of everyday usage. Indeed, Laughlin remarks in a semi-astonished vein that "in a day when the bulk of almost every American pewterer's output consisted of flatware, Coldwell advertised neither [dinner] plates nor basins."[11] That he made a living from his trade is apparent from his will, for he died solvent.

We also know from Gottesman's *The Arts and Crafts in New York, 1800–1804* (pp. 209–10) that Coldwell actually advertised his manufacture of music plates, for he published the following notice in the *New-York Gazette and General Advertiser* of August 2, 1802, and in the New York *Daily Advertiser* of the following day:

Pewterer's Work & Sale Shop, No. 7 Beekman-slip. The Subscriber takes his annual method of acquainting his numerous Candlemould Customers, he makes as usual upwards of Twenty different sizes and has lately added to his former the Apparatus for Fluted, and half Fluted Fours; can also be had at his Manufactory the following articles: appropriate vessels &c for celebration of the Holy Sacrament, Ink Stands with glass bottles, Tea Pots, Turreen Ladles, Stool and Bed Pans, Plates for Music prepared for Type, Quart and pint Beer Pots just measure, Spirit measures sealed from the gallon to handjill inclusive, with sundry other articles. N.B. The customer will not be asked at the first more than what the Goods will be sold for. George Coldwell.

---

whom he had earlier partnerships. See Sonneck–Upton (pp. 581–83) for a resumé of his pre-1800 publishing activity, and *The Bulletin of The New York Public Library LXII*, no. 1 (January 1958) for additional biographical information on him. One receipt, for the storage of trunks while he journeyed to London between June 1804 and October 1806, explains the absence of his name from New York City directories during these years.

9. See Laughlin, vol. 2, pp. 24–26, for details.

10. A spoon made by him and a photograph of his "touch" or mark appears in John Barrett Kerfoot's *American Pewter* (Boston, Houghton Mifflin, 1924) on the plate facing p. 98.

11. Vol. 2, p. 25.

And again in the *Daily Advertiser* of July 25, 1803, and in the *New-York Gazette and General Advertiser* of July 29, 1803, appeared this advertisement:

> Ice Cream Moulds, a few pair of Pewter Ice-Cream Moulds are now finished and now offered for sale at the subscriber's work-shop, No. 7 Beekman-street. They contain one gallon, are well made of the best materials, very strong and infinitely more durable than those made of Tinned Iron. Likewise for sale, quart and pint Beer Pots, Seal'd Spirit Measures, from a gallon to a half jill, Sucking Bottles for infants, Chamber Pots, Night Chair Pans, Bed do: Funnels, Sacriment vessels, common Toys, Plates for music, with upwards of twenty different sizes Candle Moulds, plain, fluted and half fluted, from threes to tens. Geo. Coldwell.

It seems evident from Kerfoot's commentary and from the above advertisements that George Coldwell earned his living mostly by manufacturing the usual commodities of everyday life. He undoubtedly accepted whatever business came his way. It would be to such an artisan that music engravers and publishers would naturally turn for the stock of plates so necessary to their work, for we have seen that these were items of simple and ordinary manufacture. The founding of music plates would hold little interest for those pewterers and metalsmiths who specialized in producing luxury goods and sophisticated materials. It follows that George Coldwell and similar pewterers in Philadelphia, Boston, Baltimore, and other cities where music was published locally[12] came to specialize in manufacturing music plates as an ordinary and continuing part of their everyday business. It is also reasonable to conclude from Coldwell's advertisements that he probably did not supply the entire music-publishing community of New York at that time with plates and that other as yet unidentified pewterers must have engaged in this work concurrently. Otherwise, why the need for him to advertise openly a commodity of such limited usage?

From the Coldwell receipt we can further conclude that the ordinary music plate of this period weighed a trifle under 1¾ pounds; that it was sold to engravers and publishers according to a weight standard and not on a per-item basis; and that the rate of exchange was set at 3 shillings (37½ cents) per pound.

12. Unfortunately, none outside of New York have as yet been identified. This, however, does not rule out conjecture. For example, H. G. and M. O. Brown's *Directory of the Book-Arts Book in Philadelphia to 1820* (p. 16) cites Thomas Barnhurst as a "copperplate maker" in 1816 and we also find Jacob Keim (p. 69) described as such during the years 1809–20. While their names do not appear in works on early American pewter, they could have made plates for Blake and Willig and other publishers, though it is more likely that pewterers or humble plumbers engaged in this business.

By referring back to the diary of Alexander Anderson, we can associate another early New York artisan with the fashioning of plates for music. In his entry for March 23, 1795, quoted on page 80 herein, Anderson noted that he had G. Youle make a plate for him so that he could engrave a musical title for George Gilfert. Admittedly, this reference does not apply to the making of a plate for the actual printing of music but for the engraving of a title only. However, Anderson's notation provides us with the name of another metalsmith who supplied engravers of an earlier period with pewter plates. This reference is good ground for conjecturing that Youle also may have been a major source of pewter plates that were used by music engravers and publishers to produce their music. Little is actually known about Youle in addition to the usual directory listings, which show him to have been a pewterer and plumber in New York City between 1793 and 1828. Like Coldwell, Youle labored at the less refined areas of metalsmithing. In the few instances when Youle actually did advertise pewter objects, he spoke with restraint, identifying these wares as distilling worms and spoon and candle molds. He appears to have concerned himself little with the manufacture of consumer goods and household objects. Rather, his activities were mostly restricted to the production of pipes and other materials of the general plumbing trade and to the less elegant aspects of pewtering.[13] The "type metal" that Anderson delivered to him for making a plate must have approximated pewter in composition, being mainly lead and tin, with antimony possibly present in a lesser amount.

A sampling of Anderson s diary for 1795 exposes several other interesting sidelights on the use of metal plates by early New York engravers, for we read:

March 30*th*, Paid Meyers 4 dollars for the 4 plates of copper
April 4*th*, Paid G. Youle 20/5 for 2 type metal plates
April 7*th*, I cast a plate of type metal
April 30*th*, Having fil'd my type metal too low, I went to Mr. Coldwell's and got it solder'd

"Myers" was evidently Judah Myers, a coppersmith in New York from 1794. He probably supplied the general engraving trade with their plateware.

While it is unlikely that copperplates were used to any considerable extent in early American music publishing after the introduction of the

13. That Youle, like Coldwell, probably restricted his everyday activities to the rougher aspects of the pewtering trade is supported by the fact that only one utensil, a ladle, bearing his "touch" is extant today.

stamping method in the late 1780s, we do know that they were used infrequently for adding titles, for title pages, and later on for vignettes and the like. The von Hagen inventory also provides evidence of the use of copperplates by American music publishers, undoubtedly for the fashioning of title pages, as follows: "The said accountant prays allowance [for] 5 large & 4 small Copper-Sheets, $4„63." In addition, copperplates are enumerated in the records of Gottlieb Graupner's estate, which is discussed in Chapter 10. Anderson's allusion to casting plates himself raises a point which would otherwise be overlooked, namely, that some engravers and publishers may have cast many of their own plates, in the earliest period at least. Entries referring to this procedure occur throughout Anderson's diary. However, for the actual finishing of plates, that is, for the planishing of them, which required a special skill possessed only by pewterers, Anderson took his plates to George Youle's shop, or, less frequently, to that of the pewterer George Coldwell.

CHAPTER VII

Engraving and Punching Tools

꧁꧂

I N T H E New York *Daily Advertiser* of January 9, 1795, William Priest, musician of the New Theatre, Philadelphia, informed the citizens of New York that "he had lately imported from Europe a compleat apparatus for engraving, printing, and publishing music in the modern stile, which is correctly executed under his immediate inspection by workmen who have many years been employed in that line in London."[1] In this all-too-brief announcement we encounter our earliest reference to the stamping and punching tools employed in early American music publishing, for Priest's allusion to the "compleat apparatus" that he had imported can only refer to the essential punches which a music engraver or publisher of 1795 used to stamp out his plates "in the modern stile." These tools are the principal part of the music engraver's outfit and the

---

1. Coincidentally, in this very issue of the *Daily Advertiser* and, in fact, on the identical page, Benjamin Carr, publisher of music in Philadelphia since July 1793, advertised the opening of his "Musical Magazine Repository" at No. 131 William Street in New York. Later on we shall question whether some sort of business relationship existed between these two personalities in the Philadelphia operation of Carr's publishing business. Priest had previously published in the *Pennsylvania Packet* of January 3, 1795, the announcement: "Music Engraving, In all its branches correctly performed by Wm. Priest, Musician of the New Theatre. For particulars enquire at No. 15 Apple Tree Alley between 4th and 5th streets." Priest's visit to America was a short one, for within four years he was back in London. In 1802 he published a book on his American experience, *Travels in the United States of America; Commencing in the Year 1793, and Ending in 1797. With the Author's Journals of the Two Voyages across the Atlantic* (London, J. Johnson, 1802). Unfortunately, Priest restricted his remarks to the curiosities he observed on this trip and made no mention of his musical or theatrical life in America or of his music-publishing experience here; his comments might have been a major source of information on our early musical and theatrical life and on our early cultural activities.

instruments most vital to the issuances of well-produced music sheets. Without them, Priest could not have published music in the style advertised. Other engraving and printing instruments necessary to this work were available to him in New York and Philadelphia at that time, so there would have been no need to import them. In fact, it was only after Priest and other musicians had begun to import the necessary "engraving apparatus," i.e., punches, that music publishing began to flourish on a continuing basis in this country.

No single aspect of the early American music-engraving and publishing trade is less documented or less understood than punching and stamping tools. We know practically nothing concrete about the nature and origin of these simple but all-important instruments. Like music plates, none of the early punches and allied tools have survived. Nor are there any known records of tools to tell us anything about them. In the absence of fact then, we are forced to rely strongly upon conjecture in order to impute shape, form, and origin to these implements. Fortunately, such conjecture can be grounded upon information gleaned from a variety of sources, including early encyclopedic works, general engraving and trade manuals, and other early printed sources; through comparisons with the instruments employed in similar or allied trades, such as typefounding, bookbinding, and metalsmithing; from information about such tools supplied by later sources, as, for instance, *A Day at a Music Publishers* and Gamble's *Music Engraving and Publishing*; from the customs and practices of the general engraving trade; from a very few early advertisements, such as Priest's, quoted before; from trade cards; through reference to a few contemporary records, such as wills and inventories; and last, but by no means least, by the telltale marks which these instruments left on extant music sheets in the form of notes, signs, lettering, etc. It is mainly upon such foundations—and, admittedly, upon a number of educated guesses—that the present chapter is constructed.

ENGRAVING TOOLS

The cutting, ruling, marking, measuring, scraping, sharpening, and other instruments which must have occupied a place in the kit of every music engraver and publisher in early America were as follows: gravers and cutting tools, a straightedge or ruling device of some kind, a marking pin, calipers or dividers, a scraper, a burnisher, an oilstone, a punching stone, and, finally, a striking and a correcting or leveling hammer. The last three tools have greater association with the punching than with the cutting (or "scratching") process, but because of their uncomplicated nature they are presented here along with the generally useful tools under discussion. The Blake inventory in Appendix B tells us that other instruments were probably used to bring plates to a state of readiness for printing and to print them: an anvil, clamps, planes, nippers, riveting irons, soldering devices, and screwdrivers and other common tools.

The most frequently used tool of every engraver, be he an engraver of music or of more general items such as prints, maps, etc., was the graver, for this was his principal cutting instrument. The music engraver mostly employed this device to cut into his plate such musical signs as were not readily stamped, including lengthened crescendos, diminuendos, and ties. In early times the graver often went under the synonymous term "burin"; often, too, in modified form it was known by the shape it suggested, such as "crook" (or, in modern terminology, "hook"). The blade of the graver was normally shaped in a V, with its cutting edge beveled out of the end furthest removed from the upper angles. Gravers were probably forged like the blades of knives and similar utensils—under fire, then brought to the proper shape and size, and afterwards polished, ground, and fit into a handle. The finished graver was then whetted on an oilstone so as to bring its cutting edge and point to an optimum state for cutting. The graver had a knob handle at its upper end and its underside was cut away so that it could be used with its cutting edge in a nearly horizontal position.

The second edition of Robert Dossie's *The Handmaid to the Arts* devotes much detail to the method of making gravers, describing the general process as follows:

The gravers should be made of the best steel, which must be drawn out into small rods, with a charcoal fire. These rods should be cut into the lengths chosen for the graver, and then softened in their temper, by heating in a charcoal fire, and suffering them to cool very slowly, either by continuing them in the fire till it extinguishes, or taking part of the burning embers out of the fire, and burying the lengths of rod in them, till the whole grow cold. They should then be filed into the form desired, and afterwards brought back to a hard temper, by heating them red hot, and, while they are so, thrusting the end into a lump of soft soap. But, in doing this, great care should be taken to put them into the soap with a true perpendicular direction; for, if they be turned in the least obliquely, the graver will warp, and be crooked. If the temper of the graver be found too hard after this treatment, and prevent the whetting it properly to an edge, it may be softened by taking a large burning piece of charcoal, and laying the end of the graver on it till it begin to grow yellow, and then thrusting it into a lump of tallow, or dipping it in water; but, if water be used, the graver must not be too hot, or it will not be softened by this treatment.[2]

2. (London, J. Nourse, 1764), vol. 2, pp. 56–59. The first edition of this anonymously

Dr. Dossie (he was a physician) further cites methods for testing the temper of the graver, for whetting it into cutting condition, and for assaying its finished form. Concerning the handle, he writes: "After the graver is mounted with its proper handle, and whetted, it is necessary to cut off that part of the knob of the handle which is in line with the edge of the graver, in order to render the whole of it so flat on that side that it may be applied in any direction to the plate." Gravers were made in several forms with respect to the shape of their points, some being round, others square, a third kind lozenge, and a fourth—restricted almost entirely to music engraving—having its point turned back by about 30 degrees so as to form a hook. This kind, which was termed a "crook graver" or simply "crook" in earlier times and which is called "hook" today, was the first tool employed by the music engraver when undertaking a plate, for with this he initially ruled off lines for staves by drawing it across the face of the plate. The next cutting tool used in the music-engraving process was the lozenge graver, which had the widest application to the entire cutting operation. The engraver used this tool to score faint but deliberate lines, such as the stems of notes, lines for bars, and thin, irregular ties. He also added in a freehand style titles, imprints, and other matter with this tool, when these were planned or called for, and utilized it for almost all of his general chores. It was his all-purpose tool. Another type of graver commonly used in music work was the square graver, which was blunt and rectangular rather than sharp and V-shaped. The impression this tool made was equal to its own thickness. It was utilized to form thick lines, such as those connecting eighth notes, and for making braces, thick ties, and other similar markings. Engravers of our early music sheets employed these cutting tools in various ways, choosing or altering them in conformity with their personal preferences for differing aspects of their work. In modern music engraving a thinner version of the lozenge graver, the "tint graver," is frequently employed.

The straightedge, calipers and dividers, and the oilstone require no

published work, which is one of the most useful compendia of information on painting, engraving, and crafts published in earlier times, appeared in 1758 and is rarely found, even in larger libraries. The second edition is a word-for-word reprint, as is a subsequent edition, published in London in 1796. The third edition is in small octavo format and was printed for A. Miller, W. Law, and R. Cater; and for Wilson, Spence, and Mawman, York. This 1796 edition, which is not found as frequently as its predecessor, proves that engravers and artisans of the late 1790s had available to them a manual of instructions on many aspects of the engraver's and craftsman's work. A number of other books containing information on the engraving and metal trades were available to American artisans of this period, some of them published or republished natively, as, for instance, the *Valuable Secrets Concerning Arts and Trades*, issued by Thomas Hubbard at Norwich, Connecticut, in 1795. This particular title was reprinted at least on two more occasions in America.

explanation, for their natures and properties are obvious. Earlier versions undoubtedly resembled or nearly resembled present-day counterparts. The marking pin was a steel rod, about ¼ inch or less in thickness and pointed at either end. With this tool the engraver marked out the position of notes onto the plate for punching after they had been measured off and proportioned through the use of calipers or dividers, and with it he also indicated the kinds of notes and signs to be punched or cut. The scraper was usually a flat piece of steel of irregular dimensions, commonly known as the "busk." A three-edged tool was sometimes used in its stead. The latter resembled a modern-day file (the "three-square" file), though its surface was smooth. The scraper was used to work off ridges and burrs raised by the pressure of the graver and punch. The burnisher must have approximated the three-edged scraper in appearance, though it was probably larger and rounder. With it the engraver rubbed down lines that had been cut too deeply, polished out scratches or holes in the face of the plate, and finished off the surface of the plate before and after corrections.

The punching stone was a flat, oblong slab on which the plate rested during the punching operation. (In ordinary copperplate printing the engraver cushioned his plate on a leather bag filled with sand; according to Dossie [vol. 2, p. 59], such cushions commonly measured 9 inches square and 3 or 4 inches in thickness.) In later times a worn-down lithographic stone may have been used for this purpose. Indeed, Gamble notes in his *Music Engraving and Printing* (p. 136) that, as of 1923, this was the practice of modern music engraving. The account attached to the will of the widow of Peter Albrecht von Hagen (1810) provides us with actual evidence of the use of punching stones in early American music engraving, for this document records delivery to the heirs of Joannetta von Hagen of "1 punching stone [valued at] 2 dolls." Finally, the striking and correcting or leveling hammer were the instruments with which the engraver struck the punches in order to impart their images into the plate and to tap down or level areas of the plate that had bulged out in the punching process. The correcting hammer was probably slightly lighter than the one used for punching the plate.

Because of the general aspects of these instruments, and because of their obvious ease of manufacture, breadth of usage, and similarity to everyday utensils and work tools, we need not discuss them further at this time. Unlike punches, these tools were not restricted to one narrow line of endeavor. In addition to their use by copperplate and music engravers, most of these instruments found employment in the hands of pewterers, coppersmiths, gold- and silversmiths, and jewelers, as well as carpenters and a host of other artisans concerned with the cutting and finishing of hard surfaces.[3] Ordinarily, gravers, scrapers, and burnishers must have come from the shops of local cutlers and allied tradesmen and were probably finished in about the manner described earlier by Dossie, though in the early period better gravers may have been imported from abroad. We know that metalworkers and cutlers abounded in America from early times on. It is also likely that some engravers fashioned their own tools in accordance with individual tastes and preferences.

A passage from Dunlap's *History of . . . Design in the United States*[4] best illustrates the conditions under which the early American engraver frequently had to labor—both with respect to his trade in general and to his tools in particular—in order to achieve success in his day-to-day quest for a livelihood. Dunlap's excerpt relates the personal narrative of David Edwin, an English engraver who had emigrated to Philadelphia in 1797, and concludes with an account of Dunlap's own experiences in the engraving trade in New York several years earlier. Dunlap's narration of Edwin's as well as his own experiences in engraving not only provides interesting insights into the early engraving trade and introduces evidence as to the availability of engraving tools in America at this time, but it underscores the need of such early artisans to rely on their own intelligence and ability to improvise their tools.

Mr. Benjamin Carr, mentioned by me in the History of the American Theatre, was a friend of Mr. Freeman's, who was then about publishing a collection of Scotch airs selected by Carr, and Edwin was employed to engrave the title page.[5] This was his first work in America; and at the time of

3. We are told by a biographer of John Fitch, of steamboat fame (Thomas Boyd, *Poor John Fitch, Inventor of the Steamboat*, New York, 1935, p. 127), that in engraving his 1785 copperplate *Map of the Northwest Parts of the United States* while on the frontier, "he had only the Graver, with which he marked powder horns for the Indians and ciphered buttons for English guards on Prison Island."

4. (1834 ed.), vol. 1, p. 67ff.

5. Dunlap's *History of the American Theatre* (New York, J. & J. Harper, 1832) contains only the most casual reference to Carr, mentioning merely his appearance on the stage in 1794. His publication of the collection of Scottish airs alluded to in Dunlap here is unknown, and no reference to it appears in Sonneck–Upton. Inasmuch as John Aitken's *The Scot's Musical Museum*, published by Aitken in 1797, the same year as Edwin's arrival into Philadelphia, contains an engraved title page signed "D. Edwin, Sculpt.," it is almost certain that Dunlap (or his source) confused Carr with Aitken when writing about Edwin some thirty years later. Little is actually known of Freeman. T. B. Freeman was in partnership with a copperplate printer named Annesly in 1795 and 1796 and was a publisher and auctioneer in Philadelphia for several decades into the nineteenth century. Dunlap denominates him simply as a publisher and later on as proprietor of auction rooms in Philadelphia, the only direct reference to him in his book being, "T. B. Freeman, Esq., was for a long time the principal encourager of the arts, by publishing engravings in Philadelphia." Several pages of Alfred C Prime's *The Arts & Crafts in Philadelphia, Maryland and South Carolina, 1721–1785* (N. p.,

commencing it he was destitute of the necessary tools, and could procure none in Philadelphia; the cause is not stated by my informant, certainly there was at that time several engravers in the city, and it would appear that some of them might have helped a brother in this state of destitution, as it regards tools. The engraver accidently found in his seaman's chest, a graver which he had thrown into it in Amsterdam and forgotten. The shank of this tool, or that part which is inserted into the handle, he shaped as well as he could to his purpose, and commenced etching the his plate therewith. As he proceded with the work, he reversed the tool, tied a rag as a substitute for the handle, round the end he used as an etching point, and with this second contrivance finished the plate.

An engraver at the time of Mr. Edwin's arrival in Philadelphia, had much to struggle with. He says in a letter before me, "copperplates were finished rough from the hammer; no tools to be purchased, he (the engraver) had to depend upon his own ingenuity to fabricate them for himself, or in directing others qualified for the work; but worse than all was the slovenly style in which printing was executed. Often have I in extreme cold weather, waited hours for a proof, till the paper, oil, and even the roller could be thawed. The work shop of the principal printer in Philadelphia, was little better than a shell, and open to the winds. I once insisted that the printer should have the plank of his press planed and levelled, as it was impossible in the state it was now in to take off a tolerable impression; and the plate I wished printed had cost me much time and trouble in the execution; the printer resisted all my arguments for a long time, being himself perfectly satisfied with the state of the press; at length, and only in consideration of my paying the expenses, it was that he gave his consent."

I have transcribed Mr. Edwin's statement of the rude imperfections attendant upon engraving and copperplate printing in Philadelphia in 1797. In New-York, before that period, there were difficulties similar, no doubt; but as early as 1790, the writer, under the direction of Mr. Peter R. Maverick, found no difficulty in procuring tools for etching and engraving and some prepared plates; and etched and scratched until he was satisfied that engraving required more skill, time, and patience, than he had to bestow upon it. Mr. Maverick was the best engraver then in New-York; his competitors were indeed few and feeble. He was his own printer, and worked off his own proofs very comfortably, at his own press, in a comfortable work shop.

PUNCHING TOOLS

The stock-in-trade of every early music engraver consisted of the cutting and finishing tools enumerated and described before, together with one or several sets of the all-important punches (or puncheons, as

---

Walpole Society, 1929, 2 vols.) are given over to advertisements by Freeman and Company of engravings newly published. A few additional references to him can be found in Mantle Fielding's "David Edwin, Engraver," *Pennsylvania Magazine of History and Biography* XXIX (1905) 79–88.

they were sometimes called). These were short rods of tempered steel, usually tapered slightly toward one end (like a chisel), with musical notes or signs and non-musical lettering standing out in relief on the smaller of their tips (see Illus. 15). It was with these instruments primarily that the engraver imparted shapes into the soft metal plates from which impressions were ultimately worked off onto music sheets. While notation could and actually had been completely cut and engraved by hand—as shown earlier, this was the dominant method employed for effecting music plates in seventeenth- and eighteenth-century Europe and in colonial America—the process was laborious and prohibitively expensive, the finished product was uneven in appearance, and it lacked esthetic quality, readability, and ease of use. Punching had all but replaced freehand engraving as the principal means of publishing music sheets in England and on the Continent at least by the middle of the eighteenth century. Indeed, the American music-publishing industry, if the uncoordinated efforts of the musician-engravers discussed here can be construed as such, may be said to have begun with the introduction of these simple tools to the newly independent states a little more than thirty-five years later.

In spite of the fact that they are the most important implements in the kit of the music engraver, none of the punches used by our earliest engravers and publishers have survived to the present day. In the absence of their physical presence we again must rely upon comparison with allied and modern tools to guess at their form, size, and even origin. About modern music punches Gamble makes the following observations on pp. 104–6 of his *Music Engraving and Printing* (which would hold true, for the most part, for tools of earlier periods): the instruments measure about 2½ to 3 inches in length and about ¼ to 5/16 inches in square section; a set of punches usually consists of from fifty to fifty-five pieces; large characters necessitate greater dimensions to give them strength to withstand the blows of the hammer and also to accommodate a larger face (the punches for brackets, clefs, slurs, etc., have considerably enlarged ends as requisite; for smaller notes and signs the ends are tapered down proportionately); a nick on one side of the punch indicates the direction in which it should be held to position its sign correctly; there are twelve sizes of punches in all, though four of these are hardly used; and, finally, punches are held in perforated wooden blocks or boxes, with their points uppermost, at a sufficient distance apart so that the engraver can readily pick them out. The Blake inventory in Appendix B shows the presence of ten frames for punches in that publisher's possession. Illustrations 15 and

16 show racks and forms of punches made in America after the middle of the nineteenth century.

Other information on the probable form and nature of early music punches can be inferred from similar instruments that were employed in related trades, such as typefounding, bookbinding, metalsmithing, coin and medal founding, saddle making, and in all those early trades which used punching tools to emboss, decorate, and finish their wares. We can also pick up scraps of information on these seemingly extinct instruments from a number of collateral sources, such as contemporary newspaper advertisements (for example, the announcement of William Priest which began this chapter), directory listings, engravers' trade cards, and other bits scattered hither and yon. Most important in the reconstruction of these early instruments are the marks they left upon the sheets they imprinted in the form of notes, signs, textual material, and directions. These give up information far in excess of their simple shapes. The method I have adopted in attempting the formidable task of defining the nature and origin of these early punching tools is directed toward discussing, and in some cases answering, the following four questions: what was the nature of these early tools and how were they made; who introduced them into America, and when, and from what source; how were they procured by our early music engravers and with what frequency; when were they first manufactured in America and by whom?

The Nature of Music Punches and How They Were Made

In former times, engraving on steel was done primarily for cutting punches and dies for striking coins, medals, and counters; for stamping and decorating metalware and other wares, such as saddles; for making the matrices or molds from which type was cast; for producing the stamps which bookbinders used for lettering and decorating the covers of books; and for a variety of other purposes, such as the making of mathematical, nautical, and scientific instruments, the cutting of metal blocks for relief printing, and general engraving. The dies or punches fashioned for these purposes must have resembled and in some cases exactly paralleled those made for stamping musical notation onto pewter plates, and the methods used to make them must have been about the same. Furthermore, it is probable that they were made by the same group of artisans: diesinkers, engravers on brass and other hard metals, and perhaps general engravers who resorted to such work to fill up their idle moments and those of their apprentices. Like the dies used in metalsmithing, particularly for chasing or embossing gold, silver, and pewter, and in typefounding and bookbinding, the punches used in the mechanical engraving of music were bits of steel or iron mixed with steel, on which, before being tempered or hardened, were cut the figures to be imparted by them. Most probably, these bits were drawn out into small rods over a charcoal fire in about the manner described previously by Dossie (p. 100 herein) and were later tempered in a similar fashion. The tools commonly employed by the engraver on steel for cutting such dies and punches included sculptors (gravers) of various kinds, chisels, flatters, files, and other related instruments.

In preparing a metal punch, the engraver first took up a piece or rod of untempered steel and drew upon one end of it the outline of the character or form it was to impart. He did this with pen and ink, if the character was large, or with the smooth, blunted end of a needle if it was to be small. He then took up a sculptor or graver and dug out the metal between the strokes he had outlined on the face of the punch, until the figure stood out in relief. He next worked the inner edges of the character, deepening the hollows carefully with the same tools. It was a general maxim of type-founding that, in cutting dies or punches or "patrices," as they are sometimes called, the letter or character had to be cut as deep as it was wide, for if the depth and width did not measure in exact proportion to one another, the letter would print black. The engraver or sculptor next smoothed down the outside of the character with files until it had been satisfactorily formed, and filed the insides as well. Finally, he finished off the punch by applying to it a very hard temper so that it could withstand repeated blows of a hammer. To make this part of the work easier he frequently used counterpunches, or dies with part of the letter or character standing in relief on their working ends. With these he could "countersink" or depress the loop of an *a* or of a clef sign, for example, with one fast operation, thus speeding up the job.

The punches used in music engraving, gold- and silversmithing, pewtering, typefounding, and bookbinding, were all prepared in about this manner. The typefounder used his punch to strike an impression into a brass block which was then inserted in a mold for forming types. The goldsmith, silversmith, pewterer, and other artisans who embossed and decorated metals and other objects like saddles, employed punches for ornamenting their wares. The bookbinder lettered and embellished the covers and spines of books with the same type of tool. And the music engraver used a similar implement for striking notation and lettering into the soft pewter plates from which editions of music were ultimately printed. The punches employed by any of the above artisans could have been

[107]

interchanged, assuming, of course, that the characters on them were suited to the job at hand. In view of this it seems odd that no one in America except the shadowy William Norman, whom Isaiah Thomas has denominated as the caster of music types about 1783, employed music punches to cast type before the Baltimore Type Foundry began this work about 1809. However, the art of typefounding developed more slowly in America than did other aspects of the printing trades, which might have accounted for the delay.

The Introduction of Punches in America

It is generally acknowledged by musicologists and others interested in early American music and music printing that the issuance of music through the punching or stamping process was first accomplished in this country by John Aitken, a Philadelphia engraver and metalsmith, in 1787.[6]

John Aitken slipped unnoticed onto the Philadelphia scene sometime before 1785. His name first appeared in city directories for that year, the first in which they were issued, with the designation "silversmith." We know nothing at all about his activities before that date, except that he was probably born in "Dulheath" [Dulkeath], Scotland, in 1744 or 1745, which would have made him somewhat less than forty years old at the time of his migration to Philadelphia. Krummel conjectures that he was probably the brother of Robert Aitken, the well-known publisher and binder in Philadelphia, but there appears to be no actual basis for this supposition.[7] John Aitken continued to be listed in Philadelphia direc-

6. Most of the facts about Aitken and about his activities in Philadelphia as a metalsmith and publisher of music have to be gleaned from a variety of sources. The hitherto most complete discussion of him appeared in Krummel's "Philadelphia Music Engraving," pp. 116–22.

7. As we shall see shortly, the designation of Aitken's birthplace comes from his grave marker. "Dulheath" is probably a misspelling or variant spelling of Dulkeath, a town about eight miles northeast of Edinburgh. Krummel imputes a relationship between John and Robert Aitken because of the similarity of their place of birth. It seems quite likely that they were related, though it would be yielding to guesswork to infer an exact relationship betwen them. There may have been a small colony of Aitkens from Dulkeath in Philadelphia at this time, for another possible relative, a woodworker named John Aitken also, will be introduced shortly. Robert Aitken, who was born at Dulkeath in 1734, is famous for having printed the first American Bible in English, the well-known "Aitken Bible" of 1787. He had a printer son named Robert Aitken, Jr., from whom he became estranged about 1797. Robert Aitken (Sr.) engaged in bookbinding, engraving, and bookselling, as well as in general printing. Following his death in 1802 his shop was taken over by his eldest daughter, Jane, thirty-eight years old at the time (she is incorrectly identified by Krummel as his widow), who continued the business for about fifteen years. Robert Aitken's activity as a bookbinder in Philadelphia has recently been the subject of two papers by William and Carol Spawn: "The Aitken Shop; Identification of an Eighteenth-Century Bindery and Its

tories as "silversmith" (except for the edition for 1794, where he was designated "copperplate printer") until 1807, when he was listed as "silversmith, goldsmith, jeweller and musical repository," being carried under this designation until 1810. In the directories for 1811 and 1813 he is listed as "silversmith, &c." and in subsequent directories as follows: 1814, coppersmith; 1816–18, sheet-copper foundry; 1819–22, sheet-copper manufacturer; 1823–24, printer; 1825, printer and copper re-finer. His name is not entered in subsequent directories.

In 1787, Aitken began publishing sheet music, and he continued in this line until about 1793, when he retired, perhaps due to the entry into Philadelphia music publishing of John Christopher Moller and subse-quently Benjamin Carr and other qualified musicians. In 1787 and again in 1791 he issued his own *Compilation of the Litanies and Vesper Hymns and Anthems As They Are Sung in the Catholic Church,* and in 1797 he issued a larger collection of vocal music entitled *The Scots Musical Museum.* In 1802 appeared a curious song of his own composition which he called *The Goldsmith's Rant* (see Frontispiece herein). This publication consists of only one page of music, containing, on its verso, a number of charming vignettes showing the metalsmith—probably Aitken himself—at work. *The Scots Musical Museum* and *The Goldsmith's Rant* were the only two publications which Aitken offered to the public between his withdrawal from publishing in 1793 or 1794 and his reentry into the field about 1807. He may have engaged in the general metalsmithing trades after 1793 and 1794, for the Mathew Carey Papers in the American Antiquarian Society associate him with doing metal repairs on Carey's presses at this time and working in other related ways. In 1807 Aitken reestablished himself as a music publisher at 76 North Second Street, from which address he continued to issue sheet music and the few collections noted below until 1811, at which time he seems to have retired from publishing altogether. (He was then about sixty years old.) During his second career in music publishing Aitken issued about 125 titles in all; a few of them were of considerable size and ambition, but the majority imitated previous issues of Blake and Willig. Krummel states in "Philadelphia Music Engraving" (p. 122) that for a time afterwards Aitken engaged in a four-way partnership with his son, William, but he does not specify in what

Tools," *Papers of the Bibliographical Society of America* LVII (1963) 422–37, and "R. Aitken, Colonial Printer of Philadelphia," *Graphic Arts Review* (January–February 1961). Another copperplate engraver who may have been related to John and Robert Aitken was James Akin, who first appeared in the Philadelphia city directories in 1794 and was listed in them for several decades afterward. No mention is made of John Aitken or James Akin in the Spawn articles.

capacity. It is obvious from the directory listings noted before that Aitken worked at coppersmithing and at other trades until he was well over eighty years old. (One cannot but wonder if, during the years when he was listed in the directories as a coppersmith and a sheet-copper founder, he manufactured copperplates for the engravers of Philadelphia.) John Aitken died in 1831, for Edward L. Clark's *A Record of the Inscriptions of the Tablets and Grave-Stones in the Burial Grounds of Christ Church, Philadelphia,* contains the following entry for him:[8]

VI

Sacred

to the Memory of

JOHN AITKEN

native of Dulheath Scotland

who departed this life

September 8th A.D. 1831

in the 86th year of his age.

Blessed are the dead who die in the Lord

for they rest from their labors.

Also

ELIZABETH, wife of

John Aitken

who departed this life

April 13th 1837

Aged 75 years.

After Aitken's break with music publishing in 1811, or, more likely, after his death in 1831, George Willig apparently acquired his plate stock, and probably his engraving tools and publishing equipment also, for we know that some of Aitken's earlier publications were reissued by Willig under his altered imprint. There is little information available on Aitken's activity as a gold-, silver-, and metalsmith. Thorn C. Jordan's *Handbook of American Silver and Pewter Marks* records him as working in Philadelphia from 1785 to 1814 and illustrates two examples of the method he employed to sign his pieces.[9] The Philadelphia Museum of Art owns two pieces of silver which were fabricated by him, a teaspoon and a creamer (shown in Illus. 17); another piece, a strainer, was entered in that institution's 1956 exhibition catalog of Philadelphia silver, 1682–1800.[10]

8. (Philadelphia, Collins, 1864), p. 468.

9. (New York, Tudor Publishing Co., 1949), p. 10.

10. Philadelphia Museum of Art, *Philadelphia Silver, 1682–1800* (Philadelphia, 1956). This piece was noted there as privately owned.

Aitken is not known to have engaged in pewtering at all, though it is obvious from the few extant examples of his silver and from the later directory listings for him that he undoubtedly engaged in the coarser aspects of the metalsmithing trades.

In order to avert future confusion, one other pertinent fact about John Aitken should be mentioned. In his "Philadelphia Music Engraving," Krummel discourses (p. 117) on a calamity that befell our John Aitken, noting that *Poulson's American Daily Advertiser* of Monday, May 12, 1806, published information on a disastrous fire two days earlier which destroyed, among other things, "a large joiner's shop, S. W. corner of Relief Alley, occupied by I. Aitken." In addition, the second volume of Alfred C. Prime's *The Arts & Crafts in Philadelphia, Maryland, and South Carolina*, which carries advertisements from 1786 through 1800, contains the following entry under cabinetmakers (p. [164]):

> AITKEN, JOHN.—The Subscriber takes this method of returning his most sincere thanks to the public, and his friends in particular, for the many favours they have conferred on him, and sollicits a continuation of their custom, which will be gratefully acknowledged. He still carries on the cabinet and chair manufactory, the south-east corner of Chesnut and Second-streets, where he has for sale, chairs of various patterns, some of which are entirely new, never before seen in this city, and finished with an elegancy of stile peculiar to themselves and equal in goodness and neatness of workmanship to any ever made here. Likewise, desks, bureaus, book cases, bed steads, tea tables, card ditto, dining ditto, &c. finished in the completest taste now prevailing in this city, which he will sell on the most reasonable terms, for cash, or a short credit.-Orders from the country punctually attended to, and executed with the quickest dispatch by the public's Very Humble servant, John Aitken.

It would appear, from the above two references, that John Aitken engaged in woodworking as well as metalsmithing and music publishing. The plain and simple fact, however, is that there were two John Aitkens active in Philadelphia at the same time, one our metalsmith and music publisher and the other a joiner and maker of furniture. The latter was listed, along with our silversmith-publisher, in Philadelphia city directories from 1791 (the second available) through 1814, under the designation "cabinet maker." It was undoubtedly he and not our John Aitken who suffered the disastrous fire in 1806, for the description "joiner"—i.e., one whose occupation is to construct articles by joining pieces of wood—leaves no doubt of this. In her *Cabinetmakers of America*, Ethel H. Bjerkoe notes that Horner calls John Aitken "President Washington's favourite cabinet-maker," possibly on the strength of the fact that Washington paid the joiner John Aitken for two dozen square-back chairs on February 21, 1797.[11] She also states that the cabinetmaker John Aitken was born in Dulkeath, Scotland, possibly confusing him in this regard, as Krummel did in another, with our silversmith and music publisher. The cabinetmaker John Aitken disappears from Philadelphia directories after 1814, and as our John Aitken is the only one listed thereafter, until 1826, it is undoubtedly he and not the furniture maker who lies buried in the Christ Church burial ground under the stone which identifies the occupant of the grave as a native of "Dulheath." It seems likely that both of these John Aitkens were related, and further, that the printer Robert Aitken was also kin. All three may have emigrated from Dulkeath, for is it not customary for relatives to congregate together when settling in strange lands? Furthermore, the city directory for 1793 lists the silversmith and cabinetmaker as living only two doors apart, the one at 50 Chestnut Street and the latter at number 48.

Although *The Goldsmith's Rant* shows that John Aitken had only the slightest knowledge of music, he obviously had a keen liking for it. was proof of this we have, in addition to this curious composition of his own creation, the knowledge that he was the first engraver on metal in America to engage in the publication of music in a serious and continuing way and the first to employ steel punches for that purpose. In addition to his publications of 1787, 1793, and 1797, described earlier, he also issued other musical works: in 1807 *Aitken's New Musical Musuem*, and between 1807 and 1816 *Aitken's Fountain of Music*, the last two being collections of instrumental music arranged for violin, flute, clarinet, etc. He also copyrighted two other sacred collections, *Aitken's Collection of Divine Music* (1806) and *A Collection of Sacred Music* (1807), neither of which is known in extant copies today. (It is entirely possible that only the title pages of these were printed and deposited for copyright, pursuant to the custom of the day, and that neither work advanced beyond this stage.) Krummel devotes a section of his discussion of Aitken to the subject of "Aitken as a Plagiarist," (pp. 121–22) contending that he copied the sheets of other publishers, particularly those of George E. Blake. While this is doubtless true; I feel that his pronouncement is unjustly harsh, for Aitken was only following established practice: Blake and Willig and other early publishers reprinted uncopyrighted music, particularly English and European titles,

11. (Garden City, N.Y., Doubleday & Co., 1957), p. 22, quoting from William MacP. Horner's *The Blue Book, Philadelphia Furniture, William Penn to George Washington* (Philadelphia, 1935). Other information of the cabinetmaker Aitken can be gleaned from Charles F. Montgomery's *American Furniture, the Federal Period, in the Henry Francis du Pont Winterthur Museum* (New York, Viking Press, 1966).

[112]

with relish. If any accusatory word can be used against Aitken in this respect, the term "imitator" would be more appropriate. He imitated rather than innovated, in the period between 1807 and 1811 at least, when he issued the bulk of his music. This practice may have been one of the factors (in addition to age or some unknown problem) which led to his retirement from active publishing in Philadelphia.

We shall now turn to a detailed examination of Aitken's activity as a music publisher between 1787 and 1797, during which time more than twenty titles issued from his hands, some of them quite large and ambitious considering the time, the place, and the circumstances under which they were produced. Sonneck–Upton lists several additional titles, but these prove to be separate issues from the larger collections that Aitken engraved. Using Sonneck–Upton as a guide, but taking cognizance of sacred and other titles not entered there, we can reconstruct the catalog of Aitken's publications during these early years (many of which years saw no other music engraver or publisher at work in America) in Table 1.[12]

It is immediately apparent from the above catalog that, with the exception of the Brown and Hopkinson works, and, of course, the collection which Aitken himself compiled, all of the known music which John Aitken engraved before about 1791 was composed by, arranged by, or printed for Alexander Reinagle. The names of John Aitken and Alexander Reinagle are connected in one way or another with twelve of the fifteen titles which Aitken engraved before 1791 or thereabout. In his *Early Concert Life in America (1731–1800)* (Leipzig, Breitkopf & Härtel, 1907), O. G. T. Sonneck, the dean of American musicologists, observed (p. 80) that "when Alexander Reinagle arrived in Philadelphia in 1786, he immediately, by virtue of his superior talent and individuality, assumed control of the musical affairs of the city." Would it be stretching the point beyond credibility to ask whether he may not have had a similar influence on the publishing of music in Philadelphia in the following year by spurring John Aitken, an advertised silversmith with no known prior connection with music, on to engraving compositions which otherwise would have had to be sent back to Europe for engraving or, if already published, would have had to be obtained from a European source.

Alexander Reinagle was born in Portsmouth, England, in 1756

12. This table includes as its final category a catalog of the treble-clef punches which Aitken employed in engraving each of these works. Its inclusion here, though premature, will facilitate an understanding of Aitken's early publishing when correlated with Table 2 herein shortly.

TABLE 1

Reconstructed Catalog of John Aitken's Early Publications

Title	Composer or Arranger	Sonneck–Upton Dating	Punches On Table 2
		1787	
A selection of the Most Favorite Scots Tunes	A. Reinagle	[1787] (p. 375); advertised August 28, 1787; printed for A. Reinagle	A, C, B
A Compilation of the Litanies and Vespers, Hymns and Anthems, etc.	J. Aitken[13]	1787; imprimatur dated Nov. 28, 1787	B
Three Rondos for the Piano Forte	William Brown	[1787] (p. 361)	C, A
		1788	
A Collection of Favourite Songs, Divided into Two Books	A. Reinagle[14]	[1789?] (p. 69); advertised in *Pennsylvania Packet* of March 17, 1788; printed for A. Reinagle	B
Seven Songs for the Harpsichord	Francis Hopkinson	[1788] (p. 403); dedication dated Nov. 20, 1788; advertised Nov. 29, 1788	B
		1789	
Adieu Thou Dreary Pile	A. Reinagle	[1789] (p. 6); advertised March, 1789; printed for A. Reinagle	B
'Tis Not the Bloom on Damons Cheek	J. Hook	[1789] (p. 212); advertised March, 1789; printed for A. Reinagle	B
Chorus Sung Before Gen Washington	A. Reinagle	[1789] (p. 63); advertised December 29, 1789	D
A Collection of Favorite Songs, Arranged for the Voice and Piano-Forte	A. Reinagle	[1789?] (p. 66)	B, D
[A Collection of Favorite Songs, Arranged for the Voice and Piano-Forte]	A. Reinagle	[1789?] (p. 67)	B, D
I'll Think of Willy Far Away	A. Reinagle	[1789?] (p. 204)	D
Tantivy Mark Forward Huzza	A. Reinagle	[1789?] (p. 422); printed for A. Reinagle	B
Twelve Favorite Pieces	A. Reinagle	[1789?] (p. 439)	B

If Tis Joy to Wound a Lover	J. Hook; arr. by A. Reinagle	[ca. 1789] (p. 204); printed for A. Reinagle	B
Was I a Shepherds Maid	C. Dibdin; arr. by A. Reinagle	[n.d.] (p. 448); "probably published in 1789"; printed for A. Reinagle	B

1790s[15]

A Compilation of the Litanies, Verpers, Hymns, and Anthems, etc.	J. Aitken[16]	1791	E, B
An Anthem for Two Voices	R. Taylor[17]	[1793] (Wolfe, No. 10347)	E
The Flowing Can	C. Dibdin	[ca. 1793] (p. 144)	E
The Scots Musical Museum	J. Aitken	[1797] (p. 370, Wolfe, No. 10170	B, E
The Bastile	Elfort	[179–?] (p. 37); printed for S. Bader	E
The Battle of Prague	Kotzwara	[179–?] (p. 39); printed for A. Reinagle	E

13. The only recorded copy of this work is in the Library Company of Philadelphia. It was reissued in facsimile in 1956 by Musical Americana (Harry Dichter).

14. As noted in H. E. Eberlein and C. V. Hubbard's "Music in the Early Federal Era," *Pennsylvania Magazine of History and Biography* LXXIX (1945) 110, Reinagle advertised this in the *Pennsylvania Packet* of March 17, 1788, as "just published . . . sold by Messers. Rice, Poyntall, Dobson and Young."

15. According to Sonneck–Upton (pp. 376–77), Aitken was also named as engraver of "A set of six sonatas for the pianoforte or harpsichord; and a book of twelve songs, with an accompaniment for the same instrument, composed by Alexander Juhan," a violinist in Philadelphia from 1783. This was advertised for publication by subscription in the *City Gazette* of Charleston, South Carolina, on June 13, 1792. No copies of either of these works are extant, and the subscription may not have been sufficiently realized to allow publication, though Dunlap's *American Advertiser* of April 10, 1793, advertised as "ready for sale at Thomas Dobson and Messrs. H. & P. Rice, A Set of Six Sonatas, composed by Alexander Juhan." As will be shown later, editions of such works were extremely small, and no copies may have survived. See also n. 17 below.

16. Evans, *American Bibliography*, No. 23106, locates a copy in the John Carter Brown Library. This title is entry no. 27 in the *Pennsylvania Registrations for Copyright, 1790–1794*, noted in F. R. Goff's "The First Decade of the Federal Act for Copyright," pp. 101–28.

17. See my "Unrecorded Eighteenth Century Imprints from the Shapiro Music Collection," *Bulletin of The New York Public Library* LXII (1958) 37–38. Aitken also is known to have advertised in the *Pennsylvania Packet* of June 15, 1791, for publishing by subscription the following set of lessons, which apparently never materialized, for no copy is now known to exist:

"New Music.-Six Lessons for the Harpsichord or Piano Forte, will be published periodically, or as soon as a sufficient number of subscribers can be got to defray the expense of engraving the Plate. Each person subscribing one dollar, will be entitled to two Copies of any one Lesson. As those are the first production of American genius that have been offered in the musical line, it is hoped that they will meet with encouragement from the Amateurs of that science in this City. Subscriptions will be received by Mr. Gardette, Dentist, Chesnut street; Mr. Rice, Bookseller, Market street, and Mr. Aitken, silversmith, who is to engrave the plates."

(baptized on April 23) and died in Baltimore on September 21, 1809. (His life span coincided with the birth of Mozart and the death of Haydn.) His parents were of Austrian nationality, and his father and two brothers were musicians. Reinagle studied in Scotland with Raynor Taylor, who later came to the United States and also became a prominent Philadelphia musician. (Another interesting aside is the fact that in 1793 Aitken engraved and published the first of Raynor Taylor's compositions issued in America, his *Anthem for Two Voices*, listed in Table 1.) Despite a shortage of information about Reinagle's European career, it is apparent that he was a respected musician before he had reached the age of twenty-one. He is also known to have been a friend of Karl Philipp Emanuel Bach, with whom he corresponded. Reinagle announced his arrival in the United States through the following advertisement which he inserted in the *New York Packet* of June 12, 1786:

> MR. REINAGLE, Member of the Society of Musicians in London . . . gives lessons in Singing, on the Harpsichord, Piano Forte, and Violin. His terms may be known by enquiring at No. 17 in Little Queen Street, and at Mr. Rivington's. He proposes to supply his Friends and Scholars with the best instruments and music printed in London. . . .

Reinagle apparently landed in New York with the intention of remaining in that city, but by the end of the year he was in Philadelphia, appearing at concerts in the company of Henry Capron, William Brown, and Alexander Juhan, who were prominently connected with the earliest concert life in that city. We need go no further into Reinagle's distinguished career, except to note that for many years he was one of the central figures in the musical life of Philadelphia. His connection with the theater there and in Baltimore was especially productive.

Is there any evidence proving that Alexander Reinagle was responsible for prodding John Aitken into music engraving in mid-1787? Indeed, there is none that can be described as direct or primary. On the other hand, the evidence arising from the circumstances is bountiful, especially when we look at the marks which Aitken's punches left on the extant sheets bearing his name as engraver or publisher. Using treble- and bass-clef signs as guides, we can classify the various sets of punches employed by Aitken to publish music throughout his career in Table 2.[18]

18. As Krummel has pointed out (p. 216ff.) in his article "Graphic Analysis," the treble-clef sign and to a lesser extent the bass-clef sign are the most distinct symbols in the music engraver's kit, the former being the largest and one of the most complex of the musical signs and the one whose variant shapes allow it the least chance of passing unnoticed. Note-heads, Krummel observes, are the most common signs in music, and because of their

TABLE 2
Clef Punches Used by John Aitken

A	B	C	D	E	F	
					1	*2*

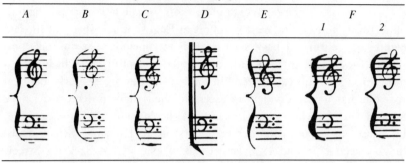

When collating Table 2 against Table 1, which indicates in what specific Aitken engraving the above punches were used, we are struck by one point immediately: in the very first publication which he engraved, and at the very outset of his career as an engraver of music, John Aitken had three sets of punches available to him. In his initial endeavor at engraving music, the *Selection of the Most Favorite Scots Tunes* (Illus. 18), by Alexander Reinagle, Aitken employed set A for punching the initial plates and set C for the concluding ones; set B was used for stamping in occasional clef signs on both. In light of what we shall observe in the next section of this chapter, namely, that some early American engraver–publishers used only one set of punches throughout their entire careers, which sometimes spanned two decades or more (Gottlieb Graupner of Boston falls into this category, as does George Willig of Philadelphia, who in 1820 was using the same style of tools he started business with in 1794), the presence of three sets of punches in the hands of Aitken in 1787 is most curious, and we are intrigued by the question of whence they came. Admittedly, Aitken could have forged and cut them himself, for he was probably capable of this feat, though it is unlikely that he actually accomplished it. More probably, Aitken's first (and later) punches were

small size are hardly distinguishable from one another. Stems, flags, and other symbols, on the other hand, are usually drawn freely and do not appear regularly enough to offer much help in distinguishing tools used in various musical publications. It is mainly on treble- and bass-clef signs that we depend in order to distinguish and identify tools used by given engravers or by an engraver for a particular period of time. In spite of the obvious value of large signs, particularly these two, in identifying engravers of music through their specific tools, the problem is somewhat more complex than Krummel allows. For one thing, engravers undoubtedly mixed sets, employing some tools in one set with those of another. In addition, the variations in the shapes of some sets are often minute, even sometimes with respect to the treble-clef sign. This problem of identification is compounded when one takes into consideration paper shrinkage (usually allowable up to 3 percent), for the paper of this early period had a high rag content, and it was printed damp.

imported from England, quite possibly with the help of Alexander Reinagle. The forms on the punches which Aitken used initially have all the aspects of contemporary English tools. Though I have not had an opportunity to examine vast numbers of English music sheets of the late eighteenth century, I have seen enough to conclude that the tools employed for punching them had very similar signs to those which Aitken used throughout his career. And in some cases they are so nearly identical that one has to use dividers to ascertain their slight differences. I have noticed that punches very similar to Aitken's were used, for example, by Elizabeth Rhames (or her engravers) at 16 Exchange Street, Dublin, between 1776 and 1778, and by B. Cooke, No. 4 Sackville Street, also of Dublin, between 1794 and 1798, to cite but two examples. Admittedly, the foregoing are only conjectures, but, as one competent historian recently observed, speculation may serve as the first step toward verification.[19]

Alexander Reinagle cannot be painted out of the picture with regard to the source of Aitken's first tools. After all, did he not advertise upon his arrival in New York in 1786 that he intended to supply his friends and scholars with music printed in London? He is the most obvious contact for supplying our immigrant silversmith with the necessary implements for commencing his new career. It does not seem at all unreasonable to conclude from Reinagle's advertisement in the *New York Packet* that, before his departure for America, he had arranged with English music sellers for a continuous supply of music to sell and distribute in the New World. Undoubtedly, he must have heard of the dearth of printed music there. Might he not, upon his arrival into Philadelphia, have perceived the possibility of greater profit as well as greater convenience through the local manufacture of music and, as a consequence, sent back to England for the necessary tools instead? The *New York Packet* advertisement of June 12, 1786, indicates that he had established contacts in London. If additional proof of this is needed, however, we need turn no further than to the Aitken edition of William Brown's *Three Rondos for the Piano Forte or Harpsichord*, the third musical publication which Aitken engraved, for we find in the list of subscribers here the names of "Mr. Reinagle" (in Philadelphia) and "Miss Reinagle, in London." By way of summation, we can restate that the combined efforts of Reinagle and Aitken accounted for almost all of our earliest musical publication; that Aitken, who had no known prior contact with music engraving or publishing, became involved

19. R. H. Shryock, "Germ Theories in Medicine Prior to 1870," *Clio Medica* VII (1972) 82.

in these activities concurrent with the arrival of Reinagle into Philadelphia; and, finally (to add a new element), that Raynor Taylor, Reinagle's teacher in England, turned to Aitken for the engraving of his first composition, which he offered to the American public following his arrival into Philadelphia in 1793, at which time there were two other music engravers at work there. One might assume that Taylor would turn to his pupil and friend for assistance in this initial project.

Table 1 exposes another possibility in the Aitken–Reinagle relationship. The eminent music master and the immigrant metalsmith may have had a falling-out about 1793 or shortly thereafter. With but one possible exception, Aitken published no more of Reinagle's compositions after that date nor did he print any music for him. Table 1 shows that the engraving of an edition of Franz Kotzwara's *The Battle of Prague* in the 1790s was the only work Aitken produced in collaboration with Alexander Reinagle after 1790. At first, it seemed possible that the Sonneck–Upton attribution of this publication to "[179–?]" was a bit conservative and, moreover, that Aitken could have engraved it as early as 1789 or 1790. The Sonneck–Upton dating of this edition appears to have been based mainly on the fact that Sonneck could find no evidence of a public performance of the Kotzwara piece before the year 1794, when it was played at Grant's Assembly Room in Philadelphia on November 27. (The fact that it appeared on the program under title alone, with no composer indicated, tends to show that it was popularly known at the time.) Moreover, as we know that *The Battle of Prague* was printed in Europe in 1789, and may have been issued there as early as 1788,[20] it would seem possible that the Aitken edition of this descriptive sonata actually appeared about 1790. However, the marks of the punches which Aitken used to engrave it—the E punches on Table 2—show rather conclusively that he did not undertake it before about 1793.

The rift with Reinagle, if such actually did occur, came possibly in late 1793, for the next known Reinagle compositions bearing American imprints were issued by Benjamin Carr in Philadelphia early in the next year. These were his *La Chasse*, advertised in January, his *Preludes*, advertised in June, and his song *America, Commerce & Freedom*, advertised in October of 1794. Reinagle employed Benjamin Carr, George Willig, and Charles Hupfield, all of Philadelphia, as his publishers before 1801, and Hupfield, Willig, and George E. Blake of Philadelphia, and Joseph

20. The biography of Kotzwara in vol. 3 (p. 46) of the third edition of *Grove's Dictionary of Music and Musicians* (New York, Macmillan, 1952), notes that a copy of John Lee's edition of this piece exists bearing the manuscript date 1788.

Carr of Baltimore after that year, the titles issued by the last-named undoubtedly dating to the period of Reinagle's residence in Baltimore. Between 1801 and 1825, about sixteen Reinagle compositions appeared under American imprints, and a few were issued in England. Only one Reinagle work ever again was published by John Aitken, a reprint edition of the song *The Bleeding Nun*, dating between 1807 and 1811, which title George E. Blake had originally "printed for the author" about 1804.

Nothing has been said heretofore regarding the participation in these earliest Reinagle–Aitken publications of one Thomas Dobson. Yet, in their *Early American Sheet Music*, Dichter and Shapiro denominate Dobson (p. xxvi) as the printer of Reinagle's *A Selection of the Most Favorite Scots Tunes*, (Illus. 18), and the Sonneck–Upton bibliography further treats Dobson as the publisher of this and of most of the other early publications which carry John Aitken's name as engraver. Thomas Dobson was an early bookseller in Philadelphia, being described thus in contemporary directories (from 1785 into the 1820s). There is no evidence to prove or even suggest that Dobson was ever a copperplate printer. Doubtless, he was not the printer of Alexander Reinagle's *Selection of the Most Favorite Scots Tunes*. Furthermore, he actually advertised most of the early Aitken–Reinagle publications as "just published and sold by Thomas Dobson" or "ready for sale at Thomas Dobson's" or in some similar way. These advertisements have been interpreted—incorrectly, I feel—to mean that he was the publisher in such instances. His advertisements only tell us that he was the distributor of these early issues, though I think there is reason for suspecting that he night have had some financial involvement in promoting them. The responsibility for issuing the majority of these earliest pieces of musical Americana rests mainly on the shoulders of Alexander Reinagle, with Aitken serving mostly as engraver and Dobson as distributor, though all three may have had some financial interest in underwriting their production. Only in the case of Francis Hopkinson's *Seven Songs for the Harpsichord or Piano Forte* can we ascribe responsibility for publication directly to Dobson, for it is stated on the title page of this that the work was "published and sold by T. Dobson." Henry and Patrick Rice, Philadelphia booksellers from at least 1785 until about 1805, were likewise involved in some of Aitken's early publications, that is, as sellers and distributors, and they were afterward similarly involved with R. Shaw.

We can conclude our treatment of John Aitken and his earliest productions with a few comments on his music punches. Aitken employed those tools which I have called A, C, and D (designated thus because of the sequence in which they appeared in his initial output) for the issuance of a few titles only. He mainly relied on the B punches for effecting plates before about 1793. About 1793 Aitken was using a new set of tools (E), with which he engraved the Taylor *Anthem* (advertised as published in December 1793), the song *The Flowing Can*, Elfort's *The Bastile*, Kotzwara's *The Battle of Prague*, and the latter half of his own compilation *The Scots Musical Museum*. The last-named did not appear until 1797 and was the last work he published in that decade. With the publication of Aitken's own song *The Goldsmith's Rant* in early 1802 we find Aitken in possession of yet another set of tools. He used this, his last set, to engrave approximately 125 pieces in the 1807–11 period, his most productive from the standpoint of number of works issued. During this time he introduced a more modern bass-clef sign, probably to keep abreast of his competition.

Punches Used by Subsequent Engravers and Publishers

All evidence now available points toward the definite conclusion that the dies or punches used in the earlier phases of American music publishing were obtained from English and European sources, and were not locally manufactured. At some point it undoubtedly became expedient for native engravers to fabricate these instruments and supply them to the trade, and eventually it proved more convenient for American music engravers to obtain their tools from a source right at hand, but this occurred at a somewhat later period. In my discussion of importation as the sole source of all of the earliest instruments, I shall refer to the specific sets of punches which were employed by several of our early musician-engravers, using few selected examples to make the point.

The January 1795 advertisement of William Priest quoted at the beginning of this chapter is the first piece of tangible evidence in proof of this argument. In this advertisement Priest announced that he had obtained from Europe his "compleat apparatus for engraving, printing, and publishing music in the modern stile." Inasmuch as the shape and style of Priest's punches, as shown on the sheets he produced, are undeniably English, and since he had started his American journey from London two years earlier, it seems certain that he must have imported his tools from some agent in that city. Strangely enough, only one music publication bearing Priest's name as engraver and publisher is extant today, his edition of Raynor Taylor's *The President's March*, which must have appeared reasonably soon after the publication of Priest's advertisement of early January 1795 (Illus. 19). Inasmuch as the imprint on this reads "Philadelphia, Engraved and Published by Wm. Priest. Sold also at the Music Stores in the United States. And by Preston and Son, No. 97 Strand London," I think we can deduce that Priest obtained his tools through if not directly from Thomas Preston and Son in London. Judging from the addition of Preston's name on his imprint, Priest probably arranged for the distribution of his music in England when negotiating to procure the necessary apparatus to engrave and publish it.[21]

Another interesting aspect of the tools Priest used to produce the sole publication bearing his name is that they appear to be almost identical to the tools which the Carrs used to engrave their edition of Alexander Reinagle's *America, Commerce and Freedom* at least three months before Priest's printing (before October 1794), their editions of William Shield's *Amidst the Illusions* and *Yankee Doodle . . . Arranged with Variations for the Piano Forte* (also reproduced in Illus. 19) in 1796, and, in fact, all the music they issued throughout the 1790s. The Carrs had engaged in music publishing and selling in London for a number of years before their departure for America in 1793 and 1794, and we would expect that they would transport a stock of English tools with them. The Carrs must have obtained their punching tools from approximately the same source as did William Priest some two years later (and it seems likely that they succeeded to William Priest's own tools upon the latter's departure from Philadelphia around 1796). Joseph Carr, who must have engraved the bulk of the music which his son Benjamin issued from his "Musical Repository" in Philadelphia during the 1790s, employed identical tools to engrave an edition of Francis Linley's *New Assistant for the Piano-Forte or Harpsichord* in London before his departure for America, and he continued to use identical tools during his entire career in Baltimore. On page [38] of Joseph Muller's *The Star Spangled Banner* is reproduced the title page of a 1794 auction catalog (Illus. 20) which tells us that Joseph Carr disposed of much of his musical merchandise, including working tools, before his departure for America. The title here reads:

A Catalog of the Valuable Stock in Trade of Mr. Joseph Carr, of Middle Row,

21. As we shall read in greater detail later on, Frederick Rausch, mentioned previously as a music publisher in New York in the 1790s and as the purchaser of pewter plates for music in 1802, negotiated with Thomas Preston, 97 Strand, London, in 1807 for the engraving and printing of twelve plates for an otherwise unidentified *Russian Air*. The fact that we can associate two of our early music publishers with this London firm suggests that Preston may have developed a connection with the American trade, possibly even acting as a source for the procurement of tools as well as articles of musical merchandise, including even perhaps English editions of music which American publishers had to procure in order to reprint them locally. We shall observe later that Gottlieb Graupner of Boston had a long association with the London firm of Clementi for the supply of English music and musical wares.

Holborn, Music Seller, Quitting Business. Consisting of a Variety of Harpsichords, Grand Piano-Fortes, Organs, Guitars, and Dulcimers, Twisting Machines, and Working Tools; an Assortment of Printed Music, by the best Composers, Copper Plates, &c. Together with the Remaining Household Furniture, Books, an Eight-day Clock, and other Effects, Which Will be Sold By Auction, By Mr. Weale, on the Premises, on Friday, the 14th of February, 1794, Precisely at Twelve o'Clock. To be Viewed on Thursday preceding the Sale. Catalogues may be had on the Premises; at Garraway's Coffee-House; and of Mr. Weale, Sworn Exchange Broker, Castle Street, Holborn.[22]

I have made every attempt to locate a copy of this catalog, both in this country and abroad, but without success. Its present unavailability is unfortunate, for it might tell us much about Carr's tools and perhaps even the names of their manufacturers.

Let us now turn our attention to Boston and look at music punching in the next decade. I discovered some years ago, when sorting through the notable collection of early American sheet music assembled by J. Francis Driscoll of Brookline, Massachusetts, to include his pertinent titles in my *Secular Music in America*, the following deposition which is quoted in full below. This was written out in longhand, possibly in the handwriting of Driscoll himself, and it constitutes a copy of a statement made by one John Weeks Moore, a nineteenth-century commentator on American music. Moore was evidently recording those facts available to him concerning the participation of Gottlieb Graupner in early Boston music publishing and especially his role in the founding of the Handel and Haydn Society of Boston. Moore's exact purpose in committing this data to paper is unknown. At the time of my examination in 1960, Driscoll's music was stored in the basement of a private dwelling in Cambridge and I had no access to photocopying equipment;[23] instead, I typed out a transcription of it. The original is undoubtedly still among Driscoll's files of music, which have since been acquired by the Newberry Library in Chicago:

> Gottlieb Graupner, musician, teacher and publisher went from Germany to England in 1791, and came from London to Boston, Mass., in 1798.

22. Inasmuch as Joseph Carr is known to have been in Baltimore as early as June 1794, he must have embarked for America shortly afterward. If the transatlantic crossing of William Priest in the prior year can be used as a yardstick, Carr must have embarked in March 1794 at the latest in order to enable him to be in Baltimore in early June. Priest sailed from London on July 31, 1793, and landed near Philadelphia the following October 1, his journey lasting about two months.

23. Driscoll's music was packed away in cartons stacked one upon the other, and I frequently struck my head on the beams of the ceiling when pulling these down for inspection of contents. It was a most unsatisfactory working arrangement, but not atypical of conditions I encountered in locating music for inclusion in my *Secular Music in America*.

One Von Hagen is mentioned as the first music printer in Boston. He was a copper plate printer, and with the graver cut out every character—a slow and expensive business. I [J. W. Moore] do not know when Mr. Von Hagen commenced printing, or where he came from; but if he used the graver in making his plates, he may have preceded Mr. Graupner who went into the publishing business because he was unable to obtain in this country a satisfactory supply of such music as he wanted for use.

He [Graupner] printed from pewter plates, the characters being stamped with steel dies, which he procured from England. He was in the business of printing music for twenty-seven years, and performed most of the labor with his own hands.

March 24, 1815, Mr. Graupner, Mr. Webb and Mr. Peabody, issued a call for a meeting, to take into consideration the expedition of forming a musical society in Boston. This meeting took place at Graupner's Hall, Franklin Street, March 30th. 1815, and was attended by sixteen persons, who then and there organized the Handel and Haydn Society. The music used by this society was purchased of Mr. Graupner, at five cents a page, being parts of Haydn's Creation. On Christmas night, 1815, a concert was given, assisted by the "Philo-harmonic Society," which had previously given concerts of instrumental music. Tickets were sold by G. Graupner, Franklin Street. At this concert Mrs. Graupner sang "With verdure clad," and "Let the bright seraphim," etc. Mr. Graupner played the double bass in the orchestra, then, and for many years.

J. W. Moore
Author of Moore's "Encyclopaedia"

Folio—March 1873

In 1852 Oliver Ditson of Boston published John W. Moore's *Complete Encyclopaedia of Music* (this was stereotyped and it went through several reissues) and in 1875 the firm of Oliver Ditson & Co. issued another edition of this work which contained an appendix. Neither the *Encyclopaedia* nor its later appendix contains the foregoing deposition nor any information from it, nor does Moore's *Historical, Biographical and Miscellaneous Gatherings . . . Relative to Printers and Printing* (Concord, N.H., 1886) repeat it or any of its contents. In discussing some of the details of Moore's statement, adding to it where we can, and correcting its few errors and discrepancies (Moore wrote at a time when sources of information were less organized, and in a day when authors frequently had to rely upon failing memories and on hearsay for many of their facts) we can learn quite a bit about the early publishing of music in Boston and about the tools employed for that purpose.

Peter Albrecht von Hagen, frequently referred to as P. A. von Hagen, Sr.,[24] indeed was *not* the first music publisher in Boston, as Moore

24. According to Sonneck–Upton (p. 508) and other sources, Peter Albrecht von Hagen was probably the son of a musician of virtually the same name (see below) who in 1740

reports. This distinction has already been allotted to William Norman, a general copperplate engraver there who cut in a freehand style the *Musical Repertory*, which he began to publish in Boston in 1796, at about the time when the von Hagens were settling in that city. However, to correct another of Moore's inaccuracies, von Hagen *was* the first to issue music in Boston using steel punches, which occurred about May of 1798. Peter Albrecht von Hagen, formerly organist of the principal church and director of the city-concert at Zutphen in Holland, came to Charleston, South Carolina, in 1774 and eventually turned up in New York City, where he and his wife taught music and appeared at concerts before migrating to Boston. Von Hagen had announced in New York in 1793 that he had imported the latest publications of music printed in Europe, and he had also dealt in the sale of general musical merchandise in that city. It is obvious that he was aware from the start of the profit to be made from the sale of music, and it is not surprising that he turned to publishing music upon his removal to Boston, a city which then lacked such a facility altogether. When examining von Hagen's early publications, one is struck immediately with two impressions: the notes and other matter actually appear, at first glance, to have been cut entirely by hand with the graver and, second, the punches or dies used to stamp them—for they actually were stamped and not cut freely by hand—were obviously of Dutch manufacture. The first point here might help explain Moore's statement regarding von Hagen's engraving, though I am inclined to suspect that his source of information confused Norman with the Dutchman. The clef signs from two of the von Hagen publications are reproduced on Table 3 below, along with those of several later Boston music publishers. These signs (A and B), it can be seen, have the distinct appearance of Dutch tools of the period, for I have seen the same sort of punch marks on contemporary sheets issued in Holland. Inasmuch as the inventory of the von Hagen estate makes reference to "Six Packages of Foreign Music originally sent from Amsterdam," it is apparent that von Hagen maintained contact with a supplier of musical merchandise in that city, and it was probably from Amsterdam that he procured the necessary punches in 1797 or 1798. Von Hagen, and afterwards his son, Peter

appeared as a violin virtuoso in Hamburg. The son is said by Burney to have studied in Paris. In 1774 he emigrated to Charleston, South Carolina, where he advertised himself as "P. A. van Hagen, jun., organist and director of the City's Concert in Rotterdam. Lately arrived from London." In 1789, on New York concert programs, he changed the "jun." to "sen." to distinguish himself from his son, who was then beginning his career as a violin virtuoso. Late in 1796, upon their removal to Boston, the family name was changed from *van* to *von* Hagen.

Albertus von Hagen, who succeeded to the family publishing business before the father's death in 1803, employed two different sets of dies during their brief careers as publishers in Boston. (As has already been noted, the younger von Hagen continued issuing music in Boston for only about a year or so following his father's death.) One set, labeled A on Table 3, was used by both the father and son from 1798 to 1802. The B set was employed by the son for the publications he issued in 1802 and 1803. Both are undeniably Dutch in appearance, and their shapes are distinct from the tools of other publishers represented on Table 3. One other fact about the von Hagen's publishing is pertinent here. Several sheets containing their imprint also contain the note that these were sold by George Gilfert in New York. Such sheets that have come to my attention were actually engraved and stamped by Gilfert in New York, for these were executed with the same tools that Gilfert used to effect the plates for the publications which bear his own New York imprint alone. Gilfert and the von Hagens obviously maintained a business relationship, the nature of which is not fully understood at this time. An example of the clef punches which Gilfert employed to accomplish the plates for one such von Hagen–Gilfert imprint is illustrated on Table 3 and again on Table 4.

From the style and appearance of the punches that Gottlieb Graupner used throughout his entire career (D and E on Table 3), which are obviously English in character, we can conclude that Moore's information regarding their origin is correct. Graupner appears to have used no other type of punch (though he may have had several sets of the same face) throughout his entire career in music publishing, which began in 1802 and lasted into the 1820s. Two examples of his clef sign are reproduced on Table 3. Although a few other publishers became active in Boston during the second decade of the nineteenth century (e.g., James Hewitt, who engraved music in Boston with the identical tools he used in New York; Hayts, Babcock & Appleton; the music master George K. Jackson; Francesco Masi; and Samuel Stockwell), Graupner so dominated the field that it was only toward 1820, when he slackened his pace, that others began to gain a toehold there. The stamps of these later publishers are shown on Table 3. Moore's statement that Graupner went into music publishing because he was unable to obtain locally a supply of music for his own use accords with the facts. While the von Hagens were publishing music in Boston at the time when Graupner commenced his own business there, the music they produced or obtained from Europe was of a different character from that which Graupner wanted or needed. In addition, the

TABLE 3
Clef Punches Used by Boston Music Publishers, 1798–1820

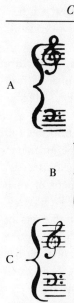

A

From *I never Would be Married*, published by P. A. von Hagen Junior & Cos., No. 62 Newbury Street, Boston, in 1798 or 1799. Also used by P. A. von Hagen, Sr., for engraving earlier publications; Sonneck–Upton, p. 201

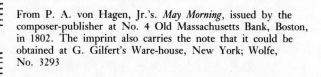

B

From P. A. von Hagen, Jr.'s. *May Morning*, issued by the composer-publisher at No. 4 Old Massachusetts Bank, Boston, in 1802. The imprint also carries the note that it could be obtained at G. Gilfert's Ware-house, New York; Wolfe, No. 3293

C

From James Hook's *Lillies and Roses*, "Printed & sold by P. A. von Hagen Junr. & Co., No. 55 Marlboro Street, Boston, and at G. Gilferts, No. 177 Broadway, New York," in 1799; Sonneck–Upton, p. 230; the plates for this were engraved by Gilfert in New York; see Table 4

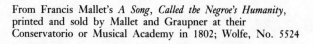

D

From Francis Mallet's *A Song, Called the Negroe's Humanity*, printed and sold by Mallet and Graupner at their Conservatorio or Musical Academy in 1802; Wolfe, No. 5524

E

From Oliver Shaw's *The Hussar's Adieu*, published by G. Graupner, No. 6 Franklin Street, Boston, ca. 1811; Wolfe, No. 7953

F

From Henry R. Bishop's *Oh! Sweet Was the Scene*, published by Simeon Wood, Boston, in 1819; Wolfe, No. 749; see also Appendix A

G

From *Picknickery*, set to the tune of Thomas Augustine Arne's *Sure Such a Day*; published by Samuel Wetherbee in Boston circa 1820; Wolfe, No. 189; another edition was issued by Graupner about that time older von Hagen was apparently ill or dying at the time and the family's publishing activity was being assumed by his son who, on the strength of later evidence, was of an irresolute character and was probably unreliable and uninterested.

The final paragraph of Moore's desposition affords a graphic picture of Gottlieb Graupner. He was the central figure in the early musical life of Boston and the sparkplug which ignited its musical machinery. He was a music publisher in the very best sense of the term.

In addition to the foregoing examples of evidence that the punches and tools used by our earliest engravers and publishers of music emanated from English and European sources, the argument can be buttressed through a few random observations regarding the employment of such tools by other early publishers. In both "Philadelphia Music Engraving" and "Graphic Analysis," Krummel attempts to reconstruct the sets of punches that were used by George E. Blake and George Willig during the first four decades of the nineteenth century; in the latter work, he has provided copious illustrations of the punch faces both men used and I will therefore omit giving examples of their tools here. However, a few remarks are in order.

George E. Blake was undoubtedly the busiest music publisher in America in the heyday of his career. By imitating the latest vogues on the London stage, he was far ahead of his competitors; he was the pacesetter of current tastes and styles with regard to American music publishing of the post-1800 era and, indirectly, of American music itself. Krummel shows that Blake employed at least four different sets of punches between 1803 and 1825. (Eight sets are listed on Blake's 1871 inventory, reproduced in Appendix B, but several of these may have been acquired after 1825.) These instruments are all in the English style, including a set of the black letter font, and I think that we can safely conclude that Blake acquired his tools from London.[25] One wonders, at first, why Blake went to the

25. Krummel states in "Graphic Analysis" (p. 231) that Blake may have succeeded to the tools that were used earlier by the peripatetic R. (Ralph?) Shaw, and in this conclusion he may be correct, for there is a distinct similarity, if not an exact identity, between some of the tools used by these two men. (Of course, it is also possible that they obtained their punches from a common source.) Shaw published music in three cities: Philadelphia (1794–96, and again 1800–1803); Baltimore (1797–1800); and Boston (1807). The punches he used to produce the song *Good Night*, by Dussek, in Baltimore between 1798 and 1800 are different from those later employed to stamp Raynor Taylor's *Moggie, or the Highland Bell*, which he issued in Philadelphia about 1801. (This is listed in Sonneck–Upton on p. 265 with the attribution "[n.d.]" but I have reattributed its publication to the year 1801 [Wolfe, No. 9269].) It is the punch face on this latter sheets which resembles the marks left on early Blake editions. The treble-clef sign here resembles that illustrated by Krummel as the second example of Blake's punches on Plate 1 (p. 221) of his "Graphic Analysis" article.

expense and trouble of acquiring so many tools. His competitor Willig acquired his punches from John Christopher Moller when the latter ceased publishing music in 1794 and later went off to New York,[26] and Willig employed these tools or identical copies of them and no others for engraving all of the music which he published between then and the 1820s. Moller's punches—later Willig's—are European in character; as Moller was born and educated in Germany, it is a reasonable assumption that he obtained these from a German source, in the same way that von Hagen obtained Dutch punches from Amsterdam. The answer to the question regarding Blake's multiplicity of tools is contained in what has already been said about him. In imitating the latest London and European fads, and in attempting to stay abreast of the best that was being done abroad in order to outpace this competition at home, Blake resorted to using a great many punch faces—far more, in fact, than anyone else in America at the time. He tended more toward experimentation and innovation than did his contemporaries, most of whom were content to issue publications of a lesser quality. Blake's sheets were neater and more modern in appearance and stood on a par with some of the best European sheets of his day. He obviously had pride in his product and could rightfully boast of the finest musical publications made in America.

The following few examples illustrate some of the customs of New York publishers with respect to their music punches. James Hewitt employed only two punch faces throughout his entire publishing career. The first he used at the outset of his activity as a music publisher in 1794 or, more likely, 1797, and he continued using it until about 1801. The marks of this same set can be found on Hewitt and Rausch's edition of James Hook's *The Flower of Yarrow* (1797); Hewitt's edition of William Reeve's *The Galley Slave* (1797–99), which contains the imprint "New York, Printed & sold by J. Hewitt at his Musical Repository, No. 131 William Street. Sold also by B. Carr Philadelphia & J. Carr Baltimore"; and even on Benjamin Carr's edition of Kotzwara's *The Battle of Prague* (1798), where the imprint reads "Philadelphia Printed for B. Carr Musical Respository High Street I. Carr Baltimore & I. Hewitt Musical Repository No. 131 William Street New York." The last-noted shows that there was more to the Hewitt–Carr relationship that has previously been realized. Hewitt used his second, more modern punch during the remainder of his New York career, between 1801 and about 1809, and he

26. When Moller recommenced issuing music in 1797 in New York, he was in possession of a new set of punches, which he continued to employ throughout his music-publishing career there, a career which probably lasted to his death in 1803.

obviously carried this set off to Boston when he moved there around 1811, for its shapes appear on the few sheets that he engraved and issued in that city between 1811 and 1817 (see Table 4). Hewitt's second punch, the one he introduced in 1801, also appears on Sarah Territt's edition of *The Battle of the Nile*, dating to the years 1804 or 1805, proving that Hewitt also engraved for other publishers. George Gilfert, who has already been mentioned with regard to some of the von Hagen publications, also used two sets or styles of punches throughout his twenty-year career. The first, which forms example C on Table 4 below, was employed by Gilfert to issue music at 191 Broadway (1794–95), 209 Broadway (1795–96), and 177 Broadway (1796–1801). During the final year of his residence at this last address he introduced a new, more modern punch (ex. D of Table 4), which he continued to use throughout the rest of his career (at No. 13 Maiden Lane) and with which he engraved plates for the von Hagens (see p. 126).

As would be expected, Edward Riley, who exchanged London for the New York scene in 1806, brought up-to-date English punches with him on his westward trek. This is evident from an examination of some of the sheets Riley produced in both cities, that is, before and after his emigration, and he continued to use identical or similar tools throughout the whole of his New York career. Inasmuch as Riley appears to have been an established music publisher before his departure for New York, one wonders what motivated him to move to New York in the first place. Regardless of the reason, his move proved successful, for by 1818 he was assuming leadership in the music-publishing field in that city, a position he maintained and even strengthened up to the time of his untimely death in 1829.

It is evident from the foregoing that a great deal more remains to be learned before our picture of early American music publishing is

TABLE 4
Clef Punches Used by James Hewitt and George Gilfert

James Hewitt		George Gilfert	
A	B	A	B
1794–1801	*1801–9 and later*	*1794–1801*	*1801–14*

anywhere near complete. For one thing, the question of availability—and price—of punches has to be more satisfactorily answered. It appears that punches could be obtained quite easily, for many sets have turned up in the hands of publishers who employed them only infrequently, sometimes for producing a few pieces only. The punches used by these individuals then disappeared, as the men themselves frequently did, and we find no more editions issued with them, even by other publishers. While the business of publishing music in Philadelphia, Baltimore, Boston, and even Charleston remained fairly stable, the trade in these localities being dominated by one or more established publishers, there cropped up time and again publishers who issued only a few publications which were engraved with punches that were not employed before or after by any known contemporaries. In addition, such "occasional" publishers sometimes turned up in the most out-of-the-way locations: Albany, New York; Frankford, Pennsylvania; Norfolk, Virginia; and, strangely enough, even Cooperstown, New York, where in 1826 an unknown engraver named Tracy punched music plates for an unknown publisher named Saxon. This phenomenon of occasional publishing in offbeat locations is all the more interesting in the light of the fact that music publishing had not yet begun to follow music-craving immigrants and migrants on their treks toward the western frontiers. That practice was to occur several decades later.

The Manufacture of Music Punches in America

We have now arrived at the final consideration of the punching tools employed by music engravers and publishers in early America. This phase poses the question when, and by whom, were such instruments first manufactured in America. The weight of evidence introduced before argues against the local manufacture of such implements in the period before about 1825. Admittedly, however, our knowledge of this subject is imperfect, and it is entirely possible that the unexpected and unknown did occur and the opposite held true. Indeed, I shall introduce shortly some facts which will tend to show that the situation could have been otherwise. The music trade was a limited one, restricted probably to a tight little group who kept things pretty much to themselves. We cannot expect to encounter general advertisements relating to the manufacture and sale of such tools. By the same token, early engravers and metal cutters who engaged in the fabrication of such tools would probably have copied English and European examples, and we could not identify native tools today through the shapes they left on extant sheets. In order to attempt to answer the questions posed in this section, I think we have to identify those artisans who would have been likely to fabricate such tools in the event that they actually were manufactured locally within our period.

In the initial section of this chapter we noted the similarity of music punches with instruments employed in a variety of allied trades: typecasting, bookbinding, jewelry making, metalsmithing, medal founding, instrument making, and like occupations. To attempt to answer the question of when and by whom music implements came to be made in America, one has to look at those other occupations and trades and determine who did or was likely to supply them with the necessary tools. In following this trail we find in every instance that the path leads to the door of the engraver on metal and brass, the artisan who advertised in earlier newspaper and trade literature that he made dies and seals; manufactured mathematical, nautical, and scientific instruments; fabricated punching tools for metalsmiths, jewelers, typefounders, bookbinders, saddle makers; and cut ornamental blocks for printers. Sometimes it turns out that a general engraver involved himself in several or perhaps in all of these sidelines in addition to his ordinary and usual industry of cutting plates for printing maps, prints, and in bookwork. From the evidence of early advertisements and the like we know that such artisans existed in colonial America long before a music-publishing trade began to flourish here. These men produced the tools that were used by colonial bookbinders, silver- and other metalsmiths, and natural philosophers, as well as by those who coined money, decorated saddles, and performed similar jobs. The invaluable cumulations of early advertisements brought together by Prime for Philadelphia, Maryland, and South Carolina, by Dow for New England, and by Gottesman for New York, as well as other sources, prove the presence of such artisans in America from the early eighteenth century on, and their numbers increased as the century progressed. In addition, their ranks were swelled through immigration after the close of the Revolutionary War.

With regard to bookbinding, for example, a case directly in point is provided by Hannah D. French in her essay "Early American Bookbinding by Hand, 1636–1820," where she reprints the following pertinent announcement from the *Pennsylvania Chronicle* of April 18, 1768: "James Smither, Engraver, At the first House in Third Street, from the Cross Keys, Corner of Chestnut-Street, Philadelphia, Performs all Manner of Engraving in Gold, Silver, Copper, Steel, and all other Metals—Coats of Arms, and Seals, done in the neatest Manner. Likewise cuts Stamps, Brands all metal cuts for Printers, and ornamental Tools for Bookbinders.

He also ornaments Guns and Pistols, both engraving and inlaying Silver, at the most Reasonable Rates."[27] She additionally notes that this was the very year that the silversmith and lapidary, Abel Buell of Killingworth, Connecticut, was making his first experiments in cutting and casting type.

Admittedly, Smithers could probably have cut music punches if the demand for them had existed at the time, as could any number of engravers before and after him.[28] Earlier in this work I discoursed briefly on the role of the silversmith as music engraver, pointing out that it was mainly this artisan who cut in a freehand manner the plates which were utilized for printing up the occasional books of sacred music that were published in America throughout the eighteenth century. Several of these men could have eased their burdens by fabricating and employing punches to facilitate such tasks, especially those men who produced plates for a number of music books. The fact that they did not resort to this aid shows once more that music publishing was only an occasional industry in the American colonies and that demand for a large and continuing supply of music did not exist before the post-Revolutionary period. Importation met the majority of requirements. Large and continuing demand had to await the blossoming of interest in music and the theater by increasing groups of amateurs, and the influx of professional musicians and actors fanned the smoldering embers of musical interest into a burning flame. With the influx of professionals and the concurrent establishment of the music-publishing trade, one might assume that local engravers and die makers would rush in to fill the tool requirements of this new-found industry, once it had implanted itself solidly and had begun to grow.

I think the following observations will show why this situation did not occur. First of all, it was probably cheaper to procure English and European punches from abroad, in spite of the inconvenience and uncertainty of transport at that time, than to have them fabricated locally. The fact that musical merchandise was shipped to America in great

27. In Helmut Lehmann-Haupt, ed., *Bookbinding in America* (Portland, Me., Southworth–Anthoensen Press, 1941), p. 28.

28. Actually, an advertisement for the manufacture of bookbinders' and printers' stamps was published by James Turner, an engraver working in Boston, as early as 1743. Turner's notice, which was quoted by Stauffer in his *American Engravers upon Copper and Steel* (pt. l, p. 278) and was recently requoted by Sinclair Hitchings in his article "Graphic Arts in Colonial New England" (p. 88), appeared in the *Boston Evening Post* in the fall of 1743 and stated that he "Engraves all sorts of Copper Plates for the Rolling Press, all sorts of stamps in Brass or Pewter for the Common Printing Press, Coats of Arms, Crests, Syphers, &c., on Gold, Silver, Steel, Copper, Brass, or Pewter. He likewise makes Watch Faces, makes and cuts Seals in Gold, Silver, or Steel: or makes Steel Faces for Seals, and sets them handsomely in Gold or Silver. He cuts all sorts of Steel Stamps, Brass Rolls and Stamps for Sadlers and Bookbinders, and does all sorts of work in Gold and Silver."

quantity and the fact that so many sets of tools appeared in America during the first years of music publishing here are indicative of this. At the same time, it can be concluded from the literature dealing with early American typefounding, a field that required similar tools, that this industry was late in gaining a toehold in this country because of the difficulty in making these tools locally. This suggests that the task of cutting the necessary punches or patrices for stamping the blanks or matrices from which type was cast was not so simple a matter as we might suppose. However, typefounding began to take a firm hold in America after 1800, and as I have noticed the presence of at least fifty individuals at work in some aspect of typefounding in Philadelphia between then and 1820 (based on the evidence of local directories), it is apparent that engravers were present then who not only cut the punches for these artisans but who would have been capable of supplying stamps and dies to the music engravers and publishers concurrently. Indeed, the Browns' *Directory of the Book-Arts . . . in Philadelphia to 1820* lists at least fifteen artisans at work in Philadelphia during this period identified as brassfounders, diesinkers, letter cutters, mathematical-instrument makers, stone and seal engravers, makers of brass ornaments for bookbinding, and the like. At least one of these not only qualified for the task of engraving music punches but may have engaged in this undertaking.

The name of Daniel H. Mason was mentioned earlier as an engraver of music in Philadelphia in the period after 1805, at least he can be found thus described in the Browns' directory (p. 82). However, as it was also noted, his name cannot be associated with any of the music published there at this time. Inasmuch as Mason was likewise carried in contemporary directories as an engraver on brass, and as he was connected in business and was probably related to Alva and William Mason, who also appear in contemporary directories with the designations "engravers of brass ornaments for bookbinding, charter and patent medicine seals, embossing plates, and brass engraving for typographical printing," it seems more likely that Daniel H. Mason's energies were directed toward the engraving of instruments for stamping music plates rather than to the actual working of them. And the other two Masons may have also engaged in this pursuit. (The advertisement of one of the Masons appears in Illus. 21.) Daniel H. Mason's name is continued in Philadelphia directories through the year 1837. My efforts to uncover tangible facts about him, or to locate his will, have met with no success. Illustration 22 shows an advertisement of the firm of Gaskill & Copper, which carried on the business of engraving tools for bookbinders from about 1837 until about 1859. I discovered this advertisement in the front of a bound collection of sheet music some years ago (though unfortunately I left its location unrecorded). And while it may have little application to the study at hand, it nonetheless shows in a graphic way the existence of another likely candidate for the fabrication of music punches in Philadelphia at a slightly later date.

Inasmuch as so many sets of punches appear to have been present in America during even the earliest phases of music publishing here, we wonder who engaged in the fabrication of these tools abroad, particularly for the English trade. Who, in fact, did supply English typefounders, bookbinders, and the like with their necessary punching and stamping tools? In attempting to answer this question I turned up the name of one engraver who made punches for bookbinders. Thomas Bewick is famous in English engraving lore. He not only raised the art of engraving on wood to the esteemed status that it achieved in the late eighteenth and early nineteenth centuries, but he produced some of the most notable plate books in the realm of English natural history. During the last seven years of his life Bewick worked on the compilation of his *Memoir*, which was published posthumously in 1828. In recounting here his early experiences as an apprentice to the Newcastle engraver Ralph Beilby, who had served his own apprenticeship as a diesinker, or seal engraver, in Birmingham, Bewick stated that Beilby refused no type of work. In addition to undertaking the coarsest kind of steel stamps, pipe molds, bottle molds, brass clockfaces, door plates, coffin plates, bookbinders' letters and stamps, steel, silver, and gold seals, mourning rings, and the like, Beilby also undertook the engraving of coats of arms, crests, and ciphers, on silver, and every kind of job from the silversmiths; also the engraving of bills of exchange, bank notes, invoices, account heads and cards. This readiness to undertake all tasks brought Beilby an overflow of work. Bewick commenced his apprenticeship with Beilby by polishing copper-plates and hardening and polishing steel seals; he later etched sword blades, cut outside and inside motto rings, and sometimes arms and crests on silver and seals of various kinds, for which he made all the new steel punches and letters. Bewick also recalled cutting bookbinders' stamps, and later on he cut the steel punches used by cast a font of type for a printer named Thomas Spence (his master Beilby actually struck them on the matrices for casting the type). While Bewick makes no mention of music punches, his memoir gives some of the flavor of the life of an engraver of this period and suggests how, in following a jack-of-all-trades existence in order to eke out his living, an early engraver could have included the cutting of music punches in the ordinary pursuit of this goal.

Further investigation turned up the name of an engraver who actually did cut music punches for the English publishing trade. In his biography, *John Bell, 1745–1831*, Stanley Morison reproduced the trade card of Richard Austin, an expert engraver who cut the punches for the fonts which Bell's foundry produced.[29] Austin is said by Morison to have brought to English typefounding an exceptional technical gift. He cut punches for other typefounders, including Vincent Figgins, during his long and fruitful career, which extended from about 1787 until 1830. Austin's trade card (Illus. 23a), which dates to the year 1787, states, in a neat copperplate hand, that he undertook a variety of jobs. It seems likely, on reflection, that a few engravers such as Austin and their apprentices probably sufficed to supply the English trade, and possibly the early American music-publishing trade also, with their necessary punches. (If the latter did occur, one can imagine that the opening up of the American trade from the 1790s on must have resulted in a spate of business for a number of foreign artisans.) In addition, music engravers are accustomed to accumulating and handing down sets of punches to succeeding engravers, and it is likely that there existed a "pool" of such devices upon which our early engravers and publishers could have drawn. In discussing the decline of the engraver's artistry, as compared with esthetic values of an earlier time, Ross in *The Art of Music Engraving* has this to say:

> The engraver's artistry of the 16th and 17th centuries has since been replaced, to a great extent, by the commercially oriented craft of the plate puncher, who, careless of the aesthetic value of his music characters, buys tools—not custom-made—but sight-unseen (one would imagine that the plate engraver would desire distinctive workmanship). Having to use so many different tools, each of which produces a different effect, the engraver often has difficulty recognizing his own work. Actually, the fault lies not entirely with the engraver, himself, for the scarcity of tool-makers has caused him a great imposition that is unlikely to be eased in the future. Younger engravers have little choice but to buy old tools from retired engravers.[30]

There actually does exist evidence attesting to the manufacture of music punches in America during the nineteenth century, although all proofs so far postdate by some decades the period under discussion. The earliest actual evidence comes in the form of a trade card of William H. Bridgens

29. P. [157].
30. P. 13.

of New York City (Illus. 23b), which dates from 1838 at the earliest and, more likely, to the period after 1850. This trade card shows that Bridgens, in addition to fabricating the necessary punches for music engraving, also undertook the other types of work so familiarly associated with the diesinker's and metal cutter's craft.

Bridgens was initially indexed in New York City directories in the issue for 1838–39, where he was located at 184 William Street and described as a diesinker. His removal to 189 William Street occurred in 1849. He was variously described in subsequent directories as a stamp cutter, engraver, or diesinker. Bridgens maintained his place of business at 189 William Street until about 1867, when he moved to 194. The above-cited card was probably printed for him either upon his move to No. 184 William Street in 1849 or to No. 189 about 1867, when he wished to inform customers of his new location. Bridgens was probably not the first in America to undertake the manufacture of music engraver's tools. It seems reasonable to conclude that he was trained by another in the craft of cutting music punches and in this sense was part of a continuing tradition. If more could be learned about his earlier life and his training, we might be able to antedate the fabrication of music-punching tools in America by some years or decades before 1838. Because Bridgens saw fit to include this article among his advertised skills, we can conclude that he was expert in the making of these instruments by about 1849 and that there existed at this time a large enough music-engraving and publishing trade to warrant such advertising.

Several additional proofs of the manufacture of music-engraver's tools in America in the later nineteenth century come in the form of extant stamps, which are owned by current engravers and sometimes still used by them. In 1962 I paid visits to several modern music-engraving establishments to gather material for this work. In one, the MV Music Engraving Company of Jersey City,[31] I was shown a set of steel punches which carried the name and address of F. Brunner, 108 Fulton Street and 65 Ann Street, on the shanks of the individual pieces. Mr. Frank Cappiello, then one of the proprietors of the firm, informed me that these were the oldest punches in his establishment and that they were said to predate the founding of the company (ca. 1900) by several decades. In checking through New York City directories over a span of years, I found Francis Brunner first entered in the issue for 1868–69, where he was described as a diesinker. Brunner was listed in directories through the

31. Attempts to renew contact with this firm in 1973 proved unsuccessful: it had either ceased business or moved.

issue for 1897–98 under several designations (diesinker, engraver, and plater) and at a variety of addresses. There was no lisiting for him at the address 108 Fulton Street, which appeared on a number of punches in the MV set. However, the address 65 Ann Street, which was stamped into other pieces, was shown by directories to have been his place of business in 1883–84 (with his home indicated as Westfield, New Jersey). This establishes the manufacture of at least some of these tools to those years. Again, it is probable that Brunner made music punches earlier in his career and that he was part of a continuing industry in this regard. The MV Music Engraving Company also owned other but later punches of American manufacture, some carrying the firm name of Dodge and Power, Boston, and a wooden rack for containing punches having the address of M. McNamara & S[on], 85 East 10th Street, New York.

Mr. Cappiello also showed me an old graver which, like the punches referred to above, was then in constant use. On the shank here appeared the name of Ezra F. Bowman & Co., Lancaster, Pa., Pat. Mar. 12, 1889. (The tool could have been made later.) Mr. Cappiello supplied me with the following facts regarding the instruments of his trade, most of them gained through the daily exercise or handed down through oral transmission. Today, punches are made only in Germany, as only German steel can withstand the constant hammering without breaking down. (American steel is too brittle in this regard.) While German tools were known to be the best, it was said that for most artistic forms English tools could not be surpassed. The MV Music Engraving Company had hundreds of sets of punches, accumulated throughout its seventy-year existence. Each of these was contained in its own rack, with point sizes corresponding to the size of printing types: 14-point roman, 12-point italic, etc. Each set has upper- and lower-case letters, plus the usual punctuation marks.

Another profitable contact with an active music engraver came in the summer of 1973, when I visited Mr. Walter Bolke in Hillsdale, New York. Throughout his lengthy career Mr. Bolke had acquired or inherited from retiring engravers a great many sets of punches, among which were some older pieces of American manufacture. One of these carried the name of F. Brunner at 78 Fulton Street, New York (Brunner worked at that address from about 1872 until about 1884) and another the name of H. Hatch, 15 Cornhill, Boston. In checking through Boston directories I found Hosea Hatch first listed as a "stencil cutter" in the number for 1868. His name continued to be listed in directories, mostly with the description "letter cutter," through 1891, and the issue for 1892 noted that he had died on November 3, 1891. Hatch moved his place of business every few years, and I found him listed at 15 Cornhill in 1886 only. Another punch in the Bolke collection carried the name of M. McNamara & S[on], 85 East 10th Street, New York, whose name has previously been mentioned as appearing on a wooden rack owned in 1962 by the MV Music Engraving Company. Mr. Bolke turned over to me several dozen of these old American punches, and I have reproduced a number of them as Illustrations 15 and 16 here, the latter showing enlargements of the makers' marks, which have been whited in to emphasize them.

Based upon available evidence, then, it appears that the punches used in America during the earliest phases of music publishing here were brought in from abroad. John Aitken's tools, for instance, probably originated in England and may have been obtained for him by Alexander Reinagle. Though Aitken theoretically was capable of making his own stamping tools, this alternative seems unlikely; it is more plausible to conclude that this backward metalsmith entered music engraving and publishing in 1786–87, or was directed into it then, not because it would have been possible for him to fabricate the all-important punches, but because his previous experience in working metals had given him the knowledge of how to handle them. Tools used by succeeding engravers—Moller, Hewitt, Gilfert, von Hagen, Graupner, the Carrs, and the rest—were imported also. Sometime in the nineteenth century, and available evidence suggests the fourth or fifth decade, native engravers and die cutters began to produce these implements for the home trade. The fabrication of music punches in America could have occurred earlier in the century. Daniel H. Mason has been mentioned as one possible maker of such implements in the initial decades of the century, but his real role in music engraving remains unsubstantiated at the present time. Punches must have accumulated, as sets were handed down from one generation of engravers to the next. In addition, we know for sure that other sets of punches continued to be imported even after American artisans had begun to produce them, for older sets abounded in 1962 and 1973, when I visited the MV Music Engraving Company and Mr. Bolke.

Our knowledge of American music punches, their history, and their makers is rudimentary at best. It is hoped that information provided on music-engraving tools here constitutes only the first steps in our progression toward greater knowledge of this area, for these tools relate in an important way to a number of collateral bibliographical fields, such as typefounding, bookbinding, and engraving. For example, the first American edition of Abraham Rees's *New Encyclopaedia; or, Universal*

[139]

Dictionary of Arts and Sciences, issued by Samuel F. Bradford at Philadelphia about 1816, contains as Plate XVI (vol. 27, pt. I), an example of a page of music and counterpoint. The music here, produced by the punching process, is contained on one side of a single sheet, at the bottom of which appears the name of its engraver, "Rich. Fairman, Sc." Richard Fairman was carried in Philadelphia directories for 1812 and from 1820 as "engraver." No information connecting him to the engraving of music has previously been known. His work here constitutes an example of a type of artisan who worked in the shadowy background of music publishing in early America. We might speculate that Fairman perhaps engraved for Blake or Willig, for his workmanship on the Rees plate was professional. This is the only occurrance of the use of these punches that has come to my notice. One would tend to think, however, that Fairman would have put them to other uses.

CHAPTER VIII

Ink and Paper

✳✳

T HE NEXT TWO articles necessary to the production of music, ink and paper, are common to all types of printing. Indeed, the need for these materials by general letterpress printers existed long before a separate and continuous music-producing trade flourished. This holds true for Europe as well as for America. In his book *The Colonial Printer*, Wroth discusses the manufacture and use of these commodities with regard to our early printing trade. Dard Hunter has provided additional information on the early manufacture of paper in this country, and several other sources treat both of ink and paper in early American printing. Because of the existence of this literature, I shall restrict my remarks on ink and paper here to those aspects which can be identified with the printing of music in this country, particularly in the period after 1787 when John Aitken began stamping plates and issuing music on a continuous basis in Philadelphia.

INK

Of all the materials employed in early American music printing, ink presents us with our greatest enigma. For although it was by for the easiest commodity to manufacture, both from the standpoint of method and materials, and the one having, along with paper, the widest application to the printing trades in general, we possess the least information with regard to its origin, its composition, and its used by our early music printers, even, for that matter, in the more general process of copperplate printing. The fact that it was so simple and common a product has contributed to a lack of documentation on it. In the absence of a detailed literature, then, we are again forced to rely on scraps of information gleaned from multiple sources to reconstruct the probable nature and use of this commodity in our early music-printing trade. We have already seen that the ink used in music printing and in general copperplate printing differed from that employed by the typographic trade in that it had to be thicker and more cohesive than ordinary printing ink. This consistency was required so that the ink would not run out of the engraved hatches and punched areas of the plate being readied for printing. Our knowledge of the nature and use of the ink employed in the printing of engraved plates is derived mainly from contemporary recipes used by the early copperplate-printing trade and from formulas employed in music publishing in later periods and even today. Information on its early makers and on suppliers of ingredients for it is supplied mostly by contemporary advertisements. These sources allow us to determine the probable nature of the ink used in early American music printing, indicate how it was probably made, and identify some of its makers or the suppliers of its components. While such evidence is sometimes circumstantial and speculative, I think it is sufficiently strong to provide us with an accurate picture of the situation as it must have existed within the period under study.

According to the literature of the day, the ink best suited to copperplate printing, and the one most widely used for it throughout the eighteenth century and well into the next, consisted of a mixture of a drying agent, such as nut oil, linseed oil, or, infrequently, suet oil, together with a carbonaceous substance usually referred to as "Frankfort black." Nut oil was extracted from almonds or walnuts and linseed oil from flaxseed, by means of a press; suet oil was derived from animal matter through heating. The blacking agent was a charred organic substance first manufactured at Frankfort-am-Main from vine twigs, or the lees or dregs of wine, or from an amalgam of peach and apricot stones, the bones of sheep, and ivory, all burned together. When the last-named ingredient was used, the compound was usually referred to as "ivory black." The use of Frankfort black yielded the very best ink known to copperplate printers. Ink of a somewhat inferior quality could be obtained by substitution lampblack (i.e., soot) in its stead.

The eighteenth-century inkmaker, or engraver, or copperplate printer —whichever of these actually compounded this product—prepared his ink in about the following way. He first measured out a quantity of oil, the principal ingredient of the ink, and poured it into an iron cauldron or pot until it filled about two-thirds of the receptacle. He next covered it and placed it over a fire, heating it until it came to a boil and stirring it the while to prevent it from boiling over. Then he removed the cover and allowed the oil to catch fire. If this did not occur spontaneously, he kindled it with a flaming paper. After the preparation had taken flame, he removed it from the fire and placed it in a corner of the chimney or in a similar place of safety and allowed it to burn for about half an hour more, again stirring it from time to time. When the preparation had burned sufficiently, its maker extinguished the flame by placing the cover back on the pot or, if this had no effect, by smothering it with a wet cloth.

He next prepared a stronger oil in about the same manner as before, though in this case he did not extinguish the flame after half an hour but allowed the preparation to continue burining until it had become thick and glutinous. He tested its consistency from time to time by drawing off samples. If, when these had cooled, they were found to be adhesive and ropy so that they could be pulled out into long threads, the oil was considered sufficiently burned and the flame was extinguished. Having prepared his oils, the inkmaker then took a quantity of the blacking stuff and ground it with a muller on an inkstone, adding only so much of the weak oil as was necessary to allow it to be worked with ease. When these had been thoroughly commingled and the mixture ground a second time, the maker then added a quantity of the stronger oil to it, mixing this until it achieved a thick, pasty consistency. The ink was then ready for use and was stored in a receptacle or ink vessel and covered. That Frankfort black and linseed oil were probably the principal constituents of the ink used for printing copperplates in America throughout the first part of the nineteenth century is evinced by three pre-1850 texts dealing with contemporary trades and occupations, all of which mention them as the basic ingredients: the *Book of Trades* (White-Hall, Pennsylvania, 1807, though this was admittedly reprinted from an earlier English edition); Edward Hazen's *The Panorama of Professions and Trades, or Everyman's Book* (Philadelphia, U. Hunt, 1836);[1] and Jacob Bigelow's *The Useful Arts* (Boston, 1840).

A formula for making the ink used in British music printing in the 1830s is recited in *A Day at a a Music Publishers.* This formula consisted of boiling linseed oil or nut oil in an iron cauldron and mixing it with a proper amount of lampblack. These were then ground together on a stone until

1. Hazen states (p. 173) that "the ink used for this kind of printing [copperplate printing] is made of a carbonaceous substance, called Frankfort black, and linseed or nut oil."

they attained the consistency of a thick paste, a drier being added during the process. The drier, which acted to make the ink set firmly on the paper, was compounded from small portions of litharge (a substance obtained by heating lead), white copperas (ferrous sulphate), and sugar of lead. The British music publisher of William Gamble's day (1923) likewise employed lampblack as his coloring agent, mixing with it "weak" and "strong copperplate oils" (otherwise unidentified, but consisting probably of linseed oil prepared in approximately the same ways as described before), these being ground together on an inkstone which was usually an old or worn-out litographic stone.[2]

It was undoubtedly a requirement in the training of every copperplate engraver and printer that he learn one or more methods for making the ink so necessary to the copperplate printing process. It was probably the custom of early engravers and especially copperplate printers—indeed, just as it was with their brethren who engaged in general typographic work—to mix up their own supplies of ink according to age-old formulas, imparted probably from generation to generation by word of mouth and through practical demonstration during the apprenticeship period. This custom no doubt prevailed from the time of the introduction of engraving and copperplate printing into the American colonies in about the year 1690, when John Coney of Massachusetts first engraved copperplates for the printing of paper money,[3] until well into the next century and perhaps thoughout most of it. During these early times the necessary oils and pigments were probably imported from English and European sources.

From about the middle of the eighteenth century on, however, there was a succession of attempts to make ink and its ingredients locally. While these ventures appear, for the most part, to have been confined to making the stuff needed for general letterpress printing, the materials used and produced could easily have been adapted to the needs and demands of copperplate printing. Wroth's investigations in this vein have shown that flaxseed was grown here and oil extraced from it for the purpose of making ink as early as 1742 and that lampblack had been made locally even before that date. Further attestation to the early manufacture of ink in America is provided by the following advertisement, which appeared in *The New-York Gazette or the Weekly Post-Boy* of September 12, 1765: "Best black and red ink, made and sold by James Watts, Book-Binder, on Rotton-Row. The Red is made of the Best Brasiletto, Gum Arabick, &c., and the black of

---

2. Gamble, *Music Engraving and Printing*, pp. 155–56.
3. For details see Richard B. Holman's "Seventeenth-century American Prints," in *Prints in and of America to 1850*, pp. 47–48.

the best Aleppo Nut Galls, Gum Arabick, &c., esteem'd by Experience. Much better than any made of the best Ink Powder; Vials to be had from 1s.6d. to 6d. Those that find Bottles preferable at 3s per Quart. And smaller quantities in Proportion." While it can be argued that Watts's advertisement refers to everyday writing ink, the fact that he was a bookbinder suggests that he might have manufactured inks for the printing trades as well. While Watts's involvement in inkmaking may have been short-lived, Wroth has pointed out that in 1792, five or six years after John Aitken had punched his first music plate and within a year of the arrival of John Christopher Moller and the Carrs and the real beginning of music publishing in the United States, Justus Fox, printer, engraver, typefounder, and inkmaker of Germantown, Pennsylvania, began to specialize in selling ready-mixed ink, not just components of it, to Matthew Carey of Philadelphia and to other printers of the middle colonies.[4]

It seems fairly certain from the evidence at hand that our early music publishers, or the copperplate printers employed by them to print music, had little difficulty obtaining the ingredients needed for making their special preparations. Those who employed lampblack as their coloring agent could obtain it from a local manufacturer together with the necessary oils. Frankfort black or ivory black were probably procured through an importer in the period before 1800, and possibly for some time afterwards—for we are informed by the *Book of Trades*, which was initially published before 1800 and was republished near Philadelphia in 1807, that "the best ink used in this business [copperplate printing] comes from Frankfort on the Maine, and it goes by the name of Frankfort black. It comes over in cakes, and is ground by the printer with a muller on an ink stone." But we learn from the following advertisement, which appeared in the Philadelphia *Aurora General Advertiser* of February 12, 1813, that this substance was manufactured locally from about that time:

Printers's Ink
Frankford and Ivory Black
Cakes and Liquid Blacking
Salts of Lemon and
Hartshorn
Made and sold at
American Paint Manufactory

4. Wroth devotes Chapter 6 of *The Colonial Printer* to the subject of printing ink. The following pertinent advertisement appeared in the *New York Daily Advertiser* of April 16, 1794, "Printers ink Manufactured and sold by Jacob Fee, No, 1 Magazine-street, near the Tea-water Pump, New York."

Fetter Lane, between Arch and
Race, N. Third St.
by
Edward Mott

According to local directories, Mott continued in the paint- and ink-manufacturing business for some decades afterwards. The fact that he not only manufactured Frankfort and ivory black but saw fit to advertise these commodities amoung his many products suggests that there existed a considerable demand for them. And while we know of no corresponding manufacturer of Frankfort and ivory black or of copperplate-printing ink in New York at that time or in other American cities where copperplate printing was carried on, we do know that by 1818, at least, there existed in New York City a large "Printers' Warehouse" and two paint manufactories, so it is likely that ready-made ink or prepared ingredients for it could be easily obtained by that date.[5] The earliest reference to the availability of Frankfort black in New York that has come to my attention appeared in *Mercien's City Directory, New-York Register and Almanac* for 1820–21 (published in June 1820), where an engraver and copperplate printer named John Ridley, who began working there in 1817, in advertising his services and wares for sale (p. 104), concluded his statement with the note, "*For Sale*, Frankfort Black, of a superior quality, Wholesale and Retail."

Information on the ink used in general engraving during the period under consideration can be gleaned from the "Memorandum and Day Book" of John Hill (1770–1850), which is preserved in the manuscript collection of the New-York Historical Society. This document lists some of Hill's expenses and receipts, among other miscellaneous entries, for work which he did on the *Hudson River Portfolio* between 1820 and 1834. (This consisted of a series of views on the Hudson, which Hill aquatinted after paintings by W. G. Wall.) Occasional entries in the early 1820s here refer to the purchase of pints, quarts, and gallons of boiled oil and to quantities of "mott's best black," Mott probably being the Edward Mott of Philadelphia whose advertisement for the sale of Frankfort and ivory black

5. C. S. Van Winkle's *Printer's Guide* (New York, 1818), the source of this information, tells us that ink was manufactured in New York at this time by Messrs. Roger Prout at the Phoenix Ink Manufactory, 63 Spring Street, and George Mather, Green, near Prince Street. According to Van Winkle (pp. 223–25), "both makers of ink boasted several years devotion to the manufacture of ink exclusively and Prout, in addition, went on to say that he had erected at considerable expense a large building of brick with seven apartments, three of which are for fires and boilers, two for making color and two stock, for the machines that are worked by horse power." The advertisement of J. Hoit, proprietor of the Printer's Warehouse, 32 Burling Slip, which appeared in the same volume, stated that he had for sale "Printing Ink, from the factories of Mather and Prout, New York, and Johnson, Philadelphia, and John I. Wells, Hartford, of various qualities."

has been quoted before. (There is good reason to suspect from this reference that Mott produced the best copperplate-printing inks and ingredients at that time and that he may have been the main supplier to the American trade.) Other entries, which relate to the pulling and sale of prints, indicate that Hill used a screw or bookbinder's press (with blankets) for pulling proofs and apparently even for producing prints which he sold.

Even after a continuing manufacture of ready-made copperplate-printing ink had begun in America it is likely that some engravers and printers continued to mix their own concoctions according to favored recipes, buying the necessary ingredients at hand. Indeed, this practice carried into William Gamble's time, for he tells us in his *Music Engraving and Printing* (p. 155) that "the ink may be purchased ready for use, but some engravers prefer to make their own." On the 1871 inventory of the estate of George E. Blake (see Appendix B herein) is mentioned a "Lot of Printer's Black," which suggests that Blake may have used lampblack for his coloring agent as well as preparing his own inks. Mr. Frank Cappiello, proprietor of the MV Music Engraving Company of Jersey City, informed me in 1962 that only rough proofs are pulled on the old iron rolling press in the back of his establishment. When a given job has been completed, the plates are sent out to a copperplate printer who pulls the final proofs from which photographs and eventually photolithographic plates are made for printing up the edition. Mr. Cappiello told me that this was done because of the special quality of ink that is needed for this procedure, the nature of which is apparently kept secret by printers specializing in this work.

PAPER

Evidence afforted by watermarks on contemporary sheets indicates that a very substantial portion of the music and song sheets issued during the earliest years of formal music publishing in America—roughly from about 1787 into the first few years of the nineteenth century was printed on foreign paper. The printers and publishers who required supplies of oversize and fine papers for copperplate work then were apparently more dependent upon import than were their brethren who engaged in the general letterpress printing trade. This situation also held true for music paper in general. Jan LaRue, who has recorded watermarks in music manuscripts preserved in the Moravian Archives in Winston-Salem, North Carolina, has concluded that "up to about 1800, American composers and copyists wrote mainly on imported paper largely Dutch and British, with some Italian papers such as those bearing the MASSO watermark, and German papers (particularly GIERSDORF) in the Moravian collection."[6]

In view of the fact that Isaiah Thomas's census of paper mills in 1810, compiled for and published in his *History of Printing*, placed the number of these establishments at 195, we tend to look upon the American papermaking industry as well developed not only at that time but for many years before that date. However, marks molded into many of our early music sheets and the appearance of the sheets themselves tend to reinforce the observations of a number of bibliographers who have pointed out that shortages of paper existed in the seaboard states, where most printing was centered, following the Revolutionary War and into the first decade of the nineteenth century. This situation is further supported by the evidence of contemporary advertisements for the sale of paper and by similar evidence. However, these same sources likewise show that the American papermaking industry made rapid strides in the period immediately after 1800 and by about 1810 (when Thomas undertook his census) was capable of supplying nearly all the paper needed, not only for the printing of books and newspapers but for copperplate printing and music printing as well. Such shortages as existed after this time were restricted mostly to frontier settlements.

In the course of compiling my *Secular Music in America*, I not only examined tens of thousands of American music sheets published between 1787 and the 1830s, but I recorded every watermark molded in them and further noted on what publications these were found. All such marks are reproduced in Appendix C herein. I shall draw upon these revealing designs to illustrate not only the early dependence upon importation for much of the paper used in American music printing through about 1800 (and to prove the contrary situation in the period after about 1802) but to show what sizes and qualities of paper were used, how paper related to the size of first editions and to their reprintings, to the cost of these, and to other factors of the early trade. But first let us review briefly the history of papermaking from its beginnings and from its introduction into America to about the year 1790.

Papermaking is an ancient craft, invented in China just short of a century after the death of Christ. Knowledge of this art was kept secret for centuries, and a millennium elapsed before the technique was introduced

6. Jan LaRue, "Watermarks and Musicology," *Acta Musicologica* II–IV (1961) 131.

into Europe, this occurring in Spain or Italy in the late twelfth or early thirteenth century. Once established, knowledge of papermaking spread rapidly, first to southern France and in the fourteenth century to northern France, Flanders, Lorraine, and the Rhine valley, which was to become the cradle of printing. (An abundant supply of paper was one of the conditions essential to the invention and rapid spread of printing; the fact that it was readily available and in frequent usage for writing by then is attested to by the many manuscripts extant which were written on paper in the fourteenth century and afterwards.)

The first paper mill was established in America about the year 1690 (within some sixty years after the initial colonization of the country and just eight years short of the first occurrence of printed music in the ninth edition of the Bay Psalm Book), when William Rittenhouse, a German emigrant papermaker, erected a mill near Germantown, Pennsylvania. One of his partners in this enterprise was William Bradford, the first printer of Pennsylvania, New York, and New Jersey. It appears that Bradford required a more substantial supply of paper for his flourishing printing businesses than importation was able to provide, and the Rittenhouse mill was a result of his collaboration with the German papermaker. The slow but steady spread of the papermaking craft in America from this time on is recorded in Dard Hunter's *Papermaking in Pioneer America*, in Wroth's *The Colonial Printer*, and in many other sources, and there is no need to discuss that subject here, beyond noting that the technique was introduced into New Jersey in 1726, into Massachusetts two years later, into Maine in the 1730s, into Virginia in 1744, into Rhode Island in 1766, into New York in 1768, into Maryland in 1776, into North Carolina a year later, and into Delaware in 1787, the year that John Aitken commenced issuing sheet music in Philadelphia. Knowledge of the craft was transported west in 1793, at about the time when John Christopher Moller and the Carrs were beginning to issue music on a wider scale in Philadelphia, when a mill was erected in Kentucky. Its manufacture in western Pennsylvania followed three years later.

Three basic requirements had to be present in order to produce paper: knowledge of the technique of papermaking itself and a few tools employed in it; a supply of raw material, which until the early or mid-nineteenth century consisted almost entirely of rags; and an abundant supply of water, to provide power for macerating the rags into pulp or "stuff" and for cleansing it. All paper made in America through 1800 and until about the third decade of the nineteenth century was fabricated by hand. The papermaker or artisan who actually fashioned the sheet (he was called the vatman) would dip a paper mold, a rectangular wooden frame interlaced with a wire mesh, into a vat of pulp or stuff, which consisted of rags macerated into a watery mass. The mold was fitted with a deckle, a separate, thin wooden frame which confined the flowing pulp and determined the size of the sheet. The vatman formed an individual sheet of paper by drawing a bit of stuff onto and over the surface of the mold, then raising the mold into a horizontal position and shaking it to throw off excess water and at the same time interlock the vegetable fibers together. He then deposited the wet sheet onto a piece of felting, which was alternated with other newly made sheets and felts to form a post, or from 125 to 144 sheets in all.[7] The vatman usually worked with a pair of molds and one deckle and was assisted by several other people, so that the process was carried on continuously. The sheets were then pressed, dried, and sized with glue before being distributed for sale. About 1790, one source tells us, approximately twenty posts (in this case, 2,500 sheets) were considered a day's work for an American papermaker and his assistants, the workday extending from dawn to dusk.[8]

While Wroth, Hunter, and others have documented the introduction of papermaking into the various colonies and states, their treatments have mostly dealt with "firsts" and little information has been published so far on the everyday manufacture of paper in America in the later eighteenth century and in the period before 1817, when Thomas and Joshua Gilpin of Delaware introduced mechanical methods for fabricating this commodity.[9] When Isaiah Thomas published in 1810 the results of his census of then-existing paper mills, he located sixty such establishments in Pennsylvania, which was the center of the industry at that time. Contrast this figure with the seventeen that Bridenbaugh reports were in existence

7. May A. Seitz's *The History of the Hoffman Paper Mills in Maryland* (p. 16) is the source of the lower figure, while Hunter's *Papermaking in Pioneer America* states (p. 15) that 144 sheets made up a post. The norm may have differed from mill to mill, depending upon the ethnic origin and training of the makers. The size of the post also varied according to the size of the paper being made.

8. Seitz, *History of the Hoffman Paper Mills*, p. 16.

9. In 1817 the Gilpins introduced the famous Fourdrinier Paper Machine into American papermaking. This device, which made paper on an endless web, had been invented by Louis Robert of France in 1798 and had been perfected by Bryan Donkin and John Hall in England and put into use there in 1804. R. H. Clapperton's *The Paper-making Machine, Its Invention, Evolution and Development* (Oxford, Pergamon Press, 1967) traces the Fourdrinier machine and its ancillaries, as well as its chief rivals, for almost a hundred years following its invention, and gives otherwise unavailable information on patents, plans, and other materials. The story of its transfer to America is told in Harold B. Hancock and Norman B. Wilkinson's "The Gilpins and Their Endless Papermaking Machine," *The Pennsylvania Magazine of History and Biography* LXXXI (1957) 391–405.

in that colony in 1773 and one can readily sense the rapid expansion that occurred in American papermaking in the intervening thirty-eight years.[10] From the evidence of advertisements and watermarks on music sheets, which we shall discuss later, it appears that paper continued to be scarce in many American localities until after 1800. The period following this date was an eventful one for American papermaking, for the majority of papermakers listed in Hunter's checklist of American papermakers, 1690–1817 (see pp. 143–69 of his *Papermaking in Pioneer America*) began working after 1800. There is no doubt that the decade from about 1800 to 1810 was one of rapid growth and development for the American papermaking industry and it was in this period that supply began to pull abreast of demand, being held back from doing so in some instances only by shortages of rags. Using the Hunter checklist of American papermakers as a guide, I have made a rough tabulation of the growth of the industry during these years, shown in Table 5.

We can readily discern from this tabulation, which is admittedly only a rough approximation but nonetheless a valid one, that the seventy-four paper mills in operation in 1798 had very nearly doubled their numbers in the years between 1799 and 1817, while they had increased by only about 40 percent between 1775 and 1798, which also can be counted as a period of growth and expansion. Regarding the difficulties encountered by papermakers before 1800, and factors which deterred more rapid expansion of papermaking during this time, Dard Hunter had the following to say: "During the 1750–1800 period innumerable small paper mills were established in almost every section of the eastern part of the country. Many of these mills had difficulty in surviving, because of the constant shortage of linen and cotton rags and the absence of trained workers who could produce papers suitable for writing and printing."[11] Wroth's *The Colonial Printer* has much to say regarding the scarcity of rags in the American colonies, a situation which continued to plague papermakers and printers into the nineteenth century, and in his *The American Printer, 1787–1825*, Rollo Silver states (p. 37) that "the search

TABLE 5
American Paper Mills in Operation

1690–1775	1776–89	1790–98	1799–1817
48	53	74	139

10. Carl Bridenbaugh *The Colonial Craftsman* (New York, New York University Press, 1950), p. 62.
11. Hunter, *Papermaking in Pioneer America*, p. 19.

for rags became so exasperating that in 1810 they were imported from Europe."

The inability of American papermakers to meet the requirements of a growing printing industry before 1800 is reflected in the census of watermarks on early American music sheets given in Appendix C herein. This documentation leads to a number of conclusions regarding the sources of supply of our earliest music printers and publishers. Admittedly, some of the paper containing music imprints of the 1790s was unwatermarked altogether, for much English and European paper of this period, particularly lesser grades, carried no marking. However, the information in Appendix C shows a healthy dependence upon Dutch and English papers for printing music in America from about 1793 until 1799 and even a few years afterwards. The marks of Budgen, Blauw, De Vries, Honig & Zoonen, Kool, Russel, Taylor, and others abound in our earliest sheet music. While I recorded in this census only titles of pieces containing such marks, it is usual to find most copies of a given work on similarly watermarked paper, though infrequently one encounters a piece on paper marked with the device of other makers (mixed sheets). There are, of course, some exceptions to this rule. It is obvious from the documentation of numbers 41 and 47 on the census (papers manufactured probably by Simon Class of Montgomery County, Pennsylvania, and Samuel Levis of Chester County) that the Carrs were able to obtain large stocks of these papers in the period 1793–99, while at the same time using much imported stock. The watermark of Simon Class, which Hunter describes as a six-pointed star, is found quite frequently on Carr publications of the 1790s.

That dependence upon importation began to ease around 1800 or slightly later, when American manufacture increased and began to meet demand, is proved by the Paffs' frequent use in the 1799–1803 period of a paper marked "WD NEW RI" (no. 47 of the census, probably the mark of an unidentified maker in or around Newport, Rhode Island) and by Blake's use of an obviously American paper watermarked "MA" (no. 27). (The Paffs also printed on a crude, unwatermarked paper of American manufacture during this time as well as using imported sheets.)[12] By the time Gottlieb Graupner commenced publishing seriously in 1803 the changeover to American sheets was becoming complete, for he and other publishers of Boston and other localities increasingly employed papers

12. It can be determined from entry nos. 12 and 13 on the census, pertaining to the papers of the Dutch makers C. & I. Honig and I. Kool, that the Paffs continued to draw upon imported stocks also during their 1799–1803 activity.

which, though unwatermarked, were undoubtedly of American manufacture. In fact, after about 1803 fine, watermarked sheets were used for special occasions and for special publications only. For example, the high-quality paper of an unidentified maker named (and watermarked) "Austin" (no. 13) was employed by Peter Weldon in 1810 for printing his *Favorita Waltz Brazilense* (Wolfe, No. 9731), undoubtedly one of the most elaborate music publications of this early period, and for issuing *Lord Wellington's March* (Wolfe, No. 5445), another extensively decorated publication, approximately a year later. Another example of the use of special paper for a special offering occurred when Blake advertised in his edition of the piano score of Handel's *Acis and Galatea* in the early 1820s that "the paper is from the manufactory of Mr. Thomas Amies, of a quality equal to his celebrated foolscap."

After about 1803 watermarked paper of any kind was rarely used by our early publishers. The identifying design of Lydig & Mesier (no. 49), who operated a paper mill on the Bronx River between 1808 and 1822,[13] constitutes a rare example of the location of a watermark in an American music sheet of the post-1805 period. While almost all the paper used for printing music in this country after 1803 or 1805 was of American manufacture, being usually coarser, thicker, and less refined than contemporary English and European sheets, watermarks can rarely be detected in it. The one main exception to the practice of using American papers entirely in the post-1805 period is George Willig. The evidence of watermarks on many of his sheets issued between 1804 and 1810 show that he acquired considerable stocks of Dutch papers manufactured at Zaandyk, Holland, by Honig & Zoonen (nos. 16, 36), and in the period around 1818 he printed on several French papers (nos. 30–33). (It should be pointed out here that I have found at least one occurrence of the use of imported paper about this time by George E. Blake also [no. 29].) However, the Honig & Zoonen paper and these French papers constituted only a small portion of the entire paper used by Willig after 1804; paper of American manufacture made up the majority of his sheets. Another interesting aspect of the paper Willig used is the fact that a few of his sheets appear with the watermark designation "G WILLIG" in them (no. 50). Either Willig owned in whole or in part a paper mill or he had such paper made up for his exclusive use. While the imprints on such sheets frequently date to Willig's early activity (before 1820), it is my

13. The Peter Mesier of this partnership must have been related to the Peter A. Mesier who sold and lithographed music in New York City from the late 1820s. The latter had been a bookseller, bookbinder, and stationer in New York from 1794.

belief that he acquired this paper at a much later date and that such early imprints on it represent restrikes or reprints from these early plates.

With respect to this last point, the publications by Carr and other publishers of the 1790s and later, which were originally issued on early watermarked paper, are sometimes found on later American paper which appears to date from the 1820s onward. These, too, represent restrikes or reprints made at a much later time. Though the same plates were employed in printing these reissues, the later paper in many cases alters their appearance to the extent that they do not look "right," in the sense that a musician says that a piece does not "sound."

A few advertisements exist which also document the growing availability of paper, and particularly of music paper, in the post-1800 period. In the New York *American Citizen and General Advertiser* of January 6, 1801, "David Dunham, Paper Ware-House, No. 26 Moore-street, Five Doors from Whitehall-Dock," advertised that he had on hand various printing and writing papers, and that "he had promise of a constant supply of assorted paper, from five different mills." In the same newspaper on the previous day had appeared this still more important notice:

STATIONARY,
MANUFACTURED AT
SAMUEL CAMPBELL'S PAPER-MILL
And for sale on moderate terms, for Cash or Credit,
AT HIS BOOK-STORE,
NO. 124 Pearl-STREET,

Writing,	Medium	
	Demy	
	Folio Post,	Equal in quality to any
	Quarto do	imported.
Gilt and plain Foolscap		
12 reams	Paper for Printing Music on,	
12 do	Copperplate do	
30 do	Cartridge	

This advertisement, which continued to be published through February 14, 1801, gives firsthand proof of the native manufacture of paper suitable for music printing in the very period under discussion. Campbell's mill, which was undoubtedly only one of several supplying the music trade after 1800, was located at Springfield, New Jersey (Dard Hunter says New York), from 1797 until 1804, when it caught fire and burned down during the last week of April. Campbell had been a bookseller and stationer in New York City from at least 1785 and undoubtedly entered papermaking in relation to his retail trade.[14] He continued in business as a printer, bookseller, and bookbinder in New York until 1818.

Little information is available regarding the cost of paper, and specifically music paper, at this time. Among the manuscripts, bills, and receipts of Frederick Rausch in the New York Public Library is a note on a receipt dated May 22, 1802, stating:

> Jany 13th 1802 $
> _____
>   "   26   "   ½ Ream of Music Paper   7,,

The above figure would place the cost of a ream of music paper at 14 dollars (and the price of a whole sheet of paper at just under 3 cents). While we do not know whether this paper was intended for writing or copying music by hand rather than for printing it, I feel sure that the same paper was used for both purposes. Old bound volumes of printed music which also contain music copied out in manuscript form and watermarks in their sheets are indicative of this. Another of Rausch's receipts (quoted fully in Chapter 10 herein) shows that Rausch was charged £1 12s 6d in 1807 by Thomas Preston of London for one hundred sheets of the best paper, upon which Preston printed an unidentified *Russian Air* for Rausch. Because of the complexities of computing meaningfully exchange values at such a time, I will refrain from speculating about the exact worth of the paper that Preston used. Suffice it to say that paper was one of the major considerations on the music publisher's expense sheet and its high cost was probably the main reason why our early publishers printed only small amounts of music at one time, resorting to reprinting as frequently as demand required.

I shall utilize the remainder of this chapter for a discussion of watermarks and their relationship to paper sizes and other factors, as indicated by the watermark evidence in Appendix C. Because of a lack of documentation, frequent changes in size and marking of paper for taxation purposes, and other factors, earlier paper and especially watermark lore is sketchy and frequently confusing. Nowhere in the literature of bibliography does there exist a reasonable definitive explanation of the relationship of watermarks to paper sizes in the field of early American printing. While our knowledge of early paper has been advanced considerably during the last several decades, thanks mainly to the work of Allan Stevenson, additional strides remain to be taken before we can rely on such

14. In a private communication to me of March 21, 1978, John Bidwell relates that, although Dard Hunter dates Samuel Campbell from 1797, Bidwell's own study of the manuscript accounts of Nathan Sellers (a maker of papermaker's molds during this period) shows that Campbell was ordering demy molds from Sellers in February 1795.

knowledge comfortably for precise bibliographical analysis, particularly in later phases of paper history. The small collection of marks in Appendix C herein recovered from early American musical publications may allow us an insight into realms which have heretofore remained restricted. Papers employed in book printing were almost always folded from one to four times (mostly three), and their watermarks, when present, became fractionated and were often wholly or partly cropped off in the binding process. Music sheets allow us a panoramic glimpse into the nature and makeup of earlier paper as it came from the mold, for early sheet music was printed on whole sheets of paper which were usually folded in half to complete the format. Because much of our early American music has remained unbound, or has been unbound from collectons of individual pieces, it is quite easy to recover marks in the sheets. Only newspapers, which because of their size have not been exploited, maps and prints, which do not exist in great numbers, and manuscripts, which were frequently penned on halves or parts of whole sheets of paper or on smaller writing paper, approximate music sheets in value for the purpose of early paper investigation. Early sheet music constitutes an ideal resource for watermark lore, especially for eighteenth-century paper, and one wonders why Churchill and Heawood and the other filigranists did not resort to this expediency. It strikes me that the tens of thousands of titles listed in the *British Union-Catalogue of Early Music Printed before the Year 1801* (London, Butterworth's Scientific Publications, 1957) constitute a treasure trove for this type of study. While LaRue and others have combed archives and manuscript repositories for telltale watermarks in earlier music paper, no one, as for as I know, has systematically researched collections of printed music in this regard.

As Philip Gaskell has pointed out in his "Notes on Eighteenth-Century British Paper"[15] and in his more recent *A New Introduction to Bibliography*, the original purpose of the watermark was probably that of a trademark. It was intended to identify the maker of the paper in which it occurred, to advertise his wares, and to guarantee their quality. (The theory has also been advanced that watermarks were originally employed in a symbolic sense, by heretical papermakers as symbols of religious propaganda.) The mark was made by stitching a wire device in the shape of the mark directly on the papermaker's mold, so that upon the formation of a sheet this mark was visible in the form of lighter lines or markings in the paper. Watermarks appear to have been common from the earliest days of

15. *The Library; Transactions of The Bibliographical Society*, 5th ser XII (1957) 34–42.

papermaking in Europe. They usually took the form of a rebus on the maker's name or of the arms of his city or guild. The mark was usually placed in one side of the rectangular whole sheet. Rarely in the early days were the name or initials on the maker included as well.

At some early date a change took place, and in addition to the watermark located in the center of one side of the sheet, a second and smaller mark, which came to be known as the countermark, was added to the other half of the sheet, so that the watermark and countermark approximately balanced one another in the mold and then in the finished sheet (see Illus. 24). The countermark generally took the form of the name or initials of the papermaker, and it probably evolved because the watermark had ceased to fulfill its function as a trademark. So many makers had imitated the marks of those who produced the finest papers that original designs had lost their meaning and intent. As a result of this practice, certain watermarks eventually came to identify certain standard sizes of paper, rather than the maker of the paper. The process probably evolved gradually, but the system was well developed by the end of the seventeenth century. Certain marks (pot, fool's cap, posthorn, etc.) became standard in England in the eighteenth century, while others were to be standardized in France and Holland. Some sizes (pot, for example) later dropped out of general use and others (foolscap was one) were replaced by totally dissimilar marks: Britannia (no. 34), Pro Patria (no. 35), and the Dutch Lion (nos. 36–37), which design appeared usually within a more elaborate background in the Pro Patria and Vryheyt marks.[16] As Gaskell has aptly put it in his "Notes on Eighteenth-Century British Paper" (p. 37),

> The conventions governing the use of watermarks during the eighteenth century were essentially the same as those described above, but the process of standardization had gone further. Whereas in the seventeenth century each country or even district where paper was made may have had its own series of marks for sizes, which might have differed from those used in neighboring areas, most eighteenth-century makers limited themselves to two or three marks for each size, which few marks, however local or national their character, were recognized everywhere and generally used. Thus paper bearing the English Royal Arms and the Arms of the City of London was made in Italy and France; Dutch Lion paper in France; Britannia paper in Holland; and paper bearing a number of Dutch national emblems in England and Scotland.

According to this same source, eighteenth-century British countermarks were generally chosen from among ten or twelve conventional and

16. I did not locate the Vryheyt design in any early American music sheet. For its design see W. A. Churchill's *Watermarks in Paper* (plates 51–75).

apparently meaningless ciphers, names, and initials. Some, such as IV (Jean Villedary) and LVG (Lucius Van Gerrevink), recalled the names of famous papermakers of the past, and all may have been based upon seventeenth-century countermarks, but they now indicated neither the maker's name nor the size of the sheet, and we have no evidence which associates their presence in the sheet with its quality.[17]

The matter is further confused by a gradual and continuing increase in the size of sheets as time went on. Paper, like tobacco today, had become an ideal medium for raising revenue. Taxes that had been placed initially on imported paper in early times under protectionist policies were gradually increased to raise revenues on homemade papers as well, for the purpose of waging wars and for other reasons. (The Stamp Act in our own history affords a fitting example of this practice.) Since the statutes which placed taxes upon paper did so according to size or type, papermakers decreased their own burden and the burden on printers by increasing the dimensions of their molds. The matter of relating watermarks to sizes of paper is further complicated by the fact that there existed three different qualities of paper (fine, second, and ordinary) and several divisions (writing paper, printing paper, copperplate or "plate" paper, and coarse papers, made for wrapping, binding, and industrial purposes), each having its own size and watermark system, though frequently the watermarks were the same on corresponding papers of each class.[18] As paper was usually difficult to obtain in colonial and post-Revolutionary America, printers used all but the very poorest types indiscriminately (and frequently these, too when necessity demanded). Printing and writing paper had identical watermarks, but the printing varieties were somewhat larger and of poorer quality than those for writing.[19] Dimensions were only approximate, as mold sizes varied slightly from maker to maker and between geographical areas. Philip Gaskell's 1957 article and Table 3 (on pp. 73–75) of his *New Introduction to Bibliography* trace the growth of the size of the sheet and the variations in watermarking it during the seventeenth and eighteenth centuries. The watermarks and size grouping detailed there relate to many of the classes of paper

17. The initials "GM" and the name "Gior. Magnani" in marks 22–23, 38–39 in Appendix C probably recall an earlier famous Italian maker.

18. The quality of paper was determined by the quality of the linen rags used to make the "stuff"; for the finest stuff only the best linen was used, while poorer linen and even scraps of other material went into poorer papers. Papers used for wrapping, bookbinding, etc. also had several classes: ordinary, blue, white-brown, and brown.

19. It has been suggested that the dimension of printing papers exceeded slightly those of the writing variety in order to allow for trimming during the binding process.

employed in early American music printing, and by collating our collection of watermarks in Appendix C against these two sources, we can determine the sizes of imported paper that were in use in American music publishing during the 1787–1830 period (see Table 6).

TABLE 6

Sizes of Imported Paper Used in Early American Music Publishing

Size or Group	Approximate dimensions	Watermark design	Number in Appendix C
Super royal	75 × 55 cm.	Strasbourg Lily	
			1–12
Writing demy	51 × 40 cm.	Strasbourg Lily	
Crown	51 × 38 cm.	Fleur-de-lis	13–19
Medium	57 × 45 cm.	Horn in crowned shield	20–26, and probably 27–28
Royal or Lombard	61 × 49 cm.	Grapes	29–33
Foolscap	45 × 35 cm.	Britannia,	34
		Pro Patria	35
		Dutch Lion	36–37

The above papers were undoubtedly imported and stocked by "paper warehouses" of the period or by stationers who distributed them to printers and publishers. (Illustration 24b shows an actual photograph of a watermark in an early American music sheet, while Illus. 25 depicts a "paper warehouse" located in Boston in the late 1820s.) All the papers in this period were fairly large, probably of the copperplate or "plate" class, since it was the custom to print two music plates, each measuring approximately 28 centimeters (11 inches) in height and 20½ centimeters (8 inches) in width, side by side so that, upon completion, they flanked one another on one side of a whole sheet of paper.[20] Allowing for margins all around and for a double margin between the two plates, where the whole sheet was eventually folded in half, we can see that a whole sheet of paper measured about 13 by 18 or 20 inches (33 by 45 to 50 centimeters). As slightly larger or smaller plates were frequently used, and as sheets were customarily trimmed after printing, any of the above papers could be

20. We have little information on early music imposition, i.e., whether plates were printed singly or two at a time. From the viewpoints of saving time and aligning pages, the latter practice would seem preferable. However, such considerations were undoubtedly controlled by custom, the size of the plank of the press, how fast ink dried, etc. We can see from Samuel Campbell's advertisement in 1801, quoted on p. 154 herein, that copperplate papers were considered appropriate for printing music. The subject of imposition is discussed more fully in the final chapter.

adapted to our early music printing.[21] The use of extremely large super royal paper is illustrated especially well in copies of James Hook's *By and Then* (Wolfe, No. 4167). which I found in the collection of early American music in the possession of the New-York Historical Society. That these sheets, which were published by the Paffs in New York in the 1801–3 period, are in the super royal category is proven by their watermarks, the Strasbourg Lily (no. 8 in Appendix C), and by their overall dimensions, which measure 75½ centimeters horizontally and 54½ centimeters vertically. Both papers have rough, deckle edges and show us an untrimmed whole sheet just as it came from the maker's mold.

While in England and some European countries the size of paper is still denominated in terms of the old watermark designations, the marks themselves began to go out of style after 1800, when machinery with "endless webbs" began to replace the papermaker's mold. As we shall see shortly, watermarks did not assume as significant a meaning with regard to the size of the sheet in this country. However, as the previously quoted advertisement of Samuel Campbell shows, watermark designations were still in use in America in 1801. A few of the marks in Appendix C display dates which were molded into the sheets with them (nos. 1, 7, 12, 13, 25). Watermark dates in European papers and in English papers before 1794 are rare. (No. 12 in Appendix C is an exception to this rule vis-à-vis Continental sheets.) The frequent discovery of dates in English paper from 1793 into the next century remained a puzzle until 1944, when C. B. Oldman published a note on them.[22] Oldman delved into the British statutes and found that a legislative enactment of 1794 (34 George III [1794], c. 20), which dealt with taxation of paper, directed that the date of the year of manufacture be added to British paper. Accordingly, it is not unusual to find watermark dates in English paper from then until the early 1800s, at which time there was less than strict adherence to the law (it was finally abrogated in 1811). The use by James Hewitt of paper marked both with the L & M Homo mark and the year 1780 is unusual not only for showing a date in European paper; the fact that he employed a paper for issuing editions fourteen and eighteen years after its manufacture does not

21. Because of variations in the dimensions of early music plates, as determined by outlines left on extant sheets, we are tempted to wonder, and rightfully so, I think, whether publishers may not have tailored their plates to accommodate foolscap and smaller sizes of paper that were available to them.

22. C. B. Oldman, "Watermark Dates in English Paper," *The Library; Transactions of The Bibliographical Society*, 4th ser XXV (1944) 70–71. Further information on the papers used in early music printing and copying is contained in Jan LaRue's "British Music Paper, 1770–1820: Some Distinctive Characteristics," *Monthly Musical Record* LXXXVII (1957) 177–80.

accord with recent bibliographical scholarship, which shows that papers were employed usually within three years after they left the maker's mill.

Let us now consider the nature and use of watermarks in American paper of the colonial and early federal periods. In the general resumé of watermarks and the discussion of their relationship to paper sizes given before, it was noted that a system of denoting papers, grades of paper, and paper dimensions according to their watermark designs gradually evolved in Europe and in England in the seventeenth century and had become standardized there in the eighteenth. No such orderly scheme emerged in America. Dard Hunter has devoted several pages of his chapter on "Ancient Watermarks, Six and a Half Centuries of Mystic Symbols" in his *Papermaking, the History and Technique of an Ancient Craft*[23] to the subject of marks in early American papers. His discussion here shows that American makers, who usually worked under more trying circumstances and with cruder implements, did not follow the European system of designating paper sizes by marks (which was evolving at the time of the beginning of American papermaking) but usually only added an identifying mark of manufacture to their molds. When designs did appear, they usually took the form of some simple device (a clover leaf, a bird, an anchor, etc.) which was placed in the mold and then into the paper as a trademark.

For example, the watermark used by William Rittenhouse, our first papermaker, from 1690 on was simply the word "Company," which denoted his partnership with William Bradford and two other interested parties in this pioneering venture. This mark continued in use until 1704. The second mark employed by the Rittenhouse mill was the monogram "WR," the initials of the principal founder, on one half of the mold, while the other half contained a clover leaf inside a shield surmounted by a crown and the word "Pennsylvania" outlined in letters beneath. This device may have been inspired by the fact that Rittenhouse was now making better paper and he wished to advertise its higher quality by marking it with a design adapted from French paper, which was then the best obtainable. The next papermark employed by this mill displayed the initials of Klaus Rittenhouse, "KR," the son of the founder, and the clover leaf alone.[24]

23. (Second ed., revised and enlarged, New York, Knopf, 1947), pp. 273–80.
24. Another discussion of the Rittenhouse watermarks appears in Hunter's *Papermaking in Pioneer America* (pp. 26–28), which points out that it is questionable that all the watermarks attributed to this mill were produced by William and Klaus Rittenhouse in their early Pennsylvania establishment. In other words, these may have been reemployed by later makers as marks of quality, much as "LVG" and "IV" on pages were in European papermaking (see p. 158 herein).

While the second paper mill in this country, the establishment of William De Wees, which dates from 1710, is not known to have used watermarks, the third mill, set up by Thomas Willcox in the colony of Pennsylvania in 1729, employed as its standard device a dove holding an olive branch and the initials "TMW," designating its founder, and afterward "MW," his son, as countermarks. (The dove design in Willcox paper is very similar to that later employed by various members of the Amies family [see no. 52 in Appendix C]; it was also used by the Gilpins and others.) This system probably reflects European watermark practices at a very early period, when watermarks were employed in the trademark sense, before they began to designate factors such as size, quality, and the like. That such was the general practice in America even a century after Rittenhouse's initial efforts is shown in the account books of Nathan Sellers, a pioneer papermold maker of Upper Darby, Pennsylvania, and after 1779 of Philadelphia, which are now preserved in the library of the American Philosophical Society in that city.[25]

Nathan Sellers was the first to draw wire in America, a commodity that is an essential ingredient in making paper molds. His skill in this art was adapted obviously very early through necessity by our early papermaking trade. The first entry in Sellers's account book relating to the manufacture by him of a paper mold appears under the date October 22, 1776, when he charged the Continental Congress the sum of £14 12d 6s "To a fine paper mould." Entries in Sellers's accounts, which in the beginning relate to nonpaper subjects such as the making of wire and nails, the repairing of watches and clocks, become more and more concerned with details regarding his manufacture of paper molds, so that after the 1790s almost all entries are on this subject. One of the earliest entries here (for February 1, 1778) relates to the making of a pair of molds (royal, demy, double foolscap, and double pot)[26] for Samuel Levis, whose inherited watermark is shown in Appendix C (no. 47), this, too, probably having been woven and placed there by Sellers. Various entries in the Sellers account book show that when a papermaker ordered markings in his mold, these usually

25. Hunter's *Papermaking, the History and Technique of an Ancient Craft* (see n. 22) devotes Chapter 21 to Sellers. Sellers's account books constitute a rather important source of our early papermaking trade; however, the extraneous material contained in them has probably deterred publication of much of the important material they contain.

26. From the beginning of the eighteenth century the production of paper was increased through the use of two-sheet molds for the smaller sizes of paper. Each mold of such a pair contained two molds made as one, with the deckle having a central bar. They were constructed so that two sheets could be fabricated side by side in a single operation. See Gaskell, *A New Introduction to Bibliography*, pp. 63–65. Also see A. H. Stevenson, "Watermarks are Twins," *Studies in Bibliography* IV (1951–52) 57–91.

consisted of his name or initials alone. The following entry, for July 25, 1779, charged againstthe account of Potts and Reynolds (of Trenton, New Jersey), is a typical one:

To a pair of Demy paper Molds with 28 letters	[$]12
To a pair of Double Fools Cap molds, with 56 letters	17

Another entry, made on March 28, 1783, against Frederick Bicking of Montgomery County, Pennsylvania, shows that Bicking employed a device along with his initials:

To a pair of fine Demy molds	9,, 0,,0
To laying 4 letters	0,,15,,0
To laying 2 flower devices, d 11/3	1,, 2,,6
	£10,,17,,6

Sellers's entries also contain much information on the size of molds. While these differed slightly according to the wants of purchasers, the following samplings from his account show that Sellers manufactured molds in the following general dimensions (in inches):

Single cap	13¼ × 16½
Royal	19⅛ × 24
Large Royal	25½ × 20½
Super Royal	20 × 27½
Medium	17½ × 22½
Post	15½ × 19
Demy	17½ × 21¾
Single Fools Cap	13½ × 16

These sizes approximate European sizes of that period. John Bidwell's recent resume of paper in post-Revolutionary America, derived from information in the Sellers manuscript accounts, shows that there was really no standard Sellers size for many of these categories, including large royal, super royal, and medium.[27] Additional information on the dimensions of American sheets of this time appears in Seitz's *History of the Hoffman Paper Mills*, which states (p. 16):

> The sizes of the sheets of papers varied. The following figures concerning sizes were taken from an old account book in the possession of the author:
> Writing paper: Pott 12½ × 15, Double Pott 15 × 25, Post 15½ × 19, Double Post 19 × 30½, Pinch Post 14½ × 18½, Large Post 16½ × 20¾, Double Large Post 20¾ × 33, Copy 16½ × 20, Medium 18 × 22½, Foolscap 13½ × 16½, Double Foolscap 16½ × 26½, Foolscap and third 13¼ × 22, Foolscap and half 13¼ × 24¾.

27. "The Size of the Sheet in America: Paper-Moulds Manufactured by N. & D. Sellers of Philadelphia," *Proceedings of the American Antiquarian Society* LXXXVII (1977) 299–342.

Book and Drawing papers: Foolscap 14 × 18¾, Demy 15½ × 20, Medium 17½ × 22½, Royal 19 × 24, Super Royal 19¼ × 27, Imperial 22 × 30¼, Columbier 23½ × 24¼, Antiquarian 31 × 53.

Printing paper: Crown 16½ × 21, Demy 17¾ × 22½, Medium 18¼ × 23, Royal 20 × 25; Super Royal 21 × 27, Double Pott 15 × 25, Double Foolscap 17 × 27, Double Crown 20 × 30 Double Demy 22½ × 35½

Cartridge paper: Foolscap 14 × 18¾, Demy 17¾ × 22½, Royal 19 × 24, Super Royal 19½ × 27½, Imperial 21 × 26, Elephand 23 × 28

Little information is available on how late into the nineteenth century such designations and sizes persisted. Doubtless the introduction of the Fourdrinier machine and its gradual adoption by the trade everywhere wreaked havoc on the age-old customs of the industry. By the time Richard Herring published the first major history of modern papermaking, his *Paper and Paper-Making, Ancient and Modern*, which first appeared at London in 1855, and by the time Henry Carey Baird had issued in translation at Philadelphia in 1866 the first comprehensive manual on this subject to be published in America, A. Proteaux's *Practical Guide for the Manufacture of Paper and Boards*, the old sizes and watermarks were no longer in use. Because the endless webb had allowed for a great increase in the size of the sheet, paper had come to be designated by weight. Watermarks were no longer put into paper through designs in molds, but were stamped on the damp continuous sheet while it was being formed through the use of a device known as the dandy roll. This was a cylinder riding on the wire mesh, which revolved and affixed not only the watermark into the paper but the wire-line and chain-line appearance of mold-made paper as well. Gaskell relates that this device came into use in England about 1825. I shall conclude this treatment of paper employed in our earlier music publishing with the observation that Jacob Perkins, an ingenious American inventor, patented on December 18, 1816, an invention for watermarking paper. Perkins had entered into partnership with Thomas Gilpin, one of the brothers responsible for introducing the Fourdrinier machine into America in 1817, in registering a patent for impressing watermarks, the principle of which was to engrave a plate bearing the device and then transfer it to a roller which left an impression on the wet paper. By using Perkins's roller, a watermark was impressed on each section of the continuous paper strip which the machine produced.[28]

28. Greville Bathe and Dorothy Bathe, *Jacob Perkins*, p. 63.

CHAPTER IX

The Copperplate or Rolling Press

꧁꧂

WHEN VIEWED in apposition with the standard printing press of the day, the copperplate or rolling press employed in early American music publishing (and for general engraving as well) was, by all standards of comparison, an extremely uncomplicated apparatus. Unlike the wooden printing press, it was not intricate in design, expensive in construction, or difficult in operation. In simple fact, it was almost identical to the body or frame of the machine employed in general letterpress printing but had none of the additional and complicating mechanisms—such as the platen, and the spindle and hose and other appurtenances needed to sustain, align, and move it; or on the carriage, the coffin, the rounce, the tympans and frisket, and similar machinery —which caused the general letterpress to be expensive to erect and which required skilled operators.[1] The construction and operation of the copperplate press was based on the simple theory of squeezing a flat surface between two rollers.

Illustration 26 presents us with a period illustration of a copperplate or rolling press. From this we are able to judge immediately that, like the

1. The reader who desires to know more about the early printing press or to compare it with the mechanism under discussion is directed to Chapter 5 of R. B. McKerrow's *An Introduction to Bibliography for Literary Students* (Oxford, 1927); to pp. 118–24 of Philip Gaskell's *A New Introduction to Bibliography;* and to Chapter 4 of Wroth's *The Colonial Printer* and the appendix to it. While details on early printing presses can be learned from a number of other sources, these are the most convenient, and the Wroth book touches directly on machines used in colonial America.

printing press of that time the machine used for printing engraved plates was made of wood and probably bore a strong resemblance to rolling presses used in England and on the Continent for a century and perhaps even two earlier. For convenience, we can divide the copperplate or rolling press into two principal parts: the body and the carriage. The body of the press consisted of two strong, upright posts called the cheeks (P), of varying dimensions but ordinarily about 4½ feet high, a foot or so thick, and 2½ feet apart. These were joined at the top and bottom by cross pieces (the top cross bar was called the head), and they were fastened by tenons (i.e., they were fitted together by mortises) into wooden feet (L,M) which supported the whole of the press. In the body of the copperplate press we see a construction approximately the same as the frame of the ordinary printing press. From each of the tips of the two feet making up the stand of the press rose vertical pieces called posts (c), which were joined at the top by other cross or horizontal ones (d). Into the cheeks above and below the posts were fitted wooden cylinders or rollers (D, E, F, [G]), set in such a way that an interval of slightly more than 1½ inches was left between them. It was from the rollers that the copperplate press derived its alternative name, which was as often as not the designation assigned to it by early American engravers and printers. The rollers measured about 6 inches in diameter and were narrowed down at their ends to form projecting pegs about 2 inches round. These end pieces were called trunnions and they turned in the cheeks. They were fitted into two half-moon-shaped pieces of wood (one above and one below) which were, in turn, lined with polished iron (or bearings) to prevent friction and to facilitate motion. The space in the half-moons left vacant by the trunnions was filled with paper, pasteboard, or some similar materials so that the rollers could be raised or lowered at will and thereby be adjusted so as to leave only enough space between them for the passage of the plank charged with the plate, paper, and blankets. The plank or table of the press was a smooth, even board (H, I, K) about 4½ feet long, 2½ feet wide (the interval between the cheeks) and 1½ inches thick. The plank rested on the upper horizontal pieces (d), and the vertical and horizontal pieces (c,d) and the plank may be considered the carriage of the press. There were no mechanisms, as in the case of the ordinary printing press, to hold the engraved and charged plate on the carriage. It lay freely on the plank and was probably pressed or "fed" into the rollers concurrent with the turning of the handle of the press. To one of the trunnions of the upper roller was fastened a cross, consisting of two levers (A, B) or pieces of wood traversing one another. By turning the cross the operator gave motion to the upper roller which then drew the plank forward and backward when it was charged with a plate, paper, and blankets to close the interval between the rollers. The lower roller moved freely, acting as a track and receiving its motion from the pressure exerted upon it by the plank as it moved back and forth. As was pointed out earlier, the plate being drawn through the rollers was pinched with considerable force and the moistened paper superimposed on it was pressed into its engraved strokes and punched areas, whence the paper took off ink and received its finished impression.

Probably the only frequent maintenance required for keeping the copperplate press in top working condition was a periodic planing and leveling of the plank, for it had a tendency to warp and splinter under continued use. When the plank could no longer be planed and leveled, by virtue of the thinness of the wood or other considerations, it had to be replaced. Reference has already been made to the operation of planing by David Edwin in his description of engraving and copperplate printing in Philadelphia in 1797. The rollers also may have required periodic replacement, and the motion of the printing operation must have placed great stress on the cheeks and cross bars, especially in the joints where these were tenoned together, so that occasional tightening or perhaps a complete renovation had to be effected.

Our earliest reference to the copperplate press in America comes from the *Autobiography* of Benjamin Franklin. In narrating here his employment by Samuel Keimer in 1728 to "print some paper money in New Jersey, which would require cuts of various types that I only could supply," he went on to say, "the New Jersey job was obtain'd, [and] I contriv'd a copperplate press for it, the first one that had been seen in this country." Wroth, whose work on the colonial printer stands as an authority on the subject of early American publishing, while not disputing the word of Franklin in this matter, leans more to the theory that the first copperplate press in America was probably one brought to Boston by the London engraver Francis Dewing upon his arrival there in 1716. And to Franklin he awards the palm for being the first to construct such an apparatus in this country. Isaiah Thomas, usually a storehouse of information on American printing "firsts," has little to say that can add to our knowledge in this instance, for he merely remarks in an offhand sort of way that "the rolling press, as it is called, by copperplate printers, was not used in England till the reign of James I [1603–25]. It was carried from Antwerp to England, by one Speed. I cannot determine when it was first brought to English America, But I believe about the beginning of the eighteenth century."[2] Inasmuch as copperplate engraving was carried on in Massachusetts as early as 1690, when John Coney engraved plates for the issuance of paper money (which, according to Stauffer "was counterfeited almost as soon as it was issued,"[3] implying additional activity in this sphere), the operation of copperplate printing must have been known and exercised in some form or other at this early date. And because money is usually issued in quantity, some sort of press was probably required. In addition, Richard B. Holman has recently pointed out in his essay, "Seventeenth Century American Prints," in *Prints in and of America to 1850* (p. 50), that a portrait of Increase Mather was engraved and issued by Thomas Emmes of Boston in 1701. And Hitchings has further noted (on p. 80 of the same source) the work of the Massachusetts silversmith Jeremiah Dummer in engraving Connecticut currency in 1709, so that it seems likely that some sort of apparatus for printing copperplates was probably in evidence even before the arrival of Francis Dewing from London in 1716. Regardless of the exact origin of the earliest copperplate presses in America, we may be sure that the rolling press flourished here immediately after its introduction or initial construction early in the eighteenth century; for to paraphrase the opinion of Wroth in this matter, in most of the chief towns of the colonies after the arrival of Dewing, the engraving and printing of copperplates slowly began to become common-place procedure.

Not only was copperplate engraving a long-established trade and the copperplate press a well-known instrument in America by the mid-1790s, when European musician-engravers began to migrate here and a few native engravers, who had previously had only the briefest contact with music publishing, began to devote more of their time to it, but the local construction of copperplate presses must have been also a fairly commonplace matter. We learn from Wroth that the printing press was first manufactured in America in 1769 by Isaac Doolittle of New Haven, a clock- and watchmaker. He further identifies its local construction with Hartford and Philadelphia in 1775; with Charleston, South Carolina, and Fayetteville, North Carolina, in 1778 and 1779 respectively; with Boston in 1792; and with New Jersey and New York in 1796.[4] If the printing press, a fairly complicated piece of machinery according to the standards of the day and one requiring of its builder a precise knowledge and skill in mechanics, metal working, and joining (it was no coincidence that the first

2. *History of Printing in America*, vol. 1, p. 37.
3. *American Engravers upon Copper and Steel*, vol. 1, p. xxii.
4. *The Colonial Printer* (1938 ed.), pp. 83–85.

such machine built in the colonies came from the hands of a watchmaker) could be obtained locally within the final decades of the eighteenth century, how much more likely it seems that the copperplate press, a child's plaything by comparison, could be ordered from local artisans at least as early and probably much earlier. Among the manuscripts of Cadwallader Colden, now in the library of the New-York Historical Society, can be found a transcription in his hand of an article from an early edition of *Chamber's Dictionary*. This describes the construction of the rolling press, together with a description of copperplate ink and an outline of the process of inking and printing copperplates.[5] This appears to date from about 1730, and I think it suggests that a press may have been erected in New York about this time according to information extracted from that English reference work.

Our treatment of the physical character of the copperplate press has shown how few materials were needed in its construction and how it could almost literally be "set up" or "erected." The only metal parts that went into it, in addition to joining devices such as nails, screws, and the like, if, indeed, such were used, were the iron pieces or bearings in the shape of half-moons which lined the wells or recesses holding the trunnions. The two rollers, which might appear at first glance to have been somewhat difficult to construct, were probably turned on an ordinary wood lathe in about the same manner as were the round posts in Illustration 26 which supported the plank. These circular pieces, as well as all other wooden parts which went into the making of a copperplate press, were probably fashioned by local cabinetmakers or furniture makers and carpenters, and it was probably to either of these classes of artisans that early engravers and copperplate printers turned in order to have their presses made to order. The fact that we know of no early newspaper advertisements announcing their manufacture, as we do in the case of the printing press, only emphasizes that their manufacture was uneventful in the everyday affairs of American cabinetmakers and carpenters. In view of the ease of construction and the requirement of few parts, we should little wonder that Benjamin Franklin was able to "contrive" a copperplate press as early as 1728 or that John Fitch of steamboat fame, as Wroth points out, printed the first copies of his 1784 copperplate *Map of the Northwest Parts of the United States* on a machine improvised from an ordinary cider press when, being on the frontier, none other was available to him.[6]

An illustration quite in point with this argument is furnished by an

5. Colden Papers, box 12, item 44.
6. *The Colonial Printer* (1938 ed.), p. 286.

advertisement of John Hutt, who had introduced himself in *Rivington's New-York Gazetteer* of June 24, 1773, as "From London, Engraver and Copper plate Printer." Hutt notified potential customers in particular and the public in general in *The New-York Journal or General Advertiser* of September 15, 1774, that he had "erected a press for that purpose [copperplate printing], by which means he will be enabled to execute every piece of engraving he is favored with, in a neater, more expeditious and reasonable manner than heretofore could be done, the printing branch being attended to with great difficulty, and an expense rather extravagant." Local manufacture can no doubt be held accountable for the apparent abundance of copperplate presses in America by the 1790s, as evidenced by newspaper advertisements such as the one inserted by James Harrison, New York's first formal music publisher, in the *New-York Daily Advertiser* of April 21, 1794, which concluded, "Copper plate Printing and engraving carried on in all its branches. N.B. Rolling press for sale"; or another inserted by Samuel Allardice in the Philadelphia *Aurora* of November 16, 1797, which commenced a general appeal for apprentices with the notice, "To be sold cheap. A complete copper-plate printing press."

What concrete evidence do we possess regarding the actual construction or manufacture of copperplate presses in America? While we have no specific information concerning their fabrication in colonial America, we do know of an advertisement which Adam Ramage, America's first major printing-press manufacturer, inserted in the *New-York Evening Post* of March 26, 1803, which reads, "To Printers, Book-Binders, &c. Adam Ramage respectfully informs his friends and the public, that he continues to make Printing-Presses, with or without rollers, Copperplate Presses, Book-binders' Presses, and Ploughs of mahogany, beach or apple-tree, on moderate terms." While Milton W. Hamilton, Ramage's most complete biographer to date, does not mention his early manufacture of copperplate presses, he does quote (p. 23) a Ramage 1829 advertisement for "Standing, Copperplate, Seal and Copying Presses of various Sizes."[7] It seems probable that Ramage manufactured copperplate or rolling presses from the very begining of his activity in Philadelphia in 1795, following his emigration from Scotland in that year.

While Ramage's advertisement indicates that copperplate presses were produced by professional press makers, a piece of direct evidence in support of the theory that engraver's presses were also erected or set up by

7. Milton W. Hamilton, *Adam Ramage and His Presses* (Portland, Me., Southworth-Anthoensen Press, 1942).

local artisans in the woodworking trades comes from the Philadelphia *United States Gazette for the Country* of February 11, 1818, where the following notice appeared:

To Printers & Book Binders
James Kent
No. 14, Greenleaf Court, Fourth Street, near Mar-
ket, Philadelphia

Respectfully informs Printers and
BookBinders, that he makes Typographical, Copper Plate, Standing, Lining and Sew-
ing Presses. He also keeps constantly on hand,
Binders' Type, ditto Press boards, Backing
and Cutting ditto, Brass Rule and Ringlet, Ball
Stocks, &c. &c.—Orders in the above business will be thankfully received and promptly
attended to.

James Kent is first encountered in the *Philadelphia Directory* for 1814, where he is listed as "carpenter, back 366 Sassafras." He reappears in the 1816 directory as "carpenter, 14 Greenleaf Court" and in the directory for 1818 as "packer of looking glasses and furniture, 14 Greenleaf Court." His name is not indexed in Philadelphia directories thereafter. But for his advertisement, we would have no inkling of his activity with regard to the making of copperplate presses. In light of this intelligence, then, it does not seem out of order to assume that copperplate or rolling presses were frequently set up by anonymous local carpenters and woodworkers from the early or mid-eighteenth century on. In fact, this was undoubtedly the situation which prevailed during most of the eighteenth century, when the country was without the services of professional or specialized press manufacturers. Carpenters and related woodworkers surely were the source of bookbinder's presses, standing presses, and other types of presses (but excluding the printing press, which was too complicated for a carpenter to undertake) as well.[8]

The fact that copperplate presses were restricted to a fairly specialized trade explains, to some degree, why we possess so little information about them. And while we have no other contemporary newspaper advertise-ments directly associating other carpenters, woodworkers, and even press

8. As Rollo Silver has pointed out in *The American Printer, 1787–1825* (p. 41), and within his article "The Costs of Mathew Carey's Printing Equipment," *Studies in Bibliography* XIX (1966) [85]–122, carpenters and metalsmiths sometimes contributed their skills concurrently to the making of a printing press, the former for effecting the necessary woodworking and the latter for fabricating and fitting metal parts.

makers with the manufacture of these machines in New York and other cities where copperplate printing was carried on, we do possess grounds for suspecting that certain such artisans probably engaged in the construction of copperplate presses. For example, Jared Beach's name appears in New York City directories for 1818–19, 1819–20 and 1821–22 with the designation "printing press maker." Previous to 1818 he was indexed here as "carpenter" and as "saddle-tree maker," and it was as "carpenter" that he appeared in the 1820–21 directory and in the issues for 1822–23 until his final listing in 1827–28. In Baltimore, our suspicions are aroused by directory listings for Henry Godd, who was described in *The Baltimore Directory and Register for the Year 1816* as "printers' joiner, 16 North Frederick Street" and as "printers' joiner and cabinet maker" at the same address in the issue for the following year.

It naturally follows that a machine so easily constructed and requiring so few parts should cost only a fraction of the price of the more complicated printing press, and two contemporary documents which contain valuations of rolling presses bear this out conclusively. One source, an account appended to the will of Peter A. von Hagen, which was finally settled upon the death of his wife Joannetta von Hagen in 1810, contains the following entry (No. 10): "[The said executor] further prays allowance for the amount, as estimated in the Inventory of the following articles, which he has delivered to the Guardians . . . . 1 Rolling Press 10 Dolls."[9] The other source, Isaiah Thomas's "Account of Stock, 1796," which can be found appended to Clifford Shipton's biography of this pioneer printer,[10] lists among his presses:

1 Laye Rolling Press	[$]10.00
1 Small do do	4.00

The small press was, in all probability, a simpler version of the usual machine, employed undoubtedly for pulling proofs and perhaps for executing lesser jobs ("jobbing") such as trade cards or invitations. The inclusion of these machines on the Thomas inventory is particularly interesting in light of Wroth's declaration that, so far as he knew, no inventories of early American letterpress establishments contained an engraver's press. In addition to a single price quotation in Wroth's *The Colonial Printer* with reference to the usual letterpress machine, that of 75 dollars cited by a New Jersey printing-press maker in his 1796

9. Probate Records, Suffolk County, Mass. No. 23410, Joannet C. E. Von Hagen, June 11, 1810.
10. Clifford K. Shipton, *Isaiah Thomas*, p. 86.

advertisement, we have in Thomas's account of stock for the same year additional grounds for emphasizing the low cost of the copperplate device, based on its simplicity, as opposed to the much higher price of the typographic press, which contained many complicated mechanisms. The Thomas inventory shows us valuations for printing presses ranging from 75 to 100 dollars for new and more elaborate models, and from 40 to 60 dollars for older and less intricate ones.

Illustration 27 depicts scenes of two early wooden copperplate presses. Illustration 27a, which emanates from *The Book of Trades*, an English publication of the late eighteenth century that was reprinted near Philadelphia in the first decade of the next (the illustration comes from the American edition), shows a typical "pull of the press." Behind the copperplate printer here can be seen the charcoal brazier which he used for heating the plate during the inking operation, and underneath the window to the right is some sort of inking apparatus, probably a "rubber" made of woolen rags tightly bound around one another. What appears to be a stock of paper sits in the background. Illustration 27b constitutes an advertisement which the copperplate printing firm of Bowen & McKenzie published in the Boston city directory for 1827.[11] Abel Bowen, one of the printers here, is mentioned in Appendix A as the printer of a number of editions of sheet music issued by Simeon Wood at Boston in 1820 and 1821. Bowen & McKenzie's press is a slightly improved version of the standard wooden press, which was still in use at this time. Suspended from the head here can be seen an apparatus for hanging the blanket around the roller, the first such depiction in American copperplate printing that has come to my attention. This practice was obviously a labor-saving device, obviating the necessity of adding blankets to the plate itself before sending it and the paper through the rollers of the press.

A reference in Joel Munsell's *Typographical Miscellany* (Albany, 1850) provides us with an interesting addendum to our discussion of the copperplate press in America and at the same time an insight into the possible working capacity of the machine used in earlier days. It is reported here that in 1813 Jacob Perkins of Newburyport, Massachusetts, patented an improvement in the rolling press whereby it could give off as many as 4,000 impressions in the space of twelve hours as opposed to 500

11. On Plate VIII of his *American Printer, 1787–1825* Rollo Silver has reproduced what may have been the first illustration of a copperplate press to appear in an American publication, in the *Encyclopaedia* published by Thomas Dobson in Philadelphia between 1790 and 1797. This was substantially a reprinting of the third edition of the *Encyclopaedia Britannica*. To effect the more than 500 plates for his edition, Dobson employed practically all the engravers in the Philadelphia area.

by the unimproved machine in the same period of time.[12] From this bit of information we can roughly estimate that the usual press operation, which included inking and cleaning the plate, required just under one minute and a half on the standard wooden machine.

The copperplate press began to undergo subtle changes from about the second decade of the nineteenth century, so that within several decades afterward it would only distantly resemble the wooden apparatus that had been in use for centuries before. The same Jacob Perkins is mentioned in Alexander Jamieson's *Dictionary of Mechanical Science, Arts, Manufactures and Miscellaneous Knowledge* (London, 1827, p. 837) as the inventor of a refinement in the rolling press whereby it utilized a steel wheel in place of the usual cross and had other subtleties and improvements in the rollers. [13] In looking into Luther Ringwalt's *American Encyclopedia of Printing* (Philadelphia, 1871), we would hardly recognize the copperplate press illustrated there as a successor of the machine shown in Illustration 27a. By this time, it had diminished in size and was composed entirely of steel. A number of metal copperplate presses of late nineteenth-century vintage can be viewed in American museums and libraries. A particularly interesting machine, which lacks manufacturer's markings but which dates undoubtedly from the latter decades of the nineteenth century, is on

12. On June 29, 1813, Perkins filed jointly with George Murray, a Philadelphia engraver and his partner in a firm specializing in the engraving of bank notes, for patent rights to a printing press for copper and steel engraving. Specifications for this were destroyed in the famous Patent Office fire of 1836, and so we know little of Perkins's actual improvements in the early copperplate press. Nor is anything said about them in his official biography, *Jacob Perkins*, by Greville and Dorothy Bathe. Munsell's reference to the fact that Perkins's machine was capable of producing 4,000 impressions in the space of a twelve-hour day seems a bit farfetched. Such a machine was probably not practical, as it would have required a small army of printers to ink and clean plates to keep that sort of operation on schedule. In any event, the day would not be long off when engraving on metal would begin to be replaced, in book work, at least, by wood engraving, which was a relief process that allowed for the printing of illustrations right along with letterpress or text. And within fifteen or twenty years the introduction of lithography on a continuing basis would displace it even more. Music printing and bank-note printing were two of the principal areas where copperplate printing survived—indeed, in cases where music engraving has not been displaced by technological substitutes, engravers use such presses today for pulling proofs and transfer copies—or had a longer life at least. Perkins is remembered today mainly for the introduction of steel engraving, especially for the prevention of bank-note forgery. He was something of a mechanical genius who built engines that used prodigious steam pressure and invented a steam gun that poured forth a devastating stream of bullets. A full list of inventions for which he sought patent protection, both in this country and later in England, to which he emigrated, is listed in Appendix 1 of the Bathe biography. His work on bank-note printing has recently been reviewed by Elizabeth Harris, "Jacob Perkins, William Congreve, and Counterfeit Printing in 1820," in *Prints in and of America to 1850*, pp. [193]–214.

13. This may have been the improvement in the machine for which Perkins and Murray sought patent protection in 1813.

permanent exhibition in the Prints Department of the Boston Public Library. On this the lower roller has been replaced by a series of short rollers which move the heavy steel table with marvelous ease. Unlike the steel press mentioned above, this has a steel cross bar rather than a wheel for hand operation. I have also seen several other American copperplate presses of the 1850–1900 period in the hands of music engravers and general engravers who use them mostly for pulling proofs. These are upright machines, and some of them bear the legend "American Bank Note Company" on their metal frames.

CHAPTER X

Customs and Conditions
of the Trade

꙳꙳꙳

B ARELY MENTIONED thus far are a number of important topics
relating to the day-to-day customs and procedures followed by our
early musician-engravers and musician-publishers in issuing sheet music,
such as the kind of music that was published, its price, the size of editions,
the use of illustrations, methods of distribution, and similar subjects. A
discussion of these themes will complete our sketch of early American
music engraving, printing, and publishing from John Aitken's time into
the mid- and late nineteenth century.

THE NATURE OF THE PRODUCT

While a detailed discussion of music published and performed in early
America is best left to a qualified musicologist, a few comments on the
nature of the product of our early musician-publishers are in order here.
As was noted in chapters 2 and 3 herein, the output during the colonial
period in America was almost entirely sacred in character. There did not
exist in the American colonies a society that was sufficiently large or
sufficiently cultivated in secular music to justify a separate trade. When
nonreligious music was performed and enjoyed in colonial America, its
rendition was restricted mostly to the homes of the musically sophisticated. Importation was capable of satisfying the needs of these few for
instruments and music. However, there occurred a slow but continual

growth of interest in nonreligious music after the middle of the eighteenth century. These sentiments, which were pent up during the American struggle for independence, burst forth after the war in a near-wild enthusiasm for the delights of the theater, opera, and program music as America began to seek an expression of its own national life. This demand was catered to and fostered by a growing influx of foreign musicians, opera companies, theatrical troupes, and similar entertainers who looked toward this untapped resource in order to achieve fame or fortune or to gain opportunities unavailable to them at home. They carried with them the musical tastes in vogue in the concert rooms of their homelands and on the stages of London, Dublin, Paris, and the other musical centers of England and Europe.

Undoubtedly the best summary of our early American musical life has been provided by Carleton Sprague Smith as an introduction to my *Secular Music in America*. Smith has pointed out in this brief but eloquent essay that there was little interest in "absolute music" in the America of the 1790s and later. The development of interest in the major works of the great composers, several of whom, like Beethoven and Haydn, were flourishing contemporaneously, had to await the refinement of goals and tastes which only began to become formalized toward the middle of the nineteenth century. While the American public of the 1780s and afterward did listen to string quartets and parts of symphonies, there did not exist a sufficiently large group of players to make it profitable for a publisher to issue the parts of string quartets and larger forms. At most, an occasional piano or violin sonata appeared locally (and, as we shall show later on, these were published only in very small editions). Piano reductions of overtures, dances, marches, and similar forms were the order of the day, as were the popular songs of the theater and semi-operatic stage. The most elaborate and demanding pieces published in America before the 1830s consisted of fantasias on popular airs. As Smith has so aptly put it, "it was the era of the embellished theme, and America heard variations on Scottish, Irish, English, French, German, Italian and their own patriotic melodies with never ending delight." Not only did they hear them; many of them played them, for the influx of great numbers of foreign music teachers had increased amateur preformance considerably. It was mainly to satisfy the tastes and interests of this group, the parlor-room amateurs, that the energies of our newly established music-publishing trade were directed. Our early American song sheets and instrumental pieces were intended for home use. This published repertory represented a manifestation and reflection of the popular or urban taste of the eastern seaboard, which imitated the vogues and tastes then rampant in England and on the Continent. While a few resident or naturalized composers did produce a body of orchestral and chamber music, this corpus remained almost entirely in manuscript, and a large part of it has since disappeared.

Alexander Reinagle, for example, composed four sonatas for the pianoforte which O. G. T. Sonneck has said "closely follow in the foot steps of Ph. Em. Bach and early Haydn without being void of individuality,"[1] and which mark Reinagle as a composer of merit. These works are extant in manuscript form only in the Library of Congress, and a few have now been recorded in disc form. Although they were performed by Reinagle on the early American concert stage, for contemporary programs indicate this, he never saw fit to commit them to print. There simply did not exist during his lifetime a sufficiently large body of amateur performers (and purchasers) to warrant the cost of engraving and printing these pieces; by the time such a musically trained and sophisticated public did exist, around the middle of the nineteenth century, Reinagle was long dead and forgotten, or, if remembered, was considered a provincial by a society whose enthusiasm was being directed toward the music of Beehoven, Chopin, Donizetti, and the like.

The same principle holds true for James Hewitt. As Sonneck–Upton and my own compilation indicate, Hewitt left an extensive corpus of printed music, most of it published by himself. (For some unexplained reason, few rival publishers saw fit to republish Hewitt's compositions, in spite of the fact that their composer hardly ever went to the trouble of copyrighting them; almost all of them were published by Hewitt himself, mostly in single editions.) Hewitt published only his smaller and less consequential works. Yet, as Irving Lowens has pointed out,[2] Hewitt is known to have composed works larger than those songs and short piano pieces with which he is identified in the published bibliographies. Hewitt, too, refrained from publishing his larger works because there did not exist in his day a market for them. This is unfortunate, since the manuscripts of his larger and more ambitious compositions have all disappeared. It is difficult, therefore, to arrive at a proper estimate of Hewitt's true musical worth as a composer. His most ambitious compositions extant today amount to a handful or two of descriptive

1. Sonneck–Upton, p. 393.
2. Irving Lowens, "James Hewitt, Professional Musician," comprising Chapter 10 of his *Music and Musicians in Early America.*

sonatas and overtures for piano which he published between 1795 and 1809. One of the earliest was written in celebration of the Battle of Trenton and another in celebration of the Fourth of July, both employing patriotic airs in keeping with the taste of the times. Similarly, his last sonata, which appeared in 1809 (Wolfe, No. 3789), was basically a set of variations on the popular air *The Plough Boy*.

Most sheet music issued in America between the time of John Aitken until the 1830s contained either light instrumental pieces, arranged for two- or, less frequently, for four-handed piano performance, or songs. Instrumental works included marches, frequently composed to mark some event or to honor a military or political personality or organization; and dances, such as waltzes, cotillions, reels, hornpipes, minuets, and works of similar form. But most frequently, especially as the nineteenth century progressed, instrumental music took the form of variations on national and popular airs. These were well suited to home entertainments and to the limited abilities of amateurs and students. Similarly, vocal music, which predominated in the total output of the period, followed the vogues established on the London, New York, and Philadelphia stages. Their songs were mostly comic, sentimental, patriotic, or national in character. They could be enjoyed and appreciated in the intimacy of the home as well as in the theater. The citizens of emerging America liked to parody and poke fun; to be stirred by noble sentiments and cry; and to celebrate their heroes, leaders, and institutions, through musical as well as verbal utterance.

From the time when John Aitken first began to strike notes into music plates, the works of immigrant and naturalized composers made up a substantial part of the printed output. These individual composed and published to satisfy their own requirements for expression; to provide music for pupils; and to make money, a concern which was then, as now, an American obsession. They relished composing songs and piano music to celebrate patriotic and national events, such as the inaugurations and deaths of presidents; the undeclared war with France; the siege of Tripoli; the battles and heroes of 1812; the Napoleonic wars and wars of national liberation of the 1820s; the Louisiana Purchase; the election of state and local officials; and the opening of the Erie Canal. The visit of General Lafayette in 1824 provoked a deluge of printed music. Bands came out to greet him wherever he went, playing *Hail LaFayette!* or *LaFayette's march* or *LaFayette's Quick Step* or some similar work of a professional or even amateur composer. As many as fifty of these songs and piano reductions of marches, quicksteps, waltzes, and the like appeared in sheet-music form, many embellished with engraved pictures and scenes.[3]

Though native composers contributed significantly to the musical expression and published output of the period, most vocal music issued in America to the 1830s consisted of reprints of the pirated compositions of foreign composers, especially of those who wrote for the contemporary English stage. The compositions of James Hook and William Shield were extremely popular in America throughout the 1790s and into the first years of the next century—Hook and Shield are represented in my *Secular Music in America* by nearly 350 and 250 editions respectively—as were songs of Stephen Storace, Samuel Arnold, Thomas Augustine Arne, Thomas Attwood, Charles Dibdin, and others. Their works eventually gave way to the songs of John Braham, John Davy, Michael King, Matthew Peter King, Joseph Mazzinghi, James Reeve, Henry Rowley Bishop, and Sir John Stevenson as the nineteenth century brought in new tastes. American society from about 1805 on was especially enamored of Irish and Scotch tunes, particularly the *Irish Melodies* of Thomas Moore, and other national music. Some of the published output of the period consisted of imitations of the music of many of the above-named composers, written for local consumption by American composers such as Hewitt, John Bray, Charles Gilfert, and, in the 1820s, by Philip Anthony Corri under the assumed name of Arthur Clifton. Books of instruction for piano, violin, flute, clarinet, and other instruments were continually popular, attesting to the existing hunger for musical knowledge. The publication of a great number of these in early America assisted in the training of a sufficiently large cadre of knowledgable amateurs by the 1820s to justify the publication of a number of large and ambitious collections of melodies and pieces for solo performance on the flute, violin, and similar instruments.

As Smith has pointed out in his essay, Beethoven, Clementi, Handel Haydn, and Mozart were known in late eighteenth- and early nineteenth-century America, but only in their lighter compositions and lesser forms. George Willig and George E. Blake probably reached the pinnacle of "absolute music" when in the second decade of the nineteenth century they issued three or four of Mozart's piano and violin sonatas. And Blake surely achieved the ultimate in early American music publishing with his

---

3. Having had the benefit of looking at all of this music, I have sometimes felt that it would be a delightful pastime to collate this mass of "LaFayette music" against published accounts of his visit and recreate his 1824 tour musically.

issuance of fifteen volumes of the vocal works of Handel. These were, however, piano scores only for such works as *Acis and Galatea, Alexander's Feast, Saul, The Messiah,* and other oratorios. Much of the lesser output of this period is dismissed now as irrelevant and unworthy of rendition. Yet, as Smith has stated, this music was written to be performed, and the patriotic marches and choruses, waltzes, reels, and cotillions served a general public that marched, sang, and danced. It should be understood and interpreted in that light today.

FORMAT AND IMPOSITION

Imposition and *format* are printing terms which indicate how pages are arranged for printing and their relationship to the size and general style or makeup of the finished work. These terms actually have relevance only to that period when handmade paper was employed in printing. Imposition refers to the number of pages that were apportioned to a single whole sheet of paper and the number of times it had to be folded to accommodate them. The format or size or, better, relationship of a given work to the original whole sheets of paper used in its printing resulted from this arrangement and folding. The greater the number of pages, the more the folding and the smaller the resultant book. For example, a quarto book resulted from the apportionment of eight pages on four leaves of text, the original whole sheet of paper having been folded twice to achieve the proper positioning and page sequence; an octavo book accommodated sixteen pages on eight leaves and necessitated another folding; and so on.

I have mentioned before that music plates, which were fairly large, were customarily arranged so that two plates or pages were printed side by side on one side of a whole sheet of paper. If the piece extended to four pages, four plates and both sides of the whole sheet were utilized. Frequently, however, and especially in the case of vocal music, only two pages were required to accommodate the whole work. In this event it was the usual practice to print both of these pages on one side of a whole sheet of paper. The paper was then folded down the middle, so that the two pages faced one another inside, and the outside pages were blank. (This arrangement may have been considered the best way of protecting the printed text.) If four pages were printed on one whole sheet of paper, the resultant format would approximate that of a folio book. However, the terms *imposition* and *format* were probably not thought of or used in early music printing.

In Chapter 8 I mentioned that we really do not know in exactly what manner early music plates were printed. Practically no information exists on this subject in early engraver's manuals, for the engraving and printing of music was a specialized field with which the general engraver concerned himself little or not at all. Engravers normally worked with larger or smaller forms which were complete in themselves, the larger forms for maps, prints, and portraits, the smaller forms for trade cards, invitations, bookplates, and the like. (Frequently, when doing small "jobbing" work, they engraved several copies or works on one large plate and printed multiple items at one time; it was easier for them to work with a large plate, and in this way they were able to ease the burdens of inking and presswork.)[4] Music printing was the only common form of copperplate printing which resulted in a paged product, and the problems and methods of effecting page sequence and registering were restricted to this field alone. Very infrequently a whole book was produced through the engraving process, as, for instance, a work on artistic anatomy or on the subject of engraving itself, where much of the text was given over to illustration. However, such books were out of the ordinary, and in most examples that have come to my attention, the engravers left these unpaged.

How, then, did our early music publishers and printers impose their plates? Singly? Two at a time? The only information I have been able to locate that has relevance to this topic comes from a French engraving manual which was issued by the publisher Roret at Paris in 1837, M. Bertilaud's *Nouveau Manuel Complet de l'Imprimerie en Taille Douce*. This devotes a few pages (128–36) to the printing of music. According to Bertilaud, whose information probably reflected the general customs of the trade, music plates were printed individually. In cases where four plates were printed, plate one was printed first. The paper was then handled and arranged in such a way that page three was printed in the opposite half and on the reverse side of the whole sheet. After waiting for about twenty-four hours, in order to alllow the ink to dry thoroughly, pages two and four were printed in a similar manner and the sheet was perfected. When two plates only were printed, each was printed individually, the initial page being run through first. In cases where title pages and illustrative matter were added, these were usually printed beforehand, prior to the printing of music. These methods were probably

---

4. For example, Illustration 57 in *Boston Prints and Printmaker, 1670–1775*, accompanying Sinclair Hitching's article "Thomas Johnston," shows two sizes of a bookbinder's trade card which were engraved and printed together on the same plate.

universal and it is likely that they carried over to American music printing as well. In some cases, our early music sheets contained only three pages of printed matter, with the fourth blank. I have noticed copies of such works with either the first page or the last page blank. Some printers may have adhered to the theory that it was better to leave the initial page blank in order to protect the first page of text, while others possibly thought that page one should be the first visible, in the manner of a modern book.

This is about all we can say with regard to the format of song sheets and the sheet music of this period. However, another format was sometimes used, in the publication of collections of tunes for performance on the violin, flute, flageolet, clarinet, etc., and for "pocket size" books of instruction. Such works were issued in a format known as "oblong quarto." This term is used to describe small music books which have longer dimensions horizontally than vertically. Such works usually measured about 7 inches from side to side and about 5 inches from top to bottom, though these dimensions varied frequently. Two illustrations of collections in oblong-quarto format can be seen as printed endpapers in the front of the second volume of my *Secular Music in America*, in the form of *Aitken's Fountain of Music* and *Blake's Evening Companion*. From many such works that I have examined I have concluded that these were normally engraved several pages to a single plate. After initial printing, two or more pages were present on one side of a sheet of paper. When the other side had been printed and perfected, the sheet was then folded one or more times to achieve proper page sequence and arrangement for binding. This was the method employed by Thomas Johnston to engrave the Boston, 1766, edition of Daniel Bayley's *A New and Compleat Introduction to the Grounds and Rules of Music*, shown in Illustration 1a, and it was the approximate method followed by Gottlieb Graupner when engraving his *Anacreontic Vocalist* (Wolfe, No. 127) around 1809. An examination of plate outlines in the copy of this piece which is now in the Free Library of Philadelphia shows that they frequently run off the tops and bottoms of pages, indicating that several pages were printed from one plate, and that sheets were then folded and cut. (This was also the approximate method used about 1625 to engrave the music plates for printing the Jacobean music collection *Parthenia In-Violata*. As I pointed out earlier in a bibliographical analysis of this work, the engraving of its plates was effected by several different hands; and, as pages were engraved two to the plate in such a manner that each ran from the center to the outer margin, it is possible that two engravers could have worked on one plate simultaneously, each sitting at opposite sides of the same table and facing one another.[5])

PROOFS

Gamble states in *Music Engraving and Printing* (p. 154) that it was formerly the custom of music engravers to pull proofs in the copperplate manner on the copperplate press. This operation consisted of inking the plate in the usual way, that is, in smearing ink into the hatches and engraved areas on it; wiping clean its surface; laying a piece of dampened paper on it, backed by a blanket; and pulling the charged plate through the press. That this was the method employed in music printing during the period under discussion is proved by two extant proofs of pages from James Hewitt's 1807 publication, *The Music of Erin*, one of which is shown in Illustration 12a. Sometime in the period after engraving and lithography were combined to produce music—engraving to effect the transfer copy, and lithography to turn out the edition[6]—this method proved less useful, for the results of proofs pulled in the copperplate manner showed a totally different effect from that which would be ultimately obtained in the lithographic printing, as the lines and notes appeared too sharp and thin.

It then became the practice of music engravers to pull proofs simply by inking the surface of the plate with a rag or dabber or "rubber" charged with green or blue ink. In this way only the surface was inked and printed from, so that the engraved parts showed white on a green or blue ground. The reason for using green or blue ink, Gamble states, is that it is easy to see any corrections marked in black ink on the proof. When green ink is utilized, the resulting proofs are referred to as "green proofs," when blue ink, "blue proofs." This is the method used today; I saw it employed during a visit to the MV Music Engraving Company in Jersey City in 1962. In assisting in the final preparations for the publication of my *Secular Music in America*, I purposely selected green as the color of the illustrated endpapers in it to simulate publisher's green proofs. A reader who refers to a copy of this work in its original trade binding will be able to visualize the approximate appearance of green proofs.

After this method of pulling proofs was introduced into America,

5. Richard J. Wolfe, "*Parthenia In-Violata*, a Seventeenth-Century Folio-Form Quarto," *Bulletin of The New York Public Library* LXV (1961) 347–64.
6. This occurred in England after 1838, in America after 1841.

Thomas Birch, who has already been noted as a publisher of music in New York City from 1825 and as an engraver there for perhaps five years before, began in the early 1840s to issue music for sale which had been printed in this manner, that is, with white staves, notes, lyrics, etc. on a colored ground. Birch printed in a variety of colors: green, blue, black, red, and others. He undoubtedly adapted this method of pulling proofs, intending to capitalize on its novelty. I do not know how long Birch continued this practice, since I have not seen enough pieces printed in this manner with copyright dates. I suspect, however, that its vogue did not last long, though Birch himself remained in business in New York for a very long time afterward. In 1853 he was joined in partnership by his son, presumably the Thomas A. Birch who continued the business alone from 1871 into the 1890s.

SIZE OF EDITIONS

While the engraving process is in so many ways unsuited to the general production of printed matter, one of the distinct advantages inherent in it is its capability of printing as few or as many copies of a given work at a given time as its user desires. The plates can then be retained indefinitely for future and continuous reprinting, until they have finally worn out. In this regard engraving held a distinct advantage over printing from type, which, before the introduction of stereotyping and electro-stereotyping by the mid-nineteenth century, required that the type of an edition be kept standing if reprinting was to occur, or that the edition be completely reset in the event that the original type was distributed. Because of the bulk involved in keeping type standing, and the frequent need to employ the type for other work, early printers rarely kept type standing for any appreciable length of time; and even after stereotyping and electroplating had solved this problem, these media were desirable only for works of immense editions, such as Bibles and textbooks. It was only much later, when stereotype plates came to be made of lighter materials (plastic is used today), that this problem was finally solved and letterpress work attained or surpassed the advantage of engraving in this respect.

Because of their ability to reprint at will from engraved plates, it follows that our early music publishers printed only as many copies of a work upon completion of its plates as experience and intuition told them were necessary to meet present and expected demand. If demand surpassed initial expectation, publishers then could happily reprint as much and as often as was necessary. This allowed them to refrain from investing in and risking expensive paper and it kept them from involving themselves more than was necessary in the tedious jobs of inking and cleaning their plates, or paying others to do this for them. All evidence available at this time indicates that in the period under discussion most editions of newly published titles were small. Of course, this factor differed from publisher to publisher, from locality to locality (the size of an edition in Philadelphia would naturally differ from one issued in Charleston, South Carolina, as there existed a much greater market potential in the northern city) and with regard to the nature and type of music published.

Our only source of information on the size of a publisher's editions at this early time comes from the manuscript account book of Simeon Wood, reproduced in transcribed form in Appendix A. This establishes with some validity and accuracy the usual sizes of editions in the 1818–21 period. Admittedly, Wood was not a major publisher in America at this time, and it appears that he was only gaining a toehold in music publishing in Boston at the time of his death. However, his figures are not inconsistent with observations and conclusions I have otherwise made. An examination of Wood's account indicates that his editions initially comprised from 50 to 100 copies and that he later reprinted in quantities of 50 and 100 as demand indicated. These figures obviously took into account his estimate of the immediate demand within Boston and the number of copies that could be disposed of through agents in other localities, such as Oliver Shaw in Providence and William M. Goodrich and Lowell Mason in Savannah, Georgia. In only two instances did Wood's initial printings exceed 100 copies. In November 1820, he had Abel Bowen print 200 copies of a song composed by an anonymous amateur entitled *My Beautiful Maid*—this may have fallen into the category of a vanity publication, its cost underwritten by its author or by the musicians Wood and Ostinell, who apparently sponsored it, and in early 1821 he had the copperplate printer Luther Stevens issue 200 copies of Frederick Granger's (a local musician) *The Star of Bethlehem*. A large edition of the latter was called for because this work had been sung at the oratorio performances of the Handel and Haydn Society and was popular.

As we can see from Wood's account, reprinting occurred frequently, though rarely did the total number of copies of his editions exceed 200. Wood's total print runs exceeded 300 in only two instances, with *This Blooming Rose*, a ballad by the ever-popular Irish vocalist Thomas Phillips, and with Haydn's *To Sigh Yet Feel No Pain*. A large edition of the Haydn song was called for because of the popularity this work achieved through its performance at the Philharmonic Society's concerts. All large editions in Wood's account book are of vocal music, which was more popular since it could be performed by a greater number of amateurs. Wood's figures for instrumental works are quite different. Except for a composition entitled the *Porcellian Club's March*, written by John Hart, a local musician and bandmaster, for the use of members of this Harvard eating society (Wood had about 300 copies of it printed, possibly by arrangement with the Club), his editions of piano music were extremely small, attesting probably to the paucity of trained pianists in Boston at the time. On August 12, 1820, Jacob Eckhard, Jr., of Charleston, South Carolina, appeared as piano soloist at a concert held in Boylston Hall for the benefit of Francis C. Schaffer, whom a newspaper advertisement for the affair describes as "an infirm, aged, and decayed Musician." Before leaving Boston, Eckhard had or let Wood engrave and publish his *Waltz*, which went on sale by the twenty-second of the month. Wood's records indicate that this was printed in eighty-six copies only, of which but fifty-three were actually sold. During this three-year period Wood published only two other instrumental works, a duet by Kozeluch (which, I am ashamed to admit, was not recorded in my *Secular Music in America*) and James Hook's *Masquerade Sonata*. In each case Wood had only twenty-five copies printed. In the course of compiling my 1801–25 bibliography, I found no copy of the Kozeluch work and I could locate only two copies of the Hook sonata. One wonders why Wood went to the trouble of engraving plates for these works when demand for them was so slight, especially when the Hook piece required ten plates.

Wood's print runs probably approximated those of many of the ordinary or lesser publishers in America from the 1790s into the 1830s, the Carrs, Hewitts, Gilferts, Paffs, and the like. However, larger and more ambitious publishers such as Blake and Willig in Philadelphia and eventually Riley in New York undoubtedly issued much of their output in larger editions, both initially and when reprinting. In addition to being located within larger market areas, these men appear to have distributed extensively through agents, and Blake apparently sent music to all parts of the then-existing country. Some of the pieces issued by Blake and these others can still be located in significant quantities. Not only did I find many copies of their individual publications in a great number of public and private institutions, but I located multiple copies (sometimes half a dozen or more) of a given title in many cases, and when one encounters bound volumes of early music on sale in the current antiquarian book market, many of these titles reappear. If Wood published an edition by printing 50 or 100 copies initially, Blake and Willig must have commenced an edition by printing up at least double that number; and I suspect that in some instances their total editions reached 500 and perhaps even 1,000 copies. The numbers of some of their publications that have survived the ravages of time, scrapdealer's heaps, wartime paper drives, and the like, indicate this. As was noted earlier, we can tell from the nature of paper at different times that frequent and continual reprinting must have gone on throughout both Blake's and Willig's lengthy careers. Blake and Willig and later Edward Riley were exceptions, however. For the most part, editions before the 1830s must have been small and in line with Wood's accounts. However, the size of editions even of ordinary publishers must have increased as populations increased, as performing amateurs grew in number, and as musical entertainment, particularly of the home variety, became more popular.

COPYRIGHT

As Silver pointed out in 1958[7] and Lowens in 1959,[8] the first copyright legislation enacted in what is now the United States occurred in 1781 when the Connecticut Assembly granted Andrew Law an exclusive patent protecting forty-two tunes and nine anthems of his entitled *Collection of the Best Tunes for the Promotion of Psalmody*. Silver has further pointed out and described how an attempt had been made by William Billings in 1772, three years before the American Revolution and while the country was still under English rule, to secure a patent from the Massachusetts House of Representatives to protect a second volume of his *New-England Psalm Singer*, the publication of which he was then contemplating and which he feared might be pirated. Silver's article provides much information on this episode, which came to nought (the bill was passed in the House and in the Governor's Council, but Governor Thomas Hutchinson refused to sign it), and speculates that Billings may have been discouraged because of this experience from continuing his scheme, for the second book of this work was not published until 1778.[9] Information furnished by Lowens and Silver shows that protection for musical compositions was not only

7. Rollo G. Silver, "Prologue to Copyright in America: 1772," *Studies in Bibliography* XI (1958) 259–62.

8. Irving Lowens, "Copyright and Andrew Law," *Papers of the Bibliographical Society of America* LIII (1959) 150–53. See also his essay, "Andrew Law and the Pirates," Chapter 4 of his *Music and Musicians in Early America*.

9. The subject of Billings's 1772 petition for copyright protection has been expanded by David P. McKay, "William Billings and the Colonial Music Patent," *Old-Time New England* LXIII (1973) 100–107. No mention is made of Silver's prior work here, and it is to be assumed that McKay was unaware of it.

being thought about in the 1770s and 1780s but was actually being pursued. However, Lowens's account of Law's experiences with regard to copyright indicate how ineffectual early protection really was or how confused the situation was in guarding against piracy throughout the individual colonies and states.

On May 2, 1783, almost four months before the signing of the Treaty of Paris which formally concluded the War for American Independence, the Colonial Congress passed a resolution recommending that the several states secure to the authors and publishers of new books the copyright of their works. This resolution probably grew out of the previous copyright legislation of three states, Connecticut (January 1783), Massachusetts (March 17, 1783), and Maryland (April 21, 1783), which had recently put such laws into their statute books. As a consequence of this congressional resolution, all but one of the original thirteen states had passed copyright legislation by 1786. Delaware alone enacted no copyright law for the protection of its citizens. Because the copyright laws of the various states differed in the period of time during which claimants were protected and in other ways, their laws must have been difficult to administer individually, and the question of jurisdiction undoubtedly complicated even further the problems which arose. As a consequence, the Senate and the House of Representatives of the United States of America in Congress assembled passed on May 31, 1790, the first formal copyright statute, "An Act for the encouragement of learning, by securing the copies of maps, charts, and books, to the authors and proprietors of such copies, during the times mentioned therein" (First Congress, Second Session, Chapter 15). In essence, this law granted copyright protection to United States citizens for a period of fourteen years, provided authors or proprietors desposited a printed copy of the title of their works in the clerk's office of the district court where they resided and that this was duly recorded by the clerk in a book kept especially for that purpose. Within six months the author or proprietor had to deliver or cause to be delivered to the Secretary of State a copy of the same title for preservation in that office. Copyright in a property could be renewed for a like term at the expiration of fourteen years, provided the title was rerecorded in the same manner.

The restriction of the 1790 statute to maps, charts, and books apparently caused problems in interpreting and administering the law, for on April 29, 1802, Congress, in laying down additional rules for the law's administration, extended its benefits to the arts of designing, engraving, and etching of historical and other prints. In 1819 such jurisdiction was broadened to cases covering patents for inventions and discoveries, and on February 3, 1831, the several acts were revised to include musical compositions as well. At the same time, the term of copyright was reset to twenty-eight years and was made renewable for fourteen years. Under this law, the author or proprietor was required to deposit a copy of the work itself in the clerk's office, which the clerk was directed to forward along with all other deposit copies in a given year to the Secretary of State for preservation in his office. It was only upon the enactment of August 10, 1846, that the author or proprietor was directed to deliver or cause to be delivered one copy of his work to the libarian of the Smithsonian Institution and another to the librarian of the Congress Library for the use of said libraries.

Information on the titles of works that were copyrighted during this earliest period is provided by the surviving record books which the clerks of the district courts prepared from 1790 until 1870 and from a few remaining title pages and copies of works which were forwarded to the Secretary of State by individual authors and proprietors, as directed. The bulk of such records are now in the Library of Congress.[10] In his checklist of "Pennsylvania Registrations for Copyright, 1790–1794," Goff notes only three musical items, as follows: "[No.] 10 Adgate, Andrew. Rudiments of Music. The Third Edition. Philadelphia: John M'Culloch, 1790; [No.] 27. Aitken, John, *comp*. A Compilation of the Litanies, Vespers, Hymns, and Anthems as they are sung in the Catholic Church. Philadelphia: John Aitken, 1791; [No.] 51. Taylor, Raynor. The Kentucky Volunteer a new Song written by a Lady of Philadelphia composed by R. Taylor. Philadelphia: Printed & Sold at Carr & Co. [1794], Benjamin Carr, *proprietor*."[11] The Aitken compilation is the first piece of stamped or punched music to be copyrighted in the United States, and the Taylor composition the first piece of sheet music. These records show that only a few musical compositions were copyrighted before 1795, and only a small number afterward. First of all, music publishing was carried on by John Aitken alone before 1793, and there was no competition nor "pirate" against whom he needed to protect his publications. Second, as we shall note in greater detail below, foreign

10. Some of the individual copyright deposit copies of early American music sheets are in the Music Division of the Library of Congress. I have seen still others, of a slightly later period, in the files of American music in the New York Public Library. These were unwittingly released by the Library of Congress during an earlier exchange program. A more complete review of our early copyright situation, together with a resumé of all extant records and their locations, can be found in G. Thomas Tanselle's "Copyright Records and the Bibliographer," *Studies in Bibliography* XXII (1969) [77]–124.

11. F. R. Goff, "The First Decade of Copyright," pp. 101–28.

compositions and publications were unprotected and could be (and were) reprinted by publishers at will. It was only to United States citizens— and, obviously, to naturalized Americans and even to composers resident here—that the privilege of copyright was offered. As there were only a handful of composers in America at this time, and as our earliest musical publications were mostly reprintings of the successes and "hits" of the English stage and of the Parisian salons, there was a limited need for copyright during this period. The protection of this law was more frequently sought by compilers or publishers of large collections of sacred music, such as the Adgate work noted by Goff before, which was printed from type.

From the few surviving records it is apparent that music was copyrighted as a book before 1802 and as a book or print afterward. Goff notes on page 107 of his essay that Benjamin Carr is recorded as author for three compositions after 1794, for copyright copies of them are in the Library of Congress. He also states that only two other pieces of sheet music were apparently recorded before 1801, both registered in Boston on October 17, 1798. These are James Davenport's *Columbia and Liberty*, set to music composed by Thomas Augustine Arne, and *The Green Mountain Farmer*, by Thomas Paine, later known as Robert Treat Paine, Jr., the son of the signer of the Declaration of Independence. That the early copyright records were scattered and are now incomplete is evidenced by the existence of copies of Alexander Reinagle's *The Music in the Historical Play of Columbus* (Wolfe, No. 10315), which bears the printed note "Copyright secured according to law" and which is known to have been registered for copyright on February 22, 1799, with Alexander Reinagle as claimant (see Sonneck–Upton, p. 80), but for which no actual record now exists. And there are several other such examples. Some editions of early American music sheets carry a copyright date, but we have no record of their entry on extant books, which suggests carelessness in recording and forwarding copies as specified by the law. Such lack of care in carrying out the letter of the law is exemplified by John and Michael Paff's edition of *The Experiment*, which they issued between 1799 and 1803. This carried a copyright notice, but record of such action is unknown.

In general, the following observations hold true for the employment of copyright protection by composers and musician-publishers in our period. Copyright was invoked to protect original compositions of composers born in or resident in the United States. And as the two Boston sheet-music publications of 1798, *Columbia and Liberty* and *The Green Mountain Farmer*, show, works were sometimes registered to protect original poetry and

[191]

lyrics as well as music. As this type of composition made up only a very small part of the total output of our music publishers before 1826, it is not surprising to find that copyright was so infrequently used. Benjamin Carr, Arthur Clifton (Philip Anthony Corri), Florant Meline, John Isaac Hawkins, Anthony Philip Heinrich, and other immigrant composers frequently resorted to copyright to protect their works (but, strangely enough, not James Hewitt; equally strange is the fact that almost none of his compositions, which he left unprotected, were pirated or reprinted by other American publishers of his time.)[12] Amateurs such as Maria Penniman (of Boston), Charles Cathrall (of Philadelphia) and James C. Drake (of Cincinnati, and Louisville, Kentucky) used it. In addition, Joseph and Bejamin Carr, George E. Blake, and Allyn Bacon as well as a few other early American music publishers invariably copyrighted all compositions or series of compositions which contained the works of native composers. Carr and Blake and Bacon in this way protected *Carr's Musical Miscellany* and Carr's *Armonia*, *Blake's Musical Miscellany* and Bacon's *American Musical Miscellany* (usually by depositing initially a title page to the series only), for these were devoted almost entirely to original works of American composers or poets. Of the more than 10,000 editions of music published in America before 1826, those copyrighted number probably only in the low hundreds. It has been suggested by others interested in the subject of early American music that after about 1818 publishers began to add copyright notices to their wares in increasing numbers. This is somewhat true, but again only with regard to original works (though one might be able to find an exception here and there). The slight increase in copyright music after about 1818 is attributable, I think, to the fact that the works of native composers and poets began at this time to constitute a slightly larger percentage of our published output and to the fact that publishers were beginning to get in the habit of resorting to copyright protection. One final observation is pertinent here. So far as I have noticed, publishers of early American music sedulously observed the restrictions against reprinting copyrighted music. I cannot recall a single violation of the law by one of our publishers of this period.

On the other hand, as Section 5 of the original Copyright Act of 1790 stated: "*And be it further enacted,* That nothing in this act shall be construed to extend to prohibit the importation or vending, reprinting or publishing

12. As noted before, Hewitt's compositions appear not to have obtained much popularity (outside his own orbit, at least) during his lifetime. Only his song *The Wounded Hussar* and his variations on the favorite air *Mark My Alford* and a few other pieces appeared in editions other than his own.

within the United States, of any map, chart, book or books, written, printed, or published by any person not a citizen of the United States, in foreign parts or places without the jurisdiction of the United States." Congress opened the door and even encouraged the pirating or reprinting of foreign music publications by American publishers (and books by book publishers as well). Foreign editions, especially the favorites of the London stage, were reprinted by American publishers (Blake, Willig, Aitken, and others) as soon as copies reached our shores. (One is inclined to suspect that, as was the custom with book publishers, some of our more enterprising publishers of music must have had arrangements with foreign agents for the transmission of copies of popular foreign compositions expressly for reprinting here.) In this regard it was "open season" all the time.

The few remaining copies of early musical titles deposited for copyright which are now preserved in the Library of Congress show how the provisions of the original act were observed. These contain deposit information written in manuscript upon the deposit sheets themselves. For example, as the copyright act directed that only the title page be deposited, I have noticed in one case at least that only the first page of a four-page publication was deposited, that page containing the title alone, and on the unprinted verso of this was written in longhand the usual deposit information.[13] Such deposit information, normally penned on the verso of the deposited title, usually indicated the date of deposit and the name of the person to whom copyright was granted, the proprietor. For example, on the verso of the deposited title page of Andrew Law's *The Art of Playing the Organ and Piano Forte* (Wolfe, No. 5323), printed from type by Jane Aitken in 1809, appears the handwritten note: "770 292. Title-page of 'The art of playing the organ or piano forte.' Deposited 19th May 1809 by Andrew Law as proprietor." And on the verso of the Library of Congress copy of the title page of Benjamin Carr's serial publication *Lyricks, or Adaptations, Arrangements & Compositions in Vocal Music* is written, "No. 11590. Title of 'Lyricks, &c.' Deposited 26 Augt. 1825 by Benjamin Carr as proprietor." During the earlier part of the period under consideration, in instances where a title was copyrighted, the phrase "Copyright" or "Copyright Secured" or "Secured according to

13. This is Benjamin Carr's composition *I am a Stranger Here* (Wolfe, no. 1607), which he himself published in 1825. The Library of Congress has only the first of its four pages. This was all that was printed and this alone was forwarded to the Secretary of State. On its verso is written in longhand: "N. 1584, Title of 'Sacred Melody. Deposited 15 July 1825 by Benjamin Carr as proprietor.'" (At the head of the title here was printed "Sacred Melody from the Southern Intelligencer.")

Law" was usually added to the published sheet, sometimes before or after the titles and sometimes at the foot of a page (usually the former). For example, the phrase "Entered according to law" can be seen at the foot of John Aitken's *The Goldsmith's Rant* (see Frontispiece herein). From about 1812 a more extensive note was frequently printed on the edition. This often occupied the center of a blank page before or after the music itself. A beautiful example of this practice is afforded by George Willig's publication of J. G. May's *The Lord's Prayer*:

DISTRICT OF PENNSYLVANIA, TO WIT:

(L.S.)

Be it remembered, That on the ninth day of May, in the forty first year of the Independence of the United States of America, A.D. 1817 George Willig of the said District, hath deposited in this office the Title of a Book the right whereof he claims as Proprietor in the words following, to wit:

"THE LORDS PRAYER Composed by J. G. May the words by the Gent C.E.

In Conformity to the Act of the Congress of the United States, intituled "An Act for the Encouragement of Learning, by securing the Copies of Maps, Charts, and Books, to the Authors and and proprietors of such Copies, during the Times therein mentioned. And also to the Act, entitled, An Act supplementary to An Act, entitled, An Act for the Encouragement of Learning, by securing the Copies of Maps, Charts, and Books, to the Authors and Proprietors of such Copies during the Times therein mentioned," and extending the Benefit to the Arts of designing, engraving, and etching historical and other Prints.

D: CALDWELL, Clerk of the
District of Pennsylvania

On some such copyright notices, the year of the publication was omitted and only the phrase "in the forty-first [or another] year of the Independence of the United States" was given. In such instances, one computes from July 4, 1776, to determine the calendar year in question. (In other words, the first year of Independence extended from July 4, 1776, to July 3, 1777, and so on.) In the period after 1820, due, perhaps, to the recent alterations of the law, a simple statement indicating the date, the jurisdiction, and the proprietor was added to publications, as, for instance, on John Cole's edition of Christopher Meineke's *President John Quincy Adams Grand March & Quick Step* (Wolfe, No. 5804), "Entered according to Act of Congress March 4th 1825 by J. Cole of Maryland."

It should be noted, in conclusion, that the dating of early American music sheets through copyright records can sometimes be misleading. In his book *The Star Spangled Banner*, Joseph Muller misdated (p. 35) James Hewitt's own compostion of *The Star Spangled Banner* (Wolfe, No. 3783) on the assumption that information added to a copyright deposit copy was correct and up-to-date. Muller's reasoning went as follows:

> In 1816 James Hewitt, an early American musician, composer and music publisher, wishing to replace the old English drinking song with native music, wrote an original tune for Key's "The Star Spangled Banner" . . . Hewitt himself first published his "Star Spangled Banner" from his "Musical Repository" at No. 156½ William Street, New York, in 1819. This date has been established from a copyright deposit in the Library of Congress of "This Blooming Rose at Early Dawn," a song by T. Philips, and issued by Hewitt and deposited for copyright May 20, 1819. The publisher was listed in New York directories as "musician" at No. 20 Harrison Street in 1818, and at No. 87 Warren Street in 1819. These two addresses were most probably Hewitt's home addresses. 156½ William Street was his place of business for that period. Hewitt disappears from city records after 1819, and went to live in Boston.

I have seen the deposit copy of *This Blooming Rose at Early Dawn* at the Library of Congress, and as I have noted in my *Secular Music in America* (No. 7016), this bears the manuscript note at the head of its title, "Recd. at Dept. of State, May 28, 1819, Danice Brent, C.C." Inasmuch as Hewitt advertised this very title in the *New York Evening Post* of November 22, 1817, as "now in publication"—he also advertised his *Star Spangled Banner* there on that same day—it is obvious that a period of almost a year and a half elapsed before his deposit copy of *This Blooming Rose at Early Dawn* was forwarded to the office of the Secretary of State, where it was duly recorded in accordance with the provision of the copyright law. It is also apparent that Hewitt resided at 156½ William Street in New York upon his return from Boston. As he was only casually involved in publishing music at this time, it is my assumption that he probably did not maintain a separate place of business then.

PLATE-NUMBERING SYSTEMS

Notice has already been taken of the description of "plate cellars" in the 1838 pamphlet *A Day at a Music Publishers*. As indicated there, large and established publishers maintained fairly expansive repositories for the storage of their engraved plates. They also kept up recording and filing systems to identify and retrieve individual titles from this mass for reprinting and for other purposes. It is doubtful that American music publishers needed such extensive facilities during the period under consideration, though George E. Blake and George Willig of Philadelphia, both of whom published extensively over long periods of time, must have come to grips eventually with the problem of storing and retrieving pieces. The 1871 auction catalog for the sale of Blake's music, plates, and engraving and printing.paraphernalia listed the entire published output of his near seventy-year career. Even though Blake had about ceased publishing by the early 1850s, the bulk and weight of the metal plates that he had accumulated must have been enormous, and it would be of great interest to know how he stored and filed them. Our curiosity here cannot be satisfied at this time, nor, I suspect, are we likely to have answers to such questions in the future. From the obituary account of Blake's life and career, as well as from the 1871 catalog of his stock, it can be concluded that he must have stored his plates in his combined residence and place of business, perhaps in the cellar. We know in the case of the Ditson firm in Boston that American music publishers came to the point where they, too, had to maintain repositories such as the one described in *A Day at a Music Publishers*, but only after the middle of the nineteenth century, when their published outputs were extensive. Before 1825, and for a decade or two afterward, music publishing continued to be conducted in small businesses and family firms.

The manuscript account book of Simeon Wood has shown us that editions which publishers issued initially were small and that they resorted to the practice of reprinting as needs and demand required. In addition to allowing publishers to avoid tying up money in paper and printing, this arrangement kept them from amassing large inventories of unsold music. In order to make such a system work efficiently, it was necessary for publishers to maintain some orderly system of registering and identifying their plates for storage. Large publishers, we are told by *A Day at a Music Publishers*, bound up all the plates of a given work and labeled the accumulated mass for deposit in their plate cellars. As early European and English publishers began to accumulate large stocks of plates, especially those firms which remained in business through several generations or which passed their enterprises on to subsequent publishers who had bought them out, there must have arisen the need for careful identification and control of their plate stocks (and perhaps stored music as well). Gradually, publishers came to identify the collective plates of a particular work by a code symbol which had been selected beforehand; and, in order to control this system better, that symbol or some variation of it was eventually added to each plate. Such an arrangement evolved because larger firms, which were constantly reprinting, undoubtedly handled the plates of many works simultaneously.

This European system of plate identification was another of the ancient customs that was eventually transferred across the Atlantic by migrating publishers and engravers, though, as was noted before, it was probably not used extensively during these early days. George E. Blake, the most prolific of our early music publishers, never added identifying symbols to his plates. Since he maintained a one-man operation, or something close to it, it seems likely that he exercised tight control over the bundles of plates which he maintained at his establishment. George Willig, who for a long time rivaled Blake with regard to the quantity of music issued, added plate marking only to a small number of his early plates, that is, to the plates of works issued early in his career, and then desisted from this practice altogether for the remainder of his long career.

I have included in my *Secular Music in America* an index of plate-numbering systems that were maintained by music publishers during the 1793–1825 period. A rapid examination of this index leads to the conclusion that only a few publishers maintained such apparatuses and that these were frequently disorganized, even chaotic. Undoubtedly, plate stocks in this early period were not sufficiently large to justify such an aid. In addition, those publishers who did maintain numbering systems sometimes added identifying symbols to their plates only upon reprinting them, which in some cases may have occurred long after the initial engraving. (In a few cases, plates, particularly for instrumental works, were never reprinted by their publishers and, as a consequence, never got into the publisher's numbering system. Because of this practice, which is especially identified with Gottlieb Graupner of Boston, it is difficult to reconstruct early plate-numbering systems to the point that they can be employed accurately for dating music, most of which appeared without an indication of year of publication.

In his "Philadelphia Music Engraving" (pp. 119–21) Krummel has observed the odd practice that John Aitken employed for organizing his plates. Aitken's system followed an alphabetical sequence. He allotted consecutive blocks of numbers to each letter of the alphabet through the number 250 and assigned appropriate numbers to each of his publications according to the first letter of its title. This system was in use only during the final phase of his career, between 1806 or 1807 and 1811, at which time his plate stock was the largest and most in need of control. For example, the numbers from 122 to 130 he set aside to accommodate works beginning with the letter O. And to the plates for the song *Oh Wander No More From Me My Love,* by James Hook (1808–11), he eventually assigned the number 123. Aitken, like Graupner, appears to have utilized this system only upon reprinting, or, at least, after having issued an initial number of copies from newly engraved plates, for sheets of a given title are frequently found with and without plate—or more correctly, publication—numbers. The want of plate or publication numbers on all known copies of an Aitken publication indicates that the plates of such titles were utilized only once for the issuance of small editions.

Of all our early publishers only Allyn Bacon of Philadelphia and John Cole of Baltimore seem to have followed any order and time sequence in establishing and maintaining plate systems. Contemporary advertisements for the sale of his publications and performance associations engraved on his pieces indicate that Bacon commenced adding numbers to his plates soon after he began publishing. His system proved invaluable to me in the compilation of the 1801–25 list in approximating the dates of his publications. His regularity and methodical approach in this regard can be recognized immediately when scanning his entry in the index of "Publishers' Plate and Publication Numbering Systems" in the third volume of my *Secular Music in America.* An interesting aspect of Bacon's system centers around the fact that it was continued by John Klemm after the latter bought out Bacon and began reissuing his earlier publications under an altered imprint. Bacon numbered his plates in approximate sequence of issue through the number 199. Klemm then numbered plates which he himself engraved or had engraved for him from number 200 on, continuing this sequence for many years afterward.

At the outset of his career in music publishing in 1821 John Cole appears to have utilized a simple alphabetical scheme for identifying his plates. He abandoned this system in early 1823 and did not resort to an identification scheme again until about two years later, by which time he had accumulated over one hundred sets of plates. He then numbered these from 1 to 104 upon reprinting them, and beginning with publication number 105 he added numbers to his plates when initially engraving them, for none of his publications after this can be found without a publication number. Cole was an active publisher in Baltimore for nearly four decades, remaining in business until his death in 1855. His plate numbers eventually ran into the thousands.

I have already mentioned that Gottlieb Graupner added publication numbers (and, earlier on, plate numbers) to his plates for a given work only upon reprinting it. Graupner at first employed no system at all.

When he accumulated a fairly large stock of plates, managing them apparently became something of a problem. He then added numbers to plates upon reprinting from them. After his plates had reached a certain number, and after much of the music they contained was less in demand, he started a new series, beginning once more with the number one. A curiosity of Graupner's system, unique in American music publishing so far as I know, is his practice of not only adding numbers upon reprinting, but of enclosing them within parentheses, upon further reprinting from them, indicating the number of times they had been reused. Graupner's system had a built-in elimination factor. Plates that were never reprinted were never numbered and may, in consequence, have been scrapped early in his career. It seems evident that he built his system to reflect, in a practical way, the use he made and could make of his plate stock.

The majority of our early publishers, such as Benjamin and Joseph Carr, James Hewitt, George Gilfert, the Paffs, etc., never numbered their plates at all. Nor did Edward Riley, who became active a decade later. Riley became the busiest and most productive publisher in New York and he must have accumulated a sizable stock of pewter plates. In addition, he had been a music engraver and publisher in London before emigrating to New York, and we would naturally assume that he maintained some system of plate recording in accordance with the current practices of music publishers of the English capital. While this must have been so, it is strange that Riley added no numbers to his plates. Other publishers who maintained plate-numbering systems were Carr & Schetky of Philadelphia, H. Dunning and John Siegling of Charleston, South Carolina, and Francesco Masi of Boston. In some of their cases their use of numbers and symbols is confusing, particularly in light of the fact that not all their publications are recorded or even extant. Resumés of their known numbered publications can be found in my *Secular Music in America*.

One final comment on plate-numbering systems is in order. In 1815 and 1816 Frederick Hill and his son, Uri K. Hill, engraved plates for several New York publishers: Adam Geib, Joseph Willson, and Peter Erben. They signed the majority of their plates with the note, "Hill, 8 Fair Street," making the exact identification of the engraver—whether it was the father or the son—in doubt. (In one instance Uri K. Hill signed his name, and in two caes "F. Hill" appears on the sheets printed from these plates.) They must have carried on a joint venture, perhaps to support the father, for their publications follow a numbering system which appears intermixed between them. This is the only instance I know of where an engraver (or engravers) employed a system for numbering plates in early American music publishing.

THE REISSUE OF MUSIC FROM EARLIER PLATES

One of the advantages of music publishing—a benefit, it has been pointed out, that was only gained for letterpress printing through the introduction of stereotyping over a century ago and which has been improved in the more modern times through the medium of photo-offset lithography—is the publisher's ability to reissue music continually from a given set of plates so long as these remained in good condition and were kept from being scratched. Because of the small editions which must have predominated in early American music publishing, plates engraved for them had a life expectancy which usually exceeded the needs of their original owners or makers. This factor gave rise to the custom of transferring plate stocks, probably along with music stocks and even tools and implements, to a subsequent publisher when a publisher quit business or died. The succeeding publisher then reused these earlier plates to issue a new edition under his own name or imprint.

Joseph Willson launched his formal publishing career in 1812 (he had previously issued a few titles on his own through James Hewitt and the brothers Paff) by reusing concurrently the earlier plates of Mrs. Bradish, John Butler, James Hewitt (who had meanwhile gone off to Boston), and Peter Weldon, together with a fresh supply of music of his own which he had Peter Smith, a sometime professor of music, engrave for him. William Dubois likewise commenced his business in 1817 by reissuing within the next nine months almost the whole of John Paff's 1811–17 catalog and a few earlier "J. & M. Paff" imprints as well. In the foregoing cases, the earlier publishers had quit business for one reason or another. Sometimes heirs sold off plates of deceased relatives when no one remained to carry on the business or perhaps the sale was occasioned by the settling of an estate.

An example of the latter is afforded by the records of the Probate Court of Suffolk County, Massachusetts, in the settling of the estate of Gottlieb Graupner of Boston. Graupner died intestate on April 16, 1836, and the court appointed his second wife and widow, Mary H. Graupner, administratrix of his estate. The court empowered her, Henry Niebuhr, trader, and Asa Fillebrown, musician, to appraise Graupner's real and personal property. On their inventory of his personal effects, which the court eventually ordered sold at auction, we find the following items and their appraised value:

Lot of Copper music plates	[$]10.00
Lot of Pewter D°.	75.00

Graupner's children by his first wife, Catherine, apparently found fault with the widow's accounting, for they filed interrogatives on the inventory. Several of these, which appear with their answers below, are of special interest to us, since they supply details concerning the final disposal of some of Graupner's plates:

[Ques.] 28 If all such property [of said deceased] has not been sold, state what parts of it have been sold, and to whom and for what price; and state each part thereof which yet remains unsold.

[Ans.] One Piano forte sold to Ward for $75.00. One double bass sold to Niebuhr for $122.00. A lot of plates sold to Parker & Ditson for 211.

[Ques.] 31 Was there a lot of pewter music plates left by said deceased? If so, have all, or any, and what part of them have been sold, and to whom, and for what price? If any remain unsold, please to give a particular of them.

[Ans.] That these were all that have been sold except some belonging to a Double Bass and a Piano Instruction which yet remain unsold[.] This is all the description she can give of them.[14]

Graupner's children were apparently still dissatisfied with several of his widow's answers, for they filed additional interrogatives on a number of them, of which Question 8 is pertinent to the subject at hand.

14. It was mainly with Graupner's plate stock that Samuel H. Parker and Oliver Ditson established a partnership for publishing music in 1836 which after 1842 became the firm of Oliver Ditson and Company, one of the country's leading music-publishing firms of the late nineteenth century. According to Waldo Selden Pratt's article on this firm, published in the *American Supplement* to *Grove's Dictionary of Music and Musicians* (New York, 1920, vol. 6, pp. 191–92), "probably from before 1850 the printing and engraving was put in charge of John H. H. Graupner, the son of Gottlieb Graupner." The fifty-one plates belonging to the "Piano Instruction Book" here was no doubt those used for issuing Graupner's 1819, 1825, and 1827 editions of his *Rudiments of the Art of Playing on the Piano Forte* (Wolfe, No. 3203–3203B). This work consisted of fifty pages of engraved music and instructions, together with an engraved title page. As far as I can tell, this was never republished by a subsequent publisher, and its plates were probably melted down after the Graupner estate had been entirely disposed of. I have never encountered a copy of the Graupner instruction book for the double bass. As no publisher appears to have been interested in the plates for this either, they too were probably melted down in 1836 or 1837. Since H. Earle Johnson does not mention this work in the inventory of Graupner's publications in his *Musical Interludes in Boston*, the theory seems plausible that Graupner never completed engraving its plates. The presence of copperplates on the above interrogatory may be explained by the fact that Graupner issued several larger works, especially after 1817, which contained engraved title pages.

[Ques. 8] 8 Please to state the number of music plates on the 31st of the former interrogative which remain unsold.

[Ans.] That she is unable to tell. That much of the music is rubbish. That there remain unsold

51 Piano Instruction book plates
45 Double Bass   "
 8 Catalogue   "

The purchase of Graupner's plate stock by the newly established firm of Parker & Ditson—Oliver Ditson had gone into the music-publishing business in 1835 and was joined by Samuel H. Parker in the following year—illustrates a custom that was entirely usual in early American music publishing: the commencing of a new venture by acquiring and using the plate stock of a retired, deceased, or defunct publisher. In addition to the cases of Willson and Dubois cited before, this happened with John G. Klemm, a member of the Philadelphia family of organ builders. Klemm started out in music publishing by acquiring and reissuing in 1823 and 1824 practically the whole of the Allyn Bacon catalog. During the first ten years of its existence, the firm of Firth & Hall, which dates from about 1827, reissued a huge amount of music from plates engraved for a number of earlier publishers. In addition to commencing a new business with old plates, active and prosperous publishers were continually absorbing into their catalogs the usable titles of retiring and defunct publishers. One of many examples of this practice, as well as a further case of the probable acquisition of music plates through the settling of an estate, is Joseph Willson's use about 1815 of some of George Gilfert's earlier plates. Gilfert had died in December of 1814 and within a year Willson was reissuing some of Gilfert's earlier titles from his shop at 16 Maiden Lane.

The reemployment of old plates not only by subsequent publishers but by subsequent publishers *in different localities* was a common practice of early music publishing. Edwin K. Jackson of Boston, whose publishing activity extended from about 1821 to 1826, provides us with an excellent example of this custom. In addition to reprinting some of James Hewitt's plates that had been engraved during Hewitt's 1811–16 residence in Boston and almost all those engraved by Simeon Wood of Boston between 1818 and 1822, Jackson reissued music from plates that had initially been utilized by Hewitt in New York between 1801 and 1810 and other plates that had been engraved for him and printed from by Peter K. Moran, also of New York (about 1822). Though it is possible that Hewitt transferred his plates to Boston upon his removal from New York about 1811, the fact that he never reprinted from them in Boston suggests that he left them in

New York, selling them to Jackson around 1820 or 1821, by which time he had ceased publishing entirely.[15] It is, however, possible, that Hewitt's plates never left New York, in spite of the fact that reissues from them later bore Jackson's Boston address, for Jackson maintained some sort of publishing operation and retail outlet in New York City during the early 1820s, and the actual reprinting of music from Hewitt's plates could have been effected there. That this very possibly occurred is suggested by the fact that many of Moran's plates, which Jackson employed to print music under his Boston imprint, were later reused by the New York firm of Firth & Hall, during the late 1820s and early 1830s. (Such sheets frequently contain both the firm's Pearl Street and Franklin Square addresses, showing that Firth & Hall reprinted from them continually.) A few of Jackson's plates were later acquired by George Willig of Philadelphia, for sheets printed from them with Willig's address are known, and it is entirely possible that they were by another publisher in the interim. Willig, like many other early American music publishers, made use of all the plates of other publishers that he could get his hands on. In addition to employing plates that had initially been used by Aitken of Philadelphia, Thomas Birch of New York, and Arthur Clifton of Baltimore, Willig also reprinted at a later date from plates originally owned by G. M. Bourne of New York, and L. Meignen and J. G. Osborne of Philadelphia. Willig's own plate stock was eventually taken over by the Philadelphia firm of Lee & Walker of Philadelphia, whose own stock was eventually absorbed by the Ditson firm in Boston.

It is evident that music plates moved about the country on a fairly casual basis. Allyn Bacon's edition of *The Star Spangled Banner* (listed as 2a in Muller, with the publication number 17) was reprinted during the Civil War, almost fifty years after it had initially appeared, within a series entitled *The Home Circle* and masked by a series title page containing the imprint, "Cincinnati, John Church., 66 West Fourth Street; Oliver Ditson & Co., Boston; Beck & Lawton, Philada.; Firth, Pond & Co., N. York; Engd. by Green & Walker, Boston." (The engraver's note here refers to the title page alone.) Another example of this later, distant reuse of plates concerns John Paff's edition of *'Tis the Last Rose of Summer*, originally issued by him in New York 1815. This was later reprinted by William Dubois in late 1817 or early 1818 and it has additionally turned

15. The fact that several of Hewitt's own post-1820 compositions were issued for him by Gottlieb Graupner and by his own son, James L. Hewitt, in Boston—*The Augusta Waltz* (Wolfe, No. 3679) and *The Boston Brigade March* (Wolfe, No. 3684) are two such works —indicates that he had ceased publishing by about 1820, after which time he probably disposed of whatever plates he had remaining.

up in the files of the American Antiquarian Society in reprint form under the series title *Gems of English Song*, with the title-page imprint "Buffalo, Published by Cottier & Denton, 215 Main St.," which dates it about 1867. We can mention, as a final example of this practice, that it is common to encounter sheets which had been initially published by George Willig in Baltimore with the subsequent imprint of "Peters, & Webb Company of Louisville, Kentucky." These reprints date to the 1850s or later and show that the Peters, & Webb Company had undoubtedly acquired some of Willig's plates after his death in 1851.[16]

One of the most unusual forms of reprinting in early American music publishing lore was Joseph Carr's edition of F. Linley's *A New Assistant for the Piano Forte or Harpsichord*. This had been initially published by Carr in England under the imprint "London, Printed by J. Carr, Middle Row, Holburn" (dating, probably, from the early 1790s, though it is not recorded in the *British Union-Catalogue of Early Music*). Carr obviously brought the plates for this work across the Atlantic in 1794, for he later utilized them to reissue an edition of this work with the imprint "Baltimore, Printed & Sold by I. Carr at his Music Store, Market Street. And by B. Carr at his Musical repositorys, Market Street, Philadelphia, & Williams St., New York." (Sonneck–Upton, p. 289, dates this 1796.) The plate used to print the final page in both editions, paged 32 and entitled "A Dictionary of Musical Terms," was employed in the interim to print the musical dictionary in Carr's 1794–96 collection *The Gentleman's Amusement* (Sonneck–Upton, pp. 157–63). This was repaged (98) in the *Amusement*, the alteration still being visible on the American edition of the Linley instructor. Copies of both editions of this work are in the Music Division of the New York Public Library.

Carr's transportation across the Atlantic Ocean of the plates of the Linley work points out rather vividly the fact that engraved plates represented money in the pockets of early music engravers and publishers, and they utilized them as frequently as demand allowed in order to keep their pockets full. Carr may have brought these Linley plates with him as a hedge against need until he could set up in business in Baltimore and commence issuing other works. The possible employment of English plates by G. Balls in Philadelphia and T. Balls in Norfolk, Virginia, in the 1817–19 period has previously been noticed. The only other instance of the use of imported plates also occurred about this time, when James

---

16. Willig had taken over Thomas Carr's plate stock about 1822 and had maintained a retail outlet there until about 1829, when it was assumed by his son, George Willig, Jr.

Hewitt obviously acquired some. After his return to New York in 1817, Hewitt issued a small amount of music from his address at 156½ William Street. Some of these offerings were newly engraved; others had been printed from plates which undoubtedly emanated from a London source. His edition of Sir John A. Stevenson's *Alas! Poor Lubin* (Wolfe, No. 8612), for example, still bears the phrase "Entd. at Stats. Hall," and the original English imprint is faintly visible, having been punched out poorly. Other such Hewitt offerings contain the original prices in pence and shillings together with parts of earlier English imprints.

THE PRICE OF MUSIC

We can determine from prices on early music sheets that for almost the entire period under discussion (1787–1825) the American music publisher charged 12½ cents or its equivalent of one shilling for each page of printed music. Publications of two pages, that had been printed from two plates—this was the most usual format for songs and vocal pieces of the stage—cost 25 cents. Three pages of music were priced at 37½ cents, and so on. Charles H. Haswell's *Reminiscences of an Octogenarian of the City of New York* (New York, 1896) provides us (pp. 57–58) with a fairly accurate picture of the price structure of the day [1816].

> Havana cigars of the best quality could be bought for 3 cents, or five for a shilling (12½ cents) . . . the fractional currency of this [New York] and all states of this period, was generally the Spanish coins of 25, 12½ and 6¼ cents and they denominated in the several states as follows . . . in this state, Ohio, and Michigan the dollar was divided into eight shillings, and the coins were termed six pence, one shilling and two shillings, accordingly.
>
> In consequence of the derangement of the currency by the war with Great Britain, and the failure of many country banks, provisions were scarce and dear: Milk, 12½ per quart [and] flour $15 per barrel.

The denomination of American money in pence and shillings remained in wide use ("dollars" and "cents" were simultaneously employed to connote values of exchange) until the 1830s, when bank reform and the standardization of currency brought about the terminology we use today. In addition to providing some sort of cost comparison to the Coldwell receipt for music plates to paper and to other commodities and equipment of the trade, Haswell's information helps us to understand why early American music sheets carried (by today's standards, at least) such odd-sounding prices: 12½ cents (one shilling); 37½ cents (3 shillings); 62½ cents (5 shillings); and 87½ cents (7 shillings). The typical music sheet, which consisted of two pages, each printed from an individual plate, was priced at 2 shillings or 25 cents each, or, colloquially speaking, at "two bits." (Present-day prices at the Fulton Market in New York City, recently relocated uptown, are said to be discussed in terms of the old-time shilling.) In the earlier period of American music publishing, before approximately 1805, some sheets issued in New York carried their prices in shillings. However, this was an infrequent practice even before 1805, and later on, when prices came more frequently to be added to music sheets, they were always denominated in terms of "cents" (or "dollars" when they exceeded eight pages). Prices in shillings on music after 1810 should arouse suspicion regarding the origin of the plates employed to print it. For example, the price "1s/7p" on James Hewitt's edition of John Braham's *The Beautiful Maid*, issued by him in New York from 156½ William Street in 1817, is a tip-off that Hewitt had acquired plates which had been imported from England. Other telltale signs, such as the phrase "Entered at Stationer's Hall" or some variation of it, and the evidence of partly punched-out English imprints beneath Hewitt's own, point this out clearly on a number of Hewitt's offerings of that period.

It would be ideal in this discussion of the price of earlier American music to be able to quote precise data on the actual cost of producing it. While I have provided some information on the cost of equipment and materials employed in this trade, our knowledge here is only partial and often inexact. It would therefore be unwise to attempt to discuss this matter with any degree of authority. Such a discourse will have to await the discovery or rediscovery of publisher's account books and other sources. (I say "rediscovery" because some such materials were known earlier, but my attempts to locate them have proved unsuccessful; for example, Joseph Muller refers in his *Star Spangled Banner* to some extant publishing records of the Carrs, and John Tasker Howard mentions in earlier editions of his *Our American Music* known correspondence of George Willig, Jr., and of James Hewitt.) We know the cost of music plates, in one instance at least, and the costs of paper, the copperplate press, and a few other items of supply. However, we lack specific information on tools, particularly punches, on ink, on the cost of engraving and printing when these were executed by agents, and on the total economic situation of the era. Since the period under discussion lasted for forty years or more, during which time there were frequent depressions and inflations, with resultant fluctuations in the value of money, goods, and services, costs and prices must have varied from time to time. The best that we can offer here are a number of observations which are based upon conclusions that can be drawn from whatever evidence there is at hand.

We have already observed in our discussion of paper that the whole sheet required for printing from two to four pages cost approximately from 2¾ to 3 cents. The following extract comes from a receipt which I found in the New York Public Library among the manuscript papers of Frederick Rausch, the early New York pianist and organist, composer, and erstwhile music publisher, whom we have encountered before. Rausch was in London between 1804 and 1806 and while there apparently contracted for the publication of an unidentified *Russian Air*. The receipt of Thomas Preston, the London publisher with American connections at this time, for this work reads as follows:

Mr Rausch

1807		To Thomas Preston 97 Strand			
Aug	1	Eng. 12 Plates of Russian Air	4	4	6
		Engraving neat Title & Plates	1	1	
	15	Printing 100 Russian Air	1	12	6
		Best Paper for D°	1	12	6
		Making up Serving L [?]		3	6

While the information here is too skimpy to allow precise conclusions, it does permit some broad generalizations. It suggests, for example, what the cost of the inking and printing operation was with regard to the cost of paper. As twelve plates were involved here, three whole sheets of paper would be required for each hundred copies printed, or a total of 300 sheets of paper was equal to the 1,200 inking and printing operations that were necessary in order to complete this work. Consequently, if a whole sheet of paper cost three cents, it cost about one-third of this—a penny—to ink a plate. While Preston's figures have relevance to the English trade, it seems logical to conclude, in light of all that we know, that they had an approximate carry-over to our own contemporary industry as well. In other words, the paper and the inking and printing of the typical two-page song cost its publisher about 5 cents for each copy issued. While, according to Preston's figures, engraving was the most expensive outlay in each publishing venture, this was a one-time operation. The costs involved here could be absorbed within the total cost of the edition and could be recouped after the sale of a certain number of copies. We can unfortunately draw no conclusions regarding the engraving of a title for this work, for Preston's reference here is ambiguous. It would appear that Preston included the cost of the twelve plates in this itemization as well.

In his deposition regarding Gottlieb Graupner's early publishing and musical activity, John Weeks Moore has stated that Graupner provided music for the initial use of the Handel and Haydn Society "at five cents a page." This figure possibly represents or at least suggests the cost to a publisher of producing a page of music (i.e., the wholesale cost). The charge of 5 cents per page would absorb the price of the paper and the cost of printing it, at least, which were the only considerations requiring financial outlay once the plates had been made. It would establish the cost of paper and printing for the typical two-page song, which sold for 25 cents, at 5 cents per copy. When one considers the expense of engraving plates, the risk involved in doing so should demand not come up to expectations, the smallness of editions at that time, and the longer time a publisher probably had to wait in order to realize a profit, this figure does not seem at all out of line. As engraving and other costs probably doubled the 5-cent figure or brought it close to 12½ cents for producing a two-page song, the pricing of 12½ cents per page probably allowed the publisher a mark-up of 100 percent, which is consistent with the pricing of merchandize from the wholesale to the retail level today.

While the field of general engraving has little relationship to the trade which produced music sheets, there is some carry-over between them with regard to the methods, tools, and materials employed by both. As a consequence, both areas shared some common costs and price factors. In his book *The Mavericks, American Engravers*, Stephens provides us (p. 64) with some idea of the cost involved in general engraving when, in discussing Peter Maverick's involvement in 1822 with Thomas Jefferson in engraving Jefferson's design of the plan of the buildings and grounds of the University of Virginia, he concluded:

> Engraving was not a cheap method of reproduction, even if enough copies were printed to make the cost of the original plate relatively small. . . . For each operation of inking the plate, wiping it clean, and running the plate and paper through the press, Maverick charged ten cents, and for the sheet of paper for this engraving of approximately sixteen by eighteen inches he charged about 5 cents. . . . In the light of such costs, it is no wonder that the cheap and easy process of lithography—though it resulted in a muddy surface and a ragged line which must have set many a good engraver's teeth on edge—pushed very rapidly to the fore.[17]

Maverick charged the University 112 dollars for engraving this work, 25 dollars for printing 250 copies, and 12 dollars for the paper used. It is

17. As will be noted shortly, lithography came into use for a short time after 1827 for producing cheaper music as well.

obvious that these figures are at variance with those provided by Preston for publishing music, which placed the cost of paper and printing on a ratio of about one to three. In addition, Maverick's charge for engraving the plate was many times that of Preston's price for effecting several. It should be remembered that Maverick was producing an artistic product with much illustration that had to be painstakingly cut by hand, and the cleaning, inking, and printing of each copy had to be attended to with equal care. Music publishing, on the other hand, entailed stamping and mass-production methods, where poor or indifferent engraving, inking, printing, and cleaning were frequently the order of the day. While these two occupations shared common tools, materials, and the like, one was carried on with a view to attaining an esthetic effect and the other, utility. Two hundred and fifty copies of the Jefferson design were ordered from Maverick in 1822, and another 25 in 1825, following a slight alteration of the plate. For this minor change Maverick charged an additional 13 dollars, raising the total engraving bill to 125 dollars. For the 500 copies that were printed, the charge for cutting the plate amounted to just under two-thirds of the entire cost of the production.

The Preston bill gives us some idea of the cost of producing music plates with regard to the other expenses involved in producing an edition. The high cost of engraving copperplates (by hand) in the period antedating the introduction of punching and stamping methods is attested to by an advertisement which William Selby, an organist and composer of Boston, published in the *Boston Evening Post* of February 2, 1782. In outlining his proposal for publishing his own work *The New Minstrel*, Selby stated that: "As all the paper expended in this work must be of a particular size and quality, and made for the purpose; as every plate will cost Mr. Selby more than eight dollars; and as each of the numbers could not be executed in London for less than five shillings, the price for each of the numbers is One Dollar and a Half."

Nicholas Tawa not only brought the above advertisement to my attention, but pointed out to me an example of another practice in music publishing, both old and new: the vanity publication. Blake, Willig, Riley, and several others of our early publishers did not always publish music on their own choice or for their own benefit. Sometimes an amateur or an interested party engaged their services for the private publication of a musical work. Such instances were probably more frequent than we now realize, and publishers must have worked out a scale of pricing for such occasions, just as early medical societies worked out standard fee schedules in order to regulate the profession. The first five items commencing my *Secular Music in America*, compositions of Frederick L. Abel of Savannah, Georgia, probably fell into this category of private or vanity publications, and the bibliography in that book contains many more examples. Though we have no information on charges for this work at this earlier period, the following notice, which appeared in the January 1, 1859, issue of *Dwight's Journal of Music* (vol. 14, no. 4 [Whole no. 352], p. 319), explains its application and cost at a later period:

REPLY TO INQUIRES RELATIVE TO PUBLICATION OF MUSIC

We are in daily receipt of manuscripts which are offered for our acceptance. But so much new music is now issued, that the sale of each piece is exceedingly limited, unless it is particularly striking or original in its character. The probability, therefore, of realizing any profit from the great majority of pieces is out of the question. Not one piece in ten pays the cost of getting up; only one in fifty proves a success. Under these circumstances, authors must not consider us illiberal or unjust either in declining to publish their works or requiring them to purchase a certain number of copies, to help defray the first expenses and introduce them to the public.

To those composers who have pupils, this requirement to purchase copies will not be burdensome, as they can readily dispose of them. Others who write for fame, will not object to this, because they have friends to whom their compositions will be a welcome gift.

Our charge for publishing music on private account are: $2.00 per page for engraving; $1.50 per 100 sheets for paper; and 75 cents per 100 pages for printing. If a full title is required, the expense will vary from $5.00 to $10.00, according to style and fancy. For a half-title, from $2.00 to $3.00. The expense of revising the manuscripts, when necessary, and of reading and correcting proofs, is included in these charges.

Authors are advised to retain copies, as in cases of the non-acceptance of Manuscripts, we cannot insure their return—the number received and the expense of postage precluding the possibility of doing so.

OLIVER DITSON & CO.

Finally, the cost of two minor pieces of equipment which were utilized both in general printing and in the printing of music are provided by Clifford Shipton in his monograph of Isaiah Thomas. In his appendix of "Isaiah Thomas's Account of Stock, 1796" (p. 90) are noted:

2 water troughts and frames	[$]4.00
22 Boards for wetting paper	3.66⅔

These boards for wetting paper were probably employed for pressing it overnight and for keeping it moist in preparation for the printing operation. Two of them are partly visible under the presses in the lefthand foreground in Illustration 11b. Such equipment was undoubtedly supplied by carpenters or other artisans who were called upon to set up the presses.

PUBLICATION BY SUBSCRIPTION

The publication of works on a subscription basis was a mechanism frequently employed in eighteenth- and early nineteenth-century printing for underwriting the cost of a publication in advance. The publisher or group sponsoring a particular work usually published in a newspaper its intention of doing so, outlining the cost and arrangements involved and inviting subscriptions to the edition. Subscribers who responded to the preliminary proposal were usually asked to pay part of the price in advance, perhaps against a smaller total than that ruling after publication day. In many cases their support of a given work earned them the right to have their names printed in a *List of Subscribers* which prefaced the edition. This practice may have had its origins in the publishing structure of early eighteenth-century England, where editions were frequently commenced and underwritten by subscribing booksellers, who pledged themselves to purchase a part of the edition, usually in unbound but roughly sewn sheets. The advantages inherent in such a system are obvious. The printer or publisher did not have to risk capital (which frequently he didn't even have), and the subscription acted as a gauge of interest in a particular work, for if the title did not arouse enough interest to attract sufficient subscribers to underwrite it, it did not have to be printed. Early newspapers abound with proposals for publishing works which never saw the light of day.

It naturally follows that such an ingenious scheme was readily adopted by our early music publishers and interested parties who wished to encourage native composers and promote local manufacture. Sometimes, as in the case of the Selby notice quoted just before, a composer himself resorted to this practice to promote his own work. Publication by subscription was also employed to assure the printing of works of extremely limited appeal and to bring out large and ambitious collections which involved too great a financial risk to undertake privately.

This mechanism was sometimes utilized to underwrite the publication of sacred collections in the American colonies. As interest in secular forms arose and grew, subscription was invoked to help nudge this type of music into print also. Two of the earliest references to the publication of secular works on a subscription basis in colonial America appeared in the

Charleston *South Carolina Gazette* in the 1760s and are indicative of the growing interest in nonreligious music at that time. The first of these, which appeared in the *Gazette* from February 13–20 of that year, reads:

> PROPOSAL for printing by subscription an *Anthem*, an *Ode* for voices and instruments, composed by Benjamin Yarnold, organist of St. Philip's Charles Town, South Carolina, being the same that was performed before the Ancient Fraternity of Free Masons, at the installation of the Hon. Benjamin Smith, Esq., Grand Master of South Carolina.
>
> That each Subscriber, on his receiving an engraved copy of each from London shall pay, or order to be paid, the sum of seven pounds current money, into the hands of Mr. Robert Wells, or Peter Timothy.

And in the same paper of October 10, 1768, appeared:

> Proposals for printing by subscription SIX SONATAS for the harpsichord or organ; with an accompaniment for a violin: composed by Peter Valton, organist of St. Philip's Charles Town, South Carolina. *Opera Prima*. To be printed on good paper, and delivered to the subscribers some time this spring, if the plates can be engraved and sent by that time. Each subscriber to pay Four pounds Carolina currency the sett, on delivery of the books. Those who subscribe to six setts to have a seventh gratis. The subscribers names to be printed. Those who intend to encourage this work, are requested to send their names to the author, to Mr. Gaines or, to Mr. David Douglas, as soon as possible.[18]

Both works, it should be noticed, were products of local talent and an appeal was made to encourage this. As no established music-publishing trade existed at this time, their plates would have to be engraved in London (but, in the case of the sonatas, probably printed in Charleston), and their publication would involve considerable expense. Hence, subscription was an ideal vehicle for producing them. However, since neither title is known in an extant copy today, these ventures probably did not come to fruition and little was risked in proposing them. The same result followed the proposal of William Selby in 1782 to publish his *The New Minstrel*, which was quoted in part above. Shelby desired to publish an extremely large work which was probably too expensive for him to undertake himself. According to Selby's proposal, this was to be issued in ten numbers, one every month, the engraving to be done "with elegance and taste by an adept in the art and educated in Europe." (The Sonneck–Upton entry for this speculates that the engraving in this case would have been undertaken by John Norman.) The fact that no copies of this work exist today is indicative of a lack of interest in promoting its

18. Both advertisements are quoted verbatim from Sonneck–Upton. The latter was also republished in the *New York Mercury* of February 20, 1769, under the byline "Charles Town, Jan. 10, 1769."

publication. In spite of this, Selby was not deterred from proposing in 1790 the publication through subscription of another compilation of his works, to be entitled *Apollo, and the Muse's Musical Compositions*. Selby's proposal for this, which he published in the Boston *Columbian Centinel* of June 16, 1790, called for 200 subscriptions. Like his *The New Minstrel* before, this work in all likelihood remained unpublished, for want of sufficient subscribers, though parts of it may have appeared in print.[19]

When John Aitken commenced issuing sheet music in this country in 1787, he forthwith invoked the subscription mechanism to assist him in this process. The first two of Aitken's endeavors, Reinagle's *A Selection of the Most Favorite Scots Tunes* and his own *Compilation of the Litanies and Vespers, Hymns and Anthems, etc.*, undoubtedly had popular appeal in that music-starved America, for these were published in the usual way. However, for the third collection he issued in 1787, William Brown's *Three Rondos for the Piano Forte*, he had to resort to the subscription arrangement, for its appeal was limited to the few who could play this music or who wished to encourage Brown's composing and Aitken's publishing. And when John Young undertook in 1793 the publication of *Young's Vocal and Instrumental Musical Miscellany*, a work that was to appear in eight numbers between 1793 and 1795 and which comprised a total of sixty-three pages, he employed the subscription method to assure himself first of sufficient interest and financial backing before undertaking the work. That he found such interest and help is proved by the existence of several copies of the work. In proposing this work Young informed potential subscribers that, "as soon as a certain number of subscribers appear, the work will be immediately commenced and executed with all possible dispatch. Such subscribers as send in their names with poetry which may be approved of, will have it set to music and introduced in the different numbers." According to the conditions of Young's proposal, which appeared in Dunlap's *Daily American Advertiser* of February 14, 1793, subscribers were to pay half a dollar upon delivery of each number.

Several others of our early publishers proposed publications by subscription throughout the 1790s. The advertisement which appeared in the *Pennsylvania Packet* of June 15, 1791, seeking subscribers for *Six Lessons for the Harpsichord or Piano Forte*, to be engraved by John Aitken, has already been mentioned. This might have been an early reference to the following work by Alexander Juhan. In 1792, Juhan, a violinist then in Charleston, sought subscribers for publication of his *Sett of Six Sonatas for*

19. See Sonneck–Upton, p. 29.

the Pianoforte or Harpsichord, a work which is unknown today in extant copies, through the first three of these were advertised as "ready for sale" in April 1793. In the following year appeared the first of *Moller & Capron's Monthly Numbers*, a periodical publication which rivaled *Young's Vocal and Instrumental Musical Miscellany*, though it contained only about half as much music. Another work proposed for publication through subscription in 1793, but apparently never published, was the *Massachusetts Musical Magazine*. Oliver Holden, its compiler, announced his intention to publish it, in the Worcester *Massachusetts Spy* of March 14 of that year, and his entire proposal can be found on pages 254–55 of the Sonneck–Upton bibliography.

In 1794, Benjamin Carr, who was to dominate Philadelphia music publishing for the next six or more years, brought out the first number of his *Gentleman's Amusement*. This, too, appeared on a subscription basis, for an advertisement of it in the *New York Daily Advertiser* of May 8, 1794, stated that a general title page and index to it would be given to subscribers only, indicating that it was also sold on the general market. In all, the *Gentleman's Amusement* ran to ninety-eight pages, being exceeded in size only by John Aitken's 1797 *Scots Musical Museum*, in which the pagination extended to 177. The year 1794 also saw the appearance in New York of James Hewitt and Mrs. Mary Ann Pownall's *Book of Songs*, a collection of ballads and duets by either of these two composers. Hewitt proposed this for publication through subscription in May 1794, and announced its publication the following March. It was priced at 12 shillings, one dollar of which was to be paid at the time of subscribing and the remainder on delivery. The price to nonsubscribers was set at 16 shillings. Two years later William Norman in Boston brought out his *Musical Repertory*, a work similar in character to the Young and Moller & Capron publications. This was priced at one dollar for each number to subscribers and $1.25 to nonsubscribers. Its five numbers totaled eighty pages, the first forty-eight of which were later reprinted by Gottlieb Graupner in his similar collection entitled *The Musical Magazine*. While, in some cases, prepayment was not required, the publisher gained an advantage in being assured of a sufficient sale before undertaking the arduous and costly tasks of engraving and printing the edition, and the subscriber reaped his *quid pro quo* through a reduced price.

In September 1796 Joseph Carr of Baltimore proposed publishing *Six Sonatas for the Pianoforte, with the accompanyment of a violin or flute ad libitum*, "composed by an amateur," a work which, for obvious reasons, never appeared in print (at least no copies are known today). In 1797, Peter A.

von Hagen considered making use of this vehicle, proposing to issue in this manner an entirely new work entitled *The Lady's Musical Miscellany*. Copies of this, too, are unknown today. Another collection intended for the fair sex, *The Ladies Magazine*, was proposed by Hewitt and Rausch in March 1797, but it likewise probably never came to publication. About the year 1800 appeared, for sale to both subscribers and nonsubscribers, *Mr. Francis's Ballroom Assistant*, "a collection of dances composed, selected and arranged by Alexander Reinagle." And in January 1800 appeared Joseph Carr's initial proposal to issue through subscription a work entitled *Musical Journal for the Piano Forte, Selected and Arranged by Benjamin Carr*. This was the major production in early American music publishing, and it is doubtful that Carr could have or would have been able to publish it otherwise. The first volume of it appeared before the following November, and by 1807 four additional volumes had come into print. In all, Carr's *Musical Journal* amounted to about 500 pages of printed music. Nothing rivaled it in magnitude until Blake commenced publishing his edition of the vocal music of Handel in the 1820s. Joseph Carr, who must have engraved the whole work, issured the initial volumes in Baltimore, while later ones appeared in Philadelphia under the imprint of (Benjamin) Carr & Schetky. In 1810, the partnership of Benjamin Carr and J. George Schetky issued by subscription in six periodical numbers a work of Carr's entitled *Six Ballads from the Poem of the Lady of the Lake*, which capitalized on the growing popularity in America of the works of Sir Walter Scott.

By then, however, the mechanism of issuing works through subscription was beginning to slow down. Either publishers had gained a sufficient toehold to allow them to dispense with this advantageous but sometimes bothersome custom, or more likely, the public had grown tired of the constant proposing and frequent failures of such schemes. The only work issued in America in this way after 1811 that has come to my notice was the 1810–11 publication by Madame LePelletier in Baltimore of her *Journal of Musick*. The custom of publishing collections of music through subscription in post-Revolutionary America continued for only about twenty years, during the first two formative decades of the music-publishing trade here. It served a useful purpose while it endured. This method was undoubtedly responsible for the publication of many large and ambitious collections, especially of instrumental music by native and naturalized composers, which otherwise would not have been economically feasible. This *modus operandi* helped bring serious music to the attention of an element of the population which, though small, was becoming more sophisticated in its tastes and needs. As a consequence there was an increase in the number of amateurs who were able to cope with the difficulties of Pleyel and Steibelt and eventually even with some of the sonatas of Mozart and Beethoven. By 1810 the sale of the sonatas and duos of such composers was becoming sufficiently frequent, even in cases where they amounted to a great many pages of music, to encourage publishers to attempt to issue such works on their own, without the crutch that the subscription technique afforded.

One last point is worthy of mention here. The lists of subscribers in early American musical publications often provided solid evidence of the musical literati of the period. Their value in this regard has yet to be fully appreciated. Although not every name on them represents a musical amateur or a lover of music, for indeed some individuals subscribed to such works out of a desire to promote American manufacture or to encourage American industry, such lists do indicate who our early performers were, private as well as public, and who our initial patrons of music were as well.

PERIODICAL AND SERIAL PUBLICATIONS

Closely allied with the process of publication by subscription were the periodical collections of music, or "musical magazines," as these were sometimes called, which a few of our pioneer musician-publishers issued during the period of their earliest activity here. These were collections of vocal or instrumental music which were published in parts periodically so that they could be bound up into a volume, usually with a collective title page, upon completion. This phenomenon of early American music publishing persisted for about ten years, roughly from 1793 to 1803, and must have come into being for a variety of reasons, the major one being the desire by our musician-publishers to put into the hands of the public compositions and arrangements of their own doing or of other American composers. Because such undertakings demanded too great an outlay of time and materials for a publisher to attempt them on his own, the subscription mechanism was invoked to underwrite the majority of them.

In addition to wishing to issue their own music and the works of native or naturalized composers, our early musician-publishers, like beginners on musical instruments, needed to sense accomplishment in their new careers by attempting the biggest forms at the very outset. Notice, for example, the several collections that appear at the very top of John Aitken's initial catalog (Table 1). When James Harrison, New York City's first music publisher, commenced his brief career in 1793, he immediately

[216]

proposed publishing by subscription a collection of the newest and most approved songs, which, he said, would eventually form a handsome folio volume of thirty pages. Likewise, two of the earliest publishers of Philadelphia, John Young and the patnership of John Christopher Moller and Henry Capron, commenced their activity through the publication of periodical collections. The majority of such works appearing in post-Revolutionary America have previously been cited in the foregoing section on subscription, and there is no need to mention every title here. Reference to the major titles will suffice.

In 1793, John Young and the partnership of Moller & Capron, all musicians of Philadelphia who had wandered over into the publishing area, commenced issuing periodical publications independent of one another but similar in design and nature. These were *Young's Vocal and Instrumental Musical Miscellany*, which was proposed for publication through subscription in February of that year, and *Moller & Capron's Monthly Numbers*, which the two musicians offered to the public exactly a month later. Both schemes were centered around the concept of issuing through subscription large and ambitious works which were designed to appear in parts or "numbers" at established intervals. Each part was to contain a specified number of pages of printed music, and upon the conclusion of a specific number of pages or sets (making up a volume) a title page and sometimes a contents page and a list of subscribers were provided, so that the accumulation could be bound up into an identifiable whole. From a perusal of the contents of *Young's Vocal and Instrumental Musical Miscellany* in the Sonneck–Upton bibliography, we can see immediately that Young concentrated on reproducing the latest favorites of the London and Philadelphia stages, though the eight numbers that appeared between early 1793 and early 1795 also contain music of the immigrant Jean Gehot and Raynor Taylor.

Moller and Capron, on the other hand, appear to have utilized their publication mainly for the issuance of their own compositions, for the four numbers which appeared contain almost nothing else. The announcement which Moller & Capron inserted in the Philadelphia *Federal Gazette* of March 13, 1793, proposing this undertaking, is worth quoting here, since it provides information on the reasoning behind the publication of such works and the methodology for carrying them out:

MUSIC. The great scarcity of well adapted music for the pianoforte or harpsichord and particularly songs, has induced the subscribers to publish by subscription in monthly numbers, all the newest vocal and instrumental music, and most favourite songs, duets, catches and glees—as also by permission of the author, a set of canzonetti, composed by a lady in Philadelphia . . . Moller & Capron.

CONDITIONS

1. Each subscriber to pay one dollar at the time of subscribing and three shillings on the delivery of each number.
2. Each number to contain six pages.
3. As soon as there is a sufficient number of subscribers, each subscriber's name will be inserted in the first number.
4. The first number to be delivered in March.

Only four numbers of the Moller & Capron publication appeared, at least only that number are extant today, and it is likely that no others were published. The work was probably never carried through to completion, for no collective title page was issued, though each number was preceded by a free leaf containing an attractive ornamental design representing St. Cecilia playing the organ, with an angel on her left playing the German flute.

Other notable periodical publications of the 1790 decade were Benjamin Carr's *The Gentleman's Amusement* and William Norman's *The Musical Repertory*. The title page of the former carried its own advertisement, which stated that "the whole [was] selected, arranged & adapted for one, two, & three German flutes or violins by *R. Shaw* of the theatre, Charlestown, & *B. Carr*. Forming the cheapest, and most complete, collection ever offered to the public; the contents being selected from the best authors, and what, purchased in any other manner would amount to more than three times the price." The initial number of *The Gentleman's Amusement* was published on the first day of April 1794, and the remaining numbers, amounting to ninety-eight pages in all, appeared by the end of that year. Norman's *Musical Repertory*, which, it has already been noted, was not stamped but was entirely engraved by hand, was issued in three numbers two years later. Much of its contents were reprinted by Gottlieb Graupner in 1803 within the pages of his *The Musical Magazine*. By far the largest and most ambitious of such early periodical works, and really the last of this genre, was the collection issued by the Carrs between 1800 and 1804 under the title of *The Musical Journal for the Piano Forte*. As noted previously, this collection amounted to about 500 pages in all, and it served as a vehicle for the publication of a great many compositions and arrangements for Benjamin Carr. Except for the publication in 1810 and 1811 of Madame LePelletier's *Journal of Musick*, a work which appears to have been devised to fulfill the requirements of a small group of French émigrés from Napoleonic France, and several of Anthony Philip

Heinrich's collections—notably *The Sylviad* and *The Western Minstrel*, appearing in 1823–26 and 1820 respectively—which were designed, like all Heinrich undertakings, on the grandest possible scale, I have noticed no major collections issued in periodical form after the completion of Carr's *Musical Journal*.

Another method for issuing works on a periodical or serial basis was established in 1812 with the publication of the first number of *Carr's Musical Miscellany in Occasional Numbers*. Like *The Musical Journal* before it, this series served as a means for publishing many of Benjamin Carr's original compositions, arrangements, and variations on the tunes of others. *Carr's Musical Miscellany* extended to eighty-five numbers in all and dated between 1812 and 1826. Titles were sold individually as they appeared. Another series, patterned on the Carr scheme, was inaugurated in 1815 by George E. Blake of Philadelphia under the title of *Blake's Musical Miscellany in Occasional Numbers*. Blake issued eighty-six numbers in this series between 1815 and 1826, almost all them works of American composition. In 1816 Allyn Bacon and his associates commenced publishing works of American composers, particularly of Thomas Van Dyke Wiesenthal, in a series entitled the *American Musical Miscellany*, eleven such works appearing under that caption between 1816 and 1819. And between 1822 and 1825 John Cole of Baltimore issued thirteen titles within the series *Cole's Piano Forte Miscellany*, this, too devoted to the compositions of Americans. The last series undertaken in this early period were also Carr (Benjamin and Thomas) enterprises, *Carr's Armonica* (or *Harmonica*) and *Lyricks, or Adaptations, Arrangements & Compositions in Vocal Music, by B. Carr*. The former, devoted to instrumental music, appeared in at least sixteen numbers between 1820 and 1824, and the other in five or more numbers in 1825. Both were nationalistic in scope and intent.

AGENTS AND DISTRIBUTORS

Our early music publishers maintained reciprocal relationships with one another and with general booksellers and general merchants in rural and frontier areas for the distribution and sale of their music; for then, as now, distribution counted as one of the major factors leading to success or failure in publishing. This interdependence of our early publishers is often reflected in their newspaper advertisements, which specified from what other individuals their music could be had, and from their imprints, into which frequently were punched the names of agents and distributors in other localities. Proof of such relationships is further evidenced by extant manuscript records, chief among which are the ever-useful account book of Simeon Wood and a small collection of invoice, order, and commission books of Gottlieb Graupner which are now preserved in the library of Brown University.

When John Aitken commenced the publication of sheet music in the United States in 1787, contemporary newspaper advertisements indicated that his products could be obtained from Thomas Dobson, William Young, Henry and Patrick Rice, and others. During the earliest period of his activity Aitken probably maintained no outlet for the sale of his publications, restricting his involvement here to engraving alone. And later on, between 1807 and 1811, when he did have some sort of shop or retail outlet, Aitken distributed many of his publications through Charles Taws, an organ builder and occasional music publisher and perhaps engraver from Philadelphia, and even added Taws's name to some of his imprints. After commencing the publication of music in Philadelphia in 1794, Benjamin Carr, the first music publisher in America who really amounted to anything, also opened up a New York branch for the sale of his printed works. He simultaneously marketed his publications through James Hewitt, who, it has been said, also commenced publishing music in New York in that year (though it was only in 1798 that he became prolific and important in this respect) and through his father, Joseph Carr, who had set up as a publisher and engraver in Baltimore. There existed a reciprocity between Hewitt and the Carrs in this early period, for some of the imprints of each carry the others' names. After moving from Philadelphia to New York in 1795 and reestablishing himself as an occasional music publisher in the latter city, John Christopher Moller issued at least one publication on which the imprint read, "New York, Printed for and Sold at I. C. Moller's Musical Store, No. 58 Vesey Street, and at T. Western's Store, Maiden Lane, and at G. Willig's Store, Market Street, Philadelphia." Greater distribution meant greater profits, or the possibility of them, at least, and Moller sent some of his new music back to Willig for sale in Philadelphia, undoubtedly on a commission basis.

Imprints are particularly illuminating in the period after 1800. Publication data on many of James Hewitt's sheets which date between 1800 and 1803 carry as sellers the names of R. [Ralph?] Shaw in Philadelphia and D. Bowen, at his "Columbian Museum," in Boston. Apparently Bowen, who was the uncle of the copperplate printer and wood engraver Abel Bowen, did not hesitate to sell music and probably other merchandise at his museum. When the building housing Bowen's museum burned down on January 15, 1803, Hewitt immediately concluded arrangements with Gottlieb Graupner for the distribution of his publications in Boston. This is indicated by the addition of Graupner's name to some of Hewitt's imprints and by some of Graupner's manuscript records. Graupner, in turn, punched Hewitt's name on the plates of some of his own offerings. It has already been noted that Peter A. von Hagen maintained an arrangement with George Gilfert of New York between 1800 and 1803. A considerable number of von Hagen's publications at this time carried the note that they were obtainable in New York from Gilfert. Some of these von Hagen editions, it has been mentioned, were actually engraved by George Gilfert in New York, though von Hagen in Boston is listed as publisher of them. Perhaps because of failing health or the irresponsibility of his son, the elder von Hagen arranged with his old friend of New York days to engrave plates for him. Would it not have been natural for Gilfert to punch in his own name as the New York distributor of this music, possibly even taking part of his engraving fee in the form of printed copies of these sheets? Gilfert, in turn, indicated von Hagen as the Boston distributor of some of his own imprints, and in a very few instances he added the name of George Willig to some of these as well.

Many of the von Hagen publications of the 1802–3 period, during which time the family business was probably under the responsibility of the son, are noteworthy for carrying the names of a great many distributors, most of whom were booksellers in outlying regions. In addition to adding to these the usual name of Gilfert in New York, von Hagen indicated that these works were available from: Daniel Hewes in Boston; D. Vinton in Providence; W. R. Wilder in Newport; B. B. Macanulty in Salem; E. M. Blunt in Newburyport; Isaac Stanwood in Plymouth; and E. A. Jenks in Portland, Maine.[20] In the period between 1800 and 1802 Joseph Carr of Baltimore marketed music in Philadelphia through John Chalk and R. Shaw and in New York through Hewitt. Benjamin Carr, who by 1803 had joined forces with George Schetky, added to their "Carr & Schetky" imprints the names of George E. Blake and George Willig as their Philadelphia agents and designated the following distributors of their music in other localities: James Hewitt in

20. We can only speculate here that there may have existed an arrangement between von Hagen and the merchants named on such imprints—as well as with the issues of other music publishers containing the names of agents on imprints—that, as was the frequent custom in general publishing, such agents had agreed to take or to guarantee sale of a given number of copies of a work, in return for which they reeeived mention on it. For an account of this practice in the general printing industry see William Charvat's *Literary Publishing in America, 1790–1850* (Philadelphia, University of Pennsylvania Press, 1959) pp. 45–46.

New York; Francis Mallet and later William Blagrove in Boston; and E. Morford in Charleston.

Among the miscellaneous receipts of Frederick Rausch in the New York Public Library is the curious one printed below. Rausch, it will be recalled, was active as a music publisher in New York, as the partner first of George Gilfert between 1794 and 1796 and then of James Hewitt for a short interlude in 1797. While no publications after 1798 carry his name, it is likely that he remained associated with music publishing in some unknown capacity. (Sonneck–Upton conjectures that he was evidently with J. & M. Paff between 1800 and 1803, as his name has been noted at their address, 127 Broadway.) We have also seen that he arranged for the purchase of music plates in 1802 and that he had music engraved in London about 1806. Rausch's receipt reads:

> Boston 2 April 1802
>
> Received of P. A. von Hagen on board the Slope Columbia one Bundle Containing Music Directed to Mr. Fred. Rausch: New York which I promise to deliver to the Said Mr. F. Rausch the danger of the Sea Excepted he paying Freight as Customary.
>
> E. Scudder
>
> Marked F: R Recd # ⁵⁰⁄₁₀₀ for Freight Joane. I Redding

While we can only speculate about Rausch's relationship with von Hagen here—for, after all, the above shipment could have related to the procurement of music for Rausch's private use, thought I think this unlikely—we do have definite evidence of the interrelaship between publishers in different localities in the form of commission and account books of Gottlieb Graupner dating to about the same period. These, it has been noted, are now preserved in the library of Brown University. These records may have passed over to John Rowe Parker (who will be discussed in greater detail below), probably following Graupner's death. Together with a few of Parker's manuscripts and accounts they came into the hands of one H. M. Reynolds, from whose estate they were purchased by the bookseller who eventually sold them to Brown. The most pertinent and interesting documents in the "Reynolds Collection" consist of an "Invoice Book," which Graupner maintained between 1802 and 1817, an "Order Book," dating between the years 1808 and 1815, and an "Invoice and Commission Book," which records music sent to Graupner from New York by James Hewitt from 1802 to 1805 to be sold on commission, with the names of ships and captains forwarding it. We learn from these documents that Graupner was accustomed to send music to outlying booksellers to be sold on commission: to Mr. Adams at Portland, Maine; "sent by Stage to Cushing & Appleton, Salem, at Commission 20 per cent"; to Henry Cushing at Providence; to William R. Wilder at New Port; to Nicholas Geffroy at New Port; to Thomas & Sappen in Portsmouth; and so on. An especially interesting aspect of the interrelationships between publishers, as reflected in these records, revolves around the exchange of music between publishers. The following entry commenced a page-and-a-half listing of forty-eight titles in the Graupner account, amounting to 334 pieces of music with a total value of $140.50:

> Philadelphia 28 April 1806
>
> Have this Day shipped in the Schooner the Lady Hope, Nathan Nicholson Master the following Music in Exchange for Yours received

While no publisher's name is present here, the titles listed prove that Graupner was in this instance exchanging music with George E. Blake in Philadelphia. Here also appear data on similar exchanges with Hewitt in New York.

The first six pages of Graupner's "Invoice and Commission Book," dating from early 1803, are devoted to a list which is titled, "Received of Mrs. D. Bowen different Music for account of Mr. J. Hewitt in New York." This contains probably an inventory of Hewitt's music which was transferred to Graupner for sale by him following the disastrous fire which destroyed Bowen's Columbian Museum in January of 1803. Hewitt apparently made haste to sign up another distributor of his music in Boston, and his relationship with Graupner, apparently a long one, ensued. The last six pages of this "Invoice and Comission Book" document music titles sent to Graupner by Hewitt to be sold on commission. The three lists here are headed respectively:

> Received by the Schooner Sally Capt. Maxfield Different Music for Mr. J. Hewitt in New York in Commission at 20 per cent . . . Febr. 10th 1803.
>
> Received by the Schooner New Forge Capt. Aaron Pratt, different Music for Account of Mr. J. Hewitt in New York at 20 per Cent Commission . . . April 22th 1803.
>
> Invoice of Music Received of Mr. J. Hewitt to sell on his Account as per his Invoice Dated New York Decr. 7 1804.

Another interesting and illuminating aspect of the Reynolds materials is the information they provide regarding the ordering of musical merchandise from London. Between 1806 and 1817 Graupner recorded many extremely large orders of music and musical merchandise purchased from or through the firm of Clementi in London. The first such transaction, which is typical, records the purchase of musical merchandise of every conceivable kind from Clementi in the amount of £116 4s 3d, a sizable sum for those days. Items ordered included instruments of every type, pianofortes, clarinets, violins, Kent bugles, etc., and music strings, mutes, cases, tuning forks and hammers, bridges, and music.

Imprints on editions in the period after 1810 shows a continuation of interrelationships between publishers and booksellers. An edition of James Hewitt's composition *Lawrence the Brave*, issued by him in Boston after his removal there, carried the imprint, "Printed & sold by J. Hewitt, & at J. Loring's, No. 1 South-row." In the period after 1815, Allyn Bacon of Philadelphia advertised on his music that it could be obtained from Vallotte and Lété in New York; from J. Robinson's circulating library, Baltimore; and from the Franklin Music Warehouse in Boston. Blake had a similar relationship with Raymond Meetz of New York for the sale of his publications in the 1818–21 period, for Meetz is named as distributor on some of these. Meetz, in turn, sometimes added Blake's name to his few publications. Blake's imprints sometimes name the following agents or sellers of his music in other localities after 1823: John Rowe Parker, Boston; J. Robinson, Baltimore; W. Cooper, Washington; W. H. Fitz-whyosonn, Richmond; Mrs. Dumotet, Charleston; W. T. Williams, Savannah; and G. Pfeiffer, New Orleans. An interesting relationship evolved from one such connection. In 1818 William Dubois of New York issued a few titles which carried on their imprints as music seller the name of W. Stodard and Company of Richmond, Virginia. In 1821 Stodard (or Stodart), who had sold pianos and music in Richmond previously, came to New York and joined Dubois in his publishing and retail business. The firm was conducted under the name of Dubois & Stodart until 1835, when Stodart dropped or sold out and Dubois was joined by another partner named Bacon (George Bacon?), the firm becoming for three years Dubois & Bacon. Probably the most intriguing agency relationship existed in the case of Thomas Balls, a publisher and music seller in Norfolk, Virginia, between 1815 and 1817, and G. Balls of Philadelphia, about 1817. A few titles are known which contain the imprint, "London, Engrav'd, Printed & Sold by J. Balls, 408 Oxford Street, & to be Had of Balls & Woodis, Norfolk, Virginia & G. Balls, Philadelphia." The name was prominent in English music publishing at this time, and it would appear that two members of the family had emigrated.

The Franklin Music Warehouse, undoubtedly the largest distribution outlet for the sale of music in early America, was established by John

Rowe Parker about 1817. Parker, who was one of the major patrons and promoters of music in Boston (he was shortly afterward publisher of *The Euterpeiad*, the country's first magazine devoted exclusively to music, and compiler of an 1824 collection of biographies of famous composers and musicians), managed his warehouse from about 1817 to about 1821 and possibly later.[21] The Franklin Music Warehouse received and sold (probably on 20-percent commission) publications of almost all of our music publishers who were active while it was in operation. This is shown conclusively by the "Day Book" kept by Parker which is now preserved in the Reynolds collection at Brown University and by an extensive *Catalog of music and musical instruments, comprising every species of musical merchandise for sale at the Franklin Music Warehouse, No. 6 Milk St. Boston, together with a great variety of the newest and most approved vocal and instrumental compositions of all the favorite authors.* This catalog, which was issued in 1820, ran to fifty-five pages and contained hundreds of titles of American music publications of that period. Also indicative of the brisk business which Parker must have done at this outlet is the distinctive oval stamp which was affixed to music sold at the Franklin Music Warehouse. This can be found on music sheets in almost every collection today. Parker's "Day Book" consists of sixty-four pages of records of music forwarded to him for sale by Blake, Bacon, Willig, the Geibs, Willson, Dubois, Riley, Benjamin Carr, Oliver Shaw, and almost every active American publisher of that period and even by Clementi and Company of London. Parker is a very interesting character. After 1823 he opened up a telegraphic office on Central Wharf in Boston and later became known as an authority on semaphore signaling, on which subject he wrote at least four books which date between 1832 and 1841. Some of his manuscript papers, I have recently been told, are in the University of Pennsylvania Library.

It can also be seen from the invaluable "Account Book of Simeon Wood," reprinted in Appendix A, that Wood sent out music for sale not only to Graupner and Parker in Boston but to Oliver Shaw in Providence and to William M. Goodrich in Savannah. Wood maintained no shop or outlet for the sale of his publications. His business evidently consisted of sending music out to agents or of selling it to local musicians, performers, and dilettanti. Had he lived longer, it seems likely that he might have succeeded Graupner as Boston's leading music publisher and seller and would, in this event, probably have enlarged his circle of distributors.

One last note regarding distribution. It is not unusual to find European

21. H. Earle Johnson refers to *The Euterpeiad* in his *Musical Interludes in Boston* as mainly a house organ for Parker's retail business.

music of this early period witb the label of an American music publisher and seller pasted over the original foreign imprint to give the appearance of freshness to the work. The extensive collection of American sheet music in the Houghton Library of Harvard University contains a fine example of this practice (or malpractice). A copy here of *The Favorite overture to the Round Tower. Accompanied on the harp by Mr. Weippert. Composed by Mr. Reeve*, which carries the imprint *London, Published for the Author and Sold at his Music Shop*, has a printed label pasted over that imprint and obliterating it, which reads:

> To be sold, at P. A. Von Hagen, Jun. and Company's Musical Magazine, No. 62 Newbury-street, Boston: There may be had—Warranted Imported Piano Fortes at different Prices—and every other Article in the Musical Line—Piano Fortes, &c. let out, conveyed and tuned, in Town and Country, on the shortest Notice—and if purchased, and payment made within three months, the hire will be abated—Also, Musical Instruments repaired in the neatest manner—and taken in Exchange.

PRINTED CATALOGS OF MUSIC

The large and extensive catalog of music sold at the Franklin Music Warehouse in Boston in the period around 1820 was printed from type by Thomas Badger, Jr., who also printed for John Rowe Parker volumes I and II of his *Euterpeiad* The issuance of catalogs such as this and by publishers of their available stock appears to have been an infrequent occurrence in pre-1840 America. Based on the few of these that have survived, it would seem that the majority of our early publishers never took the trouble to issue catalogs of their music at all. However, evidence notwithstanding, the issuance of catalogs by our early music publishers may have been far more frequent and common than we now suppose. After all, catalogs are printed ephemera, and their survival rate is far below that of other types of literature. One indication of the more common issuance and the high mortality of early American music publishers' catalogs is the reference to "8 catalogue plates" on the Graupner inventory for which no printed copies are now known to exist.

The earliest extant catalogs of music issued by our publishers appeared as supplementary pages on a number of publications of Carr & Schetky in the 1806–11 period. Many of these were actually reprintings of titles that had initially appeared in *The Musical Journal for the Piano Forte*. Instead of leaving blank pages on some of their publications, Carr & Schetky printed onto them a list of music that they had put forth. This catalog actually consisted of a single plate, to which they added new titles from time to time. Though it never became very extensive, it included most of their output during this period, and it can be used to date approximately the appearance of new works under their imprint. The first separate as well as extensive catalog of music issued in America that is known today was published by George Willig about 1808 (Wolfe, No. 9955). Three of its four pages contain an alphabetical catalog which lists Willig's stock about 1807; the final page contains another catalog, also alphabetical, which names titles issued in 1808. A great many of the titles listed in this catalog were undoubtedly published by others, and it most likely represents a list of music that Willig had for sale in 1808.

The next extant catalogs date to the period around 1817, when William Dubois issued a four-page list of all of the music that he had reprinted from the Paff plates together with some new music of his own (Wolfe, No. 2580). When Allyn Bacon issued an American edition of Neville B. Challoner's *New Preceptor for the Piano Forte* (Wolfe, No. 1756) about 1817, he devoted the final page of it to "A Catalogue of Music for the Piano Forte, Published by A. Bacon, Music and Musical Instrument Seller, No. 11 S. 4th Street, Philadelphia." This contained about two-fifths of Bacon's total output. When John Klemm assumed the Bacon plate stock in 1823 and reissued his own edition of this work, he omitted this catalog from the reprinted edition, leaving the final page blank.

The handful of other known catalogs all postdate the publication of the Parker Franklin Music Warehouse catalog of 1820. In 1822 Edward Riley issued a four-page list of "music publised [*sic*] and sold by E. Riley" (Wolfe, No. 7482), which lists publications by him and others. (The New York Public Library also has a more extensive catalog of Riley's, running to sixteen pages and containing a one-page supplement, which he probably issued about 1829, the year of his death.) About June or July 1824, George Willig issued a six-page catalog which contains only music of his own manufacture (Wolfe, No. 9956). Finally, John Cole in 1826 (late March or early April) brought out a list of all music published by him to that time (Wolfe, No. 1976). Another catalog of his musical offerings appeared about August 1830. Almost all the above-cited catalogs are known in single copies only, attesting to the low survival rate of such literature.

MUSICAL CIRCULATING LIBRARIES

Another phenomenon of the earliest period of formal American music publishing was the musical circulating library, which a few publishers and

[227]

music sellers conducted as adjuncts to their usual activities. These enterprises were probably modeled after European or English examples. Subscribers were invited to pay annual or semiannual dues, in exchange for which they were entitled to borrow individual music titles and bound volumes of music. James Harrison, who introduced music publishing to New York City in 1793, advertised such a circulating library at the very start of his publishing and selling activity. The terms outlined in his broadside announcement of this scheme can be read in Illustration 5 here. This tells us that Harrison had (or boasted of having) upwards of 1,000 volumes of music for loan. In return for a yearly subscription fee of 7 dollars, or a half-yearly fee of 4 dollars or a quarterly fee of $2.50 subscribers were entitled to borrow two volumes at any one time. Penalties were prescribed for the loan of books by borrowers to nonsubscribers, and borrowers who wrote in volumes were expected to pay for them at a pre-established valuation. (Note the reference to a catalog on Harrison's announcement.) Finally, music could also be rented by persons not subscribing to this plan, but at an inflated rate.

The scarcity of music in those early days and its great expense probably made such schemes popular, though it would appear that they were not actually as successful as we might presume. In his *Musical Interludes in Boston*, H. Earle Johnson tells us that the idea of a musical circulating library had occurred to Francis Mallet, Gottlieb Graupner, and Filippo Trajetta when they established their conservatory in 1802, from which they began to issue a little music, but that little or nothing came of the idea. We know from notices which George E. Blake added to a few of his imprints that he too conducted a circulating library from 1803 until at least 1807. Such information appeared on his editions of *A Collection of the Most Favorite Cottillions* (Wolfe, No. 2007) and on the first number of his edition of Moore's *Irish Melodies* (Wolfe, No. 8942). How long Blake continued this practice, and how extensively, are unknown at this time.

James Hewitt appears to have been the major exponent of the musical circulating library in early America. He established such an operation at his Musical Repository about November 1807, and he added to the imprints of his publications a note regarding its existence. In fact, Hewitt's publications before and after November 1807 can be distinguished by the wording of the phrase "Printed and sold at J. Hewitt's Musical Repository & Library, No. 59 Maiden Lane"; the words "& Library" are lacking from imprints of publications before about November 1807. Little else is known about Hewitt's circulating library in New York. When he migrated to Boston about 1811 and reestablished himself as a music publisher, he also set up a circulating library in that city. About this operation we know a bit more. According to Johnson (p. 231), Hewitt announced the establishment of a music rental library according to a European plan, which was similar to Harrison's. Hewitt claimed to have the largest collection of musical compositions by celebrated authors in the country, boasting several thousand volumes in all. Hewitt proposed to charge 6 dollars for a yearly subscription, $3.50 for half a year, and 2 dollars quarterly. In addition, he also handled non-musical merchandise, for the same advertisement of his library notes that he had "for sale as above—an assortment of Spanish cigars, in boxes of 250 each, of a superior quality." No further information is available on Hewitt's circulating library in Boston, but in June 1813, Samuel H. Parker informed the public that he had received a library containing several hundred volumes, including a large assortment of vocal and instrumental music which he proposed to add to his rolling stock. Samuel H. Parker, not to be confused with John Rowe Parker, publisher of the *Euterpeiad* and proprietor of the Franklin Music Warehouse, was a bookbinder and bookseller who from 1812 or 1813 conducted a general circulating library which is said to have consisted of 7,000 volumes by 1818. Parker had taken over the Union Circulating Library of William Blagrove, whose name appears as Boston agent on many of the Carr & Schetky publications of the 1807–11 period, and Parker continued the business under that title.[22] Parker also made a few attempts at publishing music between 1816 and 1823, his most notable and ambitious effort being a collection entitled *The Orphean Lyre* in 1816. The evidence indicates that Hewitt transported his New York library to Boston and that he intended to reemploy this for the circulation of music on a rental basis. That this scheme may have failed is indicated by the probable acquisition of these materials by Parker in 1813.

Other publishers and music sellers undoubtedly rented music, but to what extent we do not know. Music was expensive at this early time and available to only a few. Individuals must have utilized the circulating library in order to obtain printed music which they could copy out in manuscript form and retain for permanent use. Indeed, it has often struck me that the many manuscript transcriptions which are found in bound volumes of printed music were made from copies borrowed from such

22. Both Parker and Blagrove receive mention in Charles K. Bolton's "Circulating Libraries in Boston, 1765–1865," *Publications of the Colonial Society of Massachusetts* XI (1906–7) 196–207. Blagrove, it is pointed out there (p. 204), left Boston about 1811 and was a resident of Washington, D.C., in 1821.

establishments. Public libraries were nonexistent at this period, and rental, subscription, and "society" libraries fulfilled many of the needs of the literate public. Music sellers and publishers who conducted retail establishments frequently rented out pianos and other musical instruments, and the practice of renting music was probably practiced on a more extensive basis than we are aware of at this late date.

LITHOGRAPHED MUSIC

The practice of printing music directly from a lithographic stone was introduced into America in the third decade of the nineteenth century. The earliest known application of the lithographic process to music was made here by one Henry Stone, a little-known engraver of Washington, D.C., who lithographed a song entitled *The Generous Chief* and an unidentified collection of vocal and instrumental music in 1823.[23] Stone also executed a few other pieces of music through the lithographic process, but his efforts at reproducing music through this process were not important or enduring. The actual lithographing of music on a grander and more continuous scale really dates from the year 1827, from which time it was employed by several New York publishers: Edward S. Mesier, Anthony Fleetwood, Anthony Imbert, and George M. Bourne. Lithography remained in vogue for about a decade afterward as a medium for publishing music. In his survey article "Graphic Analysis," Krummel refers (p. 220) to lithographically produced music as though it comprised the major output of American music publishers from 1827 to 1835. This was clearly not the case. The printing of music directly from stone was restricted to the above-mentioned four publishers of New York, the other music publishers there and elsewhere continuing to print their sheets from metal plates. The output of Meiser, Fleetwood, Imbert, and Bourne, in fact, constituted only a small portion of the total output of this period. About 1826 the custom arose whereby publishers issued engraved music sheets which bore lithographically produced covers, a practice which remained in vogue for many, many decades afterward.

The lithographic process was apparently cheap when compared with the usual method of producing music: in this method music was drawn on paper and then transferred onto stone, from which an edition could be

23. The only known copy of this song is in the Clements Library of the University of Michigan (Wolfe, No. 5684). The untitled collection appears as No. 2002 in *Secular Music in America*. The most extensive information on Stone can be found in E. A. Wright and J. A. McDevitt's "Early American Sheet-Music Lithography," *Antiques* XXIII (February–March 1933) 51–53, 99–102.

printed easily; from the viewpoint of ease of operation, it was far superior to the tedious process of inking, cleaning, and printing individual plates. But it resulted in a finished sheet that was somewhat uneven in appearance and artistically inferior to music issued directly from a plate, and it never quite caught on.[24] While Krummel in his article "Graphic Analysis" (p. 220) is correct in noting that lithographically produced music was in evidence as late as the Civil War, and that the method was widely employed in the Confederacy—"probably because of the shortage of engravers there," he concluded—I am inclined toward the theory that lithography was reintroduced as a substitute for printing music in the southern states during the Civil War because of a lack of metal for plates rather than for want of engravers. Richard Harwell's checklist of Confederate music imprints on pages 101–56 of his book *Confederate Music* shows that several engravers were at work in the South during the conflict. Akin to this revival of an outmoded method for producing sheet music was the reintroduction by southern music publishers of the typographic method for the purpose of printing music sheets, which occurrence further emphasizes that substitutes were invoked because of a shortage of metal brought about by the war. In "Graphic Analysis" (p. 220) Krummel is also in error in ascribing the lithographic process to Joseph Atwell and George Endicott of New York. Both used metal plates to print their music, restricting their employment of lithography to the production of illustrated title-pages and covers. Endicott did much of Atwell's engraving in addition to his own. The later use of lithography in combination with the engraving process has already been discussed. This combined method remained dominant for producing music in America from about the middle of the nineteenth century until well into the twentieth.

ILLUSTRATED MUSIC

In her recent article on the illustration of music in America, which constitutes probably the most ambitious attempt to date to survey the decoration of American sheet-music covers in the period after 1826, Nancy R. Davison states, with regard to the musical publications issued from the 1790s through 1825, that "these early pieces of sheet music were printed from engraved plates that were rarely equipped with illustra-

24. The advertisement of Edward S. Mesier in the New York *Evening Post* of May 20, 1831, announcing that he had "lithographic music for sale at half the price of plate music," provides vivid evidence of this.

tions.[25] I have searched through the Sonneck-Upton bibliography and I have reexamined my own *Secular Music in America*—reference is made in the index there to all illustrated music of that period—and I have determined that slightly more than 220 illustrations appeared on American music sheets from 1789 through 1825, representing just over 2 percent of the total output of this period. I concluded from this survey that perhaps instead of "rarely," the word "infrequently" would better describe the situation. Admittedly, some of these decorations, about one-seventh of them, are title-page borders and ornamental frames. And while it is true, as Davison implies, that the proliferation of American illustrated music had to await the introduction of an inexpensive method of producing it (lithography), the decoration of music in the pre-1826 era was more common than she has supposed, and the precedents for the wide use of illustration which lithography engendered after 1826 can be found in the decades which preceded its introduction. It will be the objective of this section to survey the employment of illustrations on American music sheets in the pre-1826 period and to discuss the use of the *passe-partout* title page and other mechanisms for decorating such publications.

In his article "English Pictorial Music Title-pages 1820–1885," which surveys the concurrent decoration of English music covers, A. Hyatt King has appropriately noted that the year 1820, at which time lithography began to influence the development of the English pictorial music title page, may be conveniently taken as the opening of a new era in English music illustration.[26] By altering the date 1820 to 1826, approximately the same statement could be made with regard to American musical illustration. It should be noted here that illustrations on musical works serve the purpose of decoration only. Unlike illustration in books, there is little that pictorial matter can add to a musical text. The presence of illustrations and ornaments on music act more as a lure, suggesting to purchasers and others the theme in an imaginative sense. Hence, the vignette of a storm on Steibelt's *Storm Rondo*, the portrait of John Adams on *Adams and Liberty*, a representation of fighting ships on *Huzza for the*

25. "The Grand Triumphal Quick-Step; or, Sheet Music Covers in America," in *Prints in and of America to 1850*, pp. [257]–94. This attempts to do descriptively what Dichter and Shapiro's *Early American Sheet Music* does more effectively pictorially. A recent contribution to this genre, one which attempts to tell the stories behind some of our earlier songs and music, both descriptively and pictorially, is Lester S. Levy's *Grace Notes in American History, Popular Sheet Music from 1820 to 1900* (Norman, University of Oklahoma Press, 1967). And there have been other recent additions to this literature.

26. *The Library*, 5th ser IV (1950) 262–72.

Constitution, a work inspired by the undeclared war with France in 1798–1800, an engraving showing the frigate *Constellation* bombarding a Tripolitan fort on the title page of Benjamin Carr's *The Siege of Tripoli*, and so on. As King has noted in his article (see n. 26), "there are, first, decorative or ornametnal title-pages in which the design bears little, if any, relation to the subject or nature of the music, and, secondly, the descriptive or pictorial type." For purposes of convenience, I shall separate all pre-1826 decorated American music sheets into two classes: those containing illustrative or pictorial designs, regardless of whether these reflect the subject matter of their respective pieces, and those whose title pages possess ornamental borders or frames. The latter category contains about thirty-two items, comprising perhaps one-seventh of the total ornamented output of this early period.

A great many of the illustrations, pictorial ornaments, and vignettes which our earliest publishers added to their music titles were of the simplest design and were effected as inexpensively as possible. Many appear to have been added as a whim or afterthought, for example, the figure of a bird on *The Bird Waltz*, on a song entitled *The Whipperwill*, and on a piano duet entitled *The Nightingale;* the representation of a flower on *This Blooming Rose* and on *I'll Pull a Bunch of Buds and Flowers;* dancing figures (often Cupids) on sets of cotillions and other dances; musical instruments and sprays of leaves on preceptors, tutors, and some general titles; weapons and military paraphernalia on martial and patriotic pieces; and so forth. The very first sheet-music publication in America bearing an illustration or ornament, John Aitken's 1789 edition of Alexander Reinagle's *The Foederal March, as Performed in the Grand Procession in Philadelphia the 4th of July, 1788*, presents a fitting example of this practice. This work had been composed in celebration of the ratification of the Federal Constitution by the ten states, and it had also been played before George Washington by the bands of Philadelphia in the military parade of October 27, 1788. Possibly out of a desire to enhance a patriotic theme further, Aitken cut into one of the upper corners of the plate for this work the crude outline of a pole with a liberty cap.[27]

American musical illustration really begins after 1793 with the arrival of other publishers and with the more extensive publication of music and the competition which this engendered, for Aitken published no more ornamented or illustrated music until 1797. Because so many of our

27. This rather sorry excuse for an illustration can be observed on Plate 3 of Dichter and Shapiro's *Early American Sheet Music*. It seems reasonable to conclude that Aitken cut this crude illustration himself.

earliest music illustrations and ornamentations are simple and naive, I shall restrict my further remarks here to the obvious exceptions, that is, to those editions which were ornamented elaborately and in out-of-the-ordinary ways. It will also be of interest to look at the subjects that were chosen for illustration; to determine which publishers most frequently ornamented their music; to determine who the engravers were; and, finally, to discuss the use of the title page in general.

Illustration actually came to American music publishing after 1794, when Benjamin Carr, George Gilfert, and others began to add illustrations and ornaments to their more pretentious publications. The first title to which we can assign an outside engraver is Aitken's own composition of 1797 entitled *The Scots Musical Museum*, one of the largest and most ambitious collections of secular music issued in early America. The work of David Edwin in cutting the title-page ornament here has been discussed in detail before. James Hewitt's publication during that same year of his own composition, *The Battle of Trenton*, comprises one of the most ambitious attempts to illustrate music in the pre-1800 era. It is also notable for being the first work to contain an elaborate, full-page scene, showing a three-quarter portrait of Washington amid much martial imagery.

The undeclared war with France from 1798 to 1800 and the presidency of John Adams inspired a great many illustrated editions of sheet music in 1798 and 1799. On several of the latter the portraits of Washington and Adams were cut from other, separate engravings and mounted on. James Hewitt's descriptive sonata *The 4th of July* (1801) shows another major attempt at title-page illustration at this very early time, and John Aitken's 1802 edition of his own song, *The Goldsmith's Rant*, which is reproduced as the Frontispiece herein, presents us with one of the most amazing scenes in the whole literature of American music illustration. The engraver of the remarkable vignettes on the verso of this sheet is unknown, since the work is unsigned. However, because of his work in ornamenting an earlier Aitken edition, the name of David Edwin suggests itself. I have looked at several pices of silver fashioned by Aitken during his metalsmithing career and I have concluded that the caliber of workmanship in the vignettes on the verso of *The Goldsmith's Rant* was well beyond his own modest capability (see Illus. 17) The five volumes of Benjamin Carr's *Musical Journal for the Piano Forte* are notable in that Carr used two different vignettes for ornamenting title pages here, one serving for the first two and another for the final three volumes. The engraving on Benjamin Carr's *The Siege of Tripoli*, published in 1804 or 1805 and showing the *Constellation* bombarding a Tripolitan fort, is one of the most arresting scenes on an early American music sheet. George Willig, a German in origin, had John Norman of Boston engrave a scene showing a Hessian fifer for the title page of his *Compleat Tutor for the Fife*, which dates to the period between 1804 and 1809.

In 1807 George E. Blake effected an elaborate engraving for his *Blake's Collection of Duetts for Two Flutes, Clarinets, or Violins.* This is the only instance that has come to my attention of Blake's non-musical engraving and one of the few cases in which a music publisher effected a major illustration for one of his own issues. The workmanship here indicates that Blake knew how to use the graver. The title-page scene depicts the newly completed waterworks at Central Square in Philadelphia, an engineering and architectural marvel at that time. This wonder also inspired John Aitken to issue another pictorial publication, *Aitken's Fountain of Music* (1807–11), also having the waterworks as its theme. The title-page scene on Blake's issue of the collected music of John Bray's melodrama of 1808, *The Indian Princess*, is also worthy of mention. This pictures Pocahontas, the heroine of the play, before an Indian encampment. Blake also added noteworthy engravings to several other of his publications of this period. His *The Yorkshire Irishman* of 1807 presents us with one of the first comic scenes. He added an elaborate scene showing the bridge over the Schuylkill River at Philadelphia to various numbers of his collection of tunes for flute, clarinet, violin, or flageolet entitled *Blake's Evening Companion*, which appeared in nine books between 1808 and 1824.[28] Finally, his issue of Karl Kambra's *The Battle of Trafalgar* about 1808, which contains a depiction of the naval battle, indicates that Blake was something of an anglophile at this time.

Undoubtedly the most elaborate and most professionally executed engravings added to American music publications in the pre-1826 period (and perhaps for a decade or more afterward) appeared on a handful of titles issued by or for Peter Weldon in the years between 1808 and 1812. Weldon had been active as a musician, "professor of music," and sometime music publisher and perhaps music engraver in New York City from about 1797 until 1811 or slightly later, but little else is actually known about him. The handful of highly ornamented publications which he sponsored between 1808 and 1812 all have Hispanic themes, and individuals interested in him and in these particular works have theorized that he may have had a Spanish or Portuguese or Brazilian wife. Two of

28. This was probably patterned after the "Original Model of the First Bridge over the Schuylkill," listed as lot no. 2980 on the 1871 catalog of Blake's tools and music (Appendix B).

these works have reference to Brazil, and the remainder display a pro-Spanish and anti-Napoleonic fervor and celebrate Spanish victories in the Peninsular War of 1808–14. The five titles under discussion are the *Marcha del General Palofax* (1808–12), three of Weldon's own compositions, *La Battalla de Baylen* (1809), the *Favorita Waltz Brazilense* (1810), and *The Siege of Gerona* (1810–12), and an anonymous composition of about 1811 called *Lord Wellington's March*. Although all of these were issued without any indication of their publisher, Weldon's participation in the publication of each can easily be seen or inferred. In two cases, Weldon is listed as claimant for copyright. The two most elaborate title pages of this extraordinary series of publications, the scenes appearing on his *La Battalla de Baylen* and on his *Favorita Waltz Brazilense* are reproduced in Illustration 28 herein. The first one shows the massing of infantry in the city square of Seville in preparation for the Battle of Baylen and the other depicts the landing of the Royal Court of Portugal in Rio de Janeiro Harbor following its transfer there when Napoleon declared the throne of Portugal vacant.

In advertising in the *New York Evening Post* of May 16, 1812, that he had just received a few copies of the *The Siege of Gerona*, Joseph Willson stated that the work contained "elegant engravings by Leney." The reference here is to William S. Leney, an immigrant English artist, who worked in New York City between 1805 and 1820 and was one of the leading and most successful engravers of that period in America. Leney executed engravings for books contemporaneously, and it seems reasonable and logical to conclude that he was responsible for all of the illustrations in this pictorial series. There were few engravers at work in America at this time who could measure up to his artistic ability in this medium. These five publications by Weldon represent the pinnacle of American music illustration in this early period and they are among the finest pictorial American music sheets of all time.

The Anacreontic Vocalist, issued by Gottlieb Graupner at Boston in 1809 and comprising a small collection of glees, catches, canons, duets, and rounds, appropriately displayed an engraving of Anacreon and a drinking scene on its title. Although a few sheets show rather interesting illustrations after 1809, it was not until the War of 1812 that publishers again had cause to provoke public sentiment and patronage widely through picture as well as song. Illustrations were inspired by Perry's victory, by the Battle of New Orleans, by the bombardment of Fort McHenry, and by other events of that conflict. The most handsome of these War of 1812 illustrations—and many of them fall into that category—appeared on the title page of Francesco Masi's *The Battles of Lake Champlain and Plattsburg*, which is reproduced as Illustration 8a herein. (This exists in a single known copy in the Boston Public Library.) Other notable pictorial sheets of this period include several of Raynor Taylor's compositions: his music for the play *The Ethiop*, his song *The Beech Tree's Petition;* his *America and Britannia*, celebrating the resumption of peace in 1815, and his *The Martial Music of Camp Dupont.* Joseph Twibill's *On the Bosom of Night When the Weary Are Sleeping*, engraved and published probably by Bacon at Philadelphia about 1816, constitutes one of the first pictorial music sheets commemorating the fireman. It prefigured a vaster literature in this area that followed the introduction of lithography for ornamenting American music titles in 1826.

Other notable pictorial issues of the period between 1816 and 1820 include *The Two Emperors and the King of Prussia's March Entering Paris*, a Willig publication of about 1816 showing the triumphal entry into Paris of the leaders of the allied nations following the final defeat of Napoleon; Etienne Christiani's *President Monroe's March;* the depiction of a youth seated before the tomb of Mozart on the Bacon edition of *Select Airs* of that composer; and the several works of Anthony Philip Heinrich which date to 1820. For some years after 1818 comic songs came into vogue, of which a few displayed pictorial decoration. Blake, Bacon, and Riley all issued editions of a comic song entitled *Oh! Cruel*, which pictured a female ballad singer and a peg-legged violinist; Edward Riley's *O, What a Row!* of about 1822 made fun of the fragility of the newly invented steamer and played on the identical sounding of the word *row* as in oaring, and *row* as in quarreling; and Blake's offering between 1821 and 1824 of *The Ghosts of Mrs. Crookshanks & Mr. Duffy* used the supernatural to provoke laughter. About 1823 the aforementioned lithographer Henry Stone issued music sheets containing a number of illustrations, the first produced by lithography in America, though steady use of this' medium for effecting illustrations on music sheets began between 1826 and 1830.

Probably the major event in early nineteenth-century America was the return to America of the Revolutionary hero General Lafayette to receive the plaudits and thanks of a grateful nation. As was noted before, this event prompted an outpouring of musical compositions, many of which carried illustrations. A number of these showed portraits of the hero; others displayed martial and patriotic themes. The most unusual was Edward Riley's edition of Micah Hawkins's song *Massa Georgee Washington and General LaFayette.* This piece, which is one of the high spots of all American music illustration and one of the most desirable items from the viewpoint of the collector, shows a black-face Washington in the uniform of a Continental officer. The engraving here was executed by David Claypool Johnston, America's first graphic humorist. Johnston took on all sorts of jobs, as did other artists of the day, in order to earn his living. A few of his commissions were concerned with the engraving or lithographing of title scenes and vignettes for music publications. In fact, it was Johnston who lithographed the first sheet-music cover in America (see p. 241). The pictorial literature occasioned by Lafayette's visit really closed out this early period with a bang. In fact, no other event in our early history provoked a greater outpouring of music and song and of illustration to accompany it. The few other notable engravings on our music sheets antedating 1826 were William Blondell's *The Hunters of Kentucky*, a Birch publication of about 1824 which showed two Kentucky riflemen in backwoods garb and which was used as a campaign song for Andrew Jackson's unsuccessful bid for the presidency in 1824; Raymond Meetz's edition of *The Castle Garden March* of 1825, which gave New Yorkers their first musical view of this landmark of over a century; and George Willig's publication of about 1825 of *Bolivar, a Peruvian Song*, which showed a portrait of the Liberator.

Let us now consider briefly which publishers most frequently employed illustration on their sheets and the nature of the music for which they used it. The first point is best revealed by Table 7, which tells us how many times a given publisher used illustration or ornamentation on the title pages or captions of his products. This table emphasizes to what extent George E. Blake outclassed his competitors with regard to the illustration of music in this early period. George Willig, who also enjoyed a long and profitable career in music publishing, ran a poor second to him but still remained well ahead of his other contemporaries. George Gilfert, Allyn Bacon, and Benjamin Carr were the only other publishers of consequence in this respect. Inasmuch as their careers as publishers were less prolix, their use of illustration was more extensive than we would initially suppose.

Table 8 indicates that during the initial decade of music publishing here, roughly from 1789 through 1799, publishers restricted their use of illustration almost entirely to patriotic themes. This changed in the decade after 1800 with the emergence of new publishers (such as Blake and Graupner), the widening of tastes, and the growth of interest in the sophisticated, at which time scenes, views, and general ornamentation came in on a wider scale. Although patriotic themes again became the vogue between 1812 and 1816, occasioned mostly by the second war with

TABLE 7

Publishers' Use of Title Illustrations

	1786–89	1790–99	1800–1809	1810–19	1820–26	Total
John Aitken, Phila.	1	1	2			4
Benjamin Carr, Phila.		7	3		1	11
George Gilfert, N.Y.		5	11			16
Filippo Trisobio, Phila.		1				1
James Hewitt, N.Y.		3	4			7
Peter A. von Hagen, Boston		1				1
John & Michael Paff,		1	4	2		7
John Young, Phila. & N.Y.		1				1
Gottlieb Graupner, Boston			6	2	1	9
George E. Blake, Phila.			19	28	19	66
Francis Mallet, Boston			2			2
Carr & Schetky, Phila.			1			1
George Willig, Phila. & Balt.			2	16	10	28
Peter Weldon, N.Y.			2	3		5
Madame LePelletier, Baltimore				1		1
Peter Muck, Charleston				1		1
Joseph Carr, Baltimore				1		1
Edward Riley, N.Y.				2	4	6
Francesco Masi, Boston				1		1
Joseph Willson, N.Y.				1		1
George K. Jackson, Boston				1		1
Samuel H. Parker, Boston				1		1
Allyn Bacon, Phila.				8	4	12
John Klemm, Phila.				2		2
J. A. & W. Geib, N.Y.				3	2	5
William Dubois, N.Y.				2		2
Oliver Shaw, Providence				1	2	3
Thomas Carr, Baltimore					3	3
John Cole, Baltimore					8	8
C. & E. W. Jackson, Boston					1	1
Raymond Meetz, N.Y.					3	3
Henry Stone, Washington					5	5
Dubois & Stodart, N.Y.					1	1
Thomas Birch, N.Y.					1	1
William R. Coppock, Brooklyn					1	1
James L. Hewitt, Boston					1	1
Unknown					2	2
TOTAL	1	20	56	76	69	222

Great Britain, views, scenes, and ornamentation in a general sense continued to dominate the field.

Let us now consider who the engravers were. Several of these, David Edwin, George E. Blake, William S. Leney, and David Claypool Johnston, have been mentioned before. For the most part, publishers turned to the nearest and most convenient source for ornamentation. General engravers of Philadelphia, New York, and Boston were most frequently enlisted or commissioned to carry out this chore. For the most

TABLE 8
Subjects Used in Illustrations

	1786–89	1790–99	1800–1809	1810–19	1820–26	Total
Title-page borders & frames		2	8	14	9	33
American patriotic themes	1	11	2	12	2	28
Comic themes			1	4	4	9
Objects (birds, flowers, etc.)				13	9	22
Scenes, epic events, etc.		3	16	16	22	57
Dancing themes			2	1	2	5
Martial themes		2	8	5	1	16
Ornaments, sprays, music books & instruments, etc.		2	19	11	9	41
Lafayette					11	11
TOTAL	1	20	56	76	69	222

part, engravings went unsigned, the majority of them having been undertaken and executed as hackwork in the course of a day's labor. Usually, only the most elaborate or pretentious illustrations carried the names of their makers. We have already noticed in the 1795 diary of Alexander Anderson, who eventually achieved a measure of fame as America's first engraver on wood, how he was engaged by George Gilfert to engrave letters for the title of a piece of music. The cutting of fancy lettering for titles also required the services of an outside engraver. The music engraver was accustomed to stamp, punch, and cut straight or nearly straight lines into soft pewter plates. The cutting of scrolled and fancy titles in the copperplate manner, even simple ones, which were normally effected on hard copperplates and printed separately, was simply not his cup of tea. For such specialized work the publisher of music normally sought out the aid of a professional engraver, usually the closest one at hand. In a few cases, publishers sent commissions out of town. The presence of John Norman's name on the Willig flute tutor of 1809 is an example of this infrequent practice.

Biographies of the majority of those engravers whose names appeared on early American music illustrations can be found in George C. Groce and David H. Wallace's *Dictionary of Artists in America, 1564–1860* (New Haven, Yale University Press, 1957, pubd. under the auspices of the New-York Historical Society). There is no need to reiterate details here. It can be noted, by way of providing an overall profile of these workers, that they were mostly general engravers who worked in a variety of media in order to earn their daily bread. They undertook all sorts of commissions, in addition to cutting plates for making prints or for illustrating books and journals, including the engraving of buttons, tools and stamps for bookbinders, printers, and other craftsmen, dies for minting coins and plates for printing paper money, the executing of cartoons and miniature paintings, and a variety of similar projects. Many of them were immigrants who had the advantage of foreign training. Others, like William Strickland, were native-born. Some achieved a degree of notoriety or fame; others never climbed out of the depths of near-anonymity. A few of them, such as John Ritto Penniman, the engraver of the blue bird on Shaw's composition and post-1823 publication of that name, and Cephas Grier Childs, who executed the combined Indian-Alpine scene for A. P. Heinrich's *The Minstrel's Petition* of 1820, were shortly afterward involved in the introduction of the lithographic technique to America. John L. Frederick was the only music engraver, in addition to Blake, who added his name to the illustration on a sheet. Like Blake, he did this in one instance only, in this early period at least. Henry Stone has previously been mentioned with regard to the lithographing of a few music publications and a few illustrations for them in the period around 1823. It is surprising that he did not lithograph music on a wider scale after 1827, when it came into music publishing in a bigger way.

America's first lithographic house was opened in Boston in 1825 by William Pendleton and his brother, John, who had studied this art in France. In fact, they trained most of the early American lightographers and supplied them with their equipment.[29] As Davison has noted in her survey of sheet-music covers in post-1826 America, the first dated, lithographically illustrated sheet-music cover in America was issued in Boston in March 1826. This was a composition of A. P. Heinrich called *The Log House*. David Claypool Johnston drew the backwoods scene for this, and the Pendletons transferred it to stone and printed it. (The music which accompanied this scene was, of course, punched in the usual manner.) It was included in Heinrich's collection of 1823–26 entitled *The Sylviad*, where it was printed without date, and it was also issued separately.

I shall say no more about American music illustration here. For further details on this fascinating phase of music publishing the reader is referred to the Dichter-Shapiro pictorial account and to Davison's survey article of the post-1826 field, which suffers from her reliance upon the resources of a single collection of illustrated sheets, and one in a prints department

29. The best summary that I have seen on the introduction and early status of lithography in America is Peter C. Marzio's "American Lithographic Technology before the Civil War," in *Prints in and of America to 1850*, pp. 215–56. This however, is restricted to the technological side of the subject.

of a library at that. Only by examining vast amounts of pictorial American music in a variety of collections and in a number of locations, as I did in the course of compiling my *Secular Music in America*, can one fully appreciate the enormity of this form of popular expression and realize its importance in recording and chronicling the American scence of the past. Some of the major or most interesting personalities in nineteenth-century American art—David Claypool Johnston, William Rimmer, Currier and Ives, James McNeill Whistler, to mention a few—worked in this genre. The undertaking of such work was an occasional affair in the business life of many a struggling artist and engraver; they often executed such work on commission and as a sideline in order to subsidize their more important work. Sometimes, the execution of such illustrations drew them into music publishing themselves. The catalog of Peter Maverick's publications which Stephens appended to his *The Mavericks, American Engravers*, indicates that on a few occasions a general engraver and lithographer crossed over the line into music publishing as well. Maverick also turned out musical ornaments and executed a trade card for a professor of music (Samuel P. Taylor).[30]

I shall conclude this section on illustration with a few words on the use of the title page at this time. Title pages had been added to music in sheet form long before the publication of sheet music in America as a means of protecting the initial sheets of text, particularly in collections and on lengthy pieces. (The mechanism of printing a two-page song on one side of a whole sheet of paper, which was then folded in half so that the printed pages were located inside, may have served a similar purpose when title pages were not used, that is, to protect the printed text.) While the vast majority of publications in early America consisted of songs, which were brief and which did not require a separately printed introduction, title pages were commonly employed on collections and on longer instrumental works. Several of John Aitken's publications of the 1780s contained formal title pages. For one of these issues, the *Chorus Sung Before Gen. Washington As He Passed Under the Triumphal Arch Raised On the Bridge At Trenton, April 21th 1789* (a composition of Reinagle's), he enlisted the help of a local engraver, Cornelius Tiebout, for executing an ornamental title page on copper. I mention this here, as confusion is frequently caused by the presence of an engraver's name on the title page of an early sheet-music edition. Such a person is sometimes thought to be the engraver of the music, too. In compiling a master's thesis on "The His-

30. See entries 460, 548, 655, and 1035 in Stephens's book.

tory and Development of the Process of Music Printing,"[31] Mabel I. Hershberger was confused by the presence of both Tiebout's and Aitken's names on the above sheet, and she frequently interpreted the engraver named on a title page to have been the engraver of the music also. Unless one is well versed in the ways of music engraving and publishing, one has to observe caveats continually when working with early issues.

Music publishers have been fond of employing the *passe-partout* title page for introducing music of a similar nature or for issuing a number of titles in series. This involves the use of an ornamental plate having a central slot or opening reserved for putting in any desired title. It equipped them with a title page which could be used over and over for any number of publications, the text of a particular work being added freshly each time. In some instances the *passe-partout* title page was printed and in others it was engraved. George Gilfert employed a printed *passe-partout* title page for issuing in 1805 and shortly afterward a number of works: J. Delarue's *New Method of Music*; C. Berault's *A Collection of New Cotillions*; A. A. C. Meeve's compilation having that same title; and Mr. Henry's *New and Complete Preceptor for the German Flute*. Graupner utilized the *passe-partout* mechanism for issuing three of Nicolai's sonatas, opus 11, between 1803 and 1806 (Wolfe, No. 6511–13). And Dubois & Stodart followed this method for introducing two compositions of Charles Thibault which were titled *The Greek March of Liberty* in 1824. And there were many other instances of this practice in pre-1826 America. Though the use of the *passe-partout* title page was infrequent, it was by no means uncommon. A later variation on this device, utilized quite frequently in the decades after 1850, was to print a common title page listing a number of titles in series. The publisher or music seller then simply underlined or checked off the particular titles contained within. This mechanism was often employed for reprinting old music in new wrappers. The reissue of the Paff edition of about 1815 *'Tis the last Rose of Summer* in Buffalo in the 1860s under the series title *Gems of English Song* and the reissue of the Bacon, 1816, edition of *The Star Spangled Banner* in Cincinnati during the Civil War within the series entitled *The Home Circle* (see p. 203) are examples of this practice.

WOMEN PUBLISHERS

The world of the early nineteenth century is considered to have been overwhelmingly male-oriented, with little place in the commercial and

31. (Kent, Ohio, Kent State University, 1958).

professional life of the society for a woman. Her role was perceived as narrowly restricted to the home and its circle. It is therefore midly surprising to discover that a few women actually did engage in music publishing at this time. As those stand out in a rather curious way, I have included a brief comment on them here.

The first woman music publisher on the American scene was Mrs. Sarah Howe, the widow of William Howe, who had been an organ builder in New York from about 1796 and the publisher of perhaps half a dozen music titles in 1797 and 1798. Sarah succeeded to her husband's business upon his death in 1798 and continued to issue a little music for a year or two afterward under her own name. She is entered in New York City directories in 1799 and 1800 with the designation "music store," and the name "Sarah How" appears in the directory for 1803 with the description "music warehouse." (She is not mentioned in directories for 1801 and 1802 nor in annual numbers after 1803.) Her output of original editions was meager, amounting to only a few titles. Although her name was absent from the New York City directory for 1801, it is obvious that she continued to be active in this regard, for she published the following advertisement in the New York *Mercantile Advertiser* of January 22 and 23:

> Sarah Howe, Relict of William Howe, Organ Builder, no. 320 Pearl-street, Returns her thanks to her friends and the public in general for their past favours, and hopes for a continuance of the same; wish to inform them that she has for sale Finger and Barrel Organs, Harpsichords and Piano Fortes, Concert Trumpets, and Horsemen's ditto, Guitars, Dulsamore, Peddel Harp, Bassoons, Clarinets, Haut-boys, Flutes, Fifes, Bugle-Horns, Violins, Tenor and the best Roman Strings, a great variety of new Songs; the favourite Vauxhall song of "She lives in the Valley below," "I'll be True to the Lassie."
>
> Two or three Gentlemen may be accommodated with Board and lodging, in a family way.

Between 1803 and 1805 a number of music sheets appeared in New York under the name of Sarah Terrett at No. 320 Pearl Street. At the time I completed my list of American music imprints of the 1801–25 period, I treated Mrs. Terrett as a separate publisher. The advertisement quoted below, which Mrs. Terrett published in the *Mercantile Advertiser* of October 17, 1801, and continued to reprint through 1803, shows that Mrs. Howe and Mrs. Terrett were one and the same person. This and the preceding advertisement of Mrs. Howe were reprinted by Gottesman in her *The Arts and Crafts in New York, 1800–1804:* (pp. 332–33)

> Sarah Terrett (late Howe) No. 320 Pearl-street, has received by the late arrivals from London, a handsome assortment of Musical Instruments, consisting of

elegant patent Piano-Fortes from 120 to 400 dollars each; Barrel and Finger Organs, Serpents, Bazoons, Tamboreens, Clarinets, Hautboys, Patent Flutes, German Flutes of all Kinds; English Flutes, Fladganets [*sic*], Fifes, Guittars, Bass Viols, Tenors; and an elegant assortment of Bett's violins; with every other article in the musical line.

This advertisment connects the two Sarahs convincingly and shows that the widow Howe continued in the business of publishing and selling music and musical merchandise for a longer period than was previously thought. Mrs. Howe published approximately eight more pieces of music under the name Terrett at No. 320 Pearl Street between 1803 and 1805 before retiring permanently from this business.

The most prolific of the few women publishers on the early American music publishing scene was Mrs. Bradish, whose first name has eluded me thus far.[32] Like Mrs. (Howe) Terrett, Mrs. Bradish was a widow who operated a boardinghouse in New York City during the initial decades of the nineteenth century. From this establishment at No. 124 Broadway, where she also conducted a circulating library, Mrs. Bradish issued nearly twenty music titles between the years 1809 and 1811. In two cases, her name appears only as an additional retailer, on the imprints of other publishers (see, for example, the Riley–Paff–Bradish edition of John Whitaker's *The Soldier Slumb'ring* (Wolfe, No. 9867]). On the others, however, she alone appears as publisher. These she had Edward Riley engrave for her, though they were issued and sold under her own name. Although she was far more active than any other woman at this time, she endured for only three years, then transferred or sold her plate stock to Joseph Willson, who, it has been noted, used it along with the plates of other defunct publishers to gain entry into the music-publishing circle of New York City. Mrs. Bradish apparently continued on in the boardinghouse line, for she is mentioned as the proprietor of such an establishment in a book of travels published in 1819. In 1817 Henry Bradshaw Fearon was deputized by thirty-nine English families to come to America to determine the suitability of their emigration there. In the book which resulted from his experiences here,[33] he mentions that he had boarded

32. Mrs. Bradish may have been born Margaret Thompson, daughter of Colonel James Thompson of Staten Island, who was married to James Bradish, merchant, in New York City in late November 1793.

33. Henry Bradshaw Fearon, *Sketches of America; a Narrative of a Journey of Five Thousand Miles Through the Eastern and Western States of America; Contained in Eight Reports Addressed to the Thirty-Nine English Families by Whom the Author Was Deputized in June, 1817, to Accertain Whether Any, and What Part of the United States Would Be Suitable for Their Residence; with Remarks on Mr. Birbeck's "Notes and Letters"* (London, Longmans, Hurst, Reese, Orme, and Brown, 1818), pp. 6–7.

with Mrs. Bradish upon landing in New York. Stating that the streets through which he passed on the way to Mrs. Bradish's boardinghouse in State Street, opposite the battery, were narrow and dirty, he continued:

> The mode of living for those who do not keep house, is at hotels, taverns, or private boarding houses. My present residence is at one of the latter description. There are two public apartments, one for sitting, the other a dining room. At present about forty sit down to table. The lady of the house [Mrs. Bradish] presides at the head of the table, the other ladies who are boarders being placed on her left. The hours are —breakfast, eight o'clock; dinner, half past three; tea, seven; supper, ten. American breakfasts are celebrated for their profusion: there are eggs, meat of various kinds, fish, and fowls. My London habits are not yet overcome: I cannot enjoy an addition to plain bread and butter. The hours of eating are attended to by all with precision: charge, two dollars per diem, exclusive of wine. The expense of living here is about 18 dollars per week.

We do not know why Mrs. Bradish added music publishing to her boardinghouse activity in the first place, just as we do not know why she gave it up in 1811. Doubtless, she was literary and musical, and she may have involved herself in a circulating library and in the publication of music to give vent to both of these expressions. Notice that "Mrs. Bradish, late keeper of a boarding house in Broadway, New York, died in New Brunswick, N.J." appeared in the Boston *Columbian Centinel* of September 4, 1822. Oddly enough, no news of her passing was published in the *New York Evening Post* around that time.

Madame LePelletier (her Christian name is likewise unknown), whom Lubov Keefer describes in her *Baltimore's Music; The Haven of the American Composer* as "part of the Royalist ring revolving around Mrs. Jerome Bonaparte and the Baltimore belle Mme. Caton,"[34] issued an extremely ambitious collection entitled *Journal of Musick* in Baltimore in 1810 and 1811. This consisted of about 170 pages of music and, as noted before, it was sold on a subscription basis. George Willig of Philadelphia was principally responsible for engraving the plates for this work. The *Journal of Musick* contains mostly works of European composers and has a decided Latin flavor. In addition to the music of Catel, Berton, Isouard, Dussek, Boieldieu, and Handel, some of which she arranged for the piano herself, we can find several of Madame LePelletier's own compositions as well as pieces by the Englishmen Reeve and Whitaker. One might conjecture that she issued it out of nostalgia or perhaps to make available to her circle music which she herself favored but found unavailable in America. The *Journal of Musick* is her only known publication.

34. (Baltimore, 1962), p. 55.

About 1825 Mrs. Mary Weir, *née* Mary or Maria Brinckley or Brinkley (1783–1840), issued one of her own publications entitled *The Lord of the Castle*, the engraving of this having been accomplished by Thomas Birch. The imprint here reads, "New York, Published by the Author and for sale at the Music Stores." Her husband, Robert Weir, was entered in New York City directories from 1819 through 1824. Entry for "Weir, Mary, widow of Robert" appeared in the numbers from 1825 through 1840, the year of her death. She may have issued other pieces after 1825.

Finally, mention should be made of Jane Aitken, noted previously in connection with the publishing and bookbinding business of Robert Aitken of Philadelphia. Though Jane Aitken engaged in general letter-press printing, and was not connected with the musician-engravers who produced our early sheet music, she did issue an instruction book compiled by Andrew Law which was entitled *The Art of Playing the Organ and Piano Forte, or Characters Adapted to Instruments*, for which copyright was granted to her in 1809. She had previously printed in 1803 an encomium on education (see Wolfe, No. 6783) entitled *The Parents' Friend* containing one plate of music.

MUSIC BOUND IN COLLECTION

It was the custom during the period under consideration, and indeed throughout most of the nineteenth century, for individuals who had accumulated substantial quantities of music to have this bound up into volumes which resembled folio or oversize codex books. Before the modern era of mass entertainment, people had to depend upon their own devices for amusement, and the parlor piano and printed music played a significant role in their home life. Judging from the number of bound volumes that still remain intact in some of our libraries, amateurs must have accumulated songs and instrumental pieces in vogue with zest. The more fastidious or prosperous were accustomed to have their music bound in groups within covers so that they could most efficiently preserve and use it. And, of course, there was probably the element of pride in having a neat row of leather bindings set side by side on a shelf.

Usually, a collector assembled a group of favorites or of similar types of music, for example, vocal music or instrumental music, and had from twenty to forty of these (depending upon the bulk of the various pieces) bound into a collection. In the period before about 1810 the binder usually enclosed these pieces within covers that consisted of calf at the spine and corners and marbled papers over the center of the covering boards. (This is known as "half bound" in the binding trade.) Due to the scarcity of leather and to the expense of utilizing it for such large volumes, collections were rarely bound fully in a skin. Later on, morocco (imported goatskin, which was dyed in tasteful colors) or simulated morocco (a cheaper skin or even paper grained to resemble morocco) was substituted for calf, and the remainder of the boards making up the covers were covered with a marbled paper or sometimes with bookcloth. In the earlier period the binder usually added a rich, red label to the center of the front cover onto which he gilded the owner's name and the nature of the contents, for instance, "Vocal Music" or "Instrumental Music" or "Songs" or "Piano Music."

A number of libraries holding musical Americana have left such volumes intact; others have found it expedient to unbind them. As a consequence, great numbers of early American bindings have become lost. There are no standard or simple answers for collecting and storing American sheet music. Great bulk and duplication are often complicating factors. The Library of Congress is half and half in this respect. In earlier days volumes were broken up and their contents distributed, but about 150 volumes have been left intact. The present policy there, to which I myself subscribe, is to leave bound volumes intact, as these indicate tastes of past times and are representative of the type of music that was in use in the home. The Grosvenor Reference Division of the Buffalo and Erie County Public Library has preserved most of its volumes of early American sheet music in their original bound form, and the Grosvenor holdings constitute one of the largest such accumulations in existence today. A smaller but nonetheless choice collection of bound music can be found also at the Museum of the City of New York. Collectors of American sheet music usually unbind their volumes, as they are anxious to remove one or more choice pictorials from within and add these to their subject files (e.g., baseball items or patriotics).

Illustration 29 shows a title page that was actually printed up for such a collective volume. The owner, Miss Jane W. Greenwood of New York, obviously took great pride in her collection of music and owned many volumes of it. Normally, collections were bound up without title pages, though one frequently encounters manuscript indexes or tables of contents written out on the front endpapers. The example illustrated here is indicative of a very rare practice, in fact, the only instance of such a practice that I can recall encountering in the early American music field. (I came upon this particular example many years ago and unfortunately failed to record its location.) Miss Greenwood, probably a member of a prosperous family, could be called an "amateur parlor performer."

We know that she accumulated at least three other volumes which she had bound according to her tastes. All the music listed on this particular title page was issued before 1809. Some of it was printed abroad, for many of the titles listed here do not appear in the Sonneck–Upton bibliography or in my own continuation of it.

William Lloyd Keepers of New York City, who is looked upon as the dean of American music collectors, has told me that he has come upon advertisements published many decades after the period under consideration which announce the sale of bound collections at highly reduced prices. This may have been a method for remaindering old and out-of-date music. Music sellers and others possibly acquired old music sheets and bound these up in collective volumes which were sold (according to Keepers) for as little as one dollar.

It is not uncommon to discover, in volumes of early music, pieces copied out in manuscript form. Before the 1830s, at least, printed music was expensive and amateurs must have borrowed sheets from one another to copy out works which they could not afford or otherwise obtain. These were sometimes bound in collections along with other favorites. I have speculated earlier in this work that such manuscripts may have been copied from sheets that had been rented from one of the early musical circulating libraries. The popular songs of the day are frequently found in collections in manuscript form.

CHAPTER XI

Dating Early Music

✵✵

I T SEEMS APPROPRIATE to conclude this discussion of early American music engraving and printing with a few observations on the dating of early music, since it was out of a desire to understand better the methods and tools of the early trade as a means for assisting in the dating of its publications that I began the present inquiry in the first place. This topic will also afford me an opportunity to air my views regarding the bibliographical listing of the issues of our music publishers in the period after 1825 and to suggest methods which I think will have to be followed for the achievement of this goal.

I have mentioned before that the vast majority of our early sheet-music titles appeared without a date of publication on their imprints. It has been theorized that publishers followed this practice to make their music continually appear "fresh." This is undoubtedly a correct answer, but it is not the whole answer. The reason for this practice can best be found in the nature of the music-engraving and printing processes themselves. I have speculated earlier and have attempted to prove within the limitations of the evidence available that initial editions of works were usually small, gauged to satisfy an anticipated initial demand and a possible demand for a limited time thereafter. Because music plates made texts continually available through reprinting, additional issues could be made and were printed from time to time as demand required. Publishers undoubtedly desisted from placing dates on their plates because they were accustomed to employing these plates to reissue music for long periods of time, sometimes even for several decades after their initial use. Dates on music

[250]

which had been published ten and twenty or more years earlier (and publishers did reprint titles over such lengthy periods, just as long, in fact, as there was a demand for them) might act as deterrents to their later sale.

The absence of dates from early music sheets and added problems arising out of constant reprinting, frequently by subsequent publishers, have made the dating of early music something of a nightmare. In a small number of instances, particularly in the late eighteenth and very early nineteenth centuries, newspaper advertisements have aided us in this task. Additional slight aid is afforded by printed copyright notices, which began to appear infrequently on sheets in the period after 1800. For the most part, however, bibliographers, collectors, and musicologists have been dependent mainly upon street addresses which publishers invariably added to their sheets (so that their customers could find them) in order to establish time limitations within which sheets appeared. The standard directory of early American music publishers in the period from 1768 through 1889 appears in Dichter and Shapiro's *Early American Sheet Music* (pp. 165–248). This is supplemented for New York City by Virginia Larkin Redway's *Music Directory of Early New York City*,[1] which covers the period 1786–1875, and, of course, by general book-trade directories for New York, Philadelphia, Rhode Island, Boston, and Baltimore, compiled by George L. McKay, H. Glenn and Maude O. Brown, and Rollo Silver.

The fact that our earliest publishers moved frequently or stayed in business for only short periods of time has made the task of dating music less difficult in the period before roughly 1805. However, the early years of the nineteenth century brought greater stability to American music publishing, and publishers began to remain at fixed locations for longer periods of time. In addition, there followed a decline in the use of newspapers for advertising new publications during the early years of the century; and, although publishers began to copyright works with greater frequency, this practice was restricted to a small number of original compositions by American citizens, which constituted only a minute portion of the total output of the period. It has been mentioned before that George E. Blake issued music from his initial address of business (1 South Third Street) for about a decade, from 1803 until 1814, and at his subsequent address (13 South Fifth Street) for another twenty-six or twenty-seven years, from 1814 until 1841. George Willig's imprints locate their point of issue, 171 Chestnut Street, for a period of nearly thirty-five years, from 1819 until 1853. It is obvious that directory listings are of little

1. (The New York Public Library, 1941).

value in such cases; other means have to be found if we are to date or date approximately the appearance of works issued from these addresses.

The method I employed when compiling my *Secular Music in America* embodied a variety of procedures and aids, but it was essentially based on a simple inductive-deductive process which was suggested to me by John Stuart Mills's *System of Logic*, a book which lays down the basis for all scientific reasoning. This method supposes that "what we know to be true in a particular case or cases, will be true in all cases which resemble the former in certain assignable respects." In Mills's reasoning, "induction is the process by which we conclude what is true of certain individuals of a class is true of the whole class."[2] Once classes have been established in various ways, other examples (not of themselves provable) can then be deduced to belong to that class.

As an example of this method, let us consider the dating of Blake publications in the 1803–25 period. Blake, it will be remembered, occupied just two locations during the entire period (and for some years afterward). Duplicate cards containing descriptions of each of his publications, which included full title and imprint transcriptions and descriptive notes, as well as reference to punches used and other identifying matter, were filed under each of his two addresses. They were subsequently broken down in each according to similarities of punches used—Krummel has noted in his "Philadelphia Music Engraving" (pp. 105–8) and in his article "Graphic Analysis" (pp. 228–31) how important the form of the bass-clef punch is in attempting to date Blake publications; according to styles of engraving, especially for titles; by similarities of imprints and variations of addresses; and, in general, according to all other idiosyncracies. After subclasses had been established and particular publications had been assigned to them, date limitations could be inferred for each class according to the earliest and latest datable sheets within. Criteria for establishing date limits came from advertisements, copyrights, performance associations, and from the similar or nearly identical issues of other publishers who either anticipated Blake or mimicked him. (Thus, in cases where advertisements did not exist for Blake publications themselves—these were rare, as Blake hardly ever advertised—their existence for similar sheets of rival publishers served a useful purpose with regard to his own issues, particularly when both editions contained identical performance data.) Another case in point relates to the sheets of James Hewitt. Before about November 1807

2. Chapter 2, "Of Induction," in Book 3 of *System of Logic* (London, Longmans, Green, and Co., 1956), p. 188.

[252]

Hewitt published his music with the imprint "Printed & sold at J. Hewitt's Musical Repository, No. 59 Maiden Lane." After that date, he added the phrase "Musical Repository and Library" before the address. It was, in fact, from the earliest and latest advertisements of his sheets with and without such designations that I deduced that he opened his circulating library about November of 1807.

This system essentially agrees with the system of "graphic analysis" espoused by Krummel fifteen or more years ago. However, I consider it neither an identical nor a derivative method. It agrees in that it also attempts to separate publications according to an analysis of style, form of punches, addresses, performance data, advertisements, copyrights, and all other pertinent factors. It disagrees in that it does not attempt to establish such classes in nearly so dogmatic a way nor with such a degree of precision. There are actually some clear areas of divergence. For example, Krummel speculates in his "Graphic Analysis" (pp. 228–31) that Blake used certain punches during certain periods or years. I disagree with this pat conclusion. I think he used several of his many sets interchangeably. Intuition (which, studies show, is based upon unrecognized and sometimes fragmentary memories) forms an important factor in this work, and an even more important aspect of this procedure derives from the fact that it is based upon a study of the total output of an entire period, as reflected in a great number of extant collections of such material. Krummel's system flirts with the danger of overanalysis, particularly when applied to a single collection or to only a portion of the total bibliography of a given period.

The importance of analyzing the total product of a delineated time span cannot be overemphasized. It is the key to understanding and dating effectively the music issued within. It appeared to me, when I was first working with early American music imprints, that no single library or collection contained a sufficient number of these to allow for even the approximate dating of the majority of such sheets. I concluded that the only realistic way of understanding and dating these early works was to delineate an entire period and then record all of the publications within it. This was necessary in order to collect enough evidence for the inductive-deductive analysis so necessary for dating as well as recording comprehensively the activity of the early industry. The published results could be utilized not only by musicologists and by social and intellectual historians, but a record of this data in bibliographical form would relieve libraries in particular and collectors in general of the burden of attempting to date such materials through the imperfect evidence at hand. And, of

[253]

course, final library cataloging could easily follow. No one collection, not even the holdings of the Library of Congress and the New York Public Library, contained enough of this music within a given period to allow for a total understanding of that period. A project such as I undertook in compiling the issues of the 1801–25 period is, in my opinion, the only way in which dating can effectively be accomplished.[3]

Some discussion has been carried on recently regarding a continuation of our national bibliography in the secular music field in the period after 1825. Such talks, which have been mostly informal, have so far advocated only the recording of the holdings of individual collections, the output of individual publishers, the works of individual composers, and the like. Because the undertaking of a comprehensive bibliography for even a twenty-five-year period (or less) is an enormous task, a sense of defeatism pervades the field at this time. This pessimism is mostly due, I think, to the fact that the most enthusiastic advocates of further progress here are musicologists rather than bibliographers. Because a total inventory seems beyond reach at this time, partial and helter-skelter projects appear attractive on the theory that some motion is better than none. It is my feeling, however, that such undertakings will contribute little toward final solutions, and they might even produce a sense of complacency or smugness that will act as a deterrent to bringing about final solutions. Certainly, such projects will do little toward solving the problems of dating, reissue by subsequent publishers, and similar considerations.

My own list in the 1801–25 period was made possible only because a particular opportunity arose with a combination of propitious circumstances. My main interest in undertaking that list was to provide a basic tool which could be utilized by all institutions holding such materials for understanding and recording all pertinent titles within their possession. In a sense, it was an early and experimental attempt at "cooperative cataloging," a subject being investigated by libraries in greater detail at the present time. It seems likely, therefore, that further progress could be made if concerned library administrations could band together and attempt to solve common problems. Through libraries' collective sponsorship and with the added assistance of interested and concerned learned societies, financing might be obtained from private foundations and

3. The only collection I know of which contains a nearly definitive assemblage of the output of one or more individual publishers is the one brought together by Louis Dielman of Baltimore and subsequently presented to the Maryland Historical Society. This contains nearly complete runs of Willig publications (that is, of George Willig's Baltimore activity, as well as that of his son) and Cole publications as well as the output of other Baltimore publishers, frequently arranged by plate or publication number.

governmental agencies to compile and publish bibliographical tools so necessary for the study and control of large masses of records and information within the libraries' jurisdiction. It is a goal worth pursuing by administrators and scholars alike.

Illustrations

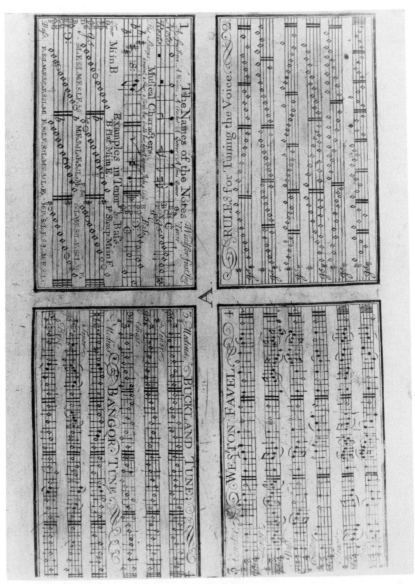

1a. Four pages of music engraved by Thomas Johnston on one side of a copperplate, for printing the Boston, 1766, edition of Daniel Bayley's *A New and Compleat Introduction to the Grounds and Rules of Musick*. Courtesy of the Essex Institute, Salem, Massachusetts.

1b. Reverse side of the copperplate shown in Illus. la, used by Johnston to engrave a clockface for Preserved Clapp.

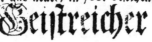

Kern

Alter und neuer, in 700. bestehender,

Geistreicher

Lieder,

Welche sowohl
Bey dem öffentlichen Gottesdienste
in denen

Reformirten Kirchen

der Hessisch-Hanauisch-Pfältzisch-Pensilvanischen
und mehrern andern angräntzenden Landen,
Als auch zur

Privat-Andacht und Erbauung

nützlich können gebraucht werden.
Nebst

JOACHIMI NEANDRI

Bundes-Liedern

Mit beygefügten
Morgen-Abend-und Comunion-Gebätern,
wie auch Catechismo und Simbolis.

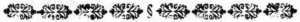

Nach dem neuesten Gesang-Buch, welches gedruckt zu Marburg,
bey Johann Henrich Stock, nun zum ersten mahl gedruckt
zu Germanton bey Christoph Saur, 1752.

2a. Title page of *Kern Alter und Neuer, in 700. Bestehender, Geistreicher Lieder*, the first music known to have been printed from type in America. Issued at Germantown, Pennsylvania, by the pioneer German-American printer Christopher Sower, 1752. From the copy in the Houghton Library, Harvard University.

3 Ach HERR! laß diese gnade mich Von deiner auffahrt spühren Das mir dem wahren glauben ich Mag meine nachfahrt zieren, Und daß einmal, wann dirs gefällt, Mit freuden scheiden aus der welt. HErr, höre doch mein flehen.

140 In eigener Melodie.
Auf diesen tag gedencken wir, Daß Christus aufgefahren, Und dancken GOtt aus höchster b'gier, Mit bitter woll bewahren Uns arme sünder hier auf erd, Allwo nichts ist als viel gefährd, Die uns macht bang nach troste, Alleluja, Alleluja, Alleluja.
2. GOtt lob, es ist der weg gemacht Uns steht der himmel offen. Christus schleußt auf mit grossem pracht, Für die so darauf hoffe Im glaubē ist man freuden=voll, Dabey man sich doch rüsten soll, Dem HErren nachzufolgen, Alleluja, Alleluja, Alleluja.
3. Wer nicht folgt, noch seinen willen thut, Dem ist nicht ernst zum HErren, Dann er wird auch vor fleisch und blut Sein himmelreich versperren: Am glauben liegts, soll der seyn recht. So wird das hertz der treuen knecht Zum himmel seyn gerichtet, Alleluja, Alleluja Alleluja
4. Solch himmelfahrt fähr

in uns an Bis wir den Vater finden, Und fliehn die welt und sündenbahn, Thun uns zu GOttes kindern: Die sehn hinauf, und GOtt herab. An treu und lieb geht ihn'n nichts ab, Bis sie zusammen kommen, Alleluja, Alleluja, Alleluja.
5. Dann wird der tag erst freudenreich, Wann uns GOtt zu ihm nehmen, Und seinem Sohn wird machen gleich, Als wir dann jetzt bekennen: Da wird sich finden freud und muth, Zu ewger zeit beym höchsten Guth: Schenck uns, o GOtt! solch leben. Alleluja, Alle. Alleluja.

141. In eigener Melodie.

Christus fuhr gen himmel,
Da sandt er uns hernieder
Den Tröster, den Heiligen
Geist, Zum trost der armen
Christenheit, Al-le-luja.
2 Christus, unser Heyland Sitzt zur rechten GOttes hand Vertritt das arm menschlich geschlecht, Daß wir durch ihn werden gerecht, Alleluja
3 Wär er nicht hingangen, Der Tröster wär nicht kommen, Seit daß er nun hingangen ist, So haben wir den Geist

H 3

2b. Internal page of the *Kern Alter und Neuer*.

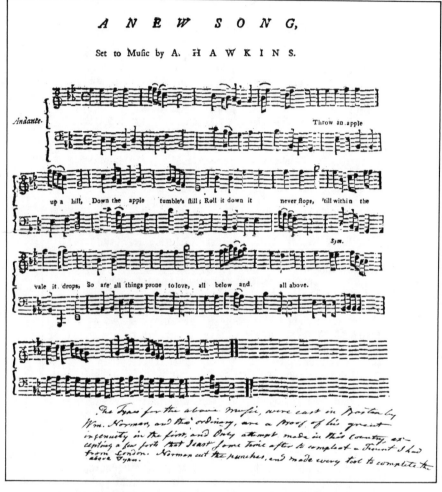

3. *A New Song, Set to Music by A. Hawkins,* published in the *Boston Magazine,* 1783. According to the note handwritten by the printer Isaiah Thomas, this was printed from the first music type cast in America by William Norman of Boston. Courtesy of the American Antiquarian Society, Worcester, Massachusetts.

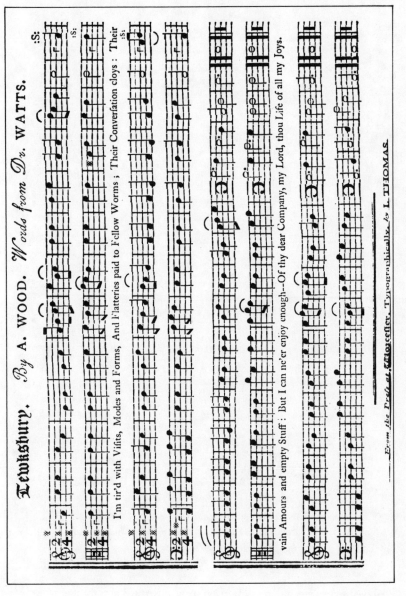

4. Sample page of music type from Isaiah Thomas's specimen book, published at Worcester about April 1785. Thomas ordered this font from the Caslon Foundry in London and employed it to print *The Worcester Collection of Sacred Harmony* and other works from 1786. From the copy in the New York Public Library.

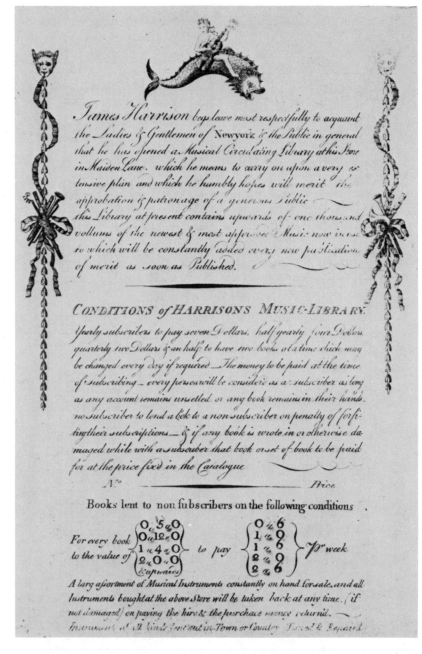

5. Engraved trade card of James Harrison, probably the first publisher of stamped music in New York, announcing the opening of his Musical Circulating Library. Courtesy of the American Antiquarian Society, Worcester, Massachusetts.

6a. Trade card of James Hewitt, advertising his Musical Repository and Musical Circulating Library in New York. This highly engraved item dates after November 1807, when he added the Library to his music-publishing and selling business. Courtesy of the American Antiquarian Society, Worcester, Massachusetts.

ADVERTISEMENT

J. A. & W. GEIB respectfully inform the inhabitants of NEW=
YORK, that they have constantly on hand, at their PIANO=FORTE WAREHOUSE,
and WHOLESALE, and RETAIL MUSIC STORE, N.º23 Maiden Lane; a large and
handsome assortment of Music, and Musical Instruments. As they import direct from
London, Paris, and Germany, they have it in their power to deal in wholesale, upon
very liberal terms. They receive PIANO FORTES of every description, by the quantity, from the Manufactories, of Broadwood, and Sons; Clementi, and Co; Astor, and
Horwood; and Stodart, and others of London; and Erard of Paris: in addition to
which the PIANO FORTES of *their own Manufacture* in this City;
which are well known for their excellent tone and workmanship, and unequal'd durability in Southern Climates: PEDAL HARPS, of Erard, Stumpf and others; Guitars;
Violins, by the box, and single; &c &c, They continue to manufacture ORGANS, of every kind; some of which, the modern Organized Piano Forte, are perhaps superior in
elegance, to any piece of musical furniture yet constructed. The newest and best music constantly on hand, by the quantity, or piece. Piano Fortes hired out by the
month, and Piano Fortes, and other Instruments repaired, tuned, and stored. Also
music Engraved, and Printed in the handsomest style.

6b. Advertisement of J(ohn), A(dam) & W(illiam) Geib, musical merchandise
sellers in New York, dating about 1818, when they began publishing jointly.
From a copy in the author's possession.

I Peter A Von Hagen of Boston in the County of Suffolk, & Commonwealth of Massachusetts, professor of music; being weak of body; but of sound disposing mind & memory; fully sensible of the uncertainty of human life, & the awful certainty of death, do make & ordain this to be my last will & testament.

Imprimis. I give & bequeath to my well beloved children, Catharina Elizabeth wife of John Christian Kahlwagen, Peter Albertus, Christina Cecilia, John Ernst, Harriet, & Louisa; & to each of them a mourning Ring or Locket, of the value of five dollars. —

Item. I give & bequeath unto my true & faithful wife Johannetta Catharina Elizabeth, & to her heirs, all the residue of my Goods, Effects & Estate, real, personal., or mixed, for the comfort & support of herself & our Childrens during their minority, the same to be entirely at her disposal; — and I hereby nominate & appoint my said Wife, to be sole Guardian of our said minor Children. —

Lastly. I hereby appoint my said beloved Wife Johannetta Catharina Elizabeth to be sole Executrix of this my last will & testament, hereby revoking all other wills by me heretofore made.

In witness whereof I have hereunto set my hand & seal this twenty second day of September in the year of our Lord, One thousand eight hundred & three. —

P. A. von Hagen

Signed, sealed, delivered, published
& declared by the Testator, to be his
last will & testament in presence
of us, who in his presence, & in the
presence of each other, hereunto
subscribed as Witnesses. —

Jos. May
Saml. May.
Charles Barrell. —

7. Last will and testament of Peter Albrecht von Hagen (Sr.), dictated and signed by him before his death in 1803. On file at the Probate Court of Suffolk County, Boston, Massachusetts.

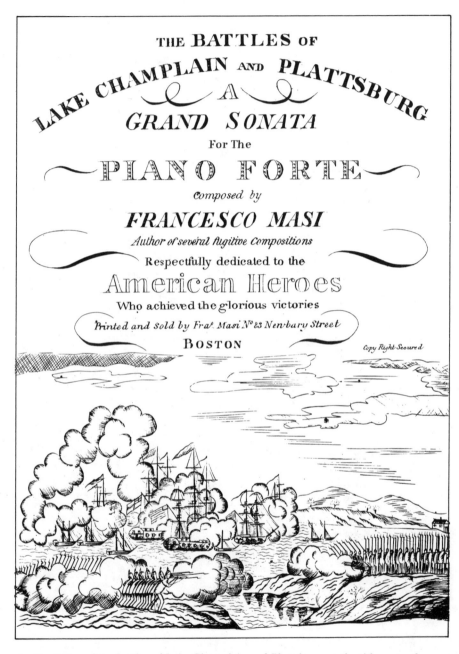

8a. Depiction of the battles of Lake Champlain and Plattsburg on the title page of Francesco Masi's descriptive sonata of 1815. From the unique copy in the Boston Public Library.

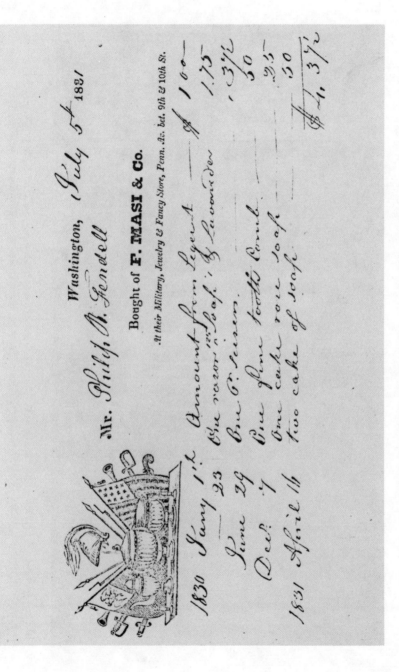

8b. Receipted bill for the purchase of dry goods at Francesco Masi's store in Washington, D.C., 1831. Courtesy of the Historical Society of Pennsylvania.

9. Lithograph of New York, ca. 1830–32, showing Trinity Church at the left, near the City Hotel, Broadway, where John and Michael Paff had conducted their music business between 1806 and 1808. This later view shows the earlier New York publisher, and R. & W. Nunns had musical merchandise establishments nearby. The photograph reproduced here was given to the author by John Tasker Howard in 1961, who had previously published it (figure 2, 160) in the first edition of his Our American Music.

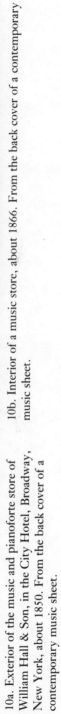

10b. Interior of a music store, about 1866. From the back cover of a contemporary music sheet.

10a. Exterior of the music and pianoforte store of William Hall & Son, in the City Hotel, Broadway, New York, about 1850. From the back cover of a contemporary music sheet.

11a. English music engraver at work. From *A Day at a Music Publishers*, ca. 1838.

11b. Interior of an English music-printing establishment. From *A Day at a Music Publishers*.

12. Proof page and final printed page from James Hewitt's *The Music of Erin*, published by him in New York, 1807. The corrections of the proof sheet may be in the hand of Hewitt himself. Courtesy of the New York Public Library.

When floating o'er th'impending steep.

OR
Cathleen Nolan

ANDANTE AFFETTUOSO

Dim

When floating o'er th'im‿pend‿ing steep, my love ap‿‿pears in

beau‿‿tys glow she's like the golden clouds that sweep light o'er the

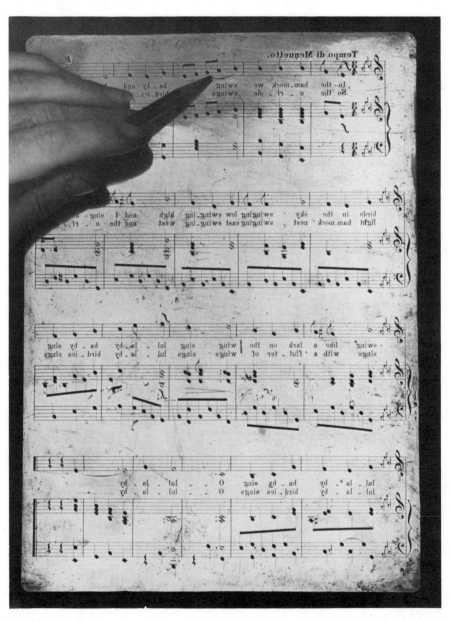

13. Pewter music plate containing an unidentified vocal work; probably late nineteenth century or early twentieth. The plate was given to the author in 1965 by Jacob Blanck.

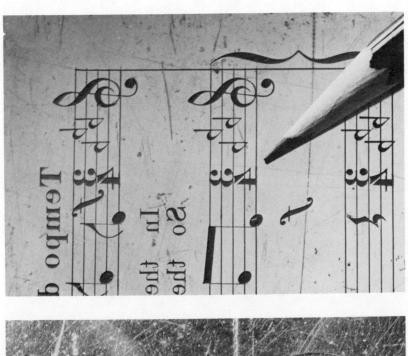

14. Blacked and unblacked enlargements of the initial staves shown in Illus. 13.

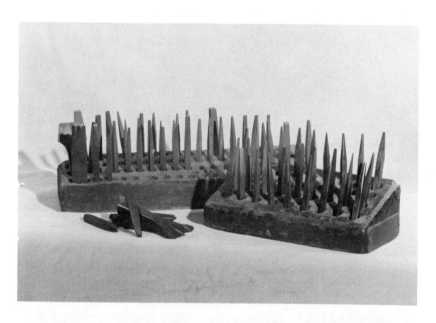

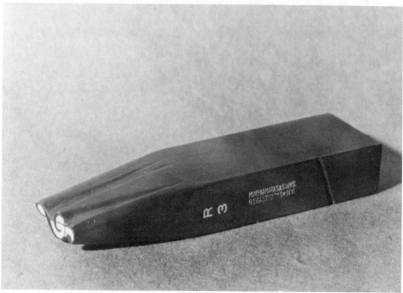

15. Punches manufactured and used in America in the late nineteenth century. Courtesy of Walter Bolke, Hillsdale, New York.

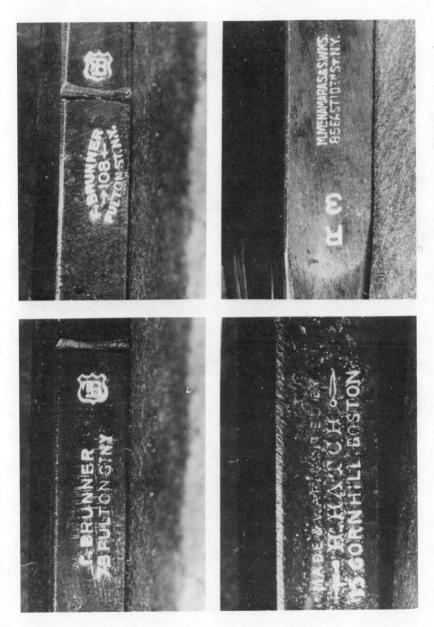

16. Enlargements of four of the punches in Illus. 15, revealing the "touches" or stamps of their American makers.

17. Silver creamer (ca. 1800) and silver spoon (undated) made by John Aitken, with enlargement showing Aitken's "touch."

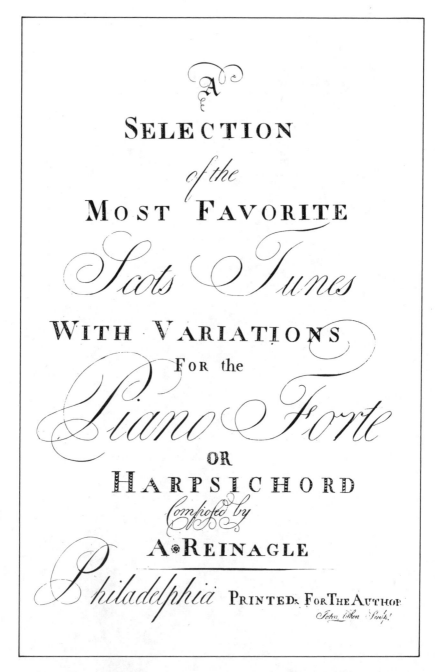

A

SELECTION

of the

MOST FAVORITE

Scots Tunes

WITH VARIATIONS

FOR the

Piano Forte

OR

HARPSICHORD

Compofed by

A.REINAGLE

Philadelphia PRINTED. FOR THE AUTHOR

John Aitken Sculp.

18. Title page and internal page of Alexander Reinagle's *A Selection of the Most Favorite Scots Tunes,* published at Philadelphia, August 1787. This was printed from the first plates on which music was stamped in America, the punching having been done by John Aitken.

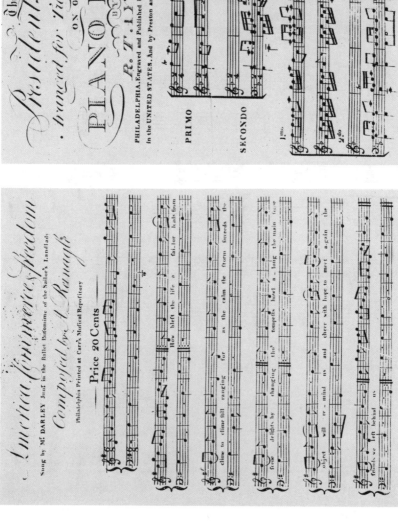

19. Publications of Benjamin Carr (1796) and William Priest (probably late 1795) showing a similarity of punch faces. From copies in the New York Public Library.

A

CATALOGUE

OF THE VALUABLE

STOCK in TRADE,

OF

Mr. Joseph Carr,

Of MIDDLE ROW, HOLBORN,

MUSIC SELLER,

QUITTING BUSINESS.

CONSISTING OF

A Variety of Harpsichords, Grand Piano-Fortes, Organs, Guitars, and Dulcimers, Twisting Machines, and Working Tools; an Assortment of Printed Music, by the best Composers, Copper Plates, &c.

TOGETHER

With the Remaining HOUSEHOLD FURNITURE, Books, an Eight-day Clock, and other Effects,

WHICH WILL BE SOLD BY AUCTION,

By Mr. WEALE,

ON THE PREMISES,

On FRIDAY, the 14th of FEBRUARY, 1794, Precisely at Twelve o'Clock.

———

To be Viewed on Thursday preceding the Sale.

Catalogues may be had on the Premises; at Garraway's Coffee-House; and of Mr. WEALE, Sworn Exchange Broker, Castle Street, Holborn.

20. Title page of the 1794 auction catalog of the sale of Joseph Carr's excess possessions just before his departure for America. From copies in the New York Public Library.

WM. G. MASON,

No. 46 Chestnut Street, three doors above Second, south side,

Philadelphia,

Continues to execute orders in the various branches of Engraving and Copper Plate Printing, Business and Visiting Cards, Checks, Notes, Bill Heads and Bills of Exchange, Door Plates, Official and Private Seals, Coats of Arms for Book Plates, &c. Jewellery and Silver Ware, engraved in the neatest manner.

STONE SEAL ENGRAVING.

Letters, Crests, Arms, Devices or Portraits engraved on Stone in the best style. Wood Engraving and Type Printing attended to. Agent for

Dickinson's Glaziers' Diamonds and Diamond Sparks.

A large assortment always on hand, and for sale at the Manufacturer's prices. Extra Diamonds made to order. Old Diamonds reset and warranted. Worn out Sparks taken in exchange. Engravers' Ruling Points made to order.

ENGRAVERS' STEEL & COPPER,

From the manufactory of J. Garside, Newark, N. J. A good assortment of Steel and Copper Plates of various sizes for sale. Orders for plates of any dimension attended to promptly and at the lowest prices.

Also, Engravers' Die Steel and Rolls made to order. Silversmiths' Rolls furnished.

White's Daguerreotype Plates, a very superior article.

All sizes constantly on hand and for sale at the lowest prices.

DAGUERREOTYPE CASES

Of every size and quality, either on hand or made to order.

An assortment of neat Fancy Articles and Novelties,

RODGERS AND WOSTENHOLM'S GENUINE CUTLERY,

Fine Stationery, Pocket Books, Card Cases, &c.,

CONSTANTLY ON HAND.

21. Page from the Philadelphia *Mercantile Register*, 1846, advertising the services and wares of William G. Mason, a member of an early Philadelphia family of brass and seal engravers.

GASKILL & COPPER,

SUCCESSORS TO M. W. BALDWIN,

BOOKBINDERS' TOOL CUTTERS,

AND

ENGRAVERS,

NO. 18 MINOR STREET,

PHILADELPHIA.

Rolls, Stamps, Polishers, Letter-boxes,

&c., &c.

Door, Coach, & Trunk Plates.

STEEL PUNCHES, BRANDS, AND MARKING PLATES.

NAME PLATES

FOR

Locomotives, Fire Engines, &c.

22. Advertisement of Gaskill & Cooper, makers of bookbinder's and other stamping tools in Philadelphia, dating probably between 1840 and 1860. Source unknown.

23a. Trade card of the English engraver Richard Austin, 1787, attesting to his manufacture of music-engraving tools. From Stanley Morison's *John Bell, 1745–1831*, p. 158.

23b. Trade card of William H. Bridgens, a New York manufacturer of music-engraver's tools after 1838. From a copy in the American Antiquarian Society, Worcester, Massachusetts.

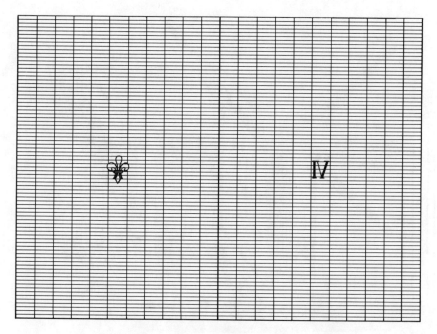

24a. Paper mold, showing watermark (left) and countermark (right).

24b. Photograph of a watermark in an early American music sheet.

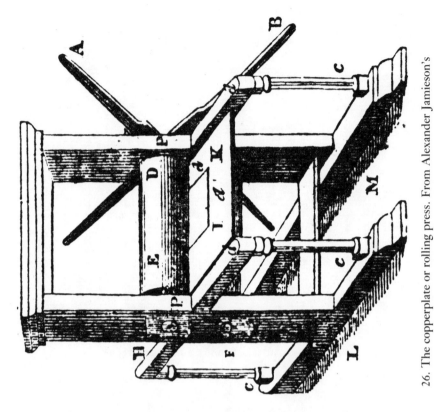

26. The copperplate or rolling press. From Alexander Jamieson's *Dictionary of Mechanical Science, Arts, Manufactures and Miscellaneous Knowledge*, London, 1827.

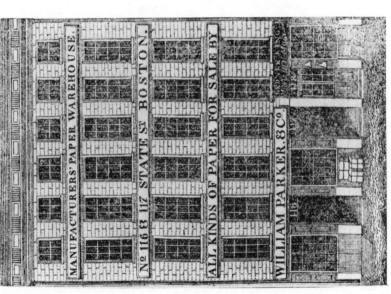

25. Advertisement of a paper-supplier's warehouse in the 1821 *Boston Directory*. From a copy in the Boston Public Library.

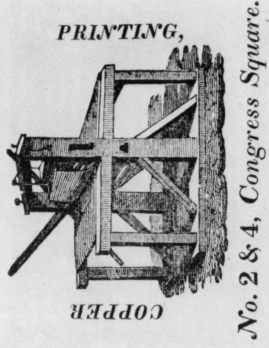

PLATE PRINTING,

COPPER

No. 2 & 4, Congress Square.

BOWEN & McKENZIE,

Hope by assiduous attention and good work, to receive a share of public patronage, and give to their employers general satisfaction.

27b. Advertisement of Bowen & McKenzie, copperplate printers, in the 1821 *Boston Directory*, showing a contemporary copperplate press. Abel Bowen, one of these partners, printed music for Boston publishers at this time. From a copy in the Boston Public Library.

27a. Typical pull of the copperplate press, from *The Book of Trades*, Whitehall, Pennsylvania, 1807. From a copy in the New York Public Library.

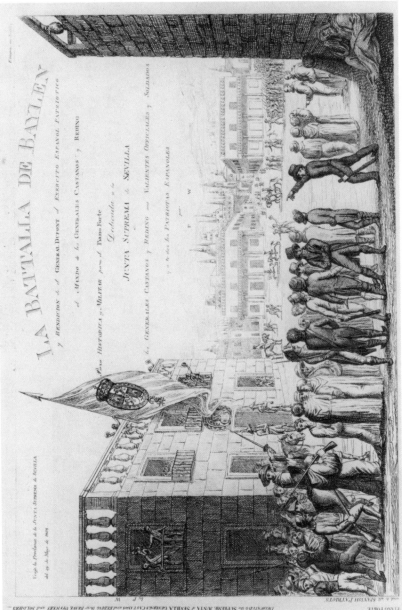

28a. Title page of Peter Weldon's *La Battalla de Baylen*, 1809. This scene and the one in Illus. 28b display the most elaborate and finely executed engraving on early American music sheets. Both were done probably by William S. Leney, an immigrant English artist. From copies in

28b. Title page of Peter Weldon's *Favorita Waltz Brazilense*, 1810.

Songs, Overtures, &c. &c.

COMPOSED FOR THE

PIANO-FORTE.

****
VOL. IV.
****

CONTAINING

OWNED BY

Miss Jane W. Greenwood,

NEW-YORK.

1809

29. Printed title page added to a collection of music privately bound for Miss Jane W. Greenwood of New York in 1809. Source unknown.

※※

Account Book of Simeon Wood, 1818–21

※※

SIMEON WOOD was a bassoonist and double-bass player in the Boston Philharmonic and Handel and Haydn Society orchestras between 1817 and 1822. His name is first indexed in Boston city directories for 1816 with the designation "musician" and in the directory for 1821 as "engraver of music." In his *Musical Interludes in Boston*, H. Earle Johnson makes only a few references to him, alluding to his orchestral activity and to his foray into music publishing, noting, in this regard, that he did not own a music store nor have an established outlet for the sale of his musical publications. Johnson also refers to Wood's irregular habits, mentioning that he lost his bassoon between Hingham and Boston one cold winter morning and that he once mislaid the bassoon part for a set of symphonies. Wood's first known attempt at music engraving took place in 1817, when he engraved the plates for the musical appendix of *The Songster's New Pocket Companion*, a collection of popular songs which was issued by T. Swan in Boston in that year. Between 1818 and 1822 he went into the business of publishing music, issuing nearly thirty titles between those dates. (His imprints almost always read "Boston, Published by S. Wood.") Simeon Wood died in Boston on May 28, 1822, aged thirty-eight, his short obituary notice stating merely that he was formerly of South Bridgewater. Papers relating to the guardianship of his minor children are on file in the Suffolk County Courthouse in Boston.[1] These show that his widow's name was Kesiah (or Keziah), and that he left three minor children, Henry Wood, Mary A. Wood, and Simeon Wood, all under fourteen years of age.

1. Case no. 26955-57, April 28, 1823. His widow was named guardian of his minor children, and the bond for this was set by Kesiah Wood, widow, Lewis Wood, musical-instrument maker, and Thomas Appleton, organ-builder.

From late December 1818 until early in 1822 Wood kept two account books into which he entered information on his music-publishing and selling activities. The first of these volumes turned up in New England some years ago and was subsequently acquired by the Music Division of the Library of Congress, where it now reposes. In this book Wood specified the titles he engraved, the customer or music seller to whom he sold them or let out copies on consignment, the number of copies printed, dates of printing and sale, and similar information. The book itself is a small volume, measuring 19½ by 16 centimeters and containing only twenty-two leaves. It is bound in red, cream, and blue marbled pasteboard covers, and on the front cover is written "S. Wood, Songs" (the rear cover is blank). Leaves within are divided into three columns denoting date, purchaser or consignee, and number of copies sold or let. Because Wood operated no music store or outlet, he mostly dealt with established dealers and distributors for the sale of his works, mainly with Gottlieb Graupner and J. R. Parker in Boston and with Oliver Shaw and others outside that city. Wood likewise did no printing, sending the plates he had engraved to two local copperplate printers, Luther Stevens and Abel Bowen or the latter's firm, Bowen & McKenzie (Alexander D. McKenzie).[2] Wood's account here provides us with our major source of information on the size of editions of our early publishers and their custom of reprinting. Because of this and the subsidiary information it contains on other practices of the early trade, I have published it here in full.

A few additional remarks are worthy of mention with regard to Wood and his music-publishing activities. Wood was obviously not a full-time music publisher, as, for instance, were Blake and Willig in Philadelphia. Rather, he represented the case so frequently encountered in early American music publishing of the musician who supplemented his income by engraving and issuing music on the side. Probably he would have become a more active and important publisher had not death intervened, for his period of activity coincided with Gottlieb Graupner's slackening pace as the major music publisher of Boston. Following Wood's death Graupner appears to have acquired the plates of one of his publications, Frederick Granger's *The Star of Bethlehem*, and to have reissued this work under his own imprint. Edwin W. Jackson, the Boston music publisher and son of the notable Dr. George K. Jackson, also acquired a few of Wood's plates and reprinted them. Some of these were later acquired by the New York firm of Firth and Hall and further reprintings of them occurred.

2. Little appears to have been published on Stephens or McKenzie, but a fairly detailed account of Bowen appeared in vol. 1 of *The Bostonian Society Publications* (1886–88), pp. [29]–56. I have seen in the society's library a scrapbook containing a great many proofs of Bowen's own engravings and woodcut illustrations. On one occasion Wood employed Samuel Wetherbee, who also engraved and published a little music, as printer.

S. WOOD, SONGS

[leaf 1, recto]

[blank]

[leaf 1, verso]

1818, Here shall soft Charity repair.

Decr.	5	O. Shaw	10
"	14	G. Graupner & co.	24
"	31	J. R. Parker	20
1819			
Decr.	14	Wm. M. Goodrich for Savannah	12
1820			
Oct.	20	Elnathan Duren	1
		Han	1
			68

[leaf 2, recto]

1818, Duett, Here shall soft Charity repair

[leaf 2, verso]

1819, Oh! sweet was the scene.

April	2d	J. R. Parker	12
"	"	G. Graupner & co.	12
"	3d	O. Shaw	6
Dec.	14	Wm. Goodrich for Savannah	12
1821			
April	2	J. R. Parker	6

[leaf 3, recto]

Oh! sweet was the scene

[leaf 3, verso]

1819, Eagle wings.

April	13	J. R. Parker	12
Dec.	14	Wm. M. Goodrich for Savannah	12
1820			
March	3	O. Shaw	4
August	25	G. Graupner	6
1821			
Sept.	1	O. Shaw	2
"	19	O. Shaw	6

[leaf 4, recto]

1819, Eagle wings.

Printed by Stevens.

1821			
Sep.	1	Printed by Stevens	50

[leaf 4, verso]

1819, This blooming rose.

August	23	J. R. Parker	20
Sept.	4	J. R. Parker	50
"	6	Brenan	12
Sept.	23	J. R. Parker	12
Nov.	2	J. R. Parker	50
"	3	O. Shaw	12
Dec.	14	Wm. M. Goodrich for Savannah	12

1820

August	25	G. Graupner	12
Dec.	8	G. Graupner	12
			192
		Missing	8
			200

1821

Dec.	14	G. Graupner	12
August	2	A. Duren	
Oct.	30	G. Graupner	6

[leaf 5, recto]

1819, This blooming rose.

	Printed by Stevens	100
	Printed by Stevens	100
		200

1821

Feb.	13	Printed by Stevens	100
June	20	Do Do Do	25
~~July~~	~~18~~	~~Do Do Do~~	

[leaf 5, verso]

1819, Porcellian Club's march.

Nov.	22		
~~August~~	~~24~~	J. Hart for G. Graupner & co.	25
Dec.	14	Wm. M. Goodrich for Savannah	50

1820

Sept.	7	G. Graupner	12
April	2	J. R. Parker	12
April	11	G. Graupner	12

[leaf 6, recto]

1819, Porcellian Club's march

Dec.	23	Printed by Wetherbee	180

[leaf 6, verso]

1820, If ye a highland laddie meet.

July	10	J. R. Parker	25

"	"	S. P. Tailor	12
"	19	O. Shaw	6
August	9	James D. Hay	6
"	25	G. Graupner	6
Nov.		Lowel Mason (Savannah)	6
			56

1821
April   2   J. R. Parker   10

[leaf 7, recto]

1820, If ye a highland laddie meet.
July   10   Printed by Wetherbee   100
               Deduct   56

1821
Feb.   15   On hand   44

[leaf 7, verso]

1820, I am wearing awa' to the land o the leal.
August   9   O. Shaw   6
"   11   J. R. Parker   40
"   22   S. P. Tailor 2—Beach 1—L. Mason
             ~~Graupner 1~~   4

1821
Janay.   6   G. Graupner   12
April   2   J. R. Parker   10
August   3   J. R. Parker   20
                                                               92

[leaf 8, recto]

1820, I am wearing awa' to the land of the leal.
August   1   Printed by Bowen   50
             Printed by Bowen   50

1821
Sept.   15   Printed by Stevens   50

[leaf 8, verso]

1820, Day of glory.
August   9   O. Shaw   6
"   11   J. R. Parker   40
"   22   S. P. Tailor   4
                                                               50

1821
Janry. 10   G. Graupner   6
March   26   Elnathan Duren   1
August   2   A. Duren   6

[leaf 9, recto]

1820, Day of glory.

August   6   Printed by Bowen   50

[leaf 9, verso]

1820, Waltz by Eckhard.

August	22	S. P. Tailor	6
"	23	O. Shaw	6
"	"	Eckhard	12
August	22	J. R. Parker (omited)	11

1821

Janry.	10	G. Graupner	6
April	2	J. R. Parker	12

[leaf 10, recto]

August	13	Printed by Bowen	36
Nov.	18	Printed by Bowen	50

[leaf 10, verso]

1820, My beautiful maid. Wood & Ostinelli.

Nov.	10	J.R. Parker	25
"	"	G. Graupner	25
		L. Ostinelli	12
Dec.	4	G. Graupner	25
			87

1821

Janry.	10	O. Shaw	2
Feb.	12	Master Ayling	1

[leaf 11, recto]

1820, My beautiful maid.

Nov.   4   Printed by Bowen   200

1821

On hand   113

[leaf 11, verso]

1820, Peace and holy love.

Dec.	30	G. Graupner	25
"	"	J. R. Parker	25
		N.Y. Th. Society Retinner	25

1821

Janry.	10	O. Shaw	2
"	18	J. Bray—and Master Ayling	8
"	19	G. Graupner	12
Febry.	12	Master Ayling	1
March	2	G. Graupner	6
"	26	Elnathan Duren	1

April	2	J. R. Parker 8 and 12	20
"	11	G. Graupner	4
		Sold and given away to sundry persons	10
			114
1821			
May	12	G. Graupner	12
August	2	A. Duren	6
"	9	G. Graupner	12

[leaf 12, recto]

1820, Peace and hold love.

		Printed by Stevens	114
1821			
April	9	Printed by Stevens	50

[leaf 12, verso]

1820, Thy cheek has borrowed from the rose. (Hay).

1821			
		Hay	
Janry.	10	O. Shaw	2

[leaf 13, recto]

1820, Thy cheek has borrowed from the rose. (Hay).
Printed by Bowen.

[leaf 13, verso]

1820, To sigh yet feel no pain.

May	22	J. R. Parker	100
1821			
Janry.	19	G. Graupner	12
"	"	J. R. Parker	50
Feb.	14	G. Graupner	12
April	11	G. Graupner	12
June	23	G. Graupner	12
			98
July	18	J. R. Parker	12
August	2	A. Duren	6
"	3	J. R. Parker	12
Sept.	1	G. Graupner	6
Oct.	23	G. Graupner	6
Nov.	3	J. R. Parker	8
1822			
Feb.	11	J. R. Parker	6
March	20	J. R. Parker	10
"	2	G. Graupner	6

[leaf 14, recto]

1820, To sigh yet feel no pain.
May		Printed by Stevens	100

1821
Janry.	19	Printed by Stevens	100
July	18	Do	50
			~~150~~
July	18	Printed by Stevens	50
Dec.		Printed by Stevens	50

[leaf 14, verso]

1821, The murderer's bride. Wood & Ostinelli.
Janry.	19	G. Graupner	12
"	"	J. R. Parker	12
"	"	Louis Ostinelli	25
Feb.	12	Master Ayling	1
"	13	Ostinelli	2
April	2	J. R. Parker	25
"	30	G. Graupner	6

[leaf 15, recto]

1821, The murderer's bride.
Janry.	19	Printed by Stevens	100

[leaf 15, verso]

1821, Erect your heads.
Febry.	15	S. P. Tailor for dedication	16
"	19	Ebenezer Shaw, Dorchester	24
March	19	Dea. Nathl. D. Gould	36
"	26	Elnathan Duren	1
April	10	Mr. Bradlee, Dorchester	1
June	16	S. P. Taylor	18
			delivered
"	"	Nathl. D. Gould Esq. (on April 22)	12

[leaf 16, recto]

1821, Erect your heads.
Febry.	15	Printed by Stevens		16.
"	19	Do	Do	24
Mar.	2	Do	Do	102

[leaf 16, verso]

1821, The star of Bethlehem. D. Duren.
April	5th	S. Wood 1, Copyright 1	2
"	"	Miss O Graupner	1
"	"	Dea. Gould	2
"	"	S. Duren	195
			200

"	10	S. Wood, 6 copies from Duren		
"	12	O. Shaw		2
July	23	J. R. Parker	paid	3
August	2	A. Duren		6
"	3	J. R. Parker	paid	7
"	13	J. R. Parker	paid	6
"	"	J. A. Dickson	paid	12
"	17	G. Graupner	paid	10
				44
"	25	Luke Eastman	paid	2
Sept.	13	J. R. Parker		2
"	18	J. R. Parker		3
"	"	C. & E. W. Jackson	paid	12

[leaf 17, recto]

1821, The star of Bethlehem.

April	4	Printed by Stevens	200
July	21	Printed by Stevens	50
Sept.	18	Printed by Stevens	50

[leaf 17, verso]

1821, Duett by Kozeluch.

June	23	J. R. Parker	6
"	"	G. Graupner	6

[leaf 18, recto]

1821, Duett by Kozeluch.

June	20	Printed by Stevens	25

[leaf 18, verso]

1821, Masquerade by [*sic*] Sonata by Hook.

June	23	G. Graupner	6

[leaf 19, recto]

1821, Masquerade sonata by Hook.

June	20	Printed by Stevens	25

[leaf 19, verso]

1821, All's well, duett.

June	23	J. R. Parker	6
"	"	G. Graupner	12
August	2	A. Duren	6

[leaf 20, recto]

1821, All's well, duett.

June	20	Printed by Stevens	25
1822		Do̶ — D̶o	
Jan.	28	Do	Do

[leaf 20, verso]

 1821, The minute gun at sea.
June	23	J. R. Parker	6
"	"	G. Graupner	12
Nov.	23	J. R. Parker	6

[leaf 21, recto]

 1821, The minute gun at sea.
| June | 20 | Printed by Stevens | 25 |

1822
| Jan. | 28 | Do   Do | 30 |

[leaf 21, verso]

 1821, The fall of Babylon.
| June | 20 | Luke Eastman, Esqr. | 16 |
| July | 13 | N. D. Gould, Esqr. | 8 |

[leaf 22, recto]

 1821, The fall of Babylon.
| June | 20 | Printed by Stevens | 16 |
| July | 13 | Do   Do | 50 |

[leaf 22, verso]

 1821, Eve's lamentation.
August	17	J. R. Parker	50
"	"	G. Graupner	6
"	"	Mrs. Martin	12
			68

"	25	Luke Eastman	8
Sept.	19	O. Shaw	2
		Carried to	
		Next Book	

[recto of rear cover]

 1821, Eve's lamentation.
| August | 17 | Printed by Stevens | 100 |

APPENDIX B

Inventory of George E. Blake, 1871

꒒꒒

D URING THE FIRST three decades of the nineteenth century—from about 1807, within four or five years after he had begun to issue music, until well into the 1830s, when his output began to slacken—George E. Blake of Philadelphia conducted the largest and busiest music-publishing and selling establishment in America. Within this period he issued year after year a large assortment of musical publications, including reprinted (pirated) editions of the latest fads of the London stage, compositions by musicians of the Philadelphia stage and by other native composers, the standard marches, dances, patriotic pieces, books of instruction, and the other usual fare of the day. In addition, he published from the mid-1820s into the early 1830s the complete vocal works of Handel, which constituted one of the largest and most ambitious projects in early American music publishing. Blake advertised at an early date that he had on hand the largest assortment of music in America, and he undoubtedly furnished the South and the then frontier areas of the United States with much of the music the early pioneers danced to, sang, and carried with them on their trek west. In the late 1830s or early 1840s he began to lessen his pace, for he was then over sixty years old. By the middle of the fifth decade of the nineteenth century he had ceased publishing music altogether. Blake spent the remaining quarter of his life in the leisurely manner described before. Upon his death in February 1871, at which time he was over ninety-five years old, he left an enormous amount of obsolete music, music plates, tools, and other paraphernalia which were sold at auction a little over three months later. The catalog of this sale, of which the only known copy is in the Free Library of Philadelphia, extends to fifty-four pages and contains the titles of probably all the music Blake published during his lengthy career. The last two pages of it list the tools with which he accomplished this remarkable production. These afford us a unique glimpse of the equipment employed by an early American music engraver

[267]

and publisher, and I have reprinted here the title page and the final two pages of that catalog.

Administrators'
Peremptory Sale,
Estate of George E. Blake, Deceased.
M. Thomas & Sons, Auctioneers.
Catalogue
of the
Large and Valuable Stock of
Music Plates,
Sheet Music,
Musical Instruments, Material, &c.,
Being the Entire Stock of the Late George E. Blake,
To Be Sold at Public Sale, Without Reserve,
by Order of Administrators,
On Monday Morning, May 22, 1871,
At 10 O'clock,
And Continuing Daily Until Sold,
At the Auction Rooms,
Nos. 138 & 141 South Fourth Street.

[page] 53 [conclusion of column 2]

Lot	Description
	TOOLS, BENCHES, &C.
2950 1/2	2 Screw Presses, small
2951 1/2	2 Iron Clamps, 19 Wooden, Assorted Sizes. 12 Mahogany, (new.)
2952 1/2	6 Planes.
2953 1/2	71 Cabinet Planes, (2 boxes.)
2954 1/2	Copper Ruling Pen.

[page] 54 [column 1]

2955 1/2	Oil Stone, 2 Spoke Shavers, 2 Gimlets, 2 Saw Setters, Nippers, Saw, Triangle, 2 Riveting Irons, Blow Pipe, Marker, 3 Hones, 2 Hammers, Small Anvil, Drawing Knife, 2 Screw Drivers, Steel Plane, 9 Extra Blades, 2 Mallets, Screw Wrench.
2956 1/2	Brace and Bits, 34 pieces. 3 Dies and Drills, 8 Pieces, 6 Markers. 2 Scales, Nipper, 3 Compasses.
2957 1/2	40 Chisels, &c.

2958 1/2	5 Squares.
2959 1/2	7 Saws.
2960	Small Grindstone and Frame.
2961	2 Rollers and Glue Pot.
2962	Anvil and Block.
2963	4 Iron Vices, Turning Lathe, Auger.
2964	3 Irons, Stone, Stamping.
2965	Large Wooden Clamp, 2 Screws.
2965 1/2	Turning Lathe, Screws, Nuts, &c.
2966	8 Sets Steel Figure Punches.
	15 do Small Letter do
	17 Capital do do
	do do (German)
	Small do do

LOT OF MISCELLANEOUS LETTERS AND FIGURES.

2967	Set Cleffs, &c., 31 Pieces.
	2 do 40 do
	2 do 36 do
	Miscell's Lot, 200 do

[column 2]

ENGRAVING INSTRUMENTS

2968	32 Gravers and Scrapers, with handles.
	4 Burnishers, 30 Heavy Scrapers.
	Music Pen, 28 Light do
	24 Round Gravers, 22 Light do
	26 Gravers, 16 Gravers, triangular.
	17 Points, &c.
2969	10 Frames for Punches.
2970	Engraving Bench and Drawer.
2971	Small do do
2972	Printing Press (To be seen at 25 S. 5th St.)
2973	3 do do do
2974	Large Screw Press, iron. do do
2975	do do wood do do
2976	Cabinet Working Bench. do do
2977	Small Press Bench.
2978	Old Velocipede. (2 wheels.)
2979	French Tool Chest, with Drawers, &c.

2980	Original Model of the First Bridge Over the Schuylkill.
2981	Lot Printer's Black. (To be seen at No. 25 S. 5th St.)
2982	Lithograph Press. do do

M. Thomas & Sons, Auctioneers

APPENDIX C

Watermarks on American Music Sheets, 1793–1830

꙰꙰

IN THE PROCESS of compiling my *Secular Music in America*, I recorded every watermark I encountered on an American music sheet of that period. My tracings of these, which have been reduced to about one third of their original size, appear herein on pp. 000–00. The list below indicates those works which were printed on watermarked paper. Grouping here is by size nomenclature in vogue at that time. The evolution of paper sizes and names and watermarks for them is conveniently furnished on Table 3 (pp. 73–75) of Philip Gaskell's *A New Introduction to Bibliography*. Further explanation is provided on the discussion of paper herein.

SUPER ROYAL AND WRITING DEMY
(Numbers 1–12)

Super royal was a known size of paper from the fourteenth century and became especially popular in the eighteenth century for printing large books and in plate work. Its watermark was the Strasbourg Lily, and its size in England after 1781 measured about 70 by 49 inches. Another paper, known as writing demy (which was used for both writing and printing) also contained the Strasbourg Lily watermark, its size approximately 51 by 40 inches.

Number 1

BLACKWELL—Ann Blackwell, an English maker. Shorter, p. 176,[1] designates her establishment as Hertfordshire Mill No. 12 and notes that she was active

1. Alfred H. Shorter, *Paper Mills and Paper Makers in England, 1495–1800* (Hilversum, Paper Publications Society, 1957). Cited as Shorter.

from 1777. Her name appears on a Britannia mark illustrated as Figure 15 there.

Found on: Phile, Hail Columbia. Boston, von Hagen, 1798. (Sonneck–Upton, p. 174)

Number 2

BLAUW—Dirk Blauw & Co., a Dutch maker. Heawood 1828[2] shows a similar mark. See numbers 14, 40.

Found on: Hewitt, The Lass of Lucerne Lake. N.Y., Gilfert, 1795. (Sonneck–Upton, p. 224)

Hook, 'Twas Pretty Poll & Honest Jack. N.Y., Gilfert, 1794–5. (Sonneck–Upton, p. 345)

Number 3

BUDGEN—Thomas Budgen, English maker. Shorter, p. 181, identifies his factory as Kent Mill No. 2, after 1778. See Figure 19 there.

Found on: Dibdin, Nancy, or the Sailor's Journal. Boston, Thomas & Andrews, ca. 1798. (Sonneck–Upton, p. 286)

Dibdin, No Good Without an Exception. Phila., Carr, 1794–6. (Sonneck–Upton, p. 298)

King, Love Comes and Goes. N.Y., Willson, 1815. (Wolfe, No. 5004)

Shield, The Green Mountain Farmer. Boston,

Linley & Moore, 1798. (Sonneck–Upton, p. 169, with watermark date "1795")

Number 4

DE VRIES—Pieter De Vries, Dutch maker.

Found on: Arnold, Little Sally. N.Y., Hewitt, 1797–9. (Sonneck–Upton, p. 234)

Dibdin, Negro Philosophy. N.Y., Hewitt, ca. 1800. (Sonneck–Upton, p. 288)

Hook, Bright Phoebus. N.Y., Hewitt, 1797–9. (Sonneck–Upton, p. 49)

Hook, He Loves His Winsome Kate. N.Y., Hewitt, 1797. (Sonneck–Upton, p. 473)

Hook, I'm In Haste. N.Y., Hewitt, 1797. (Sonneck–Upton, p. 198)

Hook, May Day Morn. N.Y., Hewitt, 1797–9. (Sonneck–Upton, p. 257)

Storace, Of Plighted Faith So Truly Kept. N.Y., Hewitt, ca. 1797. (Sonneck–Upton, p. 313)

Storace, Some Time Ago. N.Y., Hewitt, 1797–9. (Sonneck–Upton, p. 390)

2. Edward Heawood, *Watermarks Mainly of the 17th and 18th Centuries* (Hilversum, Paper Publications Society, 1950). Cited as Heawood.

Numbers 5, 6

EDMEADS & PINE—Robert Edmeads and Thomas Pine, English makers. Shorter, pp. 192–193, associates with Kent Mill No. 26 after 1785. See Figures 51–55 there.

Number 5

Found on: Hook, She Lives in the Valley Below. N.Y., Howe, 1800? (Wolfe, No. 10261)

Number 6

Found on: Taylor, Philadelphia Hymn. N.p., 179–? (Sonneck–Upton, p. 330)

Number 7

ELCAR—William Elcar, English maker. Shorter, p. 193, associates him with Kent Mill No. 27. Figures 56 and 57 there show different Elcar marks.

Found on: Dibdin, Father and Mother and Suke. Baltimore, Hupfield & Hammer, 1805–12. (Wolfe, No. 2421)

Kelly, Megen, Oh! Oh Megen Ee. Boston, Von Hagen, 1799. (Sonneck–Upton, p. 258)

New Yankee Doodle. N.Y., Hewitt, ca. 1797. (Sonneck–Upton, p. 480)

Number 8

HONIG—C. and I. Honig, Dutch makers. Heawood 1824, 1856, and similar marks under 3346 and 3348. See numbers 15, 16, 21, 36.

Found on: Colizzi, The Haunted Tower, N.p., n.d. (Wolfe, No. 1990, probably Paff)

Dignum, Fair Rosalie. N.Y., Howe, 1799–1800. (Sonneck–Upton, p. 132)

Dignum, Fair Rosalie, N.Y., Paff, 1799–1803. (Sonneck–Upton, p. 132)

Fowler, An Envious Sigh. N.Y., Paff, 1799–1803. (Sonneck–Upton, p. 125)

Gaveaux, La Pipe de Tabac. N.Y., Paff, 1799–1803. (Sonneck–Upton, p. 332)

Haydn, Adieu My Charming Fair. N.Y., Paff, 1802–3. (Wolfe No. 3478)

Hook, The Aviary. N.Y., Paff, 1799–1803. (Sonneck–Upton, p. 35)

Hook, The Blackbird. N.Y., Paff, 1799–1803. (Sonneck–Upton, p. 43)

Hook, By and By. N.Y., Paff, 1801–3. (Wolfe, No. 3967)

Hook, Dear is My Little Native Vale. N.Y., Paff, 1799–1803. (Wolfe, No. 10247)

Hook, The Linnets. N.Y., Paff, 1799–1803. (Sonneck–Upton, p. 231)

Hook, Robin Redbreast. N.Y., Paff, 1799–1803. (Sonneck–Upton, p. 356)

Hook, Within a Mile of Edinborgh. N.Y., Paff, 1802–3. (Wolfe, No. 4281)

Jackson, New Miscellaneous Musical Work. N.p., n.d. (Sonneck–Upton, p. 293–4)

Kelly, No More Love No. N.Y., Paff, 1803–7. (Wolfe, No. 4918)

Kelly, When Pensive I Thought of My Love.N.p., n.d. (Wolfe, No. 4906, probably Paff)

Playel, Beauty. N.Y., Paff, 1799–1803. (Sonneck–Upton, p. 40)

The Poor Little Child of a Tar. N.Y., Paff, 1799–1803. (Sonneck–Upton, p. 337)

Ross, I Ask Not Thy Pity. N.Y., Paff, 1799–1803. (Sonneck–Upton, p. 198)

Sanderson, The Humble Thatch'd Cottage. N.Y., Paff, ca. 1803. (Wolfe, No. 7772)

Schneider, Forget Me Not. N.p., n.d. (Sonneck–Upton, p. 145, probably Paff)

Truxton's Victory. Boston, Thomas & Andrews, 1799? (Sonneck–Upton, p. 438; variant mark, containing fleur-de-lis and crown device, with "J. Honig & Zoonen" device on no. 16).

Viguerie, The Battle of Maringo. N.Y., Paff, 1802. (Wolfe, No. 9480)

Ware, The Loud and Clear Ton'd Nightingale. N.Y., Paff, ca. 1803. (Wolfe, No. 9604)

Winter, The Peerless Maid of Buttermere. N.Y., Paff, 1799–1803. (Sonneck–Upton, p. 328)

Number 9

I K—Unidentified, probably I. (J.) Kool. See numbers 17, 37.

Found on: Marche Patriotique. Phila., Rice, 1793–6. (Wolfe, No. 10282)
Nicolai, Sonata I. N.p. n.d. (Wolfe No. 6509)
Shaw, The Gentleman's Amusement. Phila., Shaw, 1794. (Sonneck–Upton, pp. 157–163, first number only)

Number 10

J G L—Unidentified. Heawood 3016 records an "I G L."

Found on: Bishop, The Pilgrim of Love. Phila., Carr, ca. 1822. (Wolfe, No. 765)

Number 11

TAYLOR—John Taylor, English maker. Shorter, p. 196, identifies him with Kent Mill No. 35. See Figure 171 there.

Found on: Carr, Tell Me Where Is Fancy Bred. Phila., Carr, 1794. (Sonneck–Upton, p. 424, separate issue from collection)
Carr, When Icycles Hang By the Wall. Phila., Carr, 1794. (Sonneck–Upton, p. 462, separate issue from collection)

Carr, When Nights Were Cold. Phila., Carr, 1794. (Sonneck–Upton, p. 463, separate issue from collection)

Number 12

HOMO—Unidentified. Heawood 666 cites "P HOMO" on late-seventeenth-century paper.

Found on: Arnold, And Hear Her Sigh Adieu! N.Y., Hewitt, ca. 1798. (Sonneck–Upton, p. 24)
Pownall, Jemmy of the Glen. N.Y., Hewitt, 1794. (Sonneck–Upton, p. 216, separate issue from collection.

CROWN
(Numbers 13–19)

Crown paper, popular from the late seventeenth century, was manufactured for all sorts of purposes: writing, printing, copperplate work, as well as cartridge paper intended for rougher uses. Its name derived probably from a watermark design of a royal crown, found in English papers as early as 1743. Eventually, it began to contain as a countermark a bunch of grapes, and later papers normally contained this mark alone, sometimes with a crown within the stem. (Grapes were also found on an obsolete type of French paper called Lombard, which corresponded to the later size royal, and paper watermarked with the grape device is supposedly of French origin.) On the inventory of the Hoffman Mill, reported in the Seitz book, crown is designated as a printing paper only, and its size is given as 16½ by 21 inches. Gaskell sets its measurements at 15 by 20 inches, which is the recognized size today.

Number 13

AUSTIN—Unidentified maker, possibly American. Not included in Shorter nor in Churchill's alphabetical list of British papermakers and mills.[3] Hunter[4] mentions only an Austin & Carr, of Mount Holly, New Jersey (1796). Mark probably of Cyrus Austin, who ordered from Nathan Sellers in 1801 demy molds watermarked with the fleur-de-lis, 1800, AUSTIN. The dissolution of Austin's partnership with Carr must have been shortly before, as Sellers or his scribe had scratched out "Austin & Carr" for this order.

Found on: Lord Wellington's March. N.Y., ca. 1811. (Wolfe, No. 5445, probably P. Weldon)
Weldon, Favorita Waltz Brazilense. N.Y., 1810. (Wolfe, No. 7931, probably P. Weldon)

Number 14

BLAUW—Dutch maker, see number 2.

Found on: Arnold, And Hear Her Sigh Adieu! N.Y., Hewitt, ca. 1798. (Sonneck–Upton, p. 24)

3. Churchill, *Watermarks in Paper*. Cited as Churchill.
4. Hunter, *Papermaking in Pioneer America*. Cited as Hunter.

Arnold, Little Sally. N.Y., Hewitt, 1797–9. (Sonneck–Upton, p. 234)

Arnold, [Young Simon in His Lovely Sue]. N.Y., Gilfert, 1794–5. (Sonneck–Upton, p. 484)

Hook, When I Was a Chit. N.Y., Gilfert, 1794–5. (Sonneck–Upton, p. 462)

Reeve, The Lavender Girl. N.Y., Gilfert, 1794–5. (Sonneck–Upton, p. 226)

Reeve, The Market Lass. N.Y., Gilfert, 1794–5. (Sonneck–Upton, p. 251)

Shield, Hey Dance to the Fiddle & Tabor. N.Y., Hewitt, 1797–9. (Sonneck–Upton, p. 186)

[Unidentified Collection of Instrumental and Vocal Music]. N.Y., Hewitt & Rausch, 1797. (Sonneck–Upton, p. 77)

Number 15, 16

HONIG & ZOONEN—Dutch, makers, see number 8.

Number 15

Found on: Arne, Water Parted from the Sea. Phila., Trisobio, 1796–8. (Sonneck–Upton, p. 454)

Haydn, A Prey to Tender Anguish. Phila., Willig, ca. 1816. (Wolfe, No. 3535A)

Reinagle, The Volunteers. Phila., Reinagle, 1795 (Sonneck–Upton, p. 446)

Volume, Consisting of Favourite Songs, Duetts, &c. N.Y., Young, 179–. (Wolfe, No. 10351)

Number 16

See Heawood 334, 3345

Found on: Bray, The Rose. Phila., Willig, 1810? (Wolfe, No. 1332)

Davy, Yes I Remember Well the Hour. Phila., Willig, 1808–10. (Wolfe, No. 2344)

Hook, Down in the Valley. Phila., Willig, 1807? (Wolfe, No. 4018)

Jackson, Duo. Phila., Willig, 1808? (Wolfe, No. 4517)

Kelly, The Woodman. Phila., Willig, 1810? (Wolfe, No. 4929)

Shield, When Over the Billows We Go. Phila., Willig, 1809? (Wolfe, No. 8225)

Steibelt, Turkish March. Phila., Willig, 1804–10. (Wolfe, No. 8588)

Stevenson, Faithless Emma. Phila., Willig, 1808–10. (Wolfe, No. 8710)

Number 17

KOOL—Jan Kool, Dutch maker, see number 9.

Found on: Arnold, Fresh and Strong the Breeze Is Blowing, N.p., n.d. (Sonneck–Upton, p. 148, probably Carr, 1794–7)

Attwood, Ah! Once When I Was a Very Little Maid. N.Y., Hewitt, 1798. (Sonneck–Upton, p. 9)

Crazy Jane. N.Y., Weldon, 1800? (Wolfe, No. 10199)

Dignum, The Maid of the Rock. N.Y., Paff, 1799–1803. (Wolfe, No. 10207)

Hewitt, Oh Had It Been My Happy Lot. N.Y., Hewitt, ca. 1800. (Sonneck–Upton, p. 305, separate issue from collection)

Hook, Sweet Girl by the Light of the Moon. N.Y., Paff, 1802? (Wolfe, No. 4216)

Hush Every Breeze. N.p., n.d. (Sonneck–Upton, p. 301)

Reeve, The Galley Slave. N.Y., Paff, 1799–1803. (Wolfe, No. 10312)

Roslin Castle. N.Y., Paff, 1799–1803. (Sonneck–Upton, p. 363)

Weizacker, The River Patowmac. Phila., Willig, ca. 1800. (Sonneck–Upton, p. 356)

Number 18

ROGGE—Adriaan Rogge, Dutch maker of Zaandam (1704–1803). Heawood 1857–59 records his name with the Strasbourg Lily design.

Found on: Storace, Spirit of My Sainted Sire. N.Y., Carr, 1795–6. (Sonneck–Upton, p. 407)

Number 19

VAN GELDER—Dutch maker of the nineteenth century and later.

Found on: Monro, Ellen Aureen. Charleston, Siegling, 1823? (Wolfe, No. 5898)

My Dark Eyed Maid. Charleston, Siegling, ca. 1826.

MEDIUM
(Numbers 20–26 and probably 27–28)

The figure of a horn in a crowned shield designated the sort of paper known as medium, which was a popular printing and writing size in the eighteenth century, measuring approximately 58 by 45 inches. The horn by itself usually identified post paper, which approximated crown paper in size. Its relationship to the type and size of American sheets, as in numbers 27 and 28, is unknown.

Number 20

J C—English paper, maker unknown. Possibly manufactured by James Cripps or by Joseph Coles, J. Corbett or John Curteis. See Figures 25–39 in Shorter.

Found on: Dibdin, Nancy or the Sailor's Journal. Boston, Thomas & Andrews, 1799? (Sonneck–Upton, p. 438)

Von Hagen, To Arms Columbia. Boston, von Hagen, 1799. (Sonneck–Upton, p. 433)

Number 21

HONIG & ZOONEN—Dutch paper, see numbers 8, 15, 16. Heawood 2740 records a nearly identical mark. See also Churchill 322, 408.

Found on: Carr, Little Sailor Boy. Boston, von Hagen, 1799. (Sonneck–Upton, p. 234)

Hook, As Forth I Rang'd the Banks of Tweed. Boston, von Hagen, 1799. (Sonneck–Upton, p. 33)

Truxton's Victory. Boston, Thomas & Andrews, 1799? (Sonneck–Upton, p. 438)

Von Hagen, Adams & Washington. Boston, von Hagen, 1798–9. (Sonneck–Upton, p. 5)

Von Hagen, How Tedious Alas! Are the Hours. Boston, von Hagen, 1799. (Sonneck–Upton, p. 194)

Von Hagen, To Arms Columbia. Boston, von Hagen, 1799. (Sonneck–Upton, p. 433)

Young Jemmy Is a Pleasing Youth. Boston, von Hagen, 1799. (Sonneck–Upton, p. 483)

Number 22

G M—Unidentified. Probably an Italian paper. The initials may represent those of Giorgio Magnini, a famous Italian maker.

Found on: Marcha del General Palofax. N.p., n.d. (Wolfe, No. 5549, probably P. Weldon, 1808–12)

Number 23

MASSO—Italian maker. See numbers 38, 39.

Found on: Bishop, Loch Na Garr. N.Y., Geib, 1815. (Wolfe, No. 688)

Bland, The Rose of Aberdeen. N.Y., Paff, 1807. (Wolfe, No. 873)

Gilfert, Four Songs. N.Y., Appel, 1813. (Wolfe, No. 3063)

Number 24

PATCH—Christopher Patch, English maker whom Shorter, p. 237, located at Surry Mill No. 4 between 1789 and 1797. See Figure 125 there.

Found on: Pirsson, A Duetto for Two Flutes. Phila., Carr, ca. 1796. (Sonneck–Upton, p. 115, separate issue)

Number 25

RUSSELL—Edward Russell & Co., English makers. Shorter, p. 191, places him at Kent Mill No. 25. See Figure 143 there. Heawood 2759 shows identical mark dated 1799.

Found on: Dignum, Fair Rosalie. N.Y., Howe, 1799. (Sonneck–Upton, p. 132)

Number 26

WILLIAMS—Robert Williams, English maker. Shorter, p. 196, locates him at Kent Mill No. 31. See Figure 383 there and Heawood 2758 for identical mark (dated 1797).

Found on: Shield, The Green Mountain Farmer. Boston, Linley & Moore, 1798. (Sonneck–Upton, p. 169)

Number 27

M A—Unidentified American maker.

Found on: Abrams, The Shade of Henry. Phila., Willig, ca. 1800. (Sonneck–Upton, p. 377)

Bernhardt, The Beggar Boy. Phila., Willig, 1804–7. (Wolfe, No. 532)

Corri, The Bird in Yonder Cage Confin'd. Phila., Carr & Schetky, 1802–3. (Wolfe, No. 2101A–2101B)

Elfort, The Bastile. Phila., Bader, 179–? (Sonneck–Upton, p. 37)

The Female Auctioneer. Phila., Blake, 1803. (Wolfe, No. 2766)

Gretry, Overture de la Caravane. Phila., Willig, 1798–1804. (Sonneck–Upton, p. 320)

[Hark, Hark from the Woodlands] A Favorite Hunting Song. Phila., Willig, ca. 1799. (Wolfe, No. 10230)

Haydn, Sonata III. Phila., Willig, 179–? (Sonneck–Upton, p. 391)

Hewitt, The Wounded Hussar. Phila., Willig, 1798–1804. (Sonneck–Upton, p. 478)

Jordan, Blue Bell of Scotland. Phila., Willig, 1801. (Wolfe, No. 4670)

Kelly, In the Rough Blast Heaves the Billow. Phila., Blake, 1804? (Wolfe, No. 4800)

The Ladies Collection of Glees, Rounds & Chorusses. Phila., Carr & Schetky, 1804–5. (Wolfe, No. 5182)

Moulds, The Poor Village Boy. Phila., Blake, 1803–6. (Wolfe, No. 6164)

Reinagle, Ballad, Sung by Mr. Jefferson in The Tale of Terror. Phila., Blake, 1804? (Wolfe, No. 7551)

Shield, Whilst With Village Maids I Stray. Phila., Willig, n.d. [ca. 1798]. (Sonneck–Upton, p. 470)

Smith, Three Duetts. Phila., Willig, 1798–1804. (Sonneck–Upton, p. 116)

Number 28

H S—Unidentified American maker, but almost certainly Henry Sheetz, who operated a mill in Montgomery County, Pennslyvania, from 1769. Molds watermarked with the posthorn device and the initials H S were prepared for him by Nathan Sellers in 1796.

Found on: The Acquisition of Louisiana. Phila., Willig, 1804 (Wolfe, No. 89)

Storace, Captivity. Phila., Carr, 1793. (Sonneck–Upton, p. 55)

ROYAL OR LOMBARD
(Numbers 29–33)

The grape design has been employed for designating several sorts of early papers. In earlier times it marked demy and foolscap papers, as well as crown, but by the time of the period under discussion, it denominated royal and Lombard (or bastard) sheets. It was a mark particularly associated with French papers, and the marks reproduced and noted here are probably all of French origin. Royal and comparable sizes measured about 60 by 50 inches.

Number 29

G A—Unidentified, probably a French maker.

Found on: Taylor, Tell Me Not of Joys Above. Phila., Blake, 1817? (Wolfe, No. 9290)

Number 30

J B—Unidentified, probably a French maker.

Found on: The Neapolitan, Swiss & Vienna Waltzes. Phila., Blake, ca. 1817. (Wolfe, No. 6477)

Shield, O Come Sweet Mary to Me. Phila., Willig, ca. 1799. (Sonneck–Upton, p. 303)

Whitaker, Paddy Carey's Fortune. Phila., Willig, 1819? (Wolfe, No. 9859)

Number 31

BIDIRIAS—Unidentified, probably a French maker.

Found on: Braham, Is There a Heart That Never Lov'd. Phila., Willig, 1818? (Wolfe, No. 1129)

Number 32

BOWYGAR—Unidentified, probably a French maker.

Found on: Braham, Behold in His Soft Expressive Face. Phila., Willig, 1818? (Wolfe, No. 1049)

Braham, Is There a Heart That Never Lov'd. Phila., Willig, 1818? (Wolfe, No. 1129)

Kialmark, Fly to the Desert. Phila., Willig, 1818? (Wolfe, No. 4951)

Stevenson, Eveleens Bower. Phila., Willig, 1818? (Wolfe, No. 8699)

Number 33

DUMAS—B. Dumas, an unidentified French maker.

Found on: Macgaie, Donald the Pride of Dumblane. Phila., Willig, 1816–8. (Wolfe, No. 5486)

Mozart, Chicken Waltz and Turquis Waltz. Phila., Willig, 1817–8. (Wolfe, No. 6216)

FOOLSCAP

(Numbers 34–37)

Foolscap was the smallest sheet used in early American music publishing. Used also as a writing, printing, drawing, and wrapping paper, its size varied from 15 by 12¾ to 18½ by 14½ inches. It derived its name from its original watermark, which consisted of a fool's cap and bells. By the latter years of the eighteenth century, the fool's-cap design had fallen into disuse, and paper marked with the Britannia design (number 34), the Pro Patria design (number 35) and the Dutch Lion design (numbers 36–37) went under the designation "foolscap" instead, all being of an equivalent size.

Number 34

[FL]OYD—Floyd and Fellows (John Floyd and John Fellows), English makers, associated by Shorter, p. 182, with the Kent Mill No. 5. See Figure 61 there. The Britannia mark shown here was the English equivalent for the Maid of Holland mark. The figure, still seen on British pennies, has a female figure with a spear, and it continues to appear on modern British foolscap papers. The design had superceded the fool's-cap device of British papers of that size by the mid-eighteenth century, if not before.

Found on: Young's Vocal and Instrumental Musical Miscellany, No. 1. Phila., Young, 1793. (Sonneck–Upton, p. 484 and following)

Number 35

KONING & DISIARDIN—Dutch makers. The device here is the familiar Pro Patria design. The mark was Dutch in origin, being introduced probably in the late seventeenth century. Its derivation from the Maid of Holland symbol is recounted in *The Nostitz Papers*, pp. 87–90.[5] It supplanted the fool's-cap device, of which size it was an equivalent, and continued to be a popular paper throughout the eighteenth and into the nineteenth centuries. It was not only manufactured in Holland, but was widely imitated in German, English, French, Danish, Swedish, and Russian mills.

Found on: Tomlins, Fragments from Mrs. Ann Radcliff's Ode to Melancholy. Norfolk, Bosler, ca. 1807. (Wolfe, No. 9392)

Number 36

HONIG & ZOONEN—Dutch makers, noted previously in numbers 8, 15, 16, 21. The Dutch Lion is a variation of the symbol in the Pro Patria design. See Churchill, No. 120.

Found on: Abrams, The Shade of Henry. Phila., Willig, 1798–1804. (Sonneck–Upton, p. 377)

Braham, Eliza, Phila., Willig, 1808–9. (Wolfe, No. 1093)

Bray, 'Tis Her I Love! Phila., Willig, 1808–10. (Wolfe, No. 1309)

Dibdin, Monseer Non Tong Paw. Phila., Willig, 1798–1804. (Sonneck–Upton, p. 269)

Dibdin, The Soldier's Adieu. Phila., Willig, 1798–1804. (Sonneck–Upton, p. 389, separate issue from collection)

Gluck, Ouverture d'Iphigenie. Phila., Willig, 1795–7. (Sonneck–Upton, p. 317)

5. (Hilversum, Paper Publication Society, 1956).

Haydn, Overture by Haydn. Phila., Willig, ca. 1800. (Sonneck–Upton, p. 319)

Hook, Mary Once Had Lovers Two. Phila., Willig, 1806–7. (Wolfe, No. 4135)

Hook, She Lives in the Valley Below. Phila., Willig, 1801–4. (Wolfe, No. 4190)

Humphrey, Why Does Azure Deck the Sky. Phila., Willig, ca. 1808. (Wolfe, No. 4402)

King, Far Far From Me My Lover Flies. Phila., Willig, 1808–10. (Wolfe, No. 4994)

Lovely Hannah. Phila., Willig, 1798–1804. (Sonneck–Upton, p. 239)

Mozart, The Resolution. Phila., Willig, 1798–1804. (Sonneck–Upton, p. 353)

Shield, All in the Silent Convent's Cell. Phila., Willig 1808? (Wolfe, No. 8006)

Shield, Caludine Liv'd Contented. Phila., Willig, 1808? (Wolfe, No. 8023)

Shield, I Fell in Love and Lost My Place. Phila., Willig, 1808–10. (Wolfe, No. 8071)

Shield, When Over the Billows We Go. Phila., Willig, 1809? (Wolfe, No. 8225)

Steibelt, Two New Bacchanals. Phila., Willig, 1807–10. (Wolfe, No. 8530)

Thompson, The Sylphs. Phila., Willig, 1808–10. (Wolfe, No. 9363)

Number 37

KOOL—Dutch maker, noted previously in numbers 9, 17.

Found on: Arise Arise Columbia's Sons Arise. Phila., Willig, 1805? (Wolfe, No. 149)

Capron, Delia. Phila., Willig, 1798–1804. (Sonneck–Upton, p. 105)

Cooke, Nobody Coming To Marry Me. Phila., Willig, 1808? (Wolfe, No. 2073)

Gauline, Crazy Emma. Phila., Willig, 1798–1804. (Sonneck–Upton, p. 93)

Hook, Down in the Valley. Phila., Willig, 1807. (Wolfe, No. 4018)

Hook, Sonnet III [Evening]. Phila., Willig, ca 1794. (Sonneck–Upton, p. 127)

The Italian Monk Trio. Phila., Willig, 1798–1804. (Sonneck–Upton, p. 264)

Kate Kearney. Phila., Willig, 1807? (Wolfe No. 6703)

Kelly, Last Week I Took a Wife. Phila., Willig, 1809? (Wolfe, No. 4804)

The Marseilles Hymn. Phila., Willig, 1795–7. (Sonneck–Upton, p. 252)

Mozart, The Fowler. Phila., Willig, 1795–7. (Sonneck–Upton, p. 146)

Naegli, Life Let Us Cherish. Phila., Willig, 1798–1804. (Sonneck–Upton, p. 228)

Nicolai, Six Sonatas for the Piano Forte. Phila., Willig, 1793. (Sonneck–Upton, p. 394)

Nicolai, Six Sonatas for the Piano Forte. Phila., Willig, n.d. (Sonneck–Upton, p. 394, as early as 1798)

Steibelt, Two Sonatas for the Piano Forte, Phila., Willig, ca. 1800. (Sonneck–Upton, p. 395)

Taylor, Ma Cher et Mon Cher. Phila., Willig, 1798–1804. (Sonneck–Upton, p. 245)

Taylor, Rondo for the Piano Forte. Phila., Taylor, n.d. (Sonneck–Upton, p. 360, as early as 1794)

Taylor, Rustic Festivity. Phila., Taylor, n.d. (Wolfe, No. 366, as early as 1795)

Wright, A Smile from the Youth That I Love. Phila., Willig, 1798–1804. (Sonneck–Upton, p. 387)

UNIDENTIFIED AND UNCLASSIFIED MARKS

Number 38

MASSO—Italian maker, noted previously in number 23. Heawood 3748 classes a similar mark under Scroll Work.

Found on: Masonic Hymn [Unto Thee, Great God, Belong]. N.p. n.d. (Wolfe, No. 3941)

Number 39

MASSO—See preceding.

Found on: Hook, The Contented Shepherd. N.Y., Paff, 1799–1803. (Sonneck–Upton, p. 88)

Number 40

BLAUW—Dutch maker, noted previously in numbers 2, 14. Heawood 3267 and 3268 shows similar marks.

Found on: Arne, Fair Aurora. Phila., Trisobio, 1796–8. (Sonneck–Upton, p. 131)

Arnold, Happy Tawny Moor. Phila., Carr, ca. 1796. (Sonneck–Upton, p. 177)

Arnold, The Way Worn Traveller. Phila., Carr, 1794. (Sonneck–Upton, p. 455)

Capron, Come Genius of Our Happy Land. Phila., Carr, 1797–9. (Sonneck–Upton, p. 82)

Carr, The Little Sailor Boy. Phila., Carr, 1798. (Sonneck–Upton, p. 233)

Carr, The New Somebody. Phila., Carr, 1799. (Sonneck–Upton, p. 295)

Did Not Tyrant Custom Guide Me. Phila., Trisobio, 1796–8. (Sonneck–Upton, p. 108)

Hook, The Indignant Peasant. Phila., Carr, 1793. (Sonneck–Upton, p. 207)

Kelly, When Pensive I Thought On My Love. Phila., Carr, ca. 1799 (Sonneck–Upton, p. 464)

Krumpholtz, Louisa's Complaint. N.Y., Gilfert, 1794–5. (Sonneck–Upton, p. 237)

Mozart, Away with Melancholy. Phila., Carr, 1797–9. (Sonneck–Upton, p. 35)

Phile, The Favorite New Federal Song [Hail Columbia]. Phila., Carr, 1798. (Sonneck–Upton, p. 172)

Reinagle, I Have a Silent Sorrow Here. Phila., Carr, ca. 1799. (Sonneck–Upton, p. 199)

Storace, Sweet Little Barbara. Phila., Carr, 1799. (Sonneck–Upton, p. 416)

Trisobio, La Marmotte, Phila., Trisobio, 1797–8. (Sonneck–Upton, p. 251)

Von Hagen, Anna. Boston, von Hagen, 1802. (Wolfe, No. 3288)

The Cottager's Daughter. Phila., Carr, 1797–9. (Sonneck–Upton, p. 92)

Shield, The Heaving of the Lead. Phila., Carr, 1793. (Sonneck–Upton, p. 182)

Number 41

S C—American maker, possibly Simon Class, Lower Merion, Montgomery County, Pennsylvania (established 1772). Hunter described his mark as S C with a six-pointed star.

Found on: La Carmagnole. Phila., Carr, 1794. (Sonneck–Upton, p. 56, separate issue)

Carr, The Federal Overture. Phila., Carr, 19794. (Sonneck–Upton, p. 139)

Costellow, The Cherry Girl. Phila., Carr, ca. 1796. (Sonneck–Upton, p. 61)

Dear Little Kate. Phila., Reinagle, 1789? (Sonneck–Upton, p. 101, separate issue)

Dibdin, The Flowing Can. Phila., Carr, 1794. (Sonneck–Upton, p. 144)

Dibdin, Jack at the Windlass, Phila., Carr, 1793. (Sonneck–Upton, p. 213)

Dibdin, Poor Jack. Phila., Carr, n.d. (Sonneck–Upton, p. 336, as early as 1794)

Dibdin, The Vetrans. Phila., Carr, 1796. (Sonneck–Upton, p. 443)

The Dream. Phila., Carr, 1794. (Sonneck–Upton, p. 113)

Geary, Pity the Sorrows of a Poor Old Man. Phila., Carr, 1793. (Wolfe, No. 10223)

Giordani, A Concerto for the Piano Forte or Harpsichord. Phila., Moller, 1793–4. (Sonneck–Upton, p. 86)

Harington, Damon & Chlora. Phila., Carr, 1794. (Sonneck–Upton, p. 96)

Hook, The Favorite Songs Sung at Vauxhall Gardens. Phila., Carr, 1794. (Sonneck–Upton, p. 402)

Hook, Hither Mary. Phila., Carr, 1793. (Sonneck–Upton, p. 188)

Hook, Rise, Cynthia, Rise. Phila., Carr, 1793. (Sonneck–Upton, p. 355)

Hook, Sweet Lillies of the Valley. Phila., Carr, 1793. (Sonneck–Upton, pp. 415–6)

Kotzwara, The Battle of Prague. Phila., Moller, ca. 1793. (Sonneck–Upton, p. 38)

Kotzwara, The Battle of Prague. Phila., Willig, 1795–1800. (Sonneck–Upton, p. 38)

Linley, Primroses Deck. Phila., Carr, 1794. (Sonneck–Upton, p. 347)

Major Andre's Complaint. Phila., Carr, 1794. (Sonneck–Upton, p. 246)

The Match Girl. Phila., Carr, 1793. (Sonneck–Upton, p. 256)

O Dear What Can the Matter Be. Phila., Carr, 1793. (Sonneck–Upton, p. 304)

Phile, President's March and Ça Ira. Phila., Carr, 1793–4. (Sonneck–Upton, p. 342)

Pleyel, Henry's Cottage Maid. Phila., Carr, 1794. (Sonneck–Upton, p. 184)

Pownall, Six Songs for the Harpsichord or Piano Forte. N.Y., Pownall & Hewitt, 1794. (Sonneck–Upton, p. 48)

Reeve, The Desponding Negro. Phila., Carr, 1793. (Sonneck–Upton, p. 106)

Reinagle, America, Commerce & Freedom. Phila., Carr, 1794. (Sonneck–Upton, p. 15)

Reinagle, La Chasse. Phila., Carr, ca. 1794. (Sonneck–Upton, p. 59)

Rouget de Lisle. The Marseilles Hymn. Phila., Carr, 1793. (Sonneck–Upton, p. 251)

Shield, The Cheering Rosary. Phila., Carr, 1793. (Sonneck–Upton, p. 60)

Shield, Henry Cull'd the Flow'ret's Bloom. Phila., Reinagle, ca. 1789. (Sonneck–Upton, p. 184)

Storace, Captivity. Phila., Carr, 1793. (Sonneck–Upton, p. 55)

Storace, The Favorite Ballad of the Poor Black Boy. Phila., Carr, 1794. (Sonneck–Upton, p. 335)

Storace, The Favorite Duett [Ah! Tell Me Softly Breathing Gale]. Phila., Carr, 1794. (Sonneck–Upton, p. 10)

Storace, Lullaby. Phila., Carr, 1793. (Sonneck–Upton, p. 243)

Storace, The Scotch Air in the Comic Opera of The Pirates [As Wrapt in Sleep I Lay]. Phila., Carr, ca. 1793. (Sonneck–Upton, p. 33)

Storace, Whither My Love. Phila., Carr, 1793. (Sonneck–Upton, p. 470)

The Tartan Plaiddie. Phila., Reinagle, 1789? (Sonneck–Upton, p. 422, separate issue)

Taylor, Amyntor. Phila., Taylor, 1795. (Sonneck–Upton, p. 23)

Storace, The Shipwreck'd Seamans Ghost. Phila., Carr, 1793. (Sonneck–Upton, p. 380, separate issue)

Taylor, Anthem for Two Voices. Phila., Taylor, 1793. (Wolfe, No. 10347)

Taylor, The Kentucky Volunteers. Phila., Carr, 1794. (Sonneck–Upton, p. 219)

Taylor, The Lass of the Cot. Phila., Taylor, 1795. (Sonneck–Upton, p. 225)

Taylor, Nancy of the Vale. Phila., Taylor, 1795. (Sonneck–Upton, p. 286)

Taylor, Vive la Liberté. Phila., Taylor, 1795. (Sonneck–Upton, p. 444)

Taylor, The Wounded Soldier, Phila., Carr, 1794. (Sonneck–Upton, p. 478)

The Wedding Day. Phila., Carr, 1793. (Sonneck–Upton, p. 456)

Young's Vocal and Instrumental Musical Miscellany. Phila., Young, 1793–5. (Sonneck–Upton, p. 484–6)

Number 42

B—Unindentified. Possibly the mark of an American maker, or of paper manufactured for George E. Blake.

Found on: Parry, Beauty in Tears. Phila., Blake, 1814–7. (Wolfe, No. 6800) Stevenson, Flow On, Thou Shining River. Phila., Blake, 1818–20. (Wolfe, No. 8728)

Number 43

CRAIG—Unidentified. H. Craig was probably an American maker.

Found on: Smith, The Parting Kiss. Charleston, Siegling, 1821? (Wolfe, No. 8324)

Number 44

D—Unidentified. Probably an American maker.

Found on: Dear Native Home. N.Y., Bourne, ca. 1829.

Number 45

W D—Unidentified maker, probably of Newport, Rhode Island.

Found on: Abrams, A Smile and a Tear. N.Y., Paff, 1801? (Wolfe, No. 15)

[286]

Braham, Fair Ellen, N.Y., Paff, 1802? (Wolfe, No. 1097)

Dalbert, Crazy Mary. N.Y., Paff, 1799–1803. (Wolfe, No. 2250)

Fisin, I Felt the Command and Obey'd With a Sigh. N.Y., Paff, 1799–1803. (Sonneck–Upton, p. 198)

Fisin, Louisa, N.Y., Paff, 1799–1803. (Sonneck–Upton, p. 236)

Fisin, Ye Little Songsters. N.Y., Paff, n.d. (Sonneck–Upton, p. 481, possibly as early as 1799)

Giordani, The Bleeding Hero. N.Y., Paff, 1799–1803. (Sonneck–Upton, p. 44)

The Ghost of Crazy Jane. N.Y., Paff, 1801? (Wolfe, No. 5669)

Haydn, Take This Hint From a Friend. N.Y., Paff, 1799–1803. (Wolfe, No. 10236)

Heather, The Persian Maid. N.Y., Paff, 1801–3. (Wolfe, No. 3583)

Hewitt, She Hung On My Arm. N.Y., Hewitt, 1801. (Wolfe, No. 3777)

Hook, The Turtle Dove Coos Round My Cot. N.Y., Paff, 1799–1803. (Sonneck–Upton, p. 439)

Hook, When Edward Left His Native Plain, N.Y., Paff, 1799–1803. (Sonneck–Upton, p. 459)

Kreutzer, The Celebrated Overture to Ladoiska. N.Y., Hewitt & Rausch, 1797. (Sonneck–Upton, p. 322)

Mazzinghi, Calm the Winds. N.Y., Paff, 1801? (Wolfe, No. 5669)

Michele, His Majesty's Review of the Volunteer Corps of London. N.Y., Paff, 1799–1803. (Sonneck–Upton, p. 188)

Moulds, The Poor Village Boy. N.Y., Paff, 1802–3. (Wolfe, No. 6163)

Pirsson, Glide Gently on Thou Murm'ring Brook. N.Y., Pirsson, 1799–1801. (Sonneck–Upton, p. 166)

Rausch, Liberty's Throne. N.Y., Paff, 1799–1803. (Sonneck–Upton, p. 228)

Sale, The Faithful Tar. N.Y., Paff, 1799–1803. (Sonneck–Upton, p. 132)

Schroder, Everybody's March. N.Y., Paff, 1799–1803. (Sonneck–Upton, p. 129)

Spofforth, The Wood Robin. N.Y., Paff, 1801? (Wolfe, No. 8498)

Webbe, The Lass of Liverpool. N.Y., Terrett, ca. 1803. (Wolfe, No. 9662)

Willson, A Favorite Sonata. New Brunswick, N.J., Willson, 1801–2. (Wolfe, No. 10015)

Number 46

GILPIN—T. Gilpin & Co. was the firm of Thomas and Joshua Gilpin of Delaware. See Hunter, Chapter 14.

Found on: Endpapers of bound volumes of sheet music of the 1800–25 period, as, for instance, on Pelissier's *Columbian Melodies* (Wolfe, No. 6922). Not located in sheets proper.

Number 47

W L—Probably the mark of Samuel Levis or Samuel Levis, Jr., of Upper Darby, Chester County, Pennsylvania, 1775–1800. According to Hunter their watermarks included the initials W L with an eagle.

Found on: Owen. Phila., Carr, 1799. (Sonneck–Upton, p. 323)

Number 48

LYDIG & MESIER—David Lydig and Peter Mesier, Bronx Paper Mill, Bronx River, New York, 1808–22.

Found on: Thompson, Now at Moonlight's Fairy Hour. N.Y., Willson, 1814–5. (Wolfe, No. 9353C)

Number 49

TERRAZO—Unidentified maker, probably Italian.

Found on: Hopkinson, Ode from Ossian's Poems. Baltimore, Carr, 1803–7. (Wolfe, No. 4290)

Number 50

WILLIG—American paper, possibly made for George Willig, the Philadelphia music publisher.

Found on: Auld Lang Syne. Phila., Willig, 1819? (Wolfe, No. 336)
Challoner, A Duet for Two Performers on One Piano Forte [Sul Margine d'un Rio]. Phila., Willig, 1818? (Wolfe, No. 1752)
Down in the Valley My Father Dwells. Phila., Willig, 1818–9. (Wolfe, No. 2546)
Gretry, Overture de la Caravan. Phila., Willig, 1798–1804. (Sonneck–Upton, p. 320)
Jamieson, Now By My Troth. Phila., Willig, 1822–3. (Wolfe, No. 4598)
Masonic March. Phila., Willig, 1811? (Wolfe, No. 5640)
Mazzinghi, See From Ocean Rising. Phila., Willig, 1808? (Wolfe, No. 5713)
Phile, Hail! Columbia! Phila., Willig, 1819? (Wolfe, No. 6985)

Number 51

W W—Unidentified maker, probably American.

Found on: Blue Ey'd Mary. N.Y., Dubois, 1817. (Wolfe, No. 893)

Number 52

DOVE DESIGN—The watermark of Amies & Co. (William and Joseph Amies, who opened a paper mill in Montgomery County, Pennsylvania, in 1799 and became manufacturers of fine paper).

Found on: Bishop, The Little Netting Girl. N.Y., Bradish, 1811. (Wolfe, No. 686)

Mazzinghi, Huntsman Rest! Thy Chace Is Done. N.Y., Bradish, 1811. (Wolfe, No. 5690)

Moore, The Day of Love. N.Y., Bradish, 1811. (Wolfe, No. 5946)

Owen. Phila., Willig, 1798–1804. (Sonneck–Upton, p. 323)

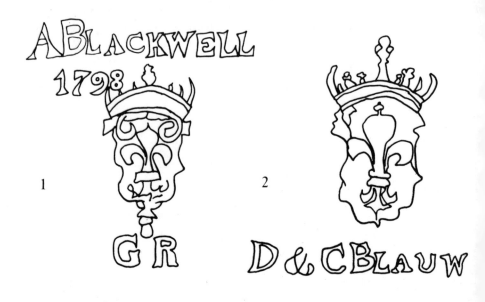

1   2

3   4

5

EDMEADS&PINE

𝒞 & 𝒫

6

EDMEADS&PINE

GR

7

WELCAR
1795

8

C&IHONIC

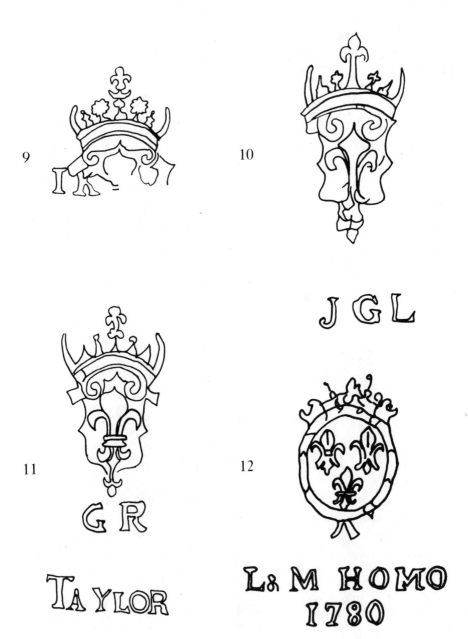

AUSTIN

13

1800

14

D & C BLAUW

15 JH&Z
I HONIC
&
ZOONEN

16 JH & Z
J HONIG
&
ZOONEN

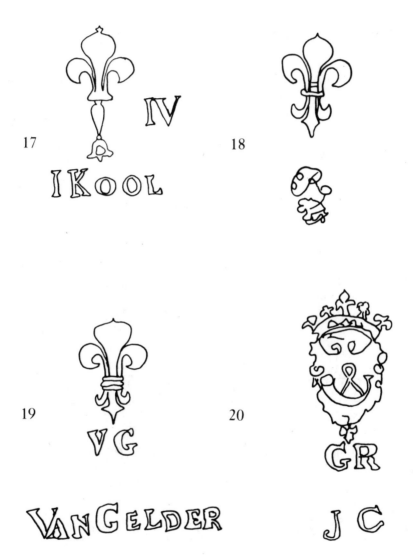

J HONIG
&
ZOONEN

21

22

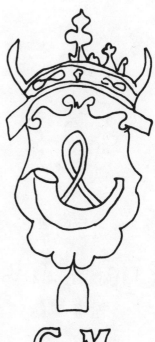

J HONIG
&
ZOONEN
AL MASSO

G M

23

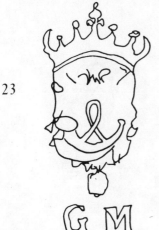

24

G M

PATCH

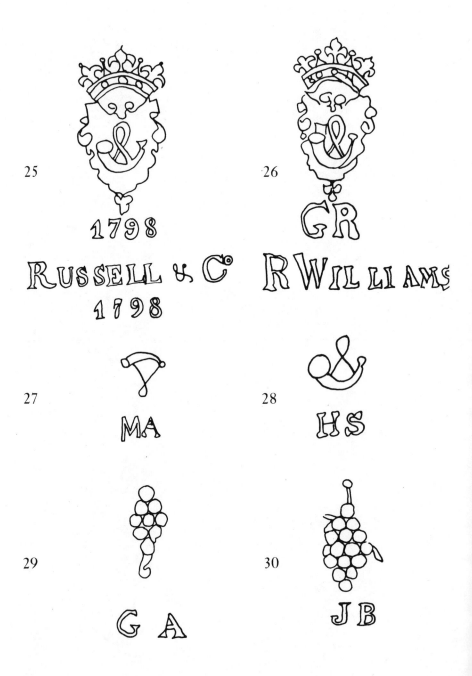

25

1798

RUSSELL & Cº
1798

26

GR

R WILLIAMS

27

MA

28

HS

29

G A

30

J B

31   32

BIDIRIAS

BOWYGAR

DL

B DUMAS

33   34

OYD & CO

35

36   37

45 W D   NEW   R I

46 T GILPIN & C°
    BRANDYWINE

47
    W L

48 LYDIG & MESIER

49 A L
    TERRAZZO

51 WW

50 G WILLIG

52

REFERENCES

Anderson, Alexander. Diary, 1795. MS. Department of Special Collections, Columbia University Library, New York.

Bathe, Greville, and Dorothy Bathe. *Jacob Perkins, His Inventions, His Times, and His Contemporaries*. Philadephia: Historical Society of Pennsylvania, 1943.

Britton, Allen P. "Theoretical Introductions in American Tune-books to 1800." Doctoral Dissertation, University of Michigan, 1949.

Brown, Harry Glenn, and Maude O. Brown. *Directory of the Book-Arts and Book Trade in Philadelphia to 1820*. New York: New York Public Library, 1950.

Churchill, W. A. *Watermarks in Paper in Holland, England, France, etc., in the XVII and XVIII Centuries and Their Interconnection*. Amsterdam: Menno Hertzberger, 1935.

A Day at a Music Publishers. London: D'Almaine and Co., ca. 1838.

Dichter, Harry, and Elliott Shapiro. *Early American Sheet Music, Its Lure and Lore, 1768–1889*. New York: R. R. Bowker, 1941.

Dunlap, William. *History of the Rise and Progress of the Arts of Design in the United States*. New York: G. P. Scott and Co., 1834; new ed., illustrated, edited, with additions, by Frank W. Bayley and Charles E. Goodspeed. Boston: C. E. Goodspeed and Co., 1918.

Dwight's Journal of Music. 41 vols. Boston, April 10, 1852–Sept. 3, 1881.

Essays Honoring Lawrence C. Wroth. Portland, Maine: Anthoensen Press, 1951.

Evans, Charles. *American Bibliography*. 14 vols. Chicago: Priv. print. for the author by the Blakely Press, 1903–59.

Gamble, William. *Music Engraving and Printing; Historical and Technical Treatise*. London: Pitman, 1923.

Gaskell, Philip. *A New Introduction to Bibliography*. Oxford: Clarendon Press, 1972.

Goff, Frederick R. "The First Decade of the Federal Act for Copyright." In *Essays Honoring Lawrence C. Wroth*.

Gottesman, Rita Susswein. *The Arts and Crafts in New York, 1800–1804; Advertisements and News Items from New York City Newspapers*. New York: New-York Historical Society, 1965.

Hitchings, Sinclair. "Graphic Arts in Colonial New England." In *Prints in and of America to 1850*.

——. "Thomas Johnston." In *Boston Prints and Printmakers, 1670–1775*. Boston: Colonial Society of Massachusetts, 1973, pp. 83–131.

Howard, John Tasker. *Our American Music; Three Hundred Years of It*. New York: Thomas Y. Crowell Co., 1931.

Hunter, Dard. *Papermaking in Pioneer America*. Philadelphia: University of Pennsylvania Press, 1952.

Johnson, H. Earle. *Musical Interludes in Boston, 1795–1830*. New York: Columbia University Press, 1943.

Krummel, Donald W. "Graphic Analysis, Its Application to Early American Engraved Music." Music Library Association *Notes*, 2nd ser. XVI (1959) 213–33.

——. "Philadelphia Music Engraving and Publishing." Doctoral Dissertation, University of Michigan, 1958.

Lowens, Irving, *Music and Musicians in Early America*. New York: W. W. Norton, 1964.

Morison, Stanley. *John Bell, 1745–1831, Bookseller, Printer, Publisher, Typefounder, Journalist, &c.*. Cambridge, England: Printed for the author by Cambridge University Press, 1930.

Muller, Joseph. *The Star Spangled Banner; Words and Music Issued between 1814 and 1864*. New York: G. A. Baker, 1935.

The Printed Note. Catalogue published by Toledo Museum of Art, 1957.

Prints in and of America to 1850. See Winterthur Conference.

Ross, Ted. *The Art of Music Engraving and Processing; a Complete Manual, Reference and Text Book on Preparing Music for Reproduction and Print*. Miami: Hansen Books, 1970.

Seitz, May A. *The History of the Hoffman Paper Mills in Maryland*. Baltimore: Printed by the Holliday Press, 1946.

Shipton, Clifford K. *Isaiah Thomas, Printer, Patriot, Philanthropist, 1749–1831*. Rochester, N.Y.: Leo Hart, 1948.

Silver, Rollo G. *The American Printer, 1787–1825*. Charlottesville: Published for the Bibliographical Society of the University of Virginia by the University Press of Virginia, 1967.

——. *Typefounding in America, 1787–1825*. Charlottesville: Bibliographical Society of the University of Virginia, 1965.

Sonneck, Oscar George Theodore. *A Bibliography of Early Secular American Music (18th Century)*. Revised and enlarged by William Treat Upton. Washington, D.C.: The Library of Congress, Music Division, 1945. Cited as Sonneck–Upton.

Spillane, Daniel. *History of the American Pianoforte: Its Technical Development and the Trade*. New York: The author, 1890.

Stauffer, David McNeely. *American Engravers upon Copper and Steel*. New York: The Grolier Club of the City of New York, 1907.

Stephens, Stephen De Witt. *The Mavericks, American Engravers*. New Brunswick: Rutgers University Press, 1950.

Thomas, Isaiah. *The History of Printing in America with a Biography of Printers, and an*

Account of Newspapers. . . . Worcester: From the press of Isaiah Thomas, jun., Isaac Stewart, printer, 1810.

Winterthur Conference on Museum Operation and Connoisseurship, 16th, 1970. *Prints in and of America to 1850.* Ed. by John D. Morse. Charlottesville: University Press of Virginia, 1970.

Wolfe, Richard J. *Secular Music in America, 1801–1825; a Bibliography.* New York: New York Public Library, 1964. Individual items from this work are cited as, e.g., Wolfe, No. 1368.

Wroth, Lawrence Counselman. *The Colonial Printer.* New York: The Grolier Club of the City of New York, 1931; second ed., revised and enlarged, Portland, Maine: The Southworth-Anthoensen Press, 1938.